Bad Apples

Identify, Prevent & Manage
Negative Behavior at Work

Adrian Furnham
*Professor of Psychology,
University College London, UK*

&

John Taylor
Consultant, UK

palgrave
macmillan

First published 2011 by
PALGRAVE MACMILLAN

Palgrave Macmillan in the UK is an imprint of Macmillan Publishers Limited,
registered in England, company number 785998, of Houndmills, Basingstoke,
Hampshire RG21 6XS.

Palgrave Macmillan in the US is a division of St Martin's Press LLC,
175 Fifth Avenue, New York, NY 10010.

Palgrave Macmillan is the global academic imprint of the above companies
and has companies and representatives throughout the world.

Palgrave® and Macmillan® are registered trademarks in the United States,
the United Kingdom, Europe and other countries.

ISBN: 978-0-230-58474-7

This book is printed on paper suitable for recycling and made from fully
managed and sustained forest sources. Logging, pulping and manufacturing
processes are expected to conform to the environmental regulations of the
country of origin.

A catalogue record for this book is available from the British Library.

A catalog record for this book is available from the Library of Congress.

Also by Adrian Furnham

The Dark Side of Behaviour at Work (2004) (with John Taylor)
Personality and Intellectual Competence (2005) (with Thomas Chamorro-Premuzic)
Learning at Work (2005) (with John Taylor)
Just for the Money (2005) (with Tom Booth)
The Psychology of Physical Attraction (2007) (with Viren Swami)
The Body Beautiful: Evolutionary and Sociocultural Perspectives (2007) (with Viren Swami)
Personality and Intelligence at Work: Exploring and Explaining Individual Differences at Work (2008)
Economic Socialisation of Young People (2008)
50 Psychology Ideas You Really Need to Know (2009)
The Elephant in the Boardroom: The Causes of Leadership Derailment (2010)
The Psychology of Personnel Selection (2010) (with Tomas Chamorro-Premuzic)
Body Language in Business (2010) (with Evgenyia Petrova)
The Wiley-Blackwell Handbook of Individual Differences (2011) (edited with Tomas Chamorro-Premuzic and Sophie von Stumm)

For Alison (AF)

For Aly (JT)

Contents

List of Illustrations

Figures

Tables

Examples

Boxes

Case study

Preface

This book is a radical revision and update of our earlier book *The Dark Side of Behaviour at Work*, published in 2004 and translated into various languages.

Much has happened since then in terms of new thinking, events and research. Alas, the figures suggest that bad behavior at work is on the increase, rather than the decrease. Despite – and sometimes because of – all modern surveillance cameras, knowledge of desirable management techniques and practices, there is abundant evidence of the steady increase in counter-productive work behaviors (CWBs).

New technology brings its own problems. We have cyber-crime and identity theft. Political changes in countries can cause destabilization, and a rise in corruption and opportunistic crime. High levels of unemployment influence people to behave badly.

> In July 2010, BDO – one of the UK's largest accountancy firms – reported that fraud broke the £1 billion barrier in the first six months of 2010, almost the same as for the whole of 2008.

Managers have a great deal to worry about along with how to increase profits and reduce costs. Law-makers do not always make it easier for the manager. The 2010 UK Bribery Act has made a number of quite normal practices overseas illegal in the UK. An employee of a company operating in the UK who pays a foreign customs official a "facilitation fee" to speed up the release of essential goods puts top management in that company at risk of imprisonment and a fine. The message to top management is clear, but how should they respond in countries where corruption is endemic?

Business is now global, technical and fast-moving. Society is changing and, with it, old loyalties and forms of behavior. Managers have to recruit, select and engage employees and set up policies and procedures that ensure efficient, effective and flexible working. And all this in an economic climate that is demanding and unpredictable, and where staff have ever-increasing demands and rights. Cyber-crime, shrinkage and fraud are on the increase – most of it conducted by people being paid by the company.

The evidence is clear: CWBs are increasing. Reports from PricewaterhouseCoopers, KPMG and BDO all show that fraud is on the increase. Shoplifting has increased and whistle-blowers continue to thrive with the ever-hungry press and the ease and universality of the Internet.

We concluded the preface to *The Dark Side of Behaviour at Work* by acknowledging that we had embarked on a journey of research, but that we were only at the beginning. We have moved on and there is greater awareness of the problems and, more importantly, what employers need to do to minimize the problems. This is another stepping stone in that journey.

ADRIAN FURNHAM, *Bloomsbury*
JOHN TAYLOR, *Fonthill Bishop*

Acknowledgements

The authors and publishers are grateful to the following for permission to reproduce copyright material: KPMG for Table 2.3 (Perpetrators of fraud, 2009), taken from the KPMG Fraud Barometer, 2010; Elsevier for extracts from M. McDaniel and D. Whetzel (2005) "Situational Judgement Test Research", *Intelligence*, 33(5), 515–25; John Wiley & Sons for Table 5.1 (Top 20 typical CWBs), taken from B. Marcus, H. Schuler, P. Quell and G. Hümpfner (2002) "Measuring Counterproductivity: Development and Initial of a German Self-Report Questionnaire", *International Journal of Selection and Assessment*, 10, 18–35; John Wiley & Sons for Table 5.3 (Items comprising the OCB and CWB measures), taken from E.K. Kelloway, C. Loughlin, J. Barling and A. Nault (2002) "Self-Reported Counterproductive Behaviors and Organizational Citizenship Behaviors: Separate but Related Constructs", *International Journal of Selection and Assessment*, 10, 143–51; John Wiley & Sons for Table 6.5 (Overview and descriptions of the non-verbal behaviors), Table 6.6 (Specific verbal indicators) and extracts, taken from A Vrij (2000) *Detecting Lies and Deceit*; Elsevier for Table 7.1 (A veiled purpose test), taken from D. Whetzel and M. McDaniel (2009) "Situational Judgement Tests: An overview of current research", *Human Resource Management Review*, 19, 188–202; and John Wiley & Sons for Case Study 4.1 ("Dave") and extracts, taken from P. Babiak (1995) "When Psychopaths Go To Work: A Case Study of an Industrial Psychopath", in *Applied Psychology*, 44, 171–88. Every effort has been made to contact all the copyright-holders, but if any have been inadvertently omitted the publishers will be pleased to make the necessary arrangement at the earliest opportunity.

List of Abbreviations

AP	antisocial potential
APD	antisocial personality disorder (also known as ASP)
CI	cognitive interview
CIB	Complaints Investigation Bureau
CV	curriculum vitae
CWB	counter-productive work behavior
FCPA	US Foreign Corrupt Practices Act
OCB	organizational citizenship behavior
PACE	Police and Criminal Evidence Act
PwC	PricewaterhouseCoopers

1 Introduction

This book is about bad behavior at work – from arson to absenteeism, sabo-tage to taking sickness leave. It seeks to describe the literature from many different sources of how, when and why people behave badly in a number of ways.

We recognize that just as there are many different forms of bad behavior, there are inevitably many different causes. We believe there are three major sources of the cause of bad behavior at work: intra-personal (i.e., bad people), inter-personal (bad groups and bad management) and organizational (how organizations are structured).

It has been suggested that it makes sense to separate two rather different kinds of "dark side" behavior at work:

▷ *Inter-personal deviance* – targeted at individuals to include gossip, theft from co-workers, violence.
▷ *Organizational deviance* – targeted towards the organization to include arson, whistle-blowing.

Other distinctions have been between "property deviance" and "pro-duction deviance". Some writers have added "political deviance" and "per-sonal aggression". The focus for *Bad Apples* is where the bad behavior has an impact on the employer or organization.

Studies in this area differ on many grounds. Vardi and Weitz (2004) note some of these. Thus, some studies and papers are entirely *theory-based*, while others are *data-based empirical studies*. Some are simply descriptive, others clearly prescriptive. Some do analysis at a macro-level, while others investigate issues at the micro-level. Some look at the structural features of counter-productive work behaviors (CWBs); others, the process by which things occur. Still others concentrate on the formal vs. informal features and aspects of corporate life.

Many studies rely on subjective data and reports, while others try to gather objective (behavioral, observational) data. Some studies concentrate on attitudes and beliefs, and others on emotional and affective responses. Finally, some researchers like to concentrate on direct vs. indirect measures of CWBs.

Management books could be accused of a sort of "Peter Pan-ism" or even "Cinderella-ism". They preferred to be upbeat, positive and blinkered about behavior at work. Hence, the research on the "dark side" and the "bad apples" was neglected. Naturally, there have been those interested in criminal behavior at work, from very specific crimes like embezzlement or sabotage, but whole other areas were neglected. The early work seemed dominated by criminologists and sociologists.

Vardi and Weitz (2004) claimed work in this area is understandable in terms of three phases. *The early phase* (1950–70) began to make distinctions between blue- and white-collar crime as individual occupational crime and group-based corporate or organizational crime.

The formative phase (1970–95) widened the area to take into consideration the workers' perspective, as well as concepts like "loyalty" and "justice". They claim the *current phase* (since 1995) had looked at very specific areas like employee deviance, workplace aggression and political behavior.

Technological, socio-economic changes and globalization have changed where and how we work. This has influenced our attitudes to, and behavior at, work, as well as how we are managed. It offers us new ways of working – and, inevitably, new ways of misbehavior.

New technology means new crimes: credit card fraud, hacking virus attacks. Individuals and whole organizations are targeted. They can cause not only considerable financial loss, but also loss of reputation. Many people seem to have lost their faith in, and trust of, organizations that seem not to have security controls and let these sorts of things happen.

Who are the perpetrators of cyber-crime – mainly hackers, former employees, organized crime and current employees. This is much more than the "help yourself" policy attitude of employees when it comes, for example, to office stationery. Can and should one have a special code of ethics at work?

Will it have any beneficial effects by, for instance, reducing CWBs? Is there a general code of ethics that one could adopt, or would it be better to devise one quite specifically for the organization? Should ethical awareness, behavior or literacy be taught in the organization? Should it be a "competency", or a factor to look for in selection? These are important – but unanswered – questions.

Business is fraught with ethical issues often portrayed as choosing between alternatives: sales vs. safety, self vs. organizational interests, in- vs. outsourcing, ecology vs. economy. There are dilemmas concerning bribery, corruption and nepotism. Ethical violations are common. The most common involve misleading and misinforming customers, violating health and safety rules, violating privacy rules, and being "careless" about confidential or proprietary information.

Marshall McLuhan is famous for his statement that "the medium is the message". By this, he meant that a medium affects people as much by its channel and processes as the message it carries. Some media are hot and high-definition, like cinema which enhances one sense and requires relatively little effort vs. cool, low-definition media which require considerable processing effort. Hot media allow for less participation than cool media. Cool media are detached, hot media involving. One is moved by hot media, not cold.

The question refers to communication by email. Consider the difference between "stealing secrets and passing them on to an interested other" – be it a consultant, journalist or spy master – when one first has to break into an office, then withdraw a file, physically remove reports, carry them out of the organization, and pass them on to another person in exchange for a reward. Compare this to sitting in the security and comfort of one's office – or, indeed, home – doing a "cut and paste" from one document to another.

In effect, they are doing exactly the same thing. Psychologically, they feel very different. To some extent, the computer-based electronic exchange of material can be seen as much "cooler, distant" even "anonymous". In fact, for many people this is a normal, everyday way of communicating.

The obvious concern with the whole integrity issue is whether integrity and its opposite (misconduct) are essentially caused by intra-personal (i.e. personality, values, morals of an individual), inter-personal (group norms) or organizational factors. It is the question central to this book. What if you put a few bad apples in a tray of good ones? Can we explain away recent corporate scandals by the actions of just a few people (Davis *et al.*, 2007)?

What happens when the highly moral, job-engaged person starts working in organizations that clearly disobeys the law? Organizational practices can strongly shape people's behavior. The most famous studies in the whole of psychology usually show how dramatically good people can do bad things. The Milgram obedience study showed that ordinary, civilized adults would, for a paltry sum paid to them for taking part in the study, literally shock to death another human being that they did not know.

Evil, corrupt organizations beget evil, corrupt behaviors. Usually, the opposite is true. A well-run, fair, open organization that is subject to good corporate governance and appropriate internal audits surely encourages good behavior. The question is whether we can explain and excuse bad behavior, as bad organizations, using bad (immoral, unfair, illegal) systems. There is always the issue of individual responsibility.

Political ideology, as well as disciplinary focus, means that some prefer to focus on the *individual* and the factors and forces that lead them to start and continue with CWBs. Others concentrate on *groups, gangs, teams and networks* that strongly influence individuals both within and outside the group. They stress social forces and pressures as main factors that shape behavior.

Still others see *socio-economic and political systems* not only in societies, but also in organizations that pre- and proscribe behavior such that good people in good groups end up doing bad things.

It is not a matter of choosing between these levels of analysis. Each can have a significant impact. There are "bad people", one can end up being influenced by the "wrong crowd", and some organizations are toxically corrupt. Clearly, each of these analyses or perspectives has different theories and recommendations for us.

It will become obvious that we, too, have our preferences. Some may want to accuse us of too individualistic an approach. So be it. However, we do not want to reject perspective differences from our own.

The apple metaphor

There are many metaphors and sayings associated with apples such as "an apple a day, keeps the doctor away". However, perhaps better known are phrases like "rotten to the core" or "one bad apple can spoil the whole barrel".

There is a *biochemistry* and *molecular biology* of apple-ripening. Is it true that one bad apple can and does accelerate the ripening and later rotting of a whole barrel, box or tray? The answer is *yes*. "One bad apple ..." But how does it work? Do they have to be in physical contact for this process to occur?

In apple trees, as in all other plants, germination, growth, development and reproduction is done through hormones that can be transported within plants (by a vascular system) or between plants by gases. Apples emit a ripening gas called *ethylene*.

> If you leave a rotten apple in a barrel of apples, the bacteria destroying it will gradually spread throughout the whole barrelful. In the same way, a person who causes difficulties or is dishonest may influence others in the community or organization he belongs to. A good example familiar to any schoolteacher is a disruptive, foul-mouthed and violent pupil whose behavior may render an otherwise easily manageable class quite unteachable, or a crooked policeman who persuades his colleagues to join him on the payroll of the local mafia.

The food industry has long known that if people pick fruit that is green and unripe, they can achieve optional ripeness by using the gas. Apples give out this gas and cause other fruit stored close to them to ripen more quickly and, by definition, spoil faster. The closer they are, the more they are exposed to the gas – but they do not have to be in direct contact. Greengrocers know that, to preserve their stock, they should first remove all over-ripe as well as rotten fruit. Next, they should store them in a cool, dark place to slow down the process.

Thus, one bad apple can accelerate the ripening and rotting of those close to them. The more bad apples randomly distributed in any storage container therefore, the more impact they have and the quicker the process accelerates. There is one more important aspect to this metaphor. The gas that over-ripe fruit give out influences many other types of fruit. Thus, a bad apple can have the same effect on bananas.

This analogy is easy to understand with regard to the topic of this book. Bad people deleteriously affect those around them. Further, the way people in organizations are "arranged" can strengthen or weaken the process.

Keep clean apples in a cool, dark, dry place and they are better preserved. Manage people in a just, open, aligned organization and they perform better.

Integrity as a trait

Before launching into the nature of the wicked, the bad and the revengeful, it is worth pausing and looking at the good, the not-so-bad and the loyal

employee. A theoretical and applied central question is the origin and stability of the concept of integrity. Can we talk of ethical, moral people who
demonstrate behaviorally very consistent evidence of following a moral code?
Is this any more than saying that people may demonstrate evidence of a
well-developed conscience or super-ego? Can people be honest and demonstrate integrity in one situation and not another? Is there any evidence of the
biological basis or inevitability of integrity? The Hobbesian vs. Rousseauian
view of morality contrasts two positions. Rousseau, along with other roman-
tics, argues that children are born good (moral) but are corrupted by *society*.
The Hobbesian view *is that people have to learn to be good*.

Few believe that one inherits integrity. There are no biological or genetic
studies that demonstrate that integrity is heritable. Certainly, genetic studies
have demonstrated the heritability of criminality. They suggest that certain
traits and abilities relate to how children are parented and how they learn,
which effects the development of their conscience.

Freudians talk of the super-ego; developmental psychologists of moral
development. Children are "polymorphous perverts" and not born with a
moral sense of socially acceptable behavior. Children learn to control their
biological urges, to distinguish between right and wrong, and to learn social
control around age five or six years.

For the Freudians, the development of the super-ego is the result of the
dual between the id and the ego. The ego checks our controls, our selfish
pleasure-seeking, amoral behavior through being disapproved of, found out
and being punished. It is the fear of consequences that leads to the development of a conscience. Children learn, from their parents, the difference
between right and wrong. They learn that transgressing moral rules leads
to punishment in some form. Parental disapproval thus generates anxiety,
which helps learning. Further, young children identify with (copy, imitate,
emulate) their parents, echoing their attitudes, beliefs and opinions. In this
sense, children come to share the morality of their parents. There is abundant evidence that children develop, over time, a moral sense.

Children learn self-control and morality primarily from their parents.
However, there are differences in the extent to which they learn these les-
sons. Some learn better than others (see Chapter 3 on the criminal personality). This accounts for the "black sheep of the family", where a child seems
not to develop personal control or a social confidence to the extent their
peers or parents did.

Parents, teachers and others notice that by the age that children start
school there are noticeable differences in their honesty and dishonesty.
Some are utterly, consistently and predictably honest in all situations, even
where they could possibly gain by dishonesty, while others are the precise
opposite.

Is integrity the opposite of "political behavior" at work? Not necessarily.
Political leaders wisely associate with powerful people and build useful coali-
tions. They work at cultivating a favorable impression and try to create obli-
gations in people who feel the need to reciprocate kindness. Less attractively,
perhaps, they seek to gain control over and use of "sensitive information".

They also, often, attack and blame others to refocus attention away from their (mis)deeds.

Work groups and counter-productive work behaviors

The study of CWBs has often been too focused on *intra*-personal, rather than *inter*-personal, determinants. Often, people need help to commit certain acts. They work in teams, groups and units that commit anti-social acts.

People with anti-social tendencies are more likely to be attracted to, and selected into, anti-social groups. Further, the group shapes the behaviors of its members, often increasing their anti-social acts. Bad apples model bad behavior which is easily copied. Groups with stronger anti-social climates have a greater ability to influence individual members' anti-social norms. The more groups have to rely on one another for task accomplishment and the more anti-social they were, the stronger the group became in its anti-social behavior.

Are people at different levels or in different work groups more or less prone to CWBs? As people climb up organizational levels, jobs change in a variety of ways. Certain senior people have more responsibility and they are likely to be (much) better rewarded. However, one characteristic that has been considered is *autonomy*. More senior managers have more freedom to determine their own work criteria, methods schedules and, even, rewards. In short, more senior people believe they have control; more junior people believe they are controlled.

It seems likely, then, that more senior jobs that offer more authority also offer easier access to all sorts of resources and easier ways to cover up CWBs. On the other hand, it could be argued that one of the criteria by which people are picked and promoted for more senior positions is their greater integrity, moral development and rule-following.

Autonomy relates to control which, in turn, relates to opportunities to restore justice, if it is perceived to be broken. Certainly, senior people can and do feel mistreated and victims of injustice on occasion but, possibly, less frequently than those with less power.

Most people work in groups that develop their own subculture and norms. These include how people feel about CWBs, to what extent they feel hard done by and to what extent they accept or flout various standards of behavior. The make-up, history and function of a team can have a profound impact on when, where, why and how frequently they engage in CWBs.

Vardi and Weitz (2004) looked at "withholding effort" in teams and showed that this behavior – or, rather, set of behaviors – was systematically related to a whole range of facts. These include:

1   The reward (and punishment) system: that is, fear of being fired
2   Group size: large groups make people less critical and easier to hide

3   Turnover rate: new, temporary, transient group members feel less commitment to groups and more prone to do less

4   Length of service: longer association means stronger ties and mutual obligation and, therefore, less "shirking"

5   Contribution to the task: the more crucial and interdependent people are in task completion, the less likely they are to withdrawal

6   Social norms: this refers to the consensus in the group about how to behave at work and when, why or how one can, or should, withhold behavior

7   Perceived fairness: this is all about whether they see others as free-riders and themselves as "suckers"; the more inequality they perceive things the more withdrawal

8   Perceived altruism: this refers to their perception of what it means to be a "good citizen" of the group.

We are all social animals. We live and work in groups which can powerfully affect our beliefs, behaviors and values.

The organization of jobs

Job advertisements sometimes give a job description. This covers the major roles and responsibilities, skills and outcomes of the job. Depending on an organization's purpose and products, jobs are designed so as to achieve those ends. They differ on many dimensions – skills required, output desired. Some people work independently, others dependently and most interdependently. Some are autonomous, others highly controlled. Some jobs place high demands on people and offer them very little control. These are clearly stressful.

Further, all jobs have usually been considered by a "compensation and benefits" spreadsheet. This is all about reward and recompense – mainly money. Some jobs are well paid, others poorly paid relative to others not only in the community at large, but also in the organization as a whole. In some, the gaps between the highest- and lowest-paid are substantial; in others, rather small.

Further, some jobs appear to offer opportunities to increase rewards. Classically, those on commission have this. However, there are often other sorts of rewards that people appreciate.

The design of jobs has been seen to be related to workplace crime. The reason is that jobs offer different opportunities for different types of rewards – formal and informal, legal and illegal.

The process

Lazy, aggressive people with low integrity can rarely, on their own, have very deleterious effects on organizations unless they are arsonists, whistle-blowers or the like. Bad apples spoil the barrel.

In a paper called "How, when and why bad apples spoil the barrel" Felps *et al.* (2006) spelt out a process whereby a dysfunctional team member (i.e. bad apple) inhibits essential group functions, processes and goals (i.e. spoils the barrel).

All work groups need members who will:

▷ contribute consistently and persistently to achieving group goals.
▷ do emotional labor to facilitate positive interactions in the group.
▷ do not violate rules or distract the group from their task.

Felps *et al.* (2006: 177) note:

> almost all of us have either had the personal experience of working with someone who displayed bad apple behaviors or had a friend, coworker, or spouse who has shared such stories with us. When this process starts to unfold at work, it consumes inordinate amounts of time, psychological resources, and emotional energy. We believe that our personal and indirect experience with such circumstances underlie many people's reluctance to fully commit to teams, despite the enthusiasm of psychologists and proclamations of popular management authors.
>
> We notice the behaviors, they offend us, reduce our enthusiasm, change our mood and may ultimately lead us to personally de-identify or leave the group, with a high likelihood that the group itself will perform poorly, fail, or disband.

Thus, bad apples can be behaviorally deferred in terms of a range of observable behaviors. *First*, bad apples withhold effort – they are shirkers, free-riders and social loafers. *Second*, they use negativity to express pessimism, anxiety, insecurity and irritation. *Third*, they are deviant: they taunt, hurt and embarrass others in their group.

These behaviors affect team-mates. Note: these do not include checking theft, vandalism or sabotage, since many of these affect the organization as a whole, rather than the team mates.

Chronic negative behaviors of any individual can have powerful effects on the team. They can engender a strong sense of inequality of damaged trust and a pervasive negative emotion throughout the team. Usually, the team responds by trying to eject or reject the bad apple, using exclusion, ostrasization or minimalization. They then try to repair and protect the group, to re-establish a sense of autonomy, self-esteem and well-being.

However, this way of coping may not succeed if the bad apple has power. He or she may be the leader, or an expert, or be protected by powerful people.

The effect of a bad apple on the barrel is, however, influenced by four moderating factors:

▷ *first*, how intense the negative behavior or social allergens.
▷ *second*, how interdependent the group – the more so, the more the effect.

▷ *third*, the seriousness, importance and consequentiability of the outcome.
▷ *fourth*, the coping skills of members of the group.

The individual action of a group member can influence by various processes, like displayed aggression. The sort of effects they can have on groups is to lower motivation, suppress creativity and learning, reduce co-operation and increase conflict. Yet, Felps *et al.* (2006: 208) note:

> It is important to note, however, that the negative member phenomenon does not explain every instance of group dysfunction. Other factors such as lack of organizational support, work–family issues, inadequate member competencies, or unclear directions provide a host of alternative causes. In other words, there is reason to be cautious in applying a bad apple label to a particular member when confronted with a dysfunctional group.

Others have pointed out important features that affect the power of bad apples on others. Gino *et al.* (2009) noted that if a person from another group, team or organization observes the bad behavior then we are more likely to do something about it. They concluded from their three studies thus:

> Unethical behavior represents a serious problem since it is detrimental to the functioning of both organizations and the broader society, as witnessed by the recent countless cases of inappropriate behavior – from the abuses in Abu Ghraib to corporate corruption on Wall Street. Our research suggests that few bad apples can indeed have a contagious effect on others around them. But, in the face of out-groups, we are willing to correct for the bad actions of our peers and compensate for them. (p. 1302)

In an important recent review, Kish-Gephart *et al.* (2010) conceived of the problem in terms of three factors: *individual differences* (bad apples), *moral issues* (bad cases) and *bad organizations* (bad barrels). Clearly, *first*, certain people could be described as bad apples: they are characterized by poor moral development, moral relativism, Machiavellianism and so on. *Second*, there is the moral issue characteristic that the person faces, such as the magnitude of effects, the social consensus that it is wrong; and the ethical climate and culture of the organization.

Kish-Gephart *et al.* (2010) found that:

> individuals who obey authority figures' unethical directives or act merely to avoid punishment, who manipulate others to orchestrate their own personal gain, who fail to see the connection between their actions and outcomes, or who believe that ethical choices are driven by circumstance are more likely to make unethical choices at work. (p. 20)

They also note:

> Our findings suggest that organizations create bad and good social environments ("barrels") that can influence individual-level unethical choices. We found

that firms promoting an "everyone for himself" atmosphere (egoistic climates) are more likely to encourage unethical choices. However, the reverse relationship is found where there is a climate that focuses employees' attention on the well-being of multiple stakeholders, such as employees, customers, and the community (benevolent climate), or on following rules that protect the company and others (principled climate). Likewise, a strong ethical culture that clearly communicates the range of acceptable and unacceptable behavior (e.g., through leader role-modeling, rewards systems, and informal norms) is associated with fewer unethical decisions in the workplace. (Kish-Gephart *et al.*, 2010: 21)

Organizational intervention

There is no shortage of papers that have attempted to provide a list of processes or procedures that an organization needs to put in place to attempt to reduce illegal, unethical CWBs. For instance, Kayes *et al.* (2007) list four characteristics of an organization with integrity:

1   It openly, honestly and frequently discusses ethics and integrity
2   There are structural supports and procedures to develop and maintain ethical decision making
3   There is a corporate culture of commitment, openness and responsibility to maintain the multiple business goals
4   Employee development really is valued.

Kayes *et al.* stress the importance of operating controls, as well as principles and processes to maintain core values and a corporate culture of integrity. They list six barriers to building an organization with integrity:

1   Fear of being ostracized for whistle-blowing
2   Companies growing too large and impersonal
3   Setting unrealistic organizational objectives that lead to a disconnection between goals and means to achieve them
4   The demographics of the workforce where certain groups (based on age, sex) seem less ethically driven than others
5   Organizations in transaction (acquisition, merger, restructuring) that seem to have fewer controls
6   Cynicism of the staff about management and regulation strategies.

Kayes *et al.* argue that integrity starts at the top of organizations. People need to know the rules and be very clear on what happens when they are broken.

Dealing with unacceptable employee behavior

It is important, first, to note that it is the behavior and not the individual that is – or, at least, should be – the focus of the intervention. That is, the "problem" employee may be more a function of a "problem" process than a "problem" personality. First, investigate how processes and procedures drive, shape and even reward problem behavior. Managers, supervisors and social norms may be a powerful, if inadvertent, contributor to a wide range of work performance issues.

Certainly, there are difficult problem people: addicts, those with mental health problems and those with strange "attitudes and values". However, the start of the intervention needs to begin with diagnosis. What is the root cause (or causes) of the performance problems? To what extent does the problem lie within the worker or is, essentially, a social or structural problem that influences many aspects of the problem. The more common, persistent and obvious the problem, the more likely its cause is external to the individual.

Diagnosis precedes cure. The next issue is having direct, specific, clear communication with the problem people. This is about good communication with the employee, hearing and understanding their perceptions but, equally, clearly stating your perceptions. It is about being open and clear, but also about being direct and subtle.

The next stage involves deciding upon a positive, effective and corrective intervention technique, rather than something fashionable, punitive and less effective. It is about finding a technique or method – ideally, acceptable to the candidate – that can and does address the problem. Options involve everything from training and coaching to performance management and target-setting. Intervention takes time and money. It needs to be well-spent. Many techniques are of very limited benefit despite overblown claims to the contrary.

Intervention may include official warnings, offering mentoring and even demotion; the "trick" is to set a realistic target for changes in behavior – deadlines, levels, and so on – with some agreement about what occurs if the target is not met.

If the intervention fails, one has to proceed to the next level, which often includes a formal discipline session followed, possibly, by dismissal. This can be a legal minefield and can, in fact, exacerbate problems because of grievances, law-suits and the like.

Conclusion

People are the core of any company, civil service or organization. They make them profitable and effective, and they deliver the results. Processes, computers and structures help make them more efficient, but they do not replace them.

Just as they make a company, staff are, too often, responsible for breaking it. CWBs are on the increase and they cost organizations in lost production, profits and reputation. Of course, there are bad people, but often the responsibility for failure lies with other people. The following chapters provide insights into the nature of the problems facing top management: the causes of, how to protect against and how to avoid CWBs. A great deal is common sense; some is counter-intuitive.

2 Counter-Productive Work Behaviors: The Nature and Size of the Problem

Introduction

This chapter addresses some definitional issues, and goes on to describe specific CWBs and their impact in the workplace.

The list of anti-social, deviant and destructive behaviors at work is long: absenteeism, accidents, bullying, corruption, fraud, disciplinary problems, drug and alcohol abuse, sabotage, sexual harassment, tardiness, theft, whistle-blowing, white-collar crime and violence are typical examples. Some are relatively trivial (occasional absenteeism, tardiness); others have much greater impact (fraud, theft, sabotage). In the US and in many academic institutions, the term "CWB" is used to cover the whole range of employee acts which have a negative effect in the workplace.

"Misbehaviors" at work, from an academic research perspective, usually come under one of the headings discussed in the following sections.

Aggression, hostility and violence

This refers to everything from workplace homicides to rude comments. Aggression can be described on various dimensions: whether it is primarily physical or verbal, whether it is active or passive, whether it is direct or indirect. It may be directed at various groups – upwards, lateral, downwards. Another distinction is whether this is targeted at the individual(s) or organizational systems, and whether it should be considered serious or not. Thus, a practical joke played on an individual may be considered a minor, personal incident, while a wildcat strike or Luddism as a major organizational incident.

It is not clear whether this sort of behavior is, indeed, on the increase or whether it is simply a function of interpretation and monitoring. Next, there is the important issue of whether there are corporate cultures that actually approve, endorse or encourage workplace violence.

Absenteeism, withdrawal and social loafing

There are many ways in which not working can be seen as counter-productive. Total absenteeism, arriving late, leaving early, sudden departures (turnover) can all be seen as having tremendous and immediate financial consequences. Added to this, it is possible to include low-quality work, slow-downs and general sloppiness which require correction.

There is also the concept of *social loafing* or the propensity to withhold effort. This has also been called shirking or *free-loading*. It means, quite simply, not pulling one's weight. Particularly in team settings, it means letting others do the work while often pretending to put in full effort.

Workplace bullying

This is behavior that deliberately targets an individual and aims to humiliate, threaten, undermine or victimize. It may be intentional or unintentional; it may involve the perpetrator being a subordinate, superior or colleague; and the cause may lie both inside and outside the organization. However, bullying does have recognizable characteristics: it is unreasonable, repeated over time and not aimed at increasing productivity.

Typical bullying acts include verbal and physical abuse; isolationism; assigning meaningless, impossible or very stressful tasks; withholding or distorting vital task relevant information. It could include hate-mail, gossip-mongering and psychologically threatening behavior. Bullying is hurtful not only in the short term, but also the long term.

Inactivity, insults and rudeness

Service businesses require and rejoice in interpersonal activity and politeness. Courteous, civil, kind behavior is valued. Could the use of rude comments or gestures, thoughtlessness or selfishness – like queue jumping or attention-seeking behavior – really be considered counter-productive work behavior?

Societies, groups and organizations have normative behavior systems or codes of conduct that people are required to follow. This includes how they dress, address each other, use profane language and help one another. These explicit and implicit rules may be broken by the use of inappropriate dress or language. One can deliberately keep people waiting, humiliate or defame them, show open and obvious favoritism or indulge in mocking. These insults could be of a racial or sexual nature. Hence, a great deal of interest in sexual harassment and racial discrimination. Both of these behaviors can easily cross the line between boisterous, high-flux bantering and flirting to serious, illegal behaviors.

Workplace sexual harassment or racial harassment comes under this group of interpersonal manifestations of CWB. The former is nearly always associated with males. It is seen as the misuse or abuse of power to humiliate or intimidate another person.

Workaholism

This is simply addiction to work – a manifestation of over-commitment and involvement. But is this really either a problem or, indeed, a counter-productive behavior at work? It seems to be a behavior encouraged in many organizations. Workaholics are not simply over-workers: both can seem and feel trapped by excessive work, but workaholics feel they have more a sense of freedom in their choice and they also feel they gain equability for their input. Over-workers, on the other hand, feel they have to work excessively (to retain their job, get paid and such) and that they do not get rewarded equitably or fairly given their input.

The question is whether the workaholic is a highly-productive, adjusted person who chooses to be very involved at work, or a frustrated, pressured, tense, troubled, uncooperative and unhappy worker avoiding things at home. Those who see workaholism as unhealthy point to its association with compulsive and perfectionistic behavior. They seem compelled to work but are not particularly happy with their work. Equally, they may be very slow or obsessional.

It has been suggested that the workaholic worker is often competitive rather than co-operative, as well as hostile and irritable. Their "super-competitiveness" and achievement orientation make them neither good colleagues nor good bosses. They may themselves encourage others to break rules and safety regulations, if they believe they get in the way of work outcome.

Substance abuse

This refers to the use (and abuse) of legal (alcohol and tobacco) and illegal drugs (stimulants, depressants) before, during or after work that may adversely affect production. Sometimes workers will take these drugs to try to make themselves work more efficiently. The night-workers or long-haul truck drivers might take a variety of stimulants to attempt to be more vigilant. Others may consume large quantities of alcohol after work to relieve stress and encourage sleep.

Others seem "addicted" to various substances that they "need" to take at work. In some organizations, the consumption of legitimate drugs is sanctioned. Many organizations accept excessive drinking on their premises during workplace parties, celebrations or special times. Unhealthy counter-productive drinking often occurs because of availability and/or poor social control. It also occurs when staff are alienated, stressed or poorly supervised. Alcohol and drug abuse is also associated with specific professions.

Yet, there are several important questions here. *First*, to what extent do ability, biographical, personality and cultural factors influence a person's use and misuse of various substances. It could be that, if there is an association between a job type and substance abuse, this could be moderated by personality. Extroverts like to drink socially and so choose jobs that offer both.

Second, there is the issue of external factors, like the individual's job and level. Group norms around drug-taking, as well as organizational culture and climate, affect substance abuse. Is it more likely that people take up and keep on taking drugs because of the situation they find themselves in?

Third, there is the obvious question of the consequences of abuse. Is there good, clear evidence that substance abuse increases absenteeism and accidents while decreasing productivity? There are, clearly, various studies that document these links (Vardi and Weitz, 2004).

Therefore, it has not been surprising that many organizations have tried to reduce abuse by introducing strict policy and discipline measures; trying to reduce stress, isolation and estrangement; and encouraging a work culture that condemns abuse of all sorts in or out of the job.

Personal revenge

It is said that "Hell has no fury like a woman scorned". This, however, does not only apply to women. The retributive, eye-for-an-eye, is well-known throughout history. It is, in essence, a form of retributive justice where an individual takes revenge for perceived mistreatment.

This can take various forms. The *first* is based on recompense. Thus, stealing from an employer can be seen as recompensing for woefully inadequate, insufficient and inequitable wages. A *second* form is posing as a victim and attempting very publicly to damage the reputation of (often very senior) people. It is very public revenge. *Third*, there is a sort of retaliatory vandalism based on the philosophy of "don't get mad: get even". It aims not to gain anything personally but to humiliate or frustrate those that brought about problems for the individual.

There are, in this scenario, various persons involved: The perpetrator(s); the avenger(s) and the bystander(s). The avenger is out to restore justice by attacking the perpetrator, while bystanders witness the episode. Revenge is about sensitivity to justice. It depends on an individual's perception of what is fair, and how justice can or should be restored.

Political behavior at work

This nearly always has a negative connotation. It usually refers to exploitative, manipulative and negative behavior that is self-serving and leads to disillusionment and difficulties. It is opportunistic, self-centered behaviors. It is about the use of particular techniques to exercise power and influence.

There are different views on office politics. On the one hand, employees talk of defamatory, self-serving, manipulative behaviors with scant regard for the welfare of others or the good of the organization as a whole. At the heart of the objection is the idea that it represents a misuse of authority and power. On the other hand, others say it is simply naïve to label organization behavior one cannot understand or influence as "political". Political behavior is about the study of power.

Vandalism

There is a relatively thin line between vandalism and sabotage. People think of vandalism in terms of graffiti, breaking public objects and scattering litter. It is a form of willful destruction and despoilment. It is more often impulsive, opportunistic excitement-seeking. It is thrill-seeking and destructive, and "normal" amongst groups of young men. More importantly, it is usually attention-seeking and demonstrative. It is sometimes about the protection or rejection of certain ideas, politics or company values.

Sabotage is more likely to be instrumental, in the sense that it aims to change certain practices or environments. Thus, eighteenth-century Luddites were saboteurs who tried to prevent mechanization. Sabotage is often planned, vengeful behavior on the part of the individuals.

Sackett (2002) lists 11 groups of CWBs. Missing from this otherwise useful classification are the CWBs associated with fraud, bribery and corruption. Table 2.1, based on Sackett's list, has therefore been adapted to include a twelfth group – corruption.

The focus in *Bad Apples* will be on CWBs which have a major impact on the organization – that is, the top four mentioned in the introduction to this chapter: theft, corruption, destruction of property, and misuse of information.

We are concerned only with those CWBs which are intentional. People who are lazy, who indulge in substance abuse (drugs and alcohol) or who have issues with other individuals (bullying, sexual harassment) fall outside the scope of this book.

CWBs cost organizations billions every year and many of them invest in ways to prevent, reduce or catch those most likely to offend. All agree it is a multi-faceted behavioral syndrome that is characterized by hostility to authority, impulsivity, social insensitivity, alienation and lack of moral integrity. People feel frustrated or powerless or unfairly dealt with, and act accordingly.

A central question for both the scientist and the manager is whether different types of CWB are discrete or related. In other words, does each CWB have its own unique characteristics, or are they are related and the product

Table 2.1 Counter-productive work behaviors

Theft	Theft of cash or property; "giving away" of goods or services, misuse of employee discount
Corruption	Fraud, bribery, abuse of employee position to achieve an unfair advantage either to self or others
Destruction of property	Deface, damage, or destroy property; sabotage
Misuse of information	Reveal confidential information; falsify records
Misuse of time and resources	Waste time, alter time card, conduct personal business during work time
Unsafe behavior	Failure to follow safety procedures; failure to learn safety procedures
Poor attendance	Unexcused absence or tardiness; misuse sick leave
Poor quality work	Intentionally slow or sloppy work
Alcohol use	Alcohol use on the job; coming to work under the influence of alcohol
Drug use	Possess, use, or sell drugs at work
Inappropriate verbal actions	Argue with customers; verbally harass co-workers
Inappropriate physical actions	Physically attack co-workers; physical sexual advances toward co-worker

of a mix of different personality types, organization situations and other external influences.

At the heart of the matter is whether people who engage in one type of CWB (i.e. sabotage) are also likely to engage in others (i.e. theft). It should, of course, be recognized that work contexts limit and provide opportunities for specific types of CWB. However, various studies using different groups have revealed a fairly strong correlation between self-reported CWBs (Sackett, 2002). Thus, it seems that people could be put on a continuum in terms of how likely they are to engage in CWBs from "very unlikely" to "very likely".

However, the choice of CWB to the individual is limited. Some thieve, others destroy, some go absent a great deal, others do shoddy work. Perhaps their personality, opportunity, level of courage or anger determines how they act, but the essential point is that people seek their vengeance where they can. Put another way, the essential causes of theft, sabotage, whistle-blowing or lying and cheating are probably the same.

Another issue is whether some organizations are more vulnerable to CWBs than others? If so, what characteristics make them more prone to having workers who perform a range of CWBs? What factors are important: large vs. small, public vs. private, high- vs. low-tech.

Vardi and Weitz (2004) reviewed various studies on utilities, health-based organizations, postal services and high-tech companies. They found leadership type important as a causal factor, but nearly all the other factors they considered, like job satisfaction, were more complex in their relationship with CWBs. However, they listed a number of organizational factors they thought relevant to high-tech companies. *First*, there is the issue of *risk and uncertainty* with demanding, competitive, unstructured work schedules. *Second*, there is *attitude to time*, which is often seen as a very valuable commodity in short supply. *Third*, there is internal and external competitiveness, which can greatly increase stress. *Fourth*, they note structural flexibility, meaning that these companies are often *virtual* and with no real boundary.

There are not many theories specifically of CWBs but one exception is that of Martinko *et al.* (2002) who developed what they called a *causal reasoning perspective*. Their aim was to demonstrate the relationships and similarities between and among various forms of CWBs. They define CWBs as those "characterized by a disregard for societal and organizational rules and values; actions that threaten the well-being of an organization and its members and break implicit and explicit rules about appropriate, civil and respectful behavior".

Martinko *et al.* (2002) reviewed over 20 relevant studies that looked at individual difference variables and situational variables that seemed to relate to CWB; individual differences included personality (e.g. neuroticism, Machiavellianism), demography (age, sex), morality (integrity), organizational experience (tenure, commitment) and self-perceptions (self-esteem, self-concept). The situational or organizational variables included organizational policies, practices, norms, rules, resource scarcity, job autonomy and appraisals.

The theory presented in Figure 2.1 goes like this. An individual in a particular work situation, say a person with low self-esteem and low integrity in a difficult competitive work environment with adverse work conditions, feels that things are not fair. The model talks of perceived disequilibria, or feelings of injustice or inequity. Associated with this feeling of unfairness is the cause or attribution that the person makes for this state of affairs. If they believe *they personally* are the cause (internal stable attribution), they are likely to take part in self-destructive behaviors, but if they feel the cause is *external* (i.e. their boss, unfair company rules) they are likely to take part in retaliation behavior. Note that the attribution must be about stable causes, meaning stable over time. Unstable causes, by definition, come and go and lead to quite different attributions. This lack of ability is a stable attribution, but being in a bad mood or having a cold is an unstable attribution.

Essentially, three things make this model attractive. *First*, it attempts to differentiate between different types of CWB, here called "self-destructive" and "retaliatory" behavior. *Second*, it offers a process whereby CWBs are likely to occur. *Third*, it describes some of the more important individual difference factors that have been associated with CWBs.

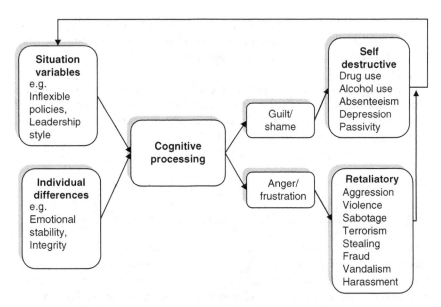

Figure 2.1   **A causal reasoning model of counter-productive work behavior**

Martinko *et al.* (2002) describe in detail six individual difference factors they believe to be heavily implicated in CWBs.

1   *Gender*: Overwhelmingly, CWBs are more likely to be the province of males, because they make more aggressive attributions and tend to be more self-serving by blaming others for their failure.
2   *Locus of control*: Those who are fatalistic, believing their lives are determined by chance or powerful others, compared with instrumentalists, who believe they control their own life outcomes, are more likely to commit CWBs.
3   *Attribution/explanation style*: Those with hostile and pessimistic attribution styles – in other words, those who attribute personal failure either to external, stable and intentional causes (i.e. a nasty boss) or internal, stable and global causes (i.e. I have no ability) – tend to cause more CWBs. In other words, how people characteristically describe their own success and failure is a good predictor of their likelihood to become involved in CWBs.
4   *Core self-evaluations*: These are fundamental beliefs about self and are similar to self-esteem. Hardy, stable, "can do" people are less likely to feel victims or experience organizational paranoia and less likely to be involved in CWBs.
5   *Integrity*: People with integrity tend to be agreeable, conscientious, emotionally stable and reliable. They are clearly less likely to get involved in CWBs.
6   *Neuroticism* (negative affectivity): This refers to the extent to which individuals experience anger, anxiety, fear and hostility. Stable individuals

tend to be more satisfied with their lives and focus on the positive. Neurotics often feel people in their environment are demanding, distant and threatening. Neurotics are more prone to CWBs.

Certainly, this model is a promising start. The authors are wary of limitations but make a good cause for specifying a reasonable process which explains how, why and when individuals in certain work situations do, and do not, get involved in CWBs.

Theft

Organizations often label theft as "inventory shrinkage" and it may represent 2–3% of retail sales. Up to half of this can be employee theft. These figures differ from country to country, sector to sector and year to year, but are serious enough for many organizations to call for expensive counter-measures. Electronic security tags, cameras and observation mirrors, locks and chain, and armed security guards are commonplace in many shops. They may or may not act as deterrents. They can, and often do, make matters worse.

The very number of synonyms for theft attests not only to how interspersed it is, but also how theft includes embezzling; filching; grand vs. petty larceny; thieving and theft; fleecing; misappropriating, liberating, peculating; pilfering; poaching; purloining and stealing.

Traditionally, people think about the theft of money (funds) or goods (materials, products, supplies). However, now perhaps the most important issues are data, intellectual property and even identities. Computerization of so many functions has lead to what one might call "new-age" CWBs.

Internet experts can it seems, with surprising ease, hack into massive databases in ways that ever-more sophisticated technologies cannot detect. It seems easier and easier to obtain, disseminate and even change various items of confidential information. This had been called *espionomics, internet piracy* or *freakery.*

No organization – big or small, public or private, successful or unsuccessful – is immune to theft. It has been argued that there are certain maxims or truisms that need to be heeded that apply to all organizations.

▷ Theft is contagious: it spreads unless controlled.
▷ Organizations concentrate too much on outsiders and not enough about insiders as potential thieves.
▷ Forgiving or ignoring theft, however small, encourages it.
▷ Organizations lose more from theft than they do from armed robberies.
▷ Caught thieves all claim it is their first time.
▷ Most, but not all, theft is retaliatory.
▷ Successful thieving soon becomes addictive.
▷ Those who lie about things tend to be thieves.
▷ Three quarters of people have stolen something of value from their employer.

▷ Some theft is actually "authorized" by supervisors.
▷ A great deal of theft is opportunistic, rather than planned.
▷ Thieves neutralize and legitimate their behavior all the time.

Self-evidently, it is difficult to obtain accurate figures on employee theft, hence the variability in estimates. Thus, some early studies suggest that about 5% of employees thieved in most work-settings but that this figure varied considerably by organization: 28% in manufacturing, 33% in hospitals, 35% for retail, 43% for supermarkets and 62% for fast foods. While some have claimed this is a preposterous, paranoid claim, others have thought it realistic. This problem inspired Wimbush and Dalton (1997) to use different methods (randomized-response technique, unmatched-count technique) to estimate the base rate for employee theft in situations with access to cash, supplies, merchandising or products. Their results suggest 50% of people steal. They note:

> Our methodology was specifically designed to estimate the base rate on theft by employees of cash, supplies, or merchandise. A reliance on these categories excludes other theft behaviours that result in lost revenues for a business as well. Consider, for example, fraudulently claiming paid sick leave, claiming pay for unworked hours (arriving late, leaving early, extended breaks), getting excessively reimbursed for expense accounts, purposefully damaging goods so that they may be purchased at discount, misusing discount privileges (purchases for friends), under-ringing cash register entries for the benefit of friends, issuing or receiving refunds for things not actually purchased, actively helping another person take company property, merchandise, or both, and deliberately overcharging or shortchanging customers for one's own advantage. (Wimbush and Dalton, 1997: 760–1)

Newspaper reports offer astounding statistics. It was claimed that, in 2009, staff from Britain's National Health Service stole £80,000,000. Another claimed the average British employee steals £400-worth of office supplies every year. An American report (Merchants Information Solutions, September 2009, www.merchantsinfo.com) noted "72,120 stealing employees were apprehended in 2008, recovering more than $69.8 million. Employee apprehension was up 3% and recovery up 9.9 % from 2007. One final interesting statistic: for every 30 employees, one was apprehended by their employer for theft."

The *Global Retail Theft Barometer* reported the following figures for 2009:

▷ Total global shrinkage cost retailers in the 41 countries **US$114,823 million**, equivalent to **1.43%** of their retail sales.
▷ The cost of crime per family was US$208.39 or €152.75.
▷ There was a rise in shrinkage and crime across the world. Shrinkage costs rose by 5.9% (from 1.35% to 1.43% the highest rate seen since the series started in 2001).

▷ Shoplifting was seen as the major problem that retailers faced, accounting for 42.5% of shrinkage or US$48.9 billion.

▷ Disloyal employees accounted for 35.5% of shrinkage or US$40.7 billion.

(Bamfield, 2009)

Commenting on the Jack L. Hayes International 2009 Survey, Mark R. Doyle, President, said:

For the 3rd consecutive year, both the apprehensions and recovery dollars from shoplifters and dishonest employees rose; up 7.26% and 21.64% respectively...While shoplifter and dishonest employee apprehensions increased 7.65% and 3.01% respectively, the increase in recovery dollars from these apprehensions was up an amazing 30.24% for shoplifting and almost 10% for dishonest employees. It should also be noted that employee theft apprehensions and recovery dollars increased for the 5th straight year...With the downturn in the economy, we have seen an increase in theft, which is having a detrimental impact on retailers' bottom-line profits. These losses drive consumer prices higher and can force unprofitable stores to close.

Table 2.2 presents a summary of the survey.

One in every 30 employees was apprehended for theft from their employer in 2008. On a per case average, dishonest employees steal a little over seven

Table 2.2 Summary of Jack L. Hayes International Survey

Participants	22 large retail companies with 19,151 stores and over $570 billion in retail sales (2008).
Apprehensions	904,226 shoplifters and dishonest employees were apprehended in 2008, up 7.26% from 2007.
Recovery dollars	Over $182 million was recovered from apprehended shoplifters and dishonest employees in 2008, up 21.64% from 2007.
Shoplifter apprehensions	832,106 shoplifters were apprehended in 2008, up 7.65% from 2007.
Shoplifter recovery dollars	Over $113 million was recovered from apprehended shoplifters in 2008, an amazing 30.24% increase from 2007. An additional $37.2 million was recovered from shoplifters where no apprehension was made, up 9.08% from 2007.
Employee apprehensions	72,120 dishonest employees were apprehended in 2008, up 3.01% from 2007.
Employee recovery dollars	Over $69.8 million was recovered from employee apprehensions in 2008, up 9.9% from 2007.

Source: Adapted from Jack L. Hayes International (2006).

times the amount stolen by shoplifters (US$969.14 vs. US$135.81) (http://www.hayesinternational.com).

Mishra and Prasad (2000: 818) listed different methods of how staff steal from their employers:

> Methods include stealing merchandise, stealing cash, retaining receipts to show stolen items were paid for, voiding a sale or making a no-sale after a customer has paid and pocketing the cash, overcharging, shortchanging, coupon stuffing, credits for nonexistent returns and sliding product through the lane without charging. Other examples include warehouse personnel stealing stocked items, and cleaning and maintenance personnel removing valuables with the trash. Employee theft also takes place at the point-of-receipt of merchandise and includes losses due to payment for goods not received.

They suggest that employee theft is the primary factor in the failure of about one third of all business. Hence the use of measures like observation mirrors, guards, CCTV and electronic surveillance to help reduce or prevent intended crime. They set out to compare the efficiency of two methods: internal controls and random inspectors using game theory. The central rationale, they point out, is the cost–benefit analysis of employing these systems.

There are all sorts of definitional issues: employers and employees have different definitions, particularly when the words "thief" and "victim" are used. Also, there is trivial theft (a few paperclips), semi-trivial (pens and paper) and non-trivial theft (computers). It is possible to distinguish between *production theft* (poor output) and *material theft* (property/money). Production theft includes work slow-downs, while material theft is, quite clearly, property theft. There is also theft of time (absenteeism) and theft of goods produced by the company.

Some have distinguished between *altruistic theft* (giving stolen goods to others) vs. *selfish theft*. This is often a post-rationalization of the thief who claims that he/she is more like Robin Hood than a common criminal. There is also *preventable* vs. *non-preventable theft*. This may be a more fuzzy distinction than can be made here. Almost no crime is totally non-preventable, though it can be significantly reduced.

In every company or organization there are staff who thieve. It may be mostly petty theft, but the extent is often surprising. The evidence is growing that employees regularly steal from their employers. Estimates vary considerably from researcher to researcher, from business sector to business sector and from country to country. But the overall picture is compelling: employee theft is significantly hurting companies and organizations.

The US Chamber of Commerce estimated, in 1999, that theft by employees costs American companies US$20 billion to US$40 billion per year. To pay for it, every man and woman working in America today contributes more than US$400 per year. The Chamber also reports that an employee is 15 times more likely than a non-employee to steal from an employer.

Unfortunately, 75% of employee-related crimes go unnoticed (http://www.inc.com).

Fraud

The difference between employee theft and fraud is largely about scale. In the previous section, "petty" theft of cash, goods on shelves or in cupboards has been discussed. Here, the theft is more determined and larger scale. There are currently over a dozen American CEOs in prison, all convicted of fraud.

Fraud comes in various forms. PricewaterhouseCoopers (PwC), in their 2009 report on economic crime, identify the following different forms of fraud:

▷ Asset misappropriation.
▷ Accounting fraud.
▷ Bribery and corruption.
▷ IP infringement.
▷ Money laundering.
▷ Tax fraud.
▷ Illegal insider-trading.
▷ Market fraud involving cartels colluding to fix prices.
▷ Espionage.

Fraud is defined by David Davies (2000) in one of the standard works on fraud as "All those activities involving dishonesty and deception that can drain value from a business, directly or indirectly, whether or not there is a personal benefit to the fraudster."

Fraud at work takes many forms. These include:

▷ Payments of false invoices.
▷ Payments to nonexistent staff.
▷ "Kickbacks" from suppliers.
▷ Internal theft of equipment, materials.

Perhaps the two most rising forms of fraud are *identity theft* and *phishing*, making it easier for people to steal personal information. Phishing occurs when fraudsters set up false sites and get people to give over personal details or move their money to them. As a result, a large percentage of the cost of developing software lies in making it secure.

Fraud, like all other CWBs, is, however, a function of three things: situational pressures on individuals; opportunity to commit and conceal fraud; and personal integrity and values.

In a recent study on organizational susceptibly to fraud Barnes and Webb (2007) found that, of all the factors that were related to fraud, the size of the organization was the most powerful. Further, some sections seem more (services) or less (manufacturing) susceptible to fraud. Surprisingly, they found that good management controls did *not* relate to losses from fraud or theft.

They concluded from their results that fraud was often sector specific and recorded separate guidelines depending on the sector concerned; also, given that individual seniority was related to fraud, that senior management should be particularly considered for monitoring.

Fraud appears to be on the increase. In 2008, more than £1.1 billion of fraud ended up in court cases – the highest level for 21 years. In a special report in the *Independent* newspaper dated 29 October 2009, the journalist Peter Archer reported: "Company managers, employees and customers were tried for some £300 million-worth of fraud last year, a threefold increase on 2007, according to investigators at KPMG. And near-record levels of recorded fraud are set to rise as the economic downturn pushes up financial crime. Investigators are also uncovering more fraud in restructuring and insolvency projects."

The worst hit sector was financial services, which suffered £388 million-worth of fraud, a tenfold increase on the £37 million recorded in 2007. However, this was boosted by an alleged £220-million attempted fraud at Sumitomo Matsui Banking Corporation, which came to court in 2008.

It is better news for the British government, however, as fraud losses were pegged back to £207 million from £833 million in 2007 – thanks largely to a crackdown on VAT carousels where tax on items such as mobile phones is fraudulently claimed back. Yet, companies have been hit badly.

According to the KPMG "Fraud Barometer", the 2000s were a decade of fraud, reaching a peak in 2009 when a record £1.3 billion of cases came to court, leading KPMG to dub the decade as the "naughty noughties" (Table 2.3).

The KPMG fraud barometer shows that 43% of fraud comes from inside the organization, costing UK business £566 million in 2009.

Table 2.3 Perpetrators of fraud, 2009

Perpetrator	Total (£)	Number of cases	Percentage of total (cost)
Management	333,610,686	65	25
Customer	26,426,554	40	2
Professional criminals	718,758,413	101	55
Employee	232,626,170	58	18
Other	1,004,312	7	<1
Total	**1,314,426,135**		

Mortgage fraud, involving organized syndicates and individuals, continues to rise as frauds perpetrated in the boom years are uncovered during the climate of falling property prices and a restricted lending market.

More and more technology is both the cause of more fraud but also better fraud detection. Company executives figure largely in many fraud statistics. They secrete high sums of money. Seniority is related to fraud for various reasons. Senior people both understand financial structures and processes better, but also have more latitude, control and decision-making power. Also, paradoxically, they are often trusted more. They are the ones who duck due diligence and override compliance regime procedures. They are trusted and clever. Instead of installing and monitoring checks, balances and safety checks, they happily abuse them.

The three most common types of economic crimes experienced in 2009 were: asset misappropriation, accounting fraud, and bribery and corruption. Accounting fraud has more than tripled since 2003.

The PwC report also shows which sectors are the most vulnerable (Figure 2.2).

People are tricked by ever-more imaginative fraudsters. Many are too embarrassed to report the issue to friends, family and the police, making the whole issue more difficult to research and manage. Credit card fraud is particularly common, with nearly a quarter of the population reporting some experience of it.

Bribery and corruption

Fraud covers a number of dishonest acts. Amongst them, bribery and corruption receive considerable attention in the press and amongst law-makers and -breakers. It is particularly relevant internationally in the context of *Bad Apples* because, in many countries, bribery seems to be

> *We can either steal it or arrest the people involved*
>
> (Flying Squad inspector to detective constables over find of £200,000)

endemic. The problem in these places is not so much the spread of one corrupt act leading to another but, rather, how to change the culture of corruption in a company or organization.

In police forces in Europe and North America, being sent to "traffic" (posted to a job responsible for the good order of traffic in a city or region) is seen as a bad career move. In countries like Indonesia, "traffic" is much sought after, because that is where real money can be made. More elite sections in Europe or North America such as counter-terrorism or even CID do not provide potential for such rich pickings. The issue, therefore, is not so much about one bad person influencing others as how to reverse the bad apple syndrome.

Corruption is defined as the abuse of entrusted power for private gain (WorldBank, http://web.worldbank.org). Transparency International (TI) further differentiates between "according to rule" corruption and "against

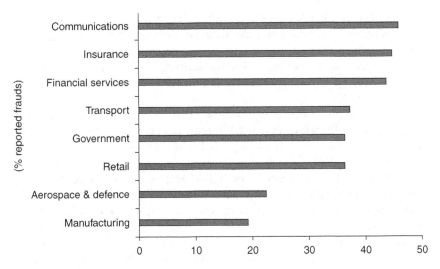

Figure 2.2   **Fraud reported by industries**
Source: PricewaterhouseCoopers (2010).

the rule" corruption. Facilitation payments, where a bribe is paid in order to receive preferential treatment for something that the bribe receiver is required to do by law, constitute the former. The latter, on the other hand, is a bribe paid to obtain services the bribe receiver is prohibited from providing.

TI publishes a list annually of the countries which are perceived to be corrupt (http://www.transparency.org). Top of their list of corrupt countries are Somalia and Afghanistan, with Kenya, Russia, Indonesia, Bangladesh and the Ukraine in the same half of the list.

It is interesting to compare this with the findings of the PwC Global Economic Crime Survey for 2009. While TI measures perceptions, PwC measures reported fraud. Kenya, Russia and Ukraine are high on PwC's list of countries suffering significant fraud, but so, too, are Canada, the UK and New Zealand. At the other end of PwC's scale are countries like Indonesia, India and Romania, which

Over half of those polled across the region, indicated that they had paid bribes to access services. 68% of those who paid bribes in Uganda did so to facilitate the delivery of services which are already catered for by their taxes while 51% of the Kenyans sampled reported paying bribes to get services. A similar trend was replicated in Tanzania where 55% of the respondents were asked for bribes while seeking services. The ranking of key public service delivery agencies, for instance the police, judiciary, immigration departments, local authorities, power utility companies, water ministries and hospitals shows that the public service in East Africa is riven with corruption.

(East African Bribery Index 2009, *Transparency International*, 2 July 2009)

recorded relatively low levels of fraud, while the perception according to TI in these countries is that there is a serious fraud problem. PwC (2009) go on to comment that:

Organizations in territories where relatively low levels of fraud were reported have either failed to detect it or have been reluctant to report it once uncovered.

Bribery and corruption is also common throughout the developed world, though its manifestations may be different. According to the PwC report, 56% of organizations in Canada reported fraud, 43% in the UK and 40% in Australia (PwC, 2009).

Corruption has concerned the UK's Metropolitan police for many years. They have done much to counter it through the establishment of the "Ghost Squad", the Complaints Investigation Bureau (CIB) and, currently, the Directorate of Public Standards. They have had varying success, but what they have uncovered is revealing. There were undoubtedly pockets of corruption where the group-think left newcomers with little choice but to conform.

Much has been written on the subject of fraud and some turned into successful Hollywood films (e.g. *Serpico*, starring Al Pacino). Frank Serpico joined the New York Police Department in 1959. He was proud to be a cop and was eager, diligent and ambitious. He felt that a police officer should be respected rather than viewed with contempt or fear. His dilemma was that he was committed to policing and keen to become a detective, but access to that area exposed him to corrupt practices (Punch, 2009).

> What Serpico found so ironic was that Stanard, Zumatto, and the other plain-clothesmen he met were really professional in the sense that they were first class investigators, and they brought to their craft all the requisites this entailed – instinct patience, technique, determination and accurate intelligence provided by a carefully nurtured network of informers. If they had wanted to, they could have wiped out a major proportion of their number one target – illegal gambling – practically overnight. But their motivation instead was that there was money it for them. Serpico was constantly impressed by the way they could ferret out operations no matter how cleverly concealed, but their purpose was always to extort money from the people they caught. (Maas, 2005: 212)

Commenting on the case, Punch says: "The operational code had effectively become elevated to the 'SOP' [Standard Operating Procedures] for the entire plain-clothes unit. Almost everyone was bent: the choice was to participate; look away or move out. This was a very rotten orchard indeed; and it was the one healthy apple that proved 'deviant'" (Punch, 2009: 60).

Some of the evidence for corruption comes from corrupt police officers who are looking to reduce their sentence by becoming informants on their former colleagues. Amongst the most notorious in the UK is Terry McGuinness, a supergrass who was then abandoned by the CIB (the

Metropolitan Police unit responsible for investigating police corruption). McLagan quotes McGuiness:

> In this situation it was impossible not to fall in with the group. Call it peer pressure if you like. Looking back there are things I would never have done if I was on my own. (McLagan, 2004)

A statement given by Neil Putnam, perhaps a more reliable witness, recalls when he joined the elite South East Regional Crime Squad (SERCS):

> He was asking me if I had any debts and things like that. I said I had credit cards and I owed money on them. And he very blatantly turned round and said "well don't worry about that. A few more months here and we'll have all your debts cleared. You won't have any debts and you'll have money..." The corruption was despicable. There was no way out. I was in it up to my neck. We felt we were untouchable. No one was going to find out we were stealing. (McLagan, 2004)

> *From the moment you became a part of the Flying Squad, you were involved in a web of corruption ... It seems that those who thought themselves an elite were all routinely engaged in stealing substantial sums of money, some approved of by much senior officers*
>
> (Judge Neil Denison, sentencing three flying squad officers to seven years in prison, 2003)

This level of corruption was confirmed to McLagan by the respected Superintendent John Yates who was asked to investigate the activities of the East Dulwich SERCS officers. He said the following to McLagan:

> I was stunned and I use the word carefully, at the scale of the corruption. I had never imagined that officers could behave like that, behaving with such impunity, being so openly corrupt and getting away with it. (McLagan, 2004)

Researchers and commentators have devoted some effort to studying corruption in the police in the UK, the US, the Netherlands and elsewhere. Maurice Punch, in the introduction to his book *Police Corruption: Deviance, Accountability and Reform in Policing*, writes:

> In a nutshell I argue that systemic corruption can become "organizational deviance" so that we can no longer talk of "Bad Apples" but rather of "Rotten Orchards". (Punch, 2003)
> In some cases the extent of the deviancy and the severity of its consequences, combined with the failure to deal with it, reach the level of "system failure". (Punch, 2009)

Dr Bryn Caless examined 149 police officer and staff cases between 1998 and 2001 which had involved corruption of some form. Using the data from his researches, Caless produced a profile of the most likely of all corrupt police officers:

> A male detective Constable, aged in his mid to late forties with no more than 18 years' service but with no hope of further promotion, whose first marriage ended in divorce and who is either embarking on remarriage or is cohabiting with a new partner. He will be a highly regarded "doer" who has a long track-record of arrest and investigation, often in informant-handling, who is regarded as a "good old boy" and is a bit of a chancer. In terms of discipline he is a maverick and will have little time for supervisors. He will have some of the socially cold characteristics of a loner and will have served in the same area for a number of years, being regarded as the expert on his local patch. His initial corrupt offence will be passing information to criminals. (Caless, 2008)

It is unfair to pick on the police, as corruption occurs in many sectors; however, as they are law enforcers, their CWBs are given much more publicity and attention.

Bribery

In April 2010, the UK passed a new Bribery Act. Until then, the US Foreign Corrupt Practices Act (FCPA) was considered to be the most demanding and stringent – that accolade now passes to the UK. The Act defines bribery as being:

> Where a person offers, promises or gives a financial or other advantage to another person to induce that person to perform improperly a relevant function or to reward a person for the improper performance of such a function or activity.
>
> Similarly a person is guilty of bribery if he or she requests, agrees to receive or accepts a financial or other advantage as a reward for the improper performance of a relevant function or activity. (Office of Public Sector Information, 2010)

The act will, amongst other things:

▷ create two general offences covering the offering, promising or giving of an advantage, and requesting, agreeing to receive or accepting of an advantage.
▷ create a discrete offence of bribery of a foreign public official.
▷ create a new offence of failure by a commercial organisation to prevent a bribe being paid for or on its behalf (it will be a defence if the organisation has adequate procedures in place to prevent bribery).

(Ministry of Justice, 2010)

This makes it an offence to offer or receive a bribe and, specifically, includes the act of offering a bribe to a foreign government official. There is also a new requirement on company officials to establish adequate procedures in a company to prevent others in the company from paying a bribe. Ignorance of what a junior member of the company is doing is not a defense if the company has done nothing to train and inform their staff how to avoid paying bribes.

It follows that, if you need to release your goods imported into a country and it is standard in those countries to pay custom officials in that country money to facilitate their release, not only is the company officially guilty of a crime in the UK, but also the company leadership and managers are also guilty, even if the individual might not be British and might never come to the UK.

The Act also applies to agents, facilitators and intermediaries of companies who may be employed by them to help win a contract. If the facilitator pays a bribe, the company is guilty. If it does not take adequate steps to make sure the facilitator knows the legal requirements and does not do everything in its power to stop the facilitator, the company is guilty.

There are, of course, many more serious issues. British Aerospace Systems aircraft deals with the Saudi government caused much controversy. The Serious Fraud Office stopped their investigations on the grounds that it was not in the public interest.

The US government was not so constrained:

> According to court documents, the "support services" that BAES provided according to the formal understanding resulted, in part, in BAES providing substantial benefits to a foreign public official of KSA, who was in a position of influence regarding sales of fighter jets, other defense materials and related support services. BAES admitted it undertook no adequate review or verification of benefits provided to the KSA official, including no adequate review or verification of more than $5 million in invoices submitted by a BAES employee from May 2001 to early 2002 to determine whether the listed expenses were in compliance with previous statements made by BAES to the U.S. government regarding its anti-corruption compliance procedures. (Jarrett and Taylor, 2010)

The new British law is much stricter and it would seem unlikely that British law enforcement agencies, whatever the political pressure, would be able to suspend legal proceedings. Not only would the specific officials be guilty, but also top managers including the CEO would be guilty.

If convicted, those in BAES would, under the new law, be liable to up to 10 years in prison and a fine. Bribery is a CWB, understanding why people do it is a significant reason for this book's existence.

Deceit

Fraud in the field of science and medical research, in particular, is surprisingly frequent and, at least over the last 30 years, reasonably well-documented. In 1981, the US House of Representatives investigated scientific misconduct. Al Gore, Chairman of the Committee on Science and Technology opened the hearing with these words:

> We need to discover whether recent incidents are merely episodes that will drift into the history of science as footnotes, or whether we are creating situations and incentives... that makes such cases as these "the tip of the iceberg".

For a thousand years astronomers credited Ptolemy with theories about the positions of planets. Historians now believe that his writings were based on the observations of an earlier astronomer: Hipparchus of Rhodes. Newton is suspected of actively trying to discredit his competitors, as well as falsifying or massaging data to fit his existing theories. Mendel was so convinced of the correctness of his theories he made the data fit his hypothesis perfectly.

The reaction from the scientific community was hostile. Phillip Handler, President of the National Academy of Sciences, called the issue "grossly exaggerated" (Lock and Wells, 1996: 5–6). But the evidence of consistent and prevalent fraud and misconduct is strong.

Lock collated details of 71 case histories broken down between Australia, Canada, the UK and the US (Table 2.4).

They include some extraordinary examples, including the notorious case of William Summerlin at the Sloan-Kettering Institute, New York, who faked transplantation results by darkening transplanted skin patches in white mice with a black felt tip pen (Lock and Wells, 1996: 15–28). In 1997, a German investigative committee uncovered evidence that two biomedical scientists had falsified data in as many as 37 publications between 1988 and 1996.

Lock himself, in 1988, conducted a small survey of 80 people in the medical research fields and, in a response rate of 100% (itself an indicator of

Table 2.4 Consistent and prevalent fraud and misconduct, by country

Country	Number of cases
Australia	4
Canada	1
United Kingdom	14
United States	52
Total	**71**

Source: Adapted from Lock and Wells (1996): 5, 6.

the interest people have in the subject), found that over half knew of some instance of fraud or misconduct. His colleague Frank Wells was responsible for reporting 26 cases to the General Medical Council in the UK.

In Australia, cases of deceit have taken on a high profile. In 1991, Dr William McBride faced 15 complaints brought against him by the Health Department. He admitted publishing false and misleading data, claiming it was "in the long term interests of humanity". He was found guilty and struck off. The Medical Tribunal said his "acts demonstrated a course of premeditated deception in the field of medical research and indicate a serious flaw or defect in his character, a trait of dishonesty" (Lock and Wells, 1996: 135).

> APATE was the spirit (daimona) of deceit, guile, fraud and deception. Her male counterpart was Dolos, the daimon of trickery and wiles. She was also a companion of the Pseudologoi (lies). Her opposite number was Aletheia, the spirit of truth.

Professor Michael Briggs was dean at Geelong University and worked in the field of oral contraceptives. He was a man with a quick wit, and an ability to attract large sums of money from drug companies. In the early 1980s, there was considerable controversy over his research, culminating in his resignation and move to Marbella in Spain. The *Sunday Times* in London drew a partial admission from him of generalizing from a small amount of data (Lock and Wells, 1996: 130).

There seem to be three types of fraud in clinical and medical research: falsification of data, concealment of data, and creation of data (Lock and Wells, 1996: 211). But the detection and prevention is still fraught with problems. There is some movement in the western world to bring the approach to fraud together and to show consistency.

Others distinguish between two types of deceivers, the straightforward crooks and the "jerks". The latter tend to be "bright but without social skills; are aggressively competitive; are idiosyncratic; drive each other hard and have a variety of unclassified characteristics including corner-cutting, self delusion, and incompetence" (Lock and Wells, 1996: 30). "Self-deception is so potent a human capability that scientists, supposedly trained to be the most objective of observers, are in fact peculiarly vulnerable to deliberate deception by others" (Broad and Wade, 1982: 116).

Deviant, dysfunctional, counter-productive behavior takes place in many organizations. Universities are one such place. Brockway *et al.* (2002) showed how student cynicism may well lead to variable behavioral problems among cynical students. Interestingly, they distinguished between policy cynicism, academic cynicism, social cynicism and institutional cynicism. Jackson *et al.* (2002) also found that personality factors, in fact, predicted student cheating behavior at university.

Deception is also frequent in business. In the late 1990s, Roger Eden and Geoffrey Brailey – former directors of Corporate Services Group Plc, dishonestly caused and permitted the company's financial statements for 1997 to be prepared in such a way as to overstate the true extent of its profitability, and that they sought to do so in 1998. In 1997, the overstatement amounted to just over £3 million. In 1998, the accounting irregularities came to light before the statements could be published. The potential overstatement of profit for 1998 is estimated to exceed at least £25 million.

Information leakage (citizenship espionage)

Information itself is a commodity which can be sold or used to damage a company or organization, though, in some cases, the perpetrators can reasonably claim that their action was for the public good. Although the individual will feel they are giving a fair account of what has happened or the data, this is often disputed and sometimes there is no attempt to tell the truth. In most cases of information leakage, a third party has to be involved. The questions to be asked are: Did the employee know he or she was passing useful information? Did the employee deliberately seek out a third person or did the third person seek out the employee?

> *Gossip is the cement which holds organizations together,* said Ms Doyle.
> *Providing communal space, such as coffee areas or lunch rooms, allows employees to share information, knowledge and build relations that benefit both the company and the employee.*
>
> (Dr Judith Doyle, author of the report "New Community or New Slavery? The Emotional Division of Labour", *Telegraph online*, 22 November 2000)

It is also possible for individuals to take information away from an organization for their personal use later. Whenever anyone moves job, they take with them information and experience which will help them make better judgments as they make decisions in their new job. They might, for example, decide to pursue (or not) a particular client because they know what they need from earlier experience with the former company. For the purposes of this chapter, we are concerned mainly with those employees who pass information to another, as this is what causes the real damage.

Hogan and Hogan (1994) make four important observations about organizational betrayal by citizenship espionage. *First*, it is rare (a low base-rate phenomenon) and therefore very hard to predict. *Second*, the greatest dangers to organizations come from those within them (not without). *Third*, people are as used to competition as opposed to co-operation at work and are experts in deceptive communication. *Fourth*, those who take part in treachery and betrayal are often unusually socially skilled (charismatic, charming, intelligent, socially poised and self-confident).

From their research, Hogan and Hogan (1994) suggested that there are four characteristics of the ideal or prototypic betrayer. They are attractive, interesting, charming and past-masters at flattery and ingratiation. However, they also have unusual degrees of egocentrism, self-absorption and selfishness. In private, however, these people experience self-doubt, and are unhappy and unsure about their self-worth. Finally, they are particularly prone to self-deception – in short, they lie to themselves. The betrayer – an essentially hollow man or woman – retains only the mask of integrity: but more of this in Chapter 3.

Whistle-blowing

Journalists love whistle-blowers. They can provide brilliant "scoops" that humiliate the rich and powerful, the secretive and the privileged. There is a lot of whistle-blowing about. In 2005, the World Bank estimated the annual cost of corruption around the world at *US$1 trillion*. Wrongdoing can often be a significant factor jeopardizing the health, safety and general well-being of others. Does whistle-blowing work, in the sense that it "corrects" or prevents wrongdoing? Are wrong practices terminated in a reasonable time period? One issue is whether issues are resolved vs. cured. A whistle-blower complaint may be investigated and controversial issues resolved. They can get worse before they (if ever) get better.

At the heart of the question of the effectiveness of whistle-blowing is whom it helps – current employees, customers, shareholders, or the particular complainant? A person whistle-blows against an organization; things happen (including retribution) and the wrongdoing ends (temporarily or totally; in part or in full). The question is: how to measure efficacy.

What sort of things do whistle-blowers complain about? These include waste of assets by bad management, illegal discrimination, stealing and theft, breaking safety codes, sexual harassment and violation of the law.

There are many serious questions regarding whistle-blowing, once it has been defined. These include how widespread it is, the sort of people who blow the whistle, reactions to the whistle-blowers and, indeed, the legal status of whistle-blowing.

Definition: This can be very broad or rather more narrow. It could be public, reporting on a range of corporate wrongdoing issues including illegal, illegitimate or immoral activity, practices or omission. This may include everything from bullying and fraud to sexual harassment and misappropriation of funds. The questions revolve around the *nature* of the wrongdoing, the *quality* of their evidence, as well as their very particular and individual *motives*.

It is essentially the disclosure of current or previous members of an organization or people, groups or teams in an organization for what they deliberately did or did not do in particular times *or* circumstances.

This is different from selling a story or leaking "tit-bits". Whistle-blowing can be *internal* or *external*. That is, one can complain or report about perceived wrongdoing from within or without the organization. It may be seen as *selfish* or *selfless*, depending on the possibility of gain for the activity. They have the same data as the whistle-blower but choose for various reasons (primarily retaliation) *not* to report on what they see or know. Thus, while some whistle-blowers are taking revenge on their employers, their employers do the same to them.

A crucial issue is whether the whistle-blower is intending to inflict damage, discomfort, humiliation, injury or punishment out of a sense of anger, injustice or embarrassment. Organizations may impose formal or informal retaliation; it may be work related or social; it may be short- or long-term; and, of course, it may be mild or severe.

How common is whistle-blowing? In which sectors is it most common – private or public sector, big vs. small companies, in tall vs. flat organizations, in growing vs. contracting parts of the economy? On the one hand, it may seem from press reports that it is reaching pandemic proportions. On the other hand, few people know a whistle-blower or have experienced it in their organization. Inevitably, the statistics are very dubious and unreliable. Is a report by an internal auditor a case of whistle-blowing? When is a complaint different from a case of whistle-blowing? Should it really be called whistle-blowing if the complainants lose their case?

Surveys which ask people if they have (ever) witnessed wrongdoing in their organization reveal that a *very* high percentage say yes, though the number drops and changes depending on precisely what behaviors are mentioned. However, if then asked whether they "blew the whistle", this number drops dramatically to less than one tenth of those who say they observed it. Equally, it is not clear how much retaliation organizations took, or attempted to take, against whistle-blowers. Some believe the percentage to be around 30% though, as always, these are "guesstimates".

Another issue is the incidence of the *efficacy* of whistle-blowing. That is, did the wrongdoing stop, continue, worsen or lessen. The act of whistle-blowing is the beginning, not the end of the problem.

There are three "actors" in every whistle blowing case: the wrong-doer, the whistle-blower and the recipient of the information. From a legal perspective, whistle-blowing is warranted if the person believes *in good faith* the wrongdoing has implications for public policy. From a philosophic perspective, the question arises as to whether the act is ethical. However, from an auditor's perspective, the central question is whether the wrongdoing is sufficient to pursue the problem. Whistle-blowers need to decide internal vs. external channels for complaint. They are clearly very different in outcome. They also need a reasonable supposition of success, in that they believe their action will lead to the wrongdoing being stopped.

Near and Miceli (1996), in an extensive review, considered two myths: "Whistle-blowers are crackpots" and "All whistle-blowers suffer retaliation".

Whistle-blowers are crackpots

The results of numerous studies, though not entirely consistent, seem to indicate the precise opposite. Compared with "silent, inactive" observers, whistle-blowers tend to be older, more senior, better-educated, with better job performance and commitment, and report they have a role responsibility to report wrongdoing through appropriate channels.

> To date, empirical evidence has shown that whistle-blowing is more likely in organizations that support whistle-blowing in various ways, but not including incentives for it, and where whistle-blowers report greater value congruence with top managers. Organizations with higher rates of whistle-blowing seem to be high performing, to have slack resources, to be relatively non-bureaucratic, and tend to cluster in particular industries or in the public rather than private or not-for-profit sectors. Finally, group size is positively related to whistle-blowing, while quality of supervisor is not. (Near and Miceli, 1996: 512–13)

Researchers have questioned whistle-blowers' morality and loyalty. The latter naturally questions who the loyalty is to. Near and Miceli (1996) conclude that there is no evidence for the myth and that most whistle-blowers simply have the opportunity to observe the wrongdoing because of the nature of their jobs.

All whistle-blowers suffer retaliation

Despite looking at all sorts of factors (personal characteristics of whistle-blowers that predict retaliation; situational factors, like organizational structure and culture), the authors found little evidence and

> can only conclude that: a) retaliation against whistle-blowers is not universal (and perhaps not even widespread); b) retaliation, when it does occur, may take many forms (ranging from less severe to more severe), all of which are highly subject to personal interpretation by the whistle-blower; and c) whistle-blowers claim that it does not deter them, either currently or in the future cases, although fear of retaliation may cause them to seek external channels for whistle-blowing, to the obvious dismay of the organization. To date, however, most state and federal legal statutes have been written with the primary goal of preventing retaliation under the assumption that retaliation will deter future whistle-blowing – despite empirical evidence to the contrary. (Near and Miceli, 1996: 523)

When are whistle-blowers effective? Most, it seems go public once organizations attempt to cover-up wrongdoing and retaliate against the whistle-blower. Where whistle-blowers are powerful with unique skills, resources and secrets the organization needs (and cannot easily replace), they are more likely to succeed. The more competent, confident, credible and objective they seem, the more they are listened to. Experts with legitimate power are likely to be more effective, particularly with internal whistle-blowing.

Near and Miceli (1995) have done an excellent job in looking at the characteristics that predict effective whistle-blowing. They divide these into individual and situational variables, and present an explanatory flow chart.

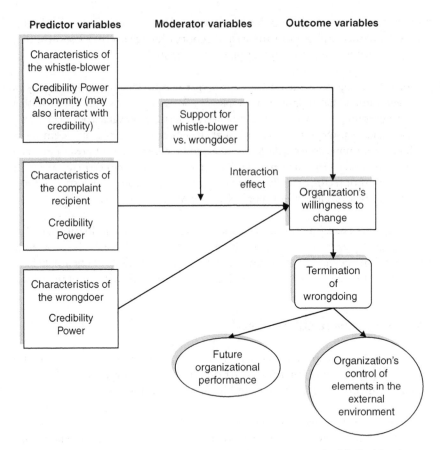

Figure 2.3   **Individual variables that affect the outcome of whistle-blowing**

The model presented in Figures 2.3 and 2.4 is based on 12 simple but crucial propositions. Whistle-blowing effectiveness is enhanced when managers, co-workers and the compliant recipient see the whistle-blower as credible and relatively powerful in the organization, and when they identify themselves at the outset rather than looking for anonymity. Effectiveness increases when the compliant recipients are supportive of the whistle-blower's actions, and when the wrong-doer has little power and credibility.

Near and Miceli (1995) assert that the greater the dependence of the organization on the wrongdoing, the less likely internal and the more likely external whistle-blowing will be. The more evidence provided and the more unambiguously illegal the acts, the more likely the effectiveness. Further, the whistle-blower needs to be seen to use appropriate channels and means. Naturally, effectiveness is enhanced in organizations where the climate discourages wrongdoing, and actually encourages whistle-blowing and discourages retaliation. It is most effective in organizations with bureaucratic structures, but only where they are formal and operating mechanisms to

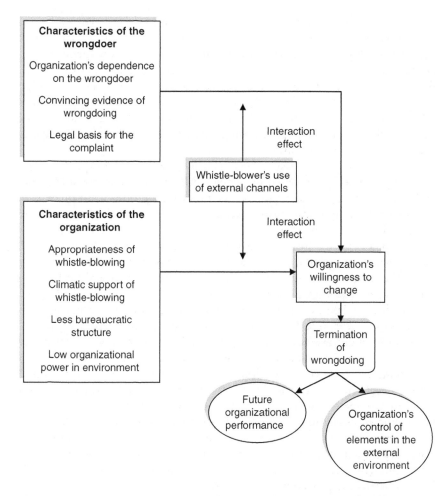

Figure 2.4   **Situational variables that affect the outcome of whistle-blowing**

encourage internal whistle-blowing. Finally, effectiveness will be enhanced in organizations that have low power in their environment, particularly if external channels of reporting are used.

The problem for the organization, the researcher and the law is to determine the *real motive* of the whistle-blower (Casal and Zalkind, 1995; Miceli *et al.*, 1991; Somers and Casal, 1994). The disgruntled, passed over, vengeful employee may take to whistle-blowing to "get even". Hopefully, close investigations of whistle-blowing accusations can help determine between just and unjust whistle-blowers. But the reputation and legal cost to an organization that has been falsely accused can be enormous. It can break organizations, as well as individuals.

Some whistle-blowers feel guilty and do so because by "telling the truth" they feel, in part, able to redeem themselves for their complicity, collusion and participation in the wrongdoing.

From the *top-down* perspectives in organizations, the whistle-blower is often seen as disloyal, a traitor, one who indulges in tittle-tattle. From the *bottom-up* perspective, they can be seen as heroes: courageous, fighters for truth. Some of the lionized whistle-blowers talk of personal sacrifice (the retaliation) for a noble cause; acting because they had no choice; being unable not to act knowing what they know. There is a great deal of talk about identification with victims, a sense of collective guilt and shame (working for the company), even being a part of history. Seeking revenge or the limelight is never discussed.

It is quite simply too easy to be a whistle-blower: media experts explain how frequently they are called by people with all sorts of impossible stories and little evidence to support them. Their motives are often a curious mix of the personal and political. Justice, ethics and fairness are concepts that are bandied about with abandon.

Bad apples at work "rot in the barrel". Corrupt managers who cheat, steal, lie and harass are potentially lethal for any organization. They can bring down the most successful and robust of organizations. If whistle-blowing can detect and eradicate them early, so much the better. But bad apples can, by their selfishness, laziness and litigiousness, bring senior managers, as well as supervisors, into bad repute by their accusation. People later judged innocent by enquiries, nevertheless go through not only extended periods of anxiety and torment, but also find they retain "dark shadows".

Essentially, then, the question is: When is whistle-blowing justified? This may refer to the manner in which it is done, as well as the reasons for it. Those who believe whistle-blowing to be a good thing and a safety-value talk of the suppression of dissent and give advice as to how to be an effective resister. It has been portrayed as an effective anti-corruption device. Some organizations clearly worried by the threat of whistle-blowing, often more euphemistically referred to as "raising concerns at work", actually have policies and procedures to deal with it. Thus, they may have a job entitled "Whistle-blowing Champion" and set out who to contact, how "the investigation" is dealt with by internal inquiry, and what occurs if this is not satisfactorily dealt with by the organization according to the whistle-blower.

In surveys, it has been shown that the over-whelming majority of people support the concept of legal protection for people who report corruption. A clear majority say they would probably or definitely not report corruption without legal protection. Clearly, job loss and other reprisals are seen to be the major deterrent to reporting corruption. Where people have faith that the management will respond to reports not by shooting the messenger but, rather, by investigating and confronting the problem, the need for whistle-blowing is significantly reduced.

It is, however, sensible to put into practice whistle-blower procedures that state that the issue of malpractice is serious and is dealt with firmly. The procedures must accept the right to raise issues confidentially and without fear of repercussions. There also need to be guidelines and time-limits for the consequent investigations. Perhaps most wisely of all, the procedures should specify consequences and penalties for making false and malicious allegations in the first place.

Some countries pass legal statutes (e.g. the British Public Interest Disclosure Act), which gives legitimate whistle-blowers legal protection against reprisal, victimization and, usually, dismissal. This Act applies to those who have "genuine concerns" about such things as criminal activity, civil offences, breaches of health and safety regulations, miscarriages of justice, environmental damage, and the like.

The Act states they must have honest and *reasonable suspicion* that a malpractice has occurred/is likely to occur and have made a *disclosure/representation* to their employer. The Act protects them if they reasonably believe they would be victimized should they raise concerns with senior people *internally* or with the *prescribed regulator*; that evidence would be concealed or destroyed if raised internally; or that they believed the disclosure was of an exceptionally serious nature.

So, when is whistle-blowing justified? This refers to the manner and matter of disclosure as well as the reasons/motives behind the whistle-blower's actions. Various criteria may be set (Table 2.5).

Espionage

Espionage is a rare crime; however, it is one that, when undetected, can have devastating consequences. Statistics are not easy to find, particularly in the UK. In the US, the Defense Security Service has researched 148 convictions since 1945, of which 83 were in the military or defense services, 30 in the intelligence agencies, 7 in other government departments, and 21 in the defense industries. Significantly, 62% were insiders who offered their services; a further 17% were recruited by close relatives (Fischer, 2000).

One of the most significant conclusions from this research was that most American spies are volunteers, not recruits, and that the most vulnerable age group is employees in their twenties. The volunteer spies are overwhelmingly in the young adult category.

The image of an ideological spy from the mid-twentieth century is no longer relevant. Burgess, Maclean and Philby belong to the Cold War. The nature of the threat now is different, and Intelligence services have moved on. There are some fundamental differences (Table 2.6).

Heuer (no date) identifies four conditions that must generally be present before a disaffected or troubled employee commits a serious betrayal of trust. He acknowledges that the same conditions apply for other insider crimes (Table 2.7).

The end of the Cold War has certainly done nothing to reduce the threat of espionage and the use by hostile intelligence services of human sources. If anything, it is more worrying because the hand of the intelligence service is harder to see and the enemy is no longer so easily identified. Personal weaknesses will play their part, but a manager's impact on a decision to betray is as important as ever.

Table 2.5 Various criteria that justify whistle-blowing

Utilitarianism	This is about working out the harm/good, ends/means ratio. There are nearly always positive and negative consequences of whistle-blowing. Whistle-blowing might cause a company to fail and innocent employees lose their jobs. If the end is not justified by the means, it probably means it is not justified. There are those who are not utilitarians and absolutists who believe that the *truth must be known* whatever the cost. It is a supposedly virtuous and moral necessity, whatever the consequences.
Correcting and preventing wrongdoing	If a whistle-blowers is clearly not interested in prevention, but only restitution (and revenge), it may be a sign of insincerity. Pessimists who talk of "the system" claim it cannot be changed, will always be corrupt and no – even altruistic – act can change that. On the other hand, if the whistle-blower seems genuinely interested in seeking that this event could (and should) not re-occur, it may be a sign of justifiability.
Responsible whistle-blowing	It may seem oxymoronic to some and quite natural to others that a code of conduct should be followed. To be responsible means things like: getting facts correct without distortion, exaggeration or fabrication; avoiding personalizing or vindictiveness; avoiding hurt, pain or embarrassment to innocent parties; consulting colleagues and relevant others before acting; choosing the appropriate time, manner and target for the whistle-blowing. Of course, all these rules must be seen in context and balanced. But the extent and reason for why they are broken gives a good insight into the real motives of the whistle-blower.
Channels exhausted	All organizations have policies and procedures about "complaints". The sincerity and honesty of a whistle-blower may be judged by the extent he/she gave the organization warnings and a chance to rectify wrongs. It is true that, within organization channels for complaints, disciplinary procedures and grievance may be absent; or obviously biased; or negative, dealing only with complaints and not prevention. Whistle-blowers often say it is dangerous, even suicidal, to try the "official" route, but that is something they must prove themselves to justify their actions.

Sabotage

Sabotage (poisoning products, arson, introducing computer viruses) is not exclusively the domain of a lunatic with explosives or a weapon. It is the cold calculation of a person intent on revenge, and there are many manifestations. Sabotage can have a wide and very specific meaning. It has, most often, two

The word "sabotage" derives from the Netherlands in the fifteenth century, when workers would throw their *sabots* (wooden shoes) into the wooden gears of the textile looms to break the cogs, feeling the automated machines would render the human workers obsolete.

Table 2.6 Fundamental differences in sensitivity to espionage

Technology	Information is no longer kept under lock and key in a senior officer's office or a heavily protected registry. More and more is held electronically. This means it can be more vulnerable to attack. It also means it can be taken in and out of a building easily. A memory stick is much easier to hide than a bundle of paper files.
End of Cold War	The threat is no longer so obvious. In the last century people in the UK were conditioned to be wary of Russians or anything that came out of communist regimes. That is no longer the case. Russians own some of our biggest football clubs and trade is now the norm not the exception.
Different techniques	Intelligence services are no longer relying on what they used to call a "conscious recruitment" – that is where they reveal to their potential recruit that they are working for an intelligence service. Increasingly intelligence officers are presenting themselves as consultants and offering their contacts a commercial deal. They continue to look for people who are greedy, disillusioned with their employer or who are lonely and seek friendship. The culprit therefore may not even know they are committing treason.

Source: Heuer (no date, "Treason 101: Insider Threat").

distinct connotations: the intention to damage company property, and/or to subvert company operations. This involves, quite simply, the destruction or tampering with (but, strictly speaking, not theft of) machinery and goods, as well as attempting to stop or slow down production. The reasons for sabotage are manifold: to protect one's job, to protect family/friends from a boss, or simply to employ the principle of an eye-for-an-eye.

Ambrose *et al.* (2002) examined the sabotage literature and identified five predominant motives:

1   A reaction to powerlessness, where people feel they have no freedom or autonomy at work – it is an attempt to attain control for its own sake

2   Chronic and acute organizational frustration that originates from such things as inadequate resources to do the job

A former IT consultant for a California oil and gas company has admitted he intentionally tampered with its computer systems after he was turned down for a permanent position there.

Mario Azar of Upland, California pleaded guilty to intentionally damaging a computer system used in interstate and foreign commerce. He was an IT consultant for Long Beach, California-based Pacific Energy Resources until around May 8, 2008.

Beginning on that date, Azar *"knowingly caused the transmission of programs"*, codes, and commands that impaired the computer systems of the company, prosecutors said. Parts of those systems were used to remotely operate giant oil platforms from the company's offices. The systems were also used to detect gas leaks.

Table 2.7 Conditions that lead to a serious betrayal of trust

Opportunity	The betrayer needs access to information or to people who have access to secret information. As already discussed, the technological age has made this easier despite vast efforts to apply the need-to-know rules through software.
Motive	Motives are complex and discussed in detail later. It is worth emphasizing here that motives are complex, rarely is there only one. Second, the real motive may be different from the appearance.
Reduced inhibitions	Most people working in the national infrastructure have high moral values and loyalty to the organization and their country; they also fear being caught. Loyalty can be stretched to breaking point by the organization and poor managers. Perceived inequities cause resentment – people feel betrayed and therefore find it easier to betray. The stigma of being caught as a traitor has no impact if they do not know the commercial proposition they have accepted is in fact the work of an intelligence service.
Triggers	Personal problems can stay with an individual throughout their career but never leading to misconduct. The decision to betray will often be triggered by some personal event or a critical incident in the workplace. Emotionally stable people cope with these incidents well – at worst, they may consider resignation. But less stable individuals may react differently and more irrationally.

3   To make work easier to accomplish, like breaking rules, restructuring social relationships – it may involve non-sanctioned means to achieve sanctioned ends

4   Boredom, entertainment and fun can certainly be had when things go wrong

5   Evening the score through a sense of injustice typically generated by disrespect, being passed over for promotion, given additional responsibilities without power.

In the world of anarchism and terrorism which exists today, there is a *sixth* reason – that of the terrorist or anarchist infiltrating organizations to sabotage key business or public services.

It is difficult, if not impossible, to obtain valid sabotage statistics for two reasons. *First*, organizations do not always know when it has occurred. *Second*, where they do, for obvious reasons of poor publicity they do not report it.

Saboteurs may be vengeful, defensive, lazy or self-promotional. Some retaliate and try to "get even", while others are more involved in self-presentation trying, somewhat bizarrely, to meet perceived expectations or requirements or organizational success.

Research shows that organizations can no longer look to prevent sabotage occurrences, but rather to anticipate and manage the event to a quick resolution. It is in management's best interest to avoid the acute and chronic stages of an event. At these stages, the organization may find the event to escalate in intensity, to fall under close media and governmental scrutiny, to interfere with the normal operations of business, to jeopardize its public image, and to damage its bottom line. Therefore once management can admit that an act may occur, it can access the impact of it on the organization and its public. With this combination of assessing an impact assuming a probability, management has developed a forecast procedure that it can make as part of a comprehensive plan to manage risk." (Di Battista, 1996)

Cyber-crime

How has new technology affected CWBs? The comparatively rapid rise of all electronic media and surveillance systems has introduced a whole new type of insider threat. There are new risks around cyber-space and the new technology. In the knowledge economy, data and formula protection are very important. Most data is now stored electronically, which contrasts to the world a few decades ago. Organizations try hard to protect their data but serious leaks are frequently seen. People "hack into" data sets; they expose private email "conversations" and steal secrets.

The question is, does this change the pattern of bad behavior at work?

Computer literacy and easier access

Most organizations historically, were extremely careful to ensure that personnel files, brand component and processing secrets, as well as financial information, was restricted to a very few senior managers on a "need-to-know basis". This is illustrated by the probably untrue modern myth that the formula for Coca Cola® is known by only two company executives, and that each knows only half of it.

"Secret Files" were kept, literally, under carefully scrutinized lock and key. To steal this secret would involve the physical act of locating them and either copying them or removing them from their place of storage. Indeed, that is the very stuff of "spy-novel" activity. What is different now is that most information is stored electronically. While every effort is usually made to protect the data, *three* things are different from the past. The *first* is that still, today, more senior people tend to be older and less computer-literate than younger people. It may well be, therefore, that people working in the IT section of organizations are "tasked" with data storage. They are often much less senior than managers who had this data in the past. Thus, computer competence and literacy, rather than seniority and position, dictates who might have access to such information.

It may well be that relatively junior, technical specialists have access to very important data in departments not well-known for their good management. Further, they may easily gain access to personnel files that hold certain personal information on performance appraisals, pay, and absenteeism. Thus, a young highly computer-literate employee could know "all about" those in the organization. This could include themselves, their colleagues and their boss. This data used to be exclusive to senior human resources executives but can now be very easily accessed by others, particularly those with Internet skills. Thus, the equity sensitive, not particularly well-paid individual may have access to sensitive information at a level never before experienced.

Related to this is the ever-developing "cat and mouse" game between data protection and hackers. Talented, determined and highly skilful young people have been able to break through into highly secret databanks, which contain, in one place, extremely important information. They are often people exploring and exploiting the data in other organizations than their own. Their motives are varied. They may be doing this out of curiosity or sheer daring, to see if they can beat the system. On the other hand, they may be doing it through political motivation, greed or revenge upon a particular group, individual or organization.

Resignations

Few companies or organizations are now able to offer young people a career for life. The emphasis from career advisors and in recruitment agencies is to move jobs regularly in order to develop talents fully. Retention of their talented, knowledgeable and hard-working employees is therefore becoming an endemic problem for employers.

The Hay Group reveals that about one third of employees surveyed worldwide plan to resign in three years. In the preceding five years, employee attrition surged by more than 25%. The Hay Group report showed that, for companies with revenues of US$500 million, the loss could amount to 4% of revenues – amounting to 40% of profits, assuming those companies earned 10% on revenues. The report gives an example from a consumer products group which recruits 100 executives a year, 25 of whom leave within 12 months. The average direct cost of recruitment and training was US$6.25 million – if they could have held on to 10 of those 25 executives, they would have saved US$2.5 million per year (Hay Group, 2001).

In the UK, a survey in 2001 showed that 22% of doctors intended to quit direct patient care in the next five years. In 1998, the figure was 14%. The principal reason was a reduction in job satisfaction (Sibbald *et al.*, 2003: 1). The cost of recruitment throughout the UK was estimated by Simon Howard in 2002 as £7 billion, "which is a lot of money in anyone's book" (Howard, 2002: 58).

There has been a great deal of research on employee turnover: why, when and how employees choose voluntarily to leave organizations. What have all these studies demonstrated? In their exhaustive meta-analysis, Griffeth *et al.* (2000) came to the following conclusions:

▷ There are *proximal* and *distal* causes that lead to the decision to leave which takes place over time in a fairly well-described dynamic process. The general decision to leave is usually initiated by job dissatisfaction. This leads to a search for an alternative. The distal factors that have been consistently shown to be important are: job content, stress, work group cohesion, autonomy, leadership, distributive justice and promotional chances. These affect commitment and satisfaction, which lead to ideas about leaving.
▷ The turnover rate in companies is not necessarily a powerful factor determining whether any one individual will leave.
▷ The turnover rate for women is quite similar to that of men.
▷ Companies that have merit-based reward systems tend to keep people longer. Where collective reward programs replace individual incentive, their introduction seems to increase turnover.
▷ Organizations (like the military) that have specific compulsory contracts to discourage resignations in a fixed period certainly experience far less turnover and a more stable workforce.
▷ Personality factors – specifically, neuroticism and conscientiousness – do predict turnover over and above other factors.

Resignations form the most frequent and perhaps the most innocent of departures, but it is often a manifestation of discontent and the one which costs most – and so many could be avoided!

Conclusion

This chapter has looked at some of the very specific types of CWBs. There is a separate research literature on these topics, yet many similar themes occur. These CWBs occur for a variety circumstances (most of which are predictable and preventable). Certainly, specific characteristics of individuals seem related to particular CWBs. A rather different sort of individual chooses to become a saboteur as opposed to a whistle-blower, though they may be motivated by very similar circumstances.

Opportunity, work group norms and management practices are the factors that most obviously account for specific CWBs. Theft, petty and serious, may be condoned by junior management; deceit maybe the norm in some settings, and mass turnover after expensive training and selection a common reaction to particular circumstances.

Integrity researchers in those specific areas offer similar advice. They maintain, with good empirical evidence, that those CWBs can be significantly reduced (though probably never eliminated). They all talk of more careful selection; better management practices; and the introduction, where appropriate, of surveillance equipment. Organizations have gone, and will go, out of business because of the preventable CWBs of the employees. No matter how good the product or service, or how hungry the market is for it, if the employees are disgruntled and vengeful because of the way they are treated, the organization may yet fail: hence the importance of taking the dark side of work behavior seriously.

CWBs are damaging; they affect profits and productivity. But disloyalty and indifference can be turned around, and with the right policies and management, organizations can create a workforce which is loyal and committed.

3 Counter-Productive Work Behaviors: Why Do They Do It?

Introduction

This chapter looks at the motivational factors that affect the behavior of employees at work. McClelland provides a basis which puts all motivation into context; Herzberg's early theory provides an understanding of the conditions that affect employee levels of satisfaction. This is followed by an explanation of equity theory that stresses the importance of "perceived fairness" on employee motivation. The section on justice at work sets this into the context of the workplace and explains why organizations need to have procedures in place to foster the impression that they are interested in justice. The chapter also looks at individual traits which make individuals more prone to engage in CWBs. The section on Persuaders identifies the role of external individuals on the motivation of insiders who commit CWBs. The section on motivational context brings the text on individual traits and Persuaders together, identifying the three overlapping fields of motivation that impact on the behavior of insiders. Theories about specific CWBs are provided, and the chapter concludes with six case studies.

The literature on human motivation is rich, of varying quality and sometimes contradictory. This chapter is not going to try and review that literature or even to identify those authors who have contributed most to the subject. But it will draw on those who have written about what makes people turn to CWBs.

It is useful to start with what motivates people, primarily in the context of the workplace. It is a complex topic, partly because people often cannot – rather than will not – explain what motivates them.

Human motivation

In one of the classics, *Human Motivation*, David McClelland says:

> It is very important to recognize at the outset that there are several kinds of answers to the question *why*, only some of which deal with the problem of motivation. A complete answer to the question *why* must include all the determinants of behavior, not just the motivational ones. (McClelland, 1987)

The external influences on the results are important in the context of CWBs, as we shall see later. Fritz Heider (1958) uses the example of a man rowing a boat across a lake. His success (or not) will depend not just on his determination and ability to achieve the task, but also on the weather and the currents which exist at the time of the attempted crossing.

A woman may have the knowledge, skills and motivation to commit sabotage on her employer's products but, if the CCTV cameras and other security measures are too intrusive to allow her to carry out the sabotage undetected, then she may not succeed. *Bad Apples* will explore some of these external factors and influences later.

Focusing on the personal determinants of behavioral outcome, McClelland breaks them down into three elements: motivational variables, skill or trait variables, and cognitive variables – beliefs, expectations and understanding. In one of the most widely accepted works on the subject, McClelland goes on to suggest that people fall into three motivational groups. Those in the first group, affiliative people, need to be liked and to have a feeling of belonging. There are people motivated by the need to achieve and they are not so worried about what others may think of them. Finally, there are those who are interested, above all else, in power. They focus on building power through influencing others (McClelland, 1987).

McClelland also discusses a fourth potential motivator: a measure of how people avoid failure or rejection. It undoubtedly exists as an emotion, but the "state of knowledge about avoidance motives is not very satisfactory ... We are not even entirely sure whether avoidance motives differ theoretically in significant ways from approach motives" (McClelland, 1987).

Affiliation, power and achievement do much to explain what motivates people at work, and helps managers and leaders (who themselves are, of course, motivated by the same things) understand what will encourage those who work for them.

The question in *Bad Apples* is whether they help us understand why people conduct CWBs. The answer is probably twofold. Some will be motivated to carry out a CWB because they want to achieve more, or because they want more power.

Thus, someone who commits fraud may be motivated by the need for more money so they can use it to increase their power over others, either within the organization or outside it. Where corruption is endemic, senior people often have to sustain their position by paying off others in the department. An academic may falsify the data to ensure his theories continue to look valid, and therefore his position and reputation in the university is maintained.

The second relevant motivator in this context is where their primary positive approach motivator is in some way thwarted and feelings of failed expectations, resentment or even revenge creep in. If a person seeks achievement, either through promotion or a particular posting, and does not succeed because of the action of a boss or the Human Resources department, they are likely to respond negatively. If the organization is lucky, this will be confined to resignation. It could become more serious and the individual could choose one of the options of CWB discussed in the preceding chapter.

Similarly, if a prime motivator is affiliation and the organization and those in the organization exclude the individual, his or her loyalty is quite likely to be undermined. While there are other more significant motivators in the case of Aldrich Ames, he clearly no longer felt part of the organization (CIA) when he decided to sell information to the KGB.

Motivations are rarely, if ever, simple. People as they go to work will do so because they want to be part of a group or team; they will also want to achieve something and to have some potential to influence others so that they have some power, if only over their own destiny and happiness. The intriguing question for practitioners and theorists alike relates to the variables between these three taken with other variables already identified by McClelland.

> Aldrich Ames (see full case study on page 268), a CIA officer who offered his services to the KGB in 1985, was generally considered to be a weak man plagued with alcohol and a wife who had very expensive tastes. His subsequent debts forced him to turn to the Russians.
>
> All that has some substance, but there is some significant evidence that he had, by 1985, become alienated from the CIA management, and his loyalty had been eroded by a number of decisions made about his career, as well as undermining his expertise on the Soviet Union – which he believed was not as big a threat as commonly believed.

Herzberg's theory

Much has been written about what motivates people to work – less on what de-motivates people or why people are destructive. Some theories concentrate on the needs, values or make-up of different individuals. Others look at the characteristics of individual jobs. One of the most significant and best-known is Herzberg, who describes what satisfies people at work and what dissatisfies people (Figure 3.1).

A quick glance at the middle boxes of Figure 3.1 shows that the manager can control much of what motivates or de-motivates people at work. And most cost nothing: recognition, applauding achievement, being a good supervisor, giving people responsibility. Herzberg's two factors are now more often described as intrinsic (to the nature of the job) and extrinsic (to external and reward factors). The more intrinsic people's motivations, the more likely they are to experience disappointment and frustration, and potentially commit CWBs.

Put another way, Herzberg's theory suggests that people at work expect good supervision, adequate pay, worthy company policies, good relationships and job security. That is why they joined the organization. If they are not satisfied with these basic needs they will quickly become dissatisfied.

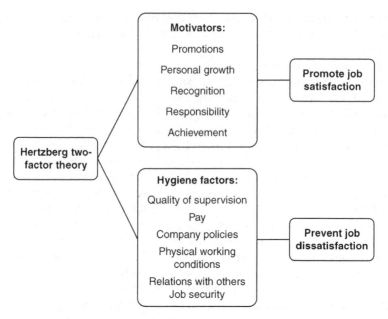

Figure 3.1 **Herzberg's theory**

A related theory, called "job facet theory" suggests that core job dimensions lead to specific psychological states which, in turn, lead to specific personal and work outcomes (Furnham, 2005). Thus, if a person uses their skills at work on a task they identify with and believe significant, they experience *meaningfulness*. Equally, if they have some autonomy, they feel responsible for the outcomes of their work. Further, if they get good feedback, they have knowledge of the results. These, in turn, lead to satisfaction and productivity.

The idea is that managers can design jobs, processes and systems which facilitate (or frustrate) satisfaction which, in turn, can lead to CWBs.

Equity theory

One of the most interesting insights into motivation comes from equity theory, which is entirely concerned with perceived fairness. Motivation for everyone is to be fairly treated. It is frequently associated with revenge. In the workplace, this is all about performance-related pay, fair treatment and non-discrimination. It is perhaps the most productive of the general theories that may usefully be applied to CWBs.

Equity theory proposes that employees are motivated to maintain fair, or "equitable", relationships among themselves and to change those relationships that are unfair or "inequitable". Equity theory is concerned with people's motivation to escape the negative feelings that result from being, or feeling, that they are unfairly treated in their jobs once they have engaged in the process of *social comparison*.

Table 3.1 Equity theory

The deal	Individuals evaluate their "deal" at work by comparing their inputs (what, how much they do) with outputs (their total "benefit package").
Compared with others	Individuals compare their input/output package with others in the workplace (superiors, colleagues/peers, subordinates).
Sense of inequality	If the ratios for peers are perceived to be *unequal*, then a deep sense of inequity exists. This could be over-rewarded or over-benefited inequity, leading to guilt; or under-rewarded or under-benefited equity, leading to anger.
The greater the inequity ...	The greater the inequity, the greater the tension, and the greater the motive to restore equity.
Remedy	Equity can be restored psychologically (cognitively by re-evaluating the circumstances, *or* by changing the comparison other, *or* by terminating the relationship).

Table 3.1 presents the arguments of equity theory.

Put simply, people at work compare themselves with others all the time. Satisfaction with pay and other benefits is almost always a function *not of absolute benefit* but (peer) *comparison benefit. It is not how much you are paid, but how much compared (or relative) to other peers.*

Equity theory suggests that people make social comparisons between themselves and others with respect to two variables – *outcomes* (benefits, rewards) and *inputs* (effort, ability). *Outcomes* refer to the things workers believe they and others get out of their jobs, including pay, fringe benefits (job security) or prestige (job titles). *Inputs* refer to the contribution employees believe they and others make to their jobs, including the amount of time at work, the amount of effort expended, the number of units produced, or the qualifications brought to the job. Equity theory is concerned with outcomes and inputs as they are *perceived* by the people involved, *not* necessarily as they actually are – although that, in itself, is often very difficult to measure. Not surprisingly, therefore, workers may disagree about what constitutes equity and inequity in the job. Equity is therefore a subjective, not objective, experience, which makes it most susceptible to being influenced by personality factors.

Employees compare themselves to others and, essentially, they have four choices (Table 3.2).

Equity theory states that people compare their outcomes and inputs to those of others in the form of a ratio. Specifically, they compare the ratio of their own outcomes and inputs, which can result in any of three states (Table 3.3).

According to equity theory, people are motivated to escape these negative emotional states of anger and guilt. Equity theory admits two major ways of

Table 3.2 Employee self-comparison

Self–inside	An employee's comparison with the experiences of others in a different position inside his or her current organization
Self–outside	An employee's comparison with the experience of others in a situation or position outside his or her organization
Other–inside	Comparison with another individual or group of individuals outside the employee's organization
Other–outside	Comparison with another individual or group of individuals inside the employee's organization

Table 3.3 Employee attitudes to outcomes and inputs

Overpayment	*Overpayment inequity* occurs when someone's outcome:input ratio is *greater than* the corresponding ratio of another person with whom that person compares himself or herself. People who are overpaid are supposed to feel *guilty*. There are relatively few people in this position.
Underpayment	*Underpayment inequity* occurs when someone's outcome:input ratio is less *than* the corresponding ratio of another person with whom that person compares himself or herself. People who are underpaid are supposed to feel *angry*. Many people feel under-benefited.
Equitable payment	*Equitable payment* occurs when someone's outcome:input ratio is *equal* to the corresponding ratio of another person with whom that person compares himself or herself. People who are equitably paid are supposed to feel *satisfied*.

resolving inequitable states. *Behavioral* reactions to equity represent things people can do to change their existing inputs and outcomes, such as working more or less hard (to increase or decrease inputs) or stealing time and goods (to increase outputs). In addition to behavioral reactions to underpayment inequity, there are also some likely *psychological* reactions. Given that many people feel uncomfortable stealing (goods or time) from their employers (to increase outputs), or would be unwilling to restrict their productivity or to ask for a salary increase (to increase inputs), they may resort to resolving the inequity by changing the way they think about the situation.

Because equity theory deals with perceptions of fairness and unfairness, it is reasonable to expect that inequity states may be redressed effectively by merely *thinking* about circumstances differently. For example, an underpaid person may attempt to *rationalize* that another's inputs are higher than his or her own, thereby convincing himself or herself that the other's higher outcomes are justified. There are various reactions to inequity: people can respond to overpayment (i.e. being under-benefited) inequities in behavioral and/or psychological ways (i.e. being over-benefited), which helps change the perceived *inequities* into a state of perceived *equity*.

If people believe they (their parents, group, ancestors) have been unfairly treated (their land taken away; their mobility blocked; victimized generally), they are motivated to correct the balance and restore justice. Justice restoration can occur via propaganda or force or, indeed, CWBs. It may involve punishing the perpetrators or their heirs, or simply changing the balance of things. Thus, if your land was "stolen", the motive to get it back will drive people to various acts, like terrorism, until their aim is achieved. Inevitably, people perceive the just or unjust situation very differently; furthermore, some restitution acts are driven by guilt, where people see their (privileged) position as being unfairly acquired (say, through inheritance).

Justice, fairness, honor, rights and reconciliation are very powerful motives. The more these words occur in the speeches, writings of individuals or groups, the more the justice motive should be considered important. As we shall see, people have used equity theory to explain theft as sabotage at work. Certainly, the concept of justice and fairness, which is at the heart of equity theory, is for all people a powerful motivator. Being thought of as unfairly treated is a primary motivator to achieve revenge.

Justice at work

The single word that dominates a great deal of debate and discussion around CWBs at work is "justice" (together with its many synonyms like "fairness"). The more people believe things are unfair and unjust, the more likely they are to attempt to regain justice. In this sense, CWBs at work may be seen to be, paradoxically, either reactions to perceived injustice or attempts to regain it.

There is abundant evidence that justice at work has powerful consequences on such things as job satisfaction/dissatisfaction, intent to leave and well-being (Dailey and Kirk, 1992; Schmitt and Dorfel, 1999). Equally people become angry and disheartened not only when they get unfairly treated, but also when they see work colleagues mistreated.

Questions of justice and fairness occur whenever decisions have to be made about the allocation of resources, whatever they are in a particular business. Concern about the outcomes of justice decisions is called *distributive* justice. However, there are also questions about how fair decisions are made, and the procedures each organization has in place to make those decisions. Concern about fairness policies is called *procedural* justice. Academically, it has been common to differentiate between three types of justice:

1   *Organizational Justice* is people's (manager and employee) perceptions of fairness in an organization's policies, pay systems and practices. The concept of justice and how justice is meted out in any organization must be fundamental to that organization's corporate culture. The

psychological literature tends to be *descriptive* (focusing on perceptions and reactions), whereas the moral philosophy writings are more *prescriptive* (specifying what should be done).

2   Research in *Distributive Justice* goes back to ideas "rules of social exchange". It is argued that rewards should be proportionate to costs, and the net rewards should be proportionate to investments. Most of the current research focuses on employee's perceptions of the fairness of the outcomes (both rewards and punishments) they receive. Results show clearly that fairness perceptions are based on relative judgments – that is, comparisons with salient others. That is, how happy one is with fairness decisions (such as decisions about pay) is dependent on the perceptions or knowledge of others' pay. It is not the absolute amount of reward people focus on but their relative rewards compared to salient others.

The question is who one compares oneself to, on what criterion of one's job, and for how long. It seems that most employees are able to distinguish between unfavorable outcomes (not as good as one hoped) and unfair outcomes. Clearly, employees react much more strongly and angrily to unfair, compared to unfavorable, outcomes. There may be various cultural factors that relate to distributive justice; that is, in collective cultures equality may be seen as more fair than equity decisions; whereas the reverse is true of individualistic cultures.

3   *Procedural Justice* concerns the means rather than the ends of social justice decisions. As predicted, all researchers have found that employees are more likely to accept organizational decisions on such things as smoking bans, parental leave policies, pay, and even disciplinary actions, if they believe the decisions are based on fair procedures.

The evaluation of procedural justice issues depends on both the environmental context within which the interaction occurs and the treatment of individuals. There are all sorts of factors built into a justice procedure which seem to be crucial – consistency, non-partiality, accuracy, correctability, representative and openness. Procedural justice requires:

Adequate notice for all interested parties to prepare

▷ A fair hearing in terms of giving all parties a fair chance to make their case.
▷ A perception of all judgments made upon good evidence rather than on intuition.
▷ Evidence of two-way (bilateral) communication.
▷ The ability and opportunity to refute supposed evidence.
▷ Consistency of judgment over multiple cases.

Although there are, or should be, general context-independent criteria of fairness, there are always special cases. All employees are very concerned with interactional justice, which is the quality of interpersonal treatment they receive at the hands of decision-makers. Two features seem important here: social sensitivity, or the extent to which people believe that they have been treated with dignity and respect, and informational justification, or the extent to which people believe they have adequate information about the procedures affecting them. (Cropanzano and Greenberg, 1997)

Quite simply, procedures matter because a good system can lead people to take a long-term view, becoming tolerant of short-term economic losses for long-term advantage.

Research has demonstrated many practical applications or consequences of organizational justice. Using fair procedures enhances employees' acceptance of institutional authorities. Further, staffing procedures (perceptions of fairness of selection devices) can have pernicious consequences.

People at work often talk of particular types of injustice: unjustified accusation/blaming; unfair grading/rating and/or lack of recognition for both effort and performance; and violations of promises and agreements. Miller (2001) argues that the perception that one has been treated disrespectfully leads to anger. A number of factors relate to people's reactions to injustice. These include the perception of the motives/state of mind of the wrong-doer (did they do it intentionally and with foresight of the consequences). Next, the offender's justification and apologies play a role along with how others reacted to the unjust act. The relationship between the harm-doer and the victim is also important, as is the public nature of the injustice. Victims of injustice want to restore their self-esteem and "educate" the offender. Usually, they retaliate by either withdrawal or attack. What is clear, however, is that people's perception of fairness and justice at work is a powerful motivator and de-motivator and, often, a major cause of negative retaliation behaviors.

Most organizations assert fair treatment of all employees and try to provide some way of dealing with complaints because they believe it directly effects employee commitment, productivity and loyalty. Table 3.4 presents typical procedural justice systems.

The key characteristics of making these systems work is:

1 simplicity – easy to use by everybody.
2 accessibility – open and comprehensive.
3 well-administered – work with follow-ups and corrections.
4 responsiveness – to needs and on time.
5 non-retributive – non-punitive.

There have been some very interesting studies that have examined employee "revenge" as a consequence of what they see to be unjust behavior. Lind *et al.* (2000) were interested in what predicted workers to complain that they had been "wrongfully" terminated after being laid off. They

Table 3.4 Typical procedural justice systems

Grievance procedures	An employee can seek a formal, impartial review of a decision that directly affects him or her.
Ombudspersons	They may investigate claims of unfair treatment, or act as intermediaries between an employee and senior management and recommend possible courses of actions to the parties.
Open-door policies	Employees can approach senior managers with problems that they may not be willing to take to their immediate supervisor. A related mechanism is a "skip-level" policy, whereby an employee may proceed directly to the next higher level of management above his or her supervisor.
Participative management	Systems that encourage employee-involvement in all aspects of organizational strategy and decision-making.
Committees or meetings	Polling employees' input on key problems and decisions.
Senior management visits	Employees meet with senior company officials and openly ask questions about company strategy, policies and practices, or raise concerns about unfair treatment.
Question/answer newsletters	Employees submit questions and concerns to a newsletter editor which, after investigation, are answered and openly reported to the organizational community.
Toll-free telephone numbers	Employees can use these anonymously to report waste, fraud, or abuse.

hypothesized that how fairly workers felt they had been tested during the course of their employment and in the termination predicted the type of claim they made. In addition, they tested such claims as claiming is related to the perception that termination of employment is the employer's fault. Further, that the relationship between claiming and blaming is stronger in those fired rather than those merely laid off.

Their study showed that three factors were directly relevant to whether people considered they would claim: fair treatment at termination, their expectation of winning the case, and their perception of fairness/justice while at work. They agreed that the results of this study, which involved interviewing 996 employed adults, have clear practical implications for all organizations, which include:

1   treating employees fairly throughout their employment and fostering the impression (and the actual belief) that the organization is interested in justice (procedural and distributive)
2   when terminating people, being honest and treating them with dignity and respect at all times for the benefit of those remaining
3   being honest about the causes of unemployment, which results in a legal saving of a significant amount

4   the enhancement of the dignity and self-respect of those terminated can be achieved by such things as providing transitional alumni status, symbols/gifts of positive regard and offers of counseling and out-placement services

5   the fact that attempts at litigation control through lobbying and particular settlement practices have only limited success and can easily backfire.

There is evidence that, to some extent, fairness is in the eye of the beholder. Thus, we know that personality factors influence perceived fairness in employee selection, especially the traits of conscientiousness and neuroticism (Bernerth *et al.*, 2006), as well as reactions to procedural fairness (Burnett *et al.*, 2009).

Justice and equity sensitivity

Are some people more sensitive to justice or equity than others? Equity theory argues thus:

1   Individuals evaluate their relationships with others by assessing the ratio of their outcomes from and inputs to the relationship against the outcome–input ratio of a comparison with others.

2   If the outcome–input ratios of the individual and comparison other are perceived to be unequal, then inequity exists.

3   The greater the inequity the individual perceives (in the form of either over reward or under reward), the more distress the individual feels.

4   The greater the distress an individual feels, the harder he or she will work to restore equity and, thus, reduce the distress. Equity restoration techniques include altering or cognitively distorting inputs or outcomes, acting on or changing the comparison other, or terminating the relationship.

At least four theories have informed this tradition, as Schmitt *et al.* (2009) have noted:

> *Relative deprivation theory* states that people judge the fairness of their outcomes in relation to their expectations. If both match, people feel justly treated. However, if outcomes fall behind expectations, they feel deprived. Expectations serve as standards of entitlement and originate from social comparisons (what do others get) and temporal comparisons (what did I get in the past). *Equity theory* predicts that people consider a distribution to be fair as long as the ratio of outcomes relative to inputs (talent, work, etc.) is equal across recipients. *Justice motive theory* assumes that people's need for justice makes them believe in a just world and motivates them to defend this belief either by action or, if that is not possible or too costly, by cognitive distortion. *Procedural fairness theory* argues that fair procedures are at least as important for people's sense of justice as are fair outcomes.

There are individual differences in the way people perceive and react to equity. Most of us pay attention to equity. Some really take it seriously. They are called *equity sensitive* (Huseman *et al.*, 1987). They adjust their inputs to that of others to ensure equity of effort and reward.

There are two other groups. Those who appear not to mind giving more than they receive are the *Benevolents*; those called the *Entitled* are pretty determined to ensure others do the lion's share.

Benevolents are those who are always socially useful. They think always more about giving than receiving. They are prepared always to contribute and cooperate. They are proto-typic altruists. Some see Benevolents as inheritors of that Calvinist Puritan tradition which perpetuates the philosophy of service-above-self. This is the tradition of maximum effort, high input without thought of reward. It is empathy and self-sacrifice.

Cynics and skeptics sometimes believe Benevolents are really simply disguising their real motives. These may be to gain social approval, or to enhance their self-image or their reputation. But this may be a small price to pay at work. If all givers want in return is praise and acceptance, it makes one's job as a manager relatively easy "slow to chide and swift to bless" works well.

The problem is, of course, never with Benevolents. It is with the Entitled. It is very unattractive and can be easily observable in spoilt children. They believe they have a right to others' total, continual and unconditional support. They have a high threshold for feeling indebted. They seem to demand help and from all around them as their due. Most importantly, they feel little or no obligation to reciprocate. They feel all are debtors but themselves.

Entitleds are exploiters and manipulators. They make or employ charm, or temper tantrums, intimidation or attention-seeking, to achieve their end. They seem insatiable "getters". They may be victims of overly permissive parenting encouraged for impulsivity. They seem to always be worried that they are not getting a better deal. They are a nightmare to manage unless, of course, they have been paired up with Benevolents.

Studies over long periods have shown that, if you put work on a piece-rate system, Entitleds do produce a great deal but, usually, at subsistence levels, and are shoddy workers to boot. Benevolents produce more and better work. This is particularly true under salaried work conditions. Benevolents are consistent and low in their absenteeism and turnover, regardless of the level and equity of reward. Entitleds will have the opposite – high absenteeism and turnover, if equity is ensured.

There is also evidence that Benevolents and Entitleds define work outcomes quite differently. Thus, doing "challenging work" may be seen as a privilege by Benevolents but as a source of stress by Entitleds.

Pay secrecy

Just after the World War I, a large American company put out a "policy memorandum" entitled "Forbidding discussion among employees of salary received". It threatened to "instantly discharge people" who disclosed their "confidential" salary in order to avoid invidious comparison and dissatisfaction. The staff would have none of it. The next day, the staff walked around with large signs around their necks showing their exact salaries.

The same issue continues to this day. People are worried that pay discussion simply fuels "hard feelings and discontentment". Does pay secrecy lead to lower motivation and satisfaction, or the other way around? Does it provoke the desire for revenge?

There have been studies on this topic that show that secrecy is prevalent in most organizations, and that workers actually want it. An organization may keep information back about an individual or pay levels and/or provide ranges or average pay rises. Or it may restrict the manner in which pay information becomes available. Or it may threaten heavy sanctions for disclosure and discussion.

There may be secrecy about pay level and structure as well as the basis and form of pay. Some employers very actively restrict the way pay information is made available. But, of course, it is pay level that is the really hot one.

Pay secrecy is not an all-or-nothing situation. There is a continuum from complete secrecy to complete openness. From *exactly* how much each individual earns in total to narrow bands (i.e. between £70,000 and £80,000) to wide bands (under £50,000; £5,000 to £100,000). For many, pay secrecy is about respectful privacy. And pay secrecy is about individualism.

Colella *et al.* (2007) looked at the costs and benefits of pay secrecy. They argued that there were various costs:

▷ Employee judgments about fairness, equity and trust may be challenged. If people don't know who is paid what, they surely infer or guess it. But uncertainty generates anxiety and vigilance about fairness. People believe that if information is withheld it is for good reason. This, in turn, affects three types of justice judgments: informational (it being withheld), procedural (lack of employee voice and potential bias), and distribution (compressing the pay range).

▷ Judgments about pay fairness will –they have to – be based on a general impression of the fairness in the organization. People see all sorts of things (hiring, firing, perks) that are vivid and memory examples of "fairness". So, even if they have a "fair but secret" pay policy, it will be judged unfair if other perhaps unrelated actions do not look fair.

▷ Secrecy breeds distrust. Openness about pay signals integrity. Secrecy may enhance a view about organizational unfairness and corruption. Further, it signals that the organization does not trust its employees. So, secrecy reduces motivation by breaking the pay for performance linkage.

▷ People need to have, and perform best when they are given, goals/ targets/key performance indicators and are rewarded for them. But, if they do not know the relative worth of the rewards (i.e. in pay secrecy), they may well be less committed to those goals.

▷ Pay secrecy could affect the labor market because it could prevent employees moving to better, fitting and rewarding jobs. Pay secret organizations may not easily lure or pull good employees from other organizations. Secrecy makes the market inefficient.

But on the other hand there can be real advantages to the organization:

▷ Secrecy can enhance organizational control and reduce conflict. Pay differentials can cause jealousy. So, hiding them may prevent problems in *esprit de corps*. Making pay open often encourages managers to reduce differences. That is, the range distribution is narrower than the performance. So, paradoxically, secrecy increases fairness in the equity sense because people can more easily be rewarded for the full range of their outputs.

▷ Secrecy prevents "political" behavior, union involvement and conflict. Openness is both economically inefficient and likely to cause conflict.

▷ Pay secrecy allows organizations more easily to "correct" historical and other pay equity. So, paradoxically, one can both minimize unfairness and discrimination, as well as perceptions of those matters, more easily by secrecy.

▷ Secrecy benefits team work, particularly in competitive individuals, organizations and cultures. It encourages interdependence rather than "superstardom".

▷ Secrecy favors organizational paternalism in that organizations can (and do) argue that employees themselves want secrecy, reducing conflict, jealousy and distress at learning about others. One can even suggest that workers might make irrational decisions if they really know what their colleagues are (really) paid. So, paternalistic secrecy increases control and the "feel good" factor.

▷ "Secrecy" is another word for privacy and increasing concern in a technologically sophisticated surveillance society. Perhaps this is why surveys show people are generally in favor of secrecy because people do not want their salaries discussed by their co-workers. People are willing to trade-off their curiosity about the pay of others for not having their own package made open.

▷ Secrecy may increase loyalty or, put more negatively, labor market immobility. If people can't compare their salaries, they maybe less inclined to switch jobs to those which are better paid. So, you get what is called "continuance commitment" through lack of poaching.

The cost–benefit ratio depends on different things. Much depends on the history of the organization. It's pretty difficult to "re-cork" the genie if it has escaped the bottle. It also depends on whether good, up-to-date, accurate industry compensation norms really exist. The public industry norm information can have a powerful effect on organizations that opt for secrecy or privacy.

The next issue is how the organization does, or claims to, determine criteria for pay allocation. Do they provide payment for years of service, for level, for performance-on-the-job or for some combination of these? The more objective the criteria (number of calls made, number of widgets sold), the more difficult it is to keep things secret. Next, appraisal systems strive to be objective, equitable and fair. The more they are, the less need for secrecy. Where objective criteria are used, staff have fewer concerns for secrecy. So, subjectivity and secrecy are comfortable bed-fellows. Under pay secrecy, people don't know what their pay is based on. And secrecy means they can't predict or believe that they can control their pay in any way.

When the pay is secret, people have to guess how they rank relative to others at the same level. That, no doubt, is why high-performers want secrecy more than low-performers; they believe they are equitably being paid more and want to avoid jealousy and conflict. So, believe you are well-paid because of your hard work and all is well with secrecy.

When pay secrecy is abolished, some people not only feel angry, they feel humiliated by exposure to relative deprivation. They feel unfairly dealt with and their easiest means of retaliation is, inevitably, to work less hard.

Three things are clear. Once you have abolished or reduced secrecy, the path back is near impossible. Next, if competitors have openness and you have secrecy, they might undermine your system. Most importantly, for openness to work you need to be pretty clear in explaining how pay is related to performance at all levels and defend your system. Otherwise, you open the most evil can of worms!

The motivational context

It is possible to identify three separate but overlapping sources of motivation (Table 3.5, Figure 3.2).

Rarely does a single motive, experience or issue encourage an individual at work to react consistently negatively at work. Many dynamic factors motivate individuals who may or may not be able to articulate their feelings. These complex motives can also change over time. The final, extreme act of leaving – thieving or deceiving – is nearly always the culmination of a number of factors and influences.

Some work experiences *trigger* bad behavior, while others simply provide too tempting and easy an opportunity for "mischief" of many kinds. Equally, some individuals have a heightened propensity to CWBs, while others have better internal controls.

Some critical incident may trigger an overwhelming feeling of revenge and the inevitability of retaliation is set. It is not unusual for people to feel angry and vengeful at work after a bad experience. The issue is how *frequent* and *intense* these triggering incidents and, more importantly, how they are dealt with.

People are likely to go through a number of processes before they are ready, emotionally and intellectually, to take action. There seem to be

Table 3.5 Sources of motivation

Personality and individual profile	How the biography, personality and values of an individual shape their very particular motivational *pattern*. For example, greed, vanity and instability can lead to very strong motives in the work-place.
The relationship between individual and employer	This is sometimes called leader–follower exchange and looks at the nature of the relationships at work; it is often a function of the leader's style. This relationship can be one of trust and support, which is associated with motivation and satisfaction or the opposite.
External influences	These can come from many sources, hence the interest in work–life balance. People can be distracted and appear de-motivated because of personal issues and problems (addictions, relationships). However, changes in the economy can affect motivation, particularly if people are worried about the future of their organization. Friends, head-hunters, media people can all influence people and influence their behavior.

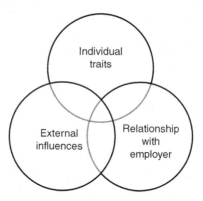

Figure 3.2   **The motivational complex**

four factors or processes that lead from specific work incidences to serious CWBs.

First, there are drivers or susceptibilities in an individual that predispose him or her to CWBs. There are the needs that come from poverty, despair and greed. There are needs stimulated by hatred, resentment and anger. There are ideological needs.

These individual qualities and factors interact with the organizational culture, management style and work of the organization. In the early days of a job, the individual is usually optimistic, sometimes a little apprehensive: Am I up to the job? Will I like the people there? As the job continues, people can measure their expectations against reality. The organization is doing the same thing, often called the "probation" period. It is all about fit: the fit between what was promised and what is delivered, between leader and follower, between team members.

People's expectations can be disappointed for a host of reasons. Many should be, but are not, made explicit before entry. If the individual asks the right questions and if the organization is honest about its business, the nature of the work and the rewards on offer, people are more likely to have realistic expectations. However, both parties at an interview are eager to impress the other and vague promises are given. Further, it sometimes happens that the person who will supervise or lead the candidate is not even present at the interview.

The management of expectations fundamentally concerns important expectations about promotion, training, salary increases. Mistakes and bad judgments are easily made at this stage, but they take time to discover. Some people will continue in a "disappointing job" because they do not want to go through another job search with all the uncertainty that it involves. They may well opt to stay with the "devil they know".

The *second* factor, therefore, is the organizational culture which may cause or condone various forms of CWB. But a more difficult issue arises when there is change (restructuring, mergers and acquisitions, change in the reporting line). Change is always said to be necessary and linked to survival and progress. However, it is often crudely done and deeply angers, frightens and depresses people.

The research shows that the appearance of discontent and CWBs is at its highest in times of change. Emotions run high; trust and justice issues come to the fore particularly when it comes to "internal communications" that maybe more PR than the truth. Once people see management communication as little more than "spin", they can easily be tempted to react, from vengeful whistle-blowing to increased absenteeism.

The two issues that affect an individual's satisfaction rating in a company are how well the company matches up to the expectations of the employee and how well it manages change. If the organization fails on either of these counts, the individual's loyalty will be weakened, resulting in some form of negative reaction.

The *third* factor is the presence of some other catalyst. Most people are subject to some form of outside influence; for some it is subtle, for others it is overt. Job advertisements that specify salaries are ubiquitous. How many people, when feeling unhappy at work, turn to the job vacancy pages? Others may be approached by head-hunters, journalists or others seeking to prey on an employee's discontent. There are good business stories to be had when famous institutions stumble. The stock market can be very jittery, and it is surprising how vulnerable the share price is to a good story about corruption or mismanagement at the top of organizations.

Fourth, after constant provocation, the employee may take some action. Initially, it may be a loss of enthusiasm, an unwillingness to put in the extra effort to complete a task or find new jobs which could be done. It can also lead to more counter-productive activities.

There is no clear moment when someone moves from stage to stage and, for some, it is possible to leap a stage. Some endure frustrations stoically; others flare up quickly. This is, in part, a function of the type of organization and the sort of people it employs. Thus, those in the health sector may show a rather different pattern of reactions to those in the manufacturing sector.

Individuals' attitudes and motives can change as they absorb new experiences and come into contact with new people. The power of the group, or of an inspirational leader or friend, cannot be over-estimated.

People can both be saved by others, or encouraged by them to commit a variety of CWBs. Similarly, being bullied or seeing someone else being badly treated (e.g. as they leave an organization) can have a lasting impact on the individual. Being humiliated by your boss deeply affects commitment to the cause.

Individual traits

What factors in an individual are likely to make him prone or susceptible to make CWBs? Employers expect that their new recruits will bring specific, desirable skills and qualities which will add value to the work of the organization, be it more profits, greater efficiency more security or better research. Some will have less-welcome qualities that can undermine, negate their advantages or even work against the company. Some of these may be recognized at recruitment.

Love of money

At work, money is much more powerful as a de-motivator than a motivator. Interestingly, the single best predictor of a person's satisfaction with their salary is their perception of their salary *compared with others*. In other words, *it is relative not absolute*. This is why some organizations keep salaries a secret and why, at "bonus time" in the city, people express such anger and fury.

The data suggest that it is often not badly-paid people who steal and commit fraud. Some do so because they can quite easily "get away with it". But many steal, pilfer and lie because they feel they are not fairly and equitably dealt with compared, say, with their peers, their boss or others in the organization.

Yet, our attitudes to money are complex. At best, it is a symbol of our worth and the contribution we make. But some will be tempted down the criminal path in order to make money, and most of us would like more money. It is therefore worth spending a little more time exploring the fascination and desire for material wealth. Most people have their price: that is, what they are prepared to do for money.

However, the role of money in motivation does depend much on the type of job people do. The results from many studies have shown that white-collar professional people who are relatively well-paid are much less motivated by money than less well-paid blue collar workers.

Money has a deep symbolic value. People are not rational about money though they are prepared to do a great deal to acquire it. For psychoanalysts money has psychological meanings: the most common and powerful of which are security, power, love and freedom (Goldberg and Lewis, 1978).

Security: In many communities, young men are brought up to believe it is their responsibility to look after the family. Building an emotional wall around themselves can lead to fear and paranoia about being hurt, rejected or deprived by others. A fear of financial loss becomes paramount because the security collector supposedly depends more and more on money for ego-satisfaction: money bolsters feelings of safety and self-esteem.

Power: Because money can be used to buy goods, services and loyalty, it can be used to acquire importance, domination and control. Money can be used to buy out or compromise enemies and clear the path for oneself. Money, some believe, is the only real means to influence and recognition. Narcissistic and vain people are therefore particularly attracted to money to fulfill their egotistical self-esteem.

Love: For some, money is given as a substitute for emotion and affection. Money is used to buy affection, loyalty and self-worth. Further, because of the reciprocity principle inherent in gift-giving, many assume that reciprocated gifts are a token of love and caring. For those who seem unsuccessful in relationships, they crave money to buy them love.

Freedom: This is a more acceptable – and, hence, more freely admitted – meaning attached to money. It buys time to pursue one's whims and interests, and frees one from the daily grind and restrictions of a paid job. For them, money buys escape from orders, commands and, even, suggestions that appear to restrict autonomy and limit independence.

Because money has so many complex psychological associations it can, and does, become a great "touchstone" for CWBs at work.

Beliefs/values

The nature of the organization: its methods, products, customers are important to many people. This could be about whether the company is pursuing a good environmental policy or uses animals to test its products. Some feel unhappy about arms manufacture, even if what they do is make products only some of which are used in the manufacture of arms. Some feel more comfortable in the public sector, others in an overtly capitalist venture; some are deeply concerned with "fair trade" or "ethical investing". Most of these factors are clearly available to candidates as they join, but some may be hidden, or there may be change. The issue here is the gap or misfit between the beliefs and values of the individual and those of the organization, which may be more about what it does, than what it "says" through mission statements, press releases and advertisements.

Table 3.6 Profiling values

Recognition	Desire to be known, seen, visible and famous: to be recognized by many others. This leads to a search for opportunities to be noticed and high achievement.
Power	Desire to succeed and out-perform the competition; to have influence and power to have one's own way.
Hedonism	The remorseless pursuit of fun and pleasure, and a lifestyle organized around personal hedonistic pleasures, including food, sex, and alcohol.
Altruism	Desire to help others provide public service and the betterment of humanity: an empathic concern for those less fortunate.
Affiliation	Needing and enjoying frequent social contact with many different types of people and being socially included in groups and societies.
Tradition	A belief in conservative virtues such as family, thrift, hard work, and etiquette.
Security	A need for predictability, social stability, structure, and efforts to avoid risk and uncertainty in the area of employment.
Commerce	Driven by a desire to earn money, realize profits, find new business opportunities, and attain a commercial lifestyle.
Aesthetics	An interest in ideas, beauty, and presentation; an interest in how things look, feel and sound – particularly the appearance of things.
Science	Being interested in science, comfortable and up-to-date with technology, preferring data-based decisions, and spending time learning how things work. A curiosity in the physical – and, to a lesser extent the social – world.

Table 3.6 presents a list of values that can be used to profile people from the work of Robert Hogan. These values determine, in part, what organizations they choose to work in and how they lead their lives. Some value recognition a great deal and, if it is not forthcoming, they might react badly. Equally, those who value security and tradition often have great problems with change.

Social needs

We are all social animals. We live and work in groups, and we need to be accepted and protected by them. They give us our identity and fulfill the deepest of our social needs.

There are those whose employment is a way of creating relationships. Maslow identified the need for "belongingness and love" in his hierarchy of needs. He suggested that people will "strive with great intensity to achieve this goal. Attaining such a place will matter more than anything else in the world and he or she may even forget that once, when hunger was foremost, love seemed unreal, unnecessary, and unimportant. Now the pangs of lone-liness, ostracism, rejection, friendlessness, and rootlessness are pre-eminent" (Maslow, 1998).

Some people go to work because it provides a social environment in which they can flourish. If they cannot satisfy these needs or they are threatened, their bitterness will grow. People even try to punish individu-als by isolating them. Solitary confinement is, after all, a form of torture. People have strong needs to be part of a group, though they can have conflicting motives to both "get along with" others as well as "get ahead of peers".

Exclusion from a group physically, or exclusion from information, can be distressing. It can lead people to develop conspiracy theories and to develop a strong hatred of those they saw as rejecting them. People differ in their need for inclusion, but the social need to be accepted and esteemed as part of a social group is universal.

Vanity

Vanity is the "excessive pride in or admira-tion of one's own appearance or achieve-ments". A person concerned does not have to have his or her accomplishment in the public eye. Often, they will be content to look at themselves in the mirror in the morning, or a saboteur might read the newspaper headlines next morning and say to himself "I did that."

Vain people seek out titles, awards, honors and attention. Their self-obsession makes them particularly uninterested in all those around them.

> *Desire for approval and recog-nition is a healthy motive but the desire to be acknowledged as better, stronger, or more intelligent than a fellow being or fellow scholar easily leads to an excessively egoistic psycho-logical adjustment ... .*
>
> (Albert Einstein (1879–1955), *Ideas and Opinions*, 1954)

Vanity usually takes on two forms: reputation and identity.

▷ *Reputation*: fame and notoriety are highly stimulating and become a major force in pushing individuals into extreme action.
▷ *Identity*: where their action provides an individual with an identity and when their actions become known, their status in and outside the com-munity increases. Their place in the community becomes more secure.

Those who seek fame and glory are more likely to be part of the insider threat. Those who seek recognition from their colleagues may be vulner-able, if such recognition is not forthcoming, but their vanity in itself is not a problem.

Table 3.7 The characteristics of the narcissist

Self-importance	They have a grandiose sense of self-importance (e.g. exaggerated achievements and talents, expectation to be recognized as superior without commensurate achievements).
Fantasies	Most are preoccupied with fantasies of unlimited success, power, brilliance and money.
Being "special"	They believe that they are "special" and unique, and can only be understood by, or should associate with, other special or high-status people (or institutions). They may try to "buy" themselves into exclusive circles.
Excessive admiration	Always, they require excessive admiration and respect from everyone at work.
Sense of entitlement	Bizarrely, often they have a sense of entitlement, i.e. unreasonable expectations of especially favorable treatment or automatic compliance with their manifest needs.
Take advantage of others	Worse, they take advantage of others to achieve their own ends, which makes them terrible managers.
Lack empathy	They lack empathy. Always unwilling to recognize or identify with the feelings and needs of others. They have desperately low EQ.
Envious of others	Curiously, they are often envious of others and believe that others are envious of them.
Arrogant, haughty behaviors	They show arrogant, haughty behaviors or attitudes all the time and everywhere at work (and home).

Many senior managers have Narcissistic Personality Disorder. This can develop over time, particularly if they are shielded from negative feedback. It is a form of extreme and pathological vanity not unknown among politicians, media people and senior managers who like the limelight. Their egocentric needs have to be met, otherwise they react badly. They can, of course, in the process seriously alienate their staff.

Table 3.7 presents the characteristics of the narcissist.

Vanity, unlike self-confidence, can be deeply unattractive, particularly in "tall poppy" societies. Vanity often leads to poor decision-making and the alienation of others.

Envy

Much is made in the Bible and in the Book of Common Prayer about the sinfulness

> *If I esteemed you less, Envy would kill Pleasure.*
>
> (Percy Bysshe Shelley to Lord Byron)

of envy. But why is it so reviled? The dictionary definition provides a clue: "Discontented or resentful longing aroused by another's possessions, qualities or luck" (*Concise Oxford Dictionary*). Yet, it is a fairly normal emotion. We look longingly at another's kitchen fittings, their clothes, their car, their spouse, their happiness or their success.

The issue is closely associated with perceived fairness; that is, how are others treated. Individuals will look at those in their peer group, but also to their seniors. The boss who is known to earn a whacking great salary or who has a large and flashy car that takes him to work can still produce feelings of envy.

Comparison with others is said to be invidious. In the civil service, there is a fairly transparent and easily perceived promotion ladder. Personnel officers have to explain the decisions of promotion boards to those who have not succeeded that year. Some are more or less content with the explanations of their own shortcomings. But many compare themselves with others and feel they deserved promotion at the same time. They were certainly disappointed and they feel justified in their complaint. They would not admit to feelings of envy, but it certainly does seem unfair.

It is not just the big issues that can eat away at an individual's contentment. The size of another's office, their job title or their benefit package can be an issue. These are containable by management – but not, we suggest, entirely. Only the manager or the personnel officer truly knows the relative value of each individual's contribution. They usually cannot share that with the discontented. The latter have to take their word for it – and this is often not enough.

We are all prone to comparisons with others, particularly those in our peer group. When the competition gets keen and there are many fighting for advancement, the decisions of management are that much more closely scrutinized. It is a thin – or, at any rate, blurred – line between fairness and envy; but managers have to tread it and get it right. Where criteria and procedures are obscure, suspicion and then envy creep in, leading to feelings of disillusion and resentment.

Ambition

Ambition, as the dictionary defines it, is good: "a strong desire to do or achieve something; desire for success, wealth or fame". If only we had more like that. But the ambition is not usually beneficial. The clever ambitious person will go to some lengths to hide the miseries which they have caused to others, but all too often

> *All ambitions are lawful except those which climb upward on the miseries or credulities of mankind.*
>
> (Joseph Conrad – A personal record)

they are found out – though few will tell them so. They continue until the boss finds the disruption amongst the rest of the workforce too great and has to ask the culprit to leave or to move him or her on elsewhere.

While ambition may be an excellent driver, it can also be a dangerous derailer under three conditions:

▷ where a person's ambition is not matched by their ability or work ethic to achieve specific goals or targets.
▷ where factors like nepotism or corruption rather than good work in an organization really determine the prizes like promotion.
▷ where they are excluded or discriminated against on the basis of race, religion, sexual orientation or some other subtle factor.

To be highly ambitious and thwarted can mean a very energetic person directing his or her ire on those they believe to be unfairly frustrating them.

Excitement and sensation-seeking

Many, but not all individuals feel both frustrated and let down when the company has no chance of providing what the individual wants. They may display signs of boredom, but there will also be something else they need. It is hard to weed out those whose sensation-seeking needs are so high that they become a problem. Adventuresome, bold, fun-lovers are often attractive people. They also are often associated with risk-taking, and companies and organizations often look for an element of this in their candidates. Usually, they look for those who know how to calculate the risk – but this is difficult to define, let alone identify in a candidate.

The dangerous sports addict is an adrenalin-seeker. Like hyper-active children, they are calmed down by excitement and risk. They need excitement to feel human. They may be prepared to break the law just for the sheer thrill of it. They need a fix, often at any cost.

The foolhardy will risk not just his or her own prosperity (or physical safety), but also that of the company. The thrill of the chase is all. It can be seen in the money markets, where managers have to leave the decisions to young and relatively inexperienced people who have to calculate profit and loss at a phenomenal speed. They clearly love it; but, if it is combined with an unsympathetic management structure that will not tolerate mistakes, then the bad deal will be hidden. Then risks to the company's profits will be great.

But it is not just the banking world which attracts the risk-taker. The armed forces admire the physically strong and the courageous. There is a fine line between that and the dangerous – not just to the soldier him/herself, but also to the men/women is leading as well.

The individual and the organization

Dysfunctional organizations

If failed expectations and poor management of change cause employee shocks, what are the elements that produce these? Most research on employee motivation concentrates on the positive: what makes employees work harder, better, more effectively, go the extra mile. There are fewer that have researched the negative motivators: why people become disillusioned, slow down, resign or, worse, start pilfering, embezzling and committing sabotage.

Top management/organizational policy and administration: Seven factors at work relate to alienation and revenge.

Today's media ensures that information, some would say too much information, is available to everyone including employees about company executives, senior civil servants and ministers. Inconsistencies and mistakes are highlighted and often publicized. The Internet makes such information available to all but, more significantly for organizations, is the proliferation of the intranet, some including provision of chat rooms for staff to air their views.

The *British Medical Journal* (*BMJ*) carried out a number of studies on job satisfaction amongst doctors working in the National Health Service in the UK. In May 2003, they published a report which concluded that "job satisfaction is an important factor underlying the intention to quit". More specifically, their survey revealed that the principal causes of general practitioner discontent lie within the wider environment. "The organization and governance of general practice has greatly changed in recent years, and doctors may be experiencing difficulties in adapting to these changes." (Sibbald *et al.*, 2003).

Whether the information that people have about their organization is accurate or not, it is often a source of immense dissatisfaction. Often, policies like chief executive pay, closing down plants or even something as simple as de-layering or going open plan can be a source of major discontent.

Day-to-day management including managerial interpersonal skills: This refers to a manager's skills and styles: IQ and EQ. They include all variants of communication skills, favoritism, the general as well as the more serious issues of bullying and harassment. The latter is particularly crucial for companies who harbor or protect such people, as they become vulnerable to legal sanctions.

Recognition, advancement, proper use of employee skills: It is part of most societies' culture to train young people to say "thank you" and show gratitude for things done or given. Failing to show gratitude to those who deserve it offends against the norms of society.

> *There are two things people want more than sex and money – recognition and praise*
>
> (Mary Kay Ash (1915–2001), US entrepreneur, business executive and founder of Mary Kay Cosmetics)

The unrecognized person in the workplace soon becomes dispirited. It is all the more extraordinary in this materialistic world because it costs nothing to ring up or go to the office and say "thank you". Recognition and praise is cheap and, done effectively and judiciously, can be particularly motivating.

Most staff opinion surveys report that staff feel unappreciated and that they do not feel valued. It is not a question of money; it is, in most cases, a lack of courtesy. Recognition and appreciation comes in other forms: job titles, certificates, pictures and interviews in the in-house magazine. For some, status is important because they want others to know they hold a senior position or have a particular expertise. Labels mean something to them.

In some organizations, status is deliberately underplayed. "Flat structures" mean fewer ranks and people becoming one of only a few homogeneous groups. For those at the bottom of the pile, this is good news – but for how long? Some more senior people may feel their contribution and experience count for nothing.

Another method of recognition is salary. Many senior executives receive proportionately huge salaries and benefits. Prolonged negotiations take place over the size of their package. The cash involved is largely immaterial; what matters is that this is a measure of how they are valued. During the heady days of the stock market boom, the bonus received each month was a symbol of success as much as a means of acquiring even more material goodies.

Just as staff enjoy recognition, gratitude and an appropriate salary, they also desire advancement and to feel that their skills are being properly exploited. In some organizations, particularly the public services and military, promotion issues dominate the thoughts of many employees as they come into the zone. For others, they only become aware of them as they see others, often their peers, being promoted and they themselves feel passed over.

Not everyone can be promoted, and this is recognized. But the systems by which people are promoted are often opaque, clouded in mystery, the rules and procedures obscure. The more they are overlooked, the more individuals not promoted will feel the "system" is against them and will feel resentful.

There is currently another trap for the employer which is becoming more frequent: over-qualification. Universities are proliferating and producing well-trained and skilled graduates, but the number of demanding jobs has not increased by the same proportion. Many employees now find themselves in jobs for which they are grossly over-qualified. Graduates can be found in most civil service departments standing for hours by the photocopier or putting basic data into a computer. Most recognize this should only be a temporary phase and they will advance. But, if the delay is too long, their motivation will fall. Their most likely course is to walk but, where the labor market is against a move, their minds might turn to more mischievous ends.

Salary: It comes as a surprise to many managers that money is not a major factor in people's motivation. A senior British political figure in the 1980s would frequently anger his civil servants by telling them that the principal motivation for everyone was money and that, by introducing a performance pay scheme, productivity would increase. In fact, within the civil service it created more resentment than almost any other management scheme introduced in the second half of the twentieth century.

It features as a dissatisfier when the employee perception is that he or she is not receiving a fair day's pay for his or her work. And the definition of "fair" is influenced by many things. In the first place, a worker needs to satisfy his standard of living – this has little to do with sufficient to live, but more to do with the repayments on a large mort-

> *A fair day's wages for a fair day's work: it is as just a demand as governed men ever made of governing*
>
> (Thomas Carlyle (1795–1881) *Past and Present*, 1843)

gage, a new car, a larger family or his annual skiing holiday. The salaries of friends or colleagues at work might also play their part in influencing someone to believe they are not being paid enough. The salary of the fat-cat CEO compared to the paltry sums paid to the workers can have negative effects.

Work itself: Where the work is boring or repetitive, the climate bullying, the management callous, staff will quickly feel disenchanted and leave. Where the nature of the work is not what they expected or offends their sensibilities, employees might feel the need to take more drastic action. Graduates of the 1980s were less concerned about the ethics of work. In the twenty-first century, they are beginning to care more about the nature of work.

Hollyforde and Whiddett (2002: 159) conclude that the following elements should be part of a satisfying job:

▷ Jobs should be interesting and significant, and give autonomy and challenge.
▷ The explicit job standards should be made clear and challenging.
▷ People should receive regular performance feedback that is accurate, behavioral, and helpful.
▷ Basic "givens" should already be in place (policies, salary, good working conditions, etc). These are hygiene factors.
▷ Those affected (or their representatives) should be involved in job design from the start – that is, they should have some autonomy over their job description.
▷ People are most likely to respond to jobs if they want to grow and develop. Those less intrinsically motivated do not respond so well.
▷ People who are seeking to meet the most basic of human needs are likely to be extrinsically motivated.

Environment, work conditions and colleagues:

The work can be intrinsically satisfying, staff are developing well, the money is good and management comes straight out of Harvard business school. But still people are unhappy. Most people spend more conscious hours at work or going to work than doing anything else. It is an important part of our social life. We need to feel comfortable there. Companies increasingly spend money on their buildings and the facilities; for good reason, they want their staff to be happy at work.

> *The job for big companies, the challenge that we all face as bureaucrats, is to create an environment where people can reach their dreams – and they don't have to do it in a garage*
>
> (Jack Welch, *Fortune*, May 1995)

It is more than just a great canteen, however. It is the atmosphere, morale, camaraderie. Some of the happiest memories are associated with some poorly maintained buildings with few facilities. But the friendships and fun are more than enough compensation. Modern, clean buildings cannot, on their own, lead to satisfaction.

Where staff find their colleagues less than conducive, where the surroundings do not offer good shopping or restaurants, where staff feel physically threatened as they leave the building, they will leave the company.

Development, growth and challenge opportunities: On its own, insufficient challenge or development will probably lead to nothing more than a speedy departure of the individuals concerned. It is, however, one of the most potent forces in keeping staff and that is why it features again as a subject later in this book.

Challenge comes in various forms. For some, it is a need to continue to learn new skills, more knowledge, a better understanding of the world or the issues facing the company. In short and modern jargon, it is the need for development. For others, it is the need for something new, excitement, the thrill of the unknown, the adventure. Harnessed, this can be a very effective force for the company. If it is unrequited, it can start to work against the company.

Others will need a different kind of challenge. The perfectionist will find it hard to work in an ambiguous environment where quality of work is not as important as quantity, for example. Some will want to apply their knowledge and skills to known problems. The analyst and the investigator will want to tackle new problems, but they may well be content without the unknown.

> *Companies... have a hard time distinguishing between the cost of paying people and the value of investing in them*
>
> (Thomas Stewart, US journalist, *Intellectual Capital*)

The need for challenge is usually associated with graduate staff. But this is an oversimplification. There are many who have the very best degrees and who run away from challenge. They wanted the safe and easy life. They needed intellectual stimulus, but this could be provided by analysis of figures or the current state of an investigation into what went wrong. All of these are dealing with existing problems and do not call for new skills or something different.

The organization, hopefully, should provide the right kind of challenge to the individual at the right moment. Where this involves new skills or knowledge, then they have to provide that as well. If employers advertise jobs as being challenging or demanding, they have the responsibility to provide that. Frequently, however, these words are used as synonyms for stress.

Without the right kind of challenge (and development or learning is challenging in its own right) staff become bored. If they can leave, that is fine – and the sooner they go, if the company cannot provide the challenge, the better. If, however, they are tied – because of a volatile and threatening job market or because the company has tied them in through some financial package – this boredom becomes destructive.

Bored members of staff will find something to distract them. This might be reading a book or the newspaper. It might become more damaging and lead to longer telephone calls to family or friends. In the modern era, it will mean long hours spent on the Internet, emailing friends or, much worse, surfing the net and exposing your computer systems to viruses or just clogging up the system with unnecessary files. The bored worker might well turn to whistle-blowing or collecting names of clients to pass on to the next company. Many incidents of sabotage, particularly of those working on conveyor-belt type activities, report that employees did it simply to relieve the unutterable tedium of their repetitive work.

The corollary to boredom is stress brought on as a result of too much challenge. Badly managed change or providing staff with too challenging work or objectives is often the cause. Again, on its own this will do little more than produce a resignation. However, the individual is unlikely to admit the reason, because they will feel it is their failure. And it is the manager's failure to recognize that he was asking too much.

In some cultures, there is pressure to produce, to achieve. Without results, people cannot progress. This can breed deceit. It might manifest itself in presenting data, which is not original in an academic environment. It might encourage individuals to commit fraud in the company, by falsifying the accounts to present them in a more favorable light. If managers set unattainable targets and provide only little support to achieve them – and, worse, threats of punishment for not achieving them – deceit and fraud are very likely to occur.

The path to revenge: People at work are remarkably resilient: they have to be. People do not move on just because of a failure. Most employees stick at the job for a long time – years if not decades, despite repeated upsets concerning or affecting work. They stay remarkably loyal and deliberate sabotage, deception or revenge never enters their minds.

Staff joining a company usually feel optimistic and anticipate working with the company with some pleasure. The recruiters will have presented a picture, hopefully accurate, which presented the organization as having the kind of qualities that the individual aspires to or admires. There are, of course, the discon-

> *Vote for the man who promises least; he'll be the least disappointing.*
>
> (Bernard Baruch (1870–1968), US Presidential advisor)

tents or criminally minded who, from day one, will take the company for all that they can get away with. (Chapter 6 addresses how organizations can protect themselves against disloyalty of all kinds). Once the excitement of the new job has died down and we have not found anything radically different from what the recruiters told us, we become satisfied.

Soon the gilt becomes tarnished; tolerance begins to thin. At some stage – and it can happen on day one – staff become disappointed, or angry and then vengeful. The office has no daylight; the people in the office are not congenial; a best friend has also started work and she is getting more money. These are not enough to upset us and we soon forget them or put them to the side because the benefits outweigh the deficits. They are temporary concerns – or, at least, manageable.

If these negatives persist because they are part of the company's culture and no one is going to change them or it is not possible to do the job properly, those feelings of disappointment become disillusionment with the company or ourselves. Those early positive feelings about the company dissipate. Staff no longer feel so committed; they put themselves first and are less willing to give that extra effort or lunch hour. They start to make excuses. They begin to think the office owes them something and they start taking from the organization. They slip from commitment to alienation.

The "breaking point" for each individual is different. Some of us can accept more "unhappiness" than others for a longer period. How many competency frameworks have inscribed "resilience" into their appraisals. "Copes with failure or disappointment" is also written into the qualities, which employers like in their staff. Recruiters look for these qualities as they select candidates. Organizational cultures often belittle those who give up on a task, let alone the company. But we each do have a breaking point, however much the culture may resist it. Indeed, the culture itself may be part of the problem.

Disappointment leads easily to disillusionment. Either the cause of disappointment is too great or has happened too frequently. The cause may not be the organization itself. Staff can be disappointed in themselves, their own per-

> *Blessed is he who expects nothing, for he shall never be disappointed*
>
> (Eighteenth-century proverb)

formance. They have committed to working for the organization but are failing, or they made a bad judgment and thought the organization would provide them with more than it did. It could have been too challenging or, more prosaically, the commute to work may have become intolerable.

Similarly, family or friends could undermine confidence in the organization. Others may be on a much higher salary or have better benefits. The adverts on TV or in the appointments pages of newspapers can cause employees to question whether they are working in the right place.

Whatever the cause, their beliefs or ideals as they joined the company have been eroded (or simply changed) and they are left with the feeling that there may be something better out there. The reaction to disillusionment is more likely to be resignation than anything more dramatic but, in the meantime, the disillusioned will tend to give less and the more unscrupulous will "take more liberties".

They will be less willing to put in the extra hours; they will spend more time on the phone; some may start to "liberate" stationery. They can justify it to themselves because they feel they have "given" a great deal to the company and this is only due to them. Most companies can accept this level of dishonesty.

When staff perceive that these things have happened because of some deliberate act by individuals in that company and who are still thriving in that company, stronger feelings emerge: those of resentment. Reactions to this emotion vary. Some will harbor their feelings; some will talk about them either to colleagues in the company, unsettling other staff, or expressing their feelings to outsiders, which can damage the company's reputation or, worse, give competitors useful insights; some will resign. Few will leave without expressing some of their disappointment to others and there is, in that act alone, retaliation. They no longer feel loyal to the company and they are seeking some kind of revenge (Figure 3.3).

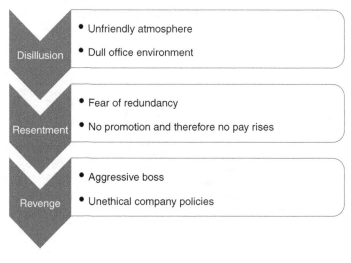

Figure 3.3 **The path to revenge**

The target varies. It can be the office itself. It may be individuals: the CEO, department head, the supervisor or possibly, though less likely, colleagues. Where the hurt is particularly deep, the individual may turn to more damaging forms of revenge: theft, fraud, deceit, sabotage or whistle-blowing.

The Persuaders

If internal bad management pushes people away from the organization, external forces can also pull the individual away. If the individual has some personal factors that make him or her vulnerable, the chances of the external force having the power to influence are that much greater. They can be enormously powerful, if played by someone with a very strong personality. If they are perceptive and can see some nascent weakness perhaps produced by resentment or an overriding personal quality, an outsider can bring havoc to the organization, significantly weaken it or, in some cases, bring it down. Thus, the perceptive head-hunter, be they professional or not, may easily seduce a talented and valuable person away from their work (see Figure 3.4).

Competition

Competition threatens companies in two ways: other companies can poach staff and they can seek information about specific products. Both can, and often do, involve persuading staff to betray their employer.

The weekend newspapers groan with tempting job offers and, now, the Internet has ever-easier ways of tempting us away from our job and into the arms of another company. Direct competitors may not necessarily be poaching staff from our company through the media, but a good many employees will be aware of what is being paid or offered elsewhere.

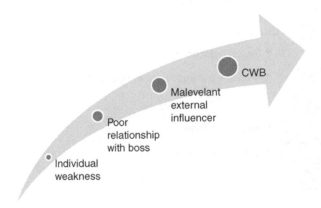

Figure 3.4   **The unsettling forces**

Where there is a group of companies whose employees know each other well – for example in journalism – competitors may well target individuals and contact them directly. In Britain, the move of Desmond Lynam from the BBC to ITV to do a very similar job demonstrates how it can be done.

Many companies are now setting up intelligence units. They scour the press and the Internet for intelligence on what the competition is doing. They may be more unscrupulous and use tactics which border on, or go beyond, the illegal. It is also possible to employ private investigators.

If they can find someone who is vulnerable, offer more money, but also flatter and offer the thrill of the change, betrayal – or, at least, resignation – is not far off.

Criminal

Criminals can use their guile to work their way into any organization which can provide them with useful information or access to cash or goods. The bank teller, a security guard or a bonds trader all have information very useful to the criminal. If a member of staff is vulnerable when he or she has some resentment or a personal weakness which the criminal can identify, the latter will take advantage.

Family

Parents and others in the family are often deeply ambitious for their offspring. This happens in Western, and particularly Eastern, society and at all levels. But it can be particularly strong in other cultures. Asian society is noted for the strength of the family, but it should not be surprising to find it elsewhere.

Whether or not families are ambitious for their children, they frequently offer advice and encouragement. When there is a problem at work, it is often to the close family that people turn. What the husband or wife says can influence employees considerably.

Parents may not approve of, or understand, the jobs their children are doing. Many prefer older and established professions like becoming a lawyer or a doctor to some modern, seemingly less secure and important job, like IT. Parents can maintain a powerful emotional source of pressure on their children for years – indeed, even after death. Adults can be seeking parental approbation for job success well into middle age. Wives can be enormously ambitious for their husbands and vice versa. The success (and failure) at work of one's spouse or relatives reflects on the individual; hence their pressure on them to succeed conspicuously, often, at any cost. Expensive spouses can often be the start on the slippery slopes to deception, fraud and theft.

Friends and minority group pressure

This group can play the same role as the family, but they can go further and tempt people into excessive social activity, drinking, clubbing and so on and thereby undermine the work culture of the organization. Peer pressure, particularly among the young, is substantial and certainly the major factor accounting for delinquency.

There is a slightly different phenomenon when an employee belongs to a minority group. We like to belong and, if we are in an alien culture or when where we feel outnumbered for whatever reason, we look for people who are like us. At its most benign and innocent, it can be Scots living in London, Brits living overseas (the "expats"), or it could be Catholics in an otherwise Protestant community. These groupings are unlikely to cause problems; indeed, they may well help the employee adjust to the society outside the office and thus make people feel more comfortable and relaxed.

Some communities are more intrusive and can lead to a conflict of loyalties. There is much suspicion about the freemasons, although the worries come about because of their secrecy, rather than their action. When we do not know what is happening, it is a natural reaction to worst-case senario and prepare for any eventuality. Pressure can be brought to bear on people because of their religion, color or nationality. We know that much undesirable behavior in young people, from binge drinking to delinquency, is sustained by their peer group norms and pressures. Groups pre- and proscribe good and bad behaviors. They can endorse CWBs or cause them to occur very rarely in an organization.

Head-hunters/recruitment agencies

These people are employed to find staff, and they nearly always find people who are already employed: by definition, most of the successful indeed crucial "knowledge workers". The employee may come into the recruitment agency or contact the head-hunter. But they are on the look out as well. Any indication that someone is not happy or is looking for a change and their names will quickly be in the carding system. Young, ambitious people soon know what they are worth, and are happy to tear up both their legal and psychological contract. Head-hunters lure and can destabilize. They can sow seeds of greed and discontent as part of their otherwise quite legitimate process. At best, they can help occupational mobility and act as a sort of vocational guidance. At worst, they sow seeds of discontent to further their own aims.

Journalists and the press

Journalists have always looked for good stories (and scoops) and found them usually amongst the discontented. They have money to pay people – often quite large sums – but they have something else they can play on most effectively: vanity. The journalist can offer public retribution for wrongs done. They can ensure either that the worker gets maximum publicity or, if they wish, anonymity. The exposure of a company or individuals in that company, when satisfaction was not possible from within, can feel enormously rewarding. If combined with flattery, the sense of importance felt by the perpetrator increases. He feels he has made a change and that it is only him that has brought this about.

Rarely does an employee leave, thieve or deceive for one of the above reasons alone. People take advice from others: friends, family and professionals. Regarding any major decision, they will usually talk with others, who may be highly skilled counselors, who will lead us down the best path for us, but mostly they are friends with no counseling skills and they offer advice. It is true, therefore, to say that however the betrayal is manifested, and however serious it is, an external force will play a part. It may be the criminal tempting someone away, or the influence of a friend or family member.

The contrary is not, however, true. An external force will rarely succeed unless there is something deficient either in the workplace or in the individual's character that predisposes him to betray.

Motivations are complex, but the elements which go to make them up are not. Everyone has experienced something similar. They are perhaps, in lesser form, recognizable. Bring all three groups together and the result can be devastating.

Theories related to specific CWBs

Theories of theft

Inevitably, the perceived cause of the problems leads to an appropriate strategy for prevention. Most researchers in the area, like Greenberg and Barling (1996), recognize that different forces together impact on when, how and why theft takes place.

There are many factors involved in employee theft. Greenberg and Barling (1998) suggest that they can be grouped into three types: person theories (Table 3.8), workplace theories (Table 3.9), and a state of interaction between both of these theories.

There must be opportunity in the case of the third factor, but it is the combination between person characteristics and workplace characteristics that probably predict theft most accurately. Thus, a morally lax individual in a morally lax workplace that offers opportunity for stealing would be an extreme case. Equally, a greedy opportunistic individual who works in an organization he or she believes to be exploitative is also a situation likely to lead to theft.

In a recent study, Greenberg (2002) showed that the moral development of an individual and the actual victim of a theft (individual vs. organization) actually determine when and why people steal money. That is, it is the particular interaction between the person and the job that leads to thieving.

So, how can the manager reduce employee theft? The first is to *break the social norms* that accept and rationalize theft. Some companies have had success with simply printing theft statistics on the intranet. It is essential to stop employees seeing their theft as appropriate and desirable. Business ethics talks can help this, but they are insufficient and can be seen as preaching.

Table 3.8 Person theories

Person theories are concerned with the essentially psychological problem of explaining why some individuals (and not others) are involved with pilfering and theft.

Financial needs	The idea is that stealing occurs as a function of financial need. But others' needs are implicated – such as social or belongingness needs, because people may steal in order to obtain goals/money that allows them to become a "club member". It is a weak theory, as it does not distinguish the origin or type of need (e.g. drug addiction, gambling, sick relatives).
Deviant personality/background	The concept is that there is a type of person that is more vulnerable to opportunities to steal as well as personally rationalize stealing behavior. The theory is weak and tautological – people who steal are the stealing type – stealing types steal!
Greed/temptation opportunities	The idea is that people are inherently greedy and steal when they can: they are trusted. However, it fails to explain why there are systematic differences in greed.
Moral laxity	Here, the theme is that some groups (especially young people) do not possess the same ethical standards or trustworthy qualities as other groups. Again, the argument is poor: it is tautological and does not explain individual differences.
Marginality	People who are marginal have less static jobs with no tenure or social standing, and steal as a way of expressing grievances. Because they have had no opportunities to develop commitment, they steal.

Profit-sharing also helps align the interests of employer and employees. Activities that lower profitability (pilfering in employee-owned companies) soon become taboo. Where this is not possible, having a clear social contract prohibiting theft may help.

If perceived (note, not actual) fairness is an issue, it is important to emphasize continually the *fairness of the company's compensation system*. Company hotlines for just whistle-blowing have been shown to have a significant effect. Some companies have suggested that the issue of theft should be brought into the open and employees should be encouraged to discuss how it is to be defined and treated. This helps to flag that the company is serious about theft and helps ensure employees commitment.

Companies are now so worried about the issue that they are attempting serious preventive, proactive – rather than reactive – methods. This involves integrity-testing and background checks at selection. It also involves employer publications but, more ominously, a tightening up of internal controls and security.

Table 3.9 Workplace theories

Workplace theories emphasize factors like:	
Organizational climate	In effect, this refers to a moral atmosphere that can even endorse dishonesty, or at least turn a blind eye towards it. The idea is that the prevailing climate sends clear messages to employees about whether, what, which and when dishonest behaviors are acceptable or not.
Deterrence doctrine	This refers to the existence, explicitness and retributive nature of company anti-theft-policies, and the perceived certainty and severity of punishment, as well as the visibility of that punishment. The idea is simple: get tough with deterrence and theft will be reduced.
Perceived organizational fairness	This "theory" suggests it is exploitation by the employer that causes pilferage. Note that it is perceived to be unfairness on the part of the organization that is the crucial factor. Pay cuts, in particular, lead to this activity.

Most employers would prefer to avert the problem in the first place, perhaps with some pre-employment testing – like giving people integrity tests. Yet, Greenberg and Barling (1996: 59) point to some severe limitations with that idea.

> Although integrity tests have been shown to predict on-the-job theft, they still need to be used with caution for several reasons: it is ironical and unreasonable to expect dishonest people to answer questions truthfully about their own attitudes toward theft and past dishonest behavior. Attitudes about theft or personality tendencies are only moderately correlated with theft behaviors. Opportunity for theft does not necessarily lead to greater occurrences of theft. In fact, most employees in various occupations have access to money or merchandise but choose not to steal. Labelling someone a "thief" may become a self-fulfilling prophesy and would certainly make it more difficult for that person to obtain alternative employment. This approach ignores the potential contribution of workplace factors that might lead to employee theft.

Greenberg (1998) has argued that there are forces that both encourage and discourage theft at various levels (see Figure 3.5). They work first at the level of the individual. Thus, the personality and the moral development of the individual maybe either an encouraging or inhibiting force, while various life pressures (for more money to fund gambling debts, secret love affairs etc.) may encourage the individual to thieve.

Individuals have to make the decision to thieve, which then usually results in their justifications (to self and others) of that act. After the theft,

Figure 3.5 **Different forces on theft**

they then usually try to manage the interpretation of that action and label it according to their own ends. Many try to legitimise a clearly illegitimate act. Their personality, morality and intelligence are powerful determinants in how, when and why this is done.

At the group level, there may well be peer pressure to take part in group organized and accepted thieving. Equally, there may well be peer-based pressure not to take part in any or specific types of theft. Paradoxically, some organizations encourage theft by tacitly accepting it as an invisible wage structure. Most verbalize – or, indeed, try to induce inhibiting forces by – a mixture of a code of ethics, ethical leadership and having a non-bureaucratic structure.

Deceit

Some work has been done to analyze the motivations of scientific research-ers, though the frustrations of those investigating are apparent. "What we do not know far outweighs what we do know. Most of the wrongdoers have been bright, accomplished scientists who have engaged sometimes in hon-est and, other times dishonest research...No obvious link seems to exist between a predilection for unethical behavior and any particular type of training or institutional employer" (Lock and Wells, 1996: 9).

Iain Gillespie (1996) identifies five principal reasons for deceit in medical research (Table 3.10).

Table 3.10 Five principal reasons for deceit in medical research

Personal ambition	There is a natural desire to please the boss. Ambition is also honed by comparing one's rate of progress with that of contemporaries (i.e. making social comparisons). Employees often feel resentful at a colleague's much more rapid progress.
Need to publish	There are pressures to publish a great deal of high quality material. There are also the pressures of the deadline and of obtaining grants that might be reliant on the published material.
Financial pressures	When a payment is offered for each subject introduced into a trial, some find it difficult to resist fudging the books.
Health problems: **Gillespie separates this into two parts**	The first act of fraud may be a clear manifestation of a personality disorder.
	The temptation to fake a figure just for sheer excitement also occurs.

Broad and Wade focus more on the self-deception argument. "The desire to win credit, to gain the respect of one's peers, is a powerful incentive for almost all scientists... The thirst for recognition has brought with it the temptation to 'improve' a little on the truth" (Broad and Wade, 1988: 24). Self-deception, they believe, is a problem of "pervasive importance in science. The most rigorous training in objective observation is often a feeble defense against the desire to obtain a particular result" (Broad and Wade, 1988: 109).

Information leakage

Information leakage which is the responsibility of employees, as opposed to external stealing, can be for the six reasons (Table 3.11).

Accidental loss can be put down to carelessness and the responsibility of the individual. The employers would have to accept some responsibility if they had not trained the individual concerned sufficiently, or was working them so hard that mistakes begin to happen out of tiredness or out of having too much to do.

People at work spy on their bosses. They may betray their colleagues, their bosses or the company as a whole. They may even become a traitor by committing treason. Countries have laws about treason, espionage, sedition and mutiny to discourage their enemies.

The enemy within can be a thief but is often worse: a betrayer of trust. They are the sort of industrial or organizational spies that tend to be portrayed in novels: they tend to be, in some sense, outside conventional society;

Table 3.11 Six reasons for information leakage

Accidental	The loss of papers or electronic data, which might be found by other interested parties, or indiscrete comments made over the phone or overheard in a bar.
Casual gossip	A discussion motivated by someone's desire to discuss either the private lives of others (which may be salacious) or the company's business (which may be intended to damage).
Deliberate gossip or bad-mouthing	This occurs when a person feels hurt or betrayed about something that happened in the office that they feel was deliberately unfair.
Deliberate	Passing of information to interested parties to expose some wrongdoing in the company or organization (classic whistle-blowing).
Deliberate and clandestine	Passing of information that benefits the business of a third party, such as a journalist or competitor.
Taking confidential information on departure	Stealing information from an organization that will be of direct benefit to the thief in their new employment.

they are somehow invisible; their attachment to others is superficial; they are fascinated with the power of secrecy and they are individualistic (autonomous, self-reliant). The enemy within, the citizen spy, is often after selling trade secrets.

Eoyang (1994: 85–6) believes that, classically, there is a behavior chain (typical sequence of events) that occurs:

> The chain begins with *intention*, which is some level of interest and motivation in violating security. Next is the formulation of *plans* either along or with others to transform the intentions into concrete actions. The third essential step is to gain access to locations, persons, or sources that retain restricted information. Once access has been achieved, the actual *acquisition* of the information must be effected. Since most perpetrators of espionage wish to minimize the risks of their trade, they typically engage in deception to hide their activities and their responsibility for it. As most consumers of espionage products are government, spies must have *contact* with some foreign agency to whom they can confer the stolen information and from whom they can receive their compensation (*exchange*). The actual transmittal of the information may take many forms, some of which have been celebrated in innumerable spy novels. Although the rewards of espionage are rarely munificent, the consumption of the gains from espionage can sometimes arouse suspicions when it shows as unusual or unexplained affluence. Finally, it may be necessary for spies to flee (escape) to avoid capture and punishment or to enjoy the fruits of their clandestine endeavours without retribution.

Whistle-blowing

It is possible to conceive of the motives of whistle-blowers along one simple dimension: from *prosocial, altruistic* and *selfless* to *vengeful, spiteful* and *selfish*. Inevitably, whistle-blowing is motivationally complex. It is an act not taken lightly, and an act often involving courage.

The perception of whether a whistle-blowing action is altruistic or vengeful no doubt depends on who makes the judgment – press or public, employee or owner, customer or lawyer. In hindsight, it is easy to point out that it is in an organization's best interest to act.

From what we know, what individual difference variables have been shown to be related to whistle-blowing? Does it relate to the whistle-blower's personality, moral values, and demography or job status, like rank, pay level or job performance?

If *personality* factors are important, the question is which studies have examined self-esteem, neuroticism, authoritarianism and locus of control. Results have shown very weak effects. Certainly, one may expect stable rather than neurotic people to deal better with the stress of whistle-blowing. Conscientious individuals may seem more "justice-sensitive". However, so far, results are mixed or disappointing, suggesting personality effects are low.

Surely, *morality, ideology* and *values* relate to whistle-blowing? While that would certainly be the case, the academic research literature has found surprisingly little evidence of it.

The studies on demography, however, have been more forthcoming. Some studies have shown that whistle-blowers tend to be older, more senior and better-educated, but this observation has been challenged. Equally, the studies on rank, pay, job performance and supervisory status correlates of whistle-blowing have not shown clear relationships. The lack of clear findings in this area may be for various reasons. The *first* concerns the quality and quantity of the research studies in this area, which remain few and modest in nature. The *second* is that maybe there are various different types of whistle-blower and that this leads to the impression of equivocal data. *Third*, few of the studies looked at the *motives* of whistle-blowers – or, indeed, their job history.

It has been suggested that particular organizational factors are related to whistle-blowing. These include:

▷ the organizational climate, particularly the tolerance of wrongdoing.
▷ the perceived general fairness of management practices and processes.
▷ the existence and use of ethical procedures.
▷ corporate cultural values – like individualism, uncertainty avoidance and tolerance of ambiguity.
▷ the distribution, interaction, procedural and distributive justice that actually exists and is perceived to exist in organizations.
▷ industry type – private vs. public.
▷ national culture.

Various studies have attempted to investigate these issues.

Miceli *et al.* (2008) developed a model based on the famous bystander research to try to predict who will blow the whistle. It has three phases:

▷ *First,* there is the question of noting the focal/specific activity as wrongful or not. Different individuals may label identical behavior quite differently: Is flirting sexual harassment? Is tax evasion tax avoidance? If a behavior is thought of as wrongdoing, any person or group in the organization has the power and responsibility to do something about it. An observer may perceive wrongdoing and believe they know who is responsible (any "why") but fail to report it. However, if they do report it, we move on to the next phase.

▷ *Second,* how an organization responds to a whistle-blower incident sends clear signals to others inside and outside the organization. Does the organization deny, downplay or try to hide the complaint? Is it hyper- or hyposensitive? Does it have processes and procedures designed to deal with these issues? Inevitably, whistle-blowers can have a demoralizing effect on the organization, depending on the response and *who* makes *what* decision regarding how to react.

▷ *Third,* there are questions for any individual as to whether they believe it is *their* responsibility to act. Further, they need to believe that any action available to them will be effective in reducing or eliminating that wrongdoing. If they believe either that it is not primarily their responsibility or that any intervention will not work, they are unlikely to act. If they decide to act and whistle-blowing the issue is the potential cost–benefit analysis of such an activity. If costs like sacking, demotion, and humiliation occur, they may decide not to act.

The model has been successfully used to understand the whole issue of whistle-blowing.

The normalization of both wrongdoing and whistle-blowing

How common, frequent and normal a behavior is has profound implications for how people react to it. Corruption, theft and bribery can be part of everyday organizational life, neither exceptional nor unusual. People accept the wrongdoing as normal. Wrongdoing can certainly be *institutionalized*. It is embedded, routine and acceptable. It is not thought of as odd or wrong. There are many interesting, historical examples of when this has occurred. Organizations self-censor and, if they have no clear moral or ethical behavioral codes, it is easy for people in the organization to become, normatively, wrongdoers.

Most individuals and organizations have an impressive rationalization process by which they explain away wrongdoing. They can argue:

▷ the behavior is not wrong; the law is an ass.

▷ they have little choice but to take part in wrongful behaviors.

▷ nobody anywhere is actually hurt or damaged by their actions.
▷ if people are affected by wrongdoing, they effectively deserve their fate.
▷ they are no worse than their competitors who do the same, if not worse.
▷ they need to engage in the wrongdoing to save (or help prosper) the company and all those dependent on the people who work there.
▷ they can indulge in those petty and minor issues because, overall, they are good.
▷ they can easily refocus their attention away from bad behavior into good.

The problem is that, over time, employees become fully socialized into the "wicked, wrongdoing" ways of organizations. They accept the benefits of corruption, easily and quickly compromising their moral sense. Often by coercion, sometimes by fear, they begin to accept things as they are and, in fact, encourage others likewise. Over time, they can and do become very committed to wrongdoing organizations and groups.

This is why so many people work so long – and, often, so happily – in organizations that perform wrongdoing. Psychological processes change the perceptions of employees so much so that it takes a real outsider, in some sense of the word, to eventually blow the whistle on what is going on around them.

Constructive, beneficial deviance or sour, pusillanimous, revenge

The person who reports on his or her own organization that is fraudulent or corrupt potentially could be seen to be traitorous or deviant. While it is clearly deviant (from norms) it could be seen as courageous. Hence the view of the whistle-blower as a hero, as a person prepared to "fight for the right", as David against Goliath, as the beacon of hope in the dark world. That type of whistle-blower does exist. However, there is another version of the whistle-blower. This is of the disenchanted, alienated and under-productive worker "unhappy with their lot", whose sole aim it is to punish those whom they (incorrectly) see as the cause of their predicament. They are often vengeful individuals with a long history of complaining. They are supersensitive to insults, harassment and unfairness.

To some extent, one can distinguish between these two extremes by looking at the outcomes. If we live in a just world, differences between the constructive and destructive, the pro-social and anti-social deviant may be seen. However, one person's flirting is another's sexual harassment; one's firm management another's bullying; one's staff privileges another's theft. The best predictor of the future is the past. What is known about whistle-blowers to indicate whether they are serious, moral individuals eager to right wrongs, or are serial litigious complainants out to take revenge for their perceived failures?

A problem with this area is the often-implicated idea that all whistle-blowing is honestly motivated by courageous, moral individuals willing to stick up for principles against probable retaliation. Speak to a person on the end of a whistle-blower hotline and you hear a very different story. That is, not so much of a wrongdoing but, rather, hurt pride, jealousy, narcissism and spitefulness. This is all the more the case if complaints are made anonymously.

Sabotage

In the world of anarchism and terrorism which exists today there is a sixth reason – that of the terrorist or anarchist infiltrating organizations to sabotage key business or public services.

It is quite impossible to get valid sabotage statistics for two reasons. *First*, organizations do not always know when it has occurred. *Second*, where they do, for obvious reasons of poor publicity they do not report it.

Saboteurs may be vengeful, defensive, lazy or self-promotional. Some want retaliation and try to "get even"; others are more involved in self-presentation, trying (somewhat bizarrely) to meet perceived expectations or requirements, or organizational success.

Using interesting examples, Crino (1994) listed various motivations for sabotage:

1   To make a statement or send a message. They hope to gain maximum publicity and sympathy for their position which may be based on political, moral or religious beliefs.
2   To prevent or encourage corporate change. Some want to stop mergers or stock sales by scaring off bidders. Others sabotage old equipment forcing a company to buy new machines.
3   To establish personal worth or simply be the centre of attention. They may want to increase their status or join particular subcultures. This is rarely politically motivated sabotage but more likely pathologically motivated sabotage.
4   To gain a competitive advantage over co-workers. They may destroy others work or, withholding or lying about important information, losing important documents; compromising others reputation (rumour, blame, altered records) or encouraging them to take part in self-defeating behaviors. The idea is to enhance ones' own reputation at the expense of others.
5   To gain revenge against management and co-workers. Workers who have been shown disrespect, passed over for promotion, given added responsibility but no commensurate reward, or not been given support from colleagues become disgruntled. Arson, bomb threats and attempted poisoning is not unusual for these saboteurs.
6   To have an impact in a large, faceless, distant bureaucracy. People are loyal to their local group and resent the interference by anonymous people from head office often many miles away. Curiously sabotage can increase a sense of control: they (personally) can slow down production,

make errors, let faulty products leave the factory. It allows them to think, quite negatively, that they can make a difference.

7 *To obtain thrills and satisfy a need to destroy.* Bored sensation seekers love a fire, a line of cars with slashed tyres, a building with broken windows. Sabotage is a game and an exciting one at that. One can beat the system and outsmart pompous authority figures.

8 *To avoid responsibility for failure, incompetence or to avoid work.* Sabotage can refocus attention away from them. It can also be used to intimidate or implicate others or even encourage them to conspire to avoid work.

9 *For personal gain.* Sabotage may well create conditions for additional compensation, compromising data, setting up good jobs with competitors. Clever IT sabotage can lead to access to data on managed funds, customer records, etc.

10 *To vent anger created by one's personal life.* The disappointed, disillusioned and frustrated may take out their anger at work quite simply because they spend a lot of their time there. The acts are random, unplanned and gratuitous aimed simply to vent anger and feel more control.

Conclusion

The motives for disruptive behavior in the workplace can originate for a variety of reasons, and there is unlikely to be only one cause. These motives can be grouped under three headings:

▷ *Personal*, ranging from strongly held beliefs and values to greed and personality disorders such as narcissism.
▷ *Revenge* against a dysfunctional organization, caused by such factors as poor management, lack of recognition and dull work.
▷ *External persuaders*, including family, journalists and criminals.

The unsettling forces, strengths and weaknesses in individuals are recognizable; that staff should become occasionally resentful or disillusioned should not come as a surprise; some minor infringements are inevitable. And the consequences are usually met with resilience by the employees, who also recognize that the world is not perfect. But when employers and their managers persist in negative behavior, or fail to notice and react to an individual's problems, the reaction escalates.

That may be enough. The ambitious individuals who seek thrills and excitement in their work will not tolerate a company where advancement and new challenges are absent. They will resign and, depending on the severity of their poor management experiences, will bad-mouth the company, seek to take with them information or clients, or seek some other form of revenge.

If during the process of disillusionment an external "persuader" discovers what is happening, the consequences could be accelerated and turned into a more damaging act of sabotage.

The solutions for employers are not hard to grasp. It may be that the fault lies entirely with the individual and some external malevolent force. But, before seeking refuge in this rather comfortable explanation, employers might pause and ask themselves whether their own management skills and styles might have contributed to the process.

4   Bad Eggs and Bad Apples

Introduction

This chapter is about individualistic, person-centered explanations for CWBs. Some people – but fortunately very few – are, for want of a better theoretical and non-psychological term, evil. They are morally corrupt and capable of inflicting physical and mental pain on others. They are more than difficult or nasty or incompetent. Indeed, they are often more than simply bad. They appear to have criminal and psychopathic tendencies. Their lack of conscience and an absence of a sense of right and wrong make them able to inflict great harm on others without regret or remorse.

Three basic points need to be made. *First*, people commit CWBs because of the way they are treated and because of the workplace culture. This tends to explain the vast majority of CWBs. It is not that they start off bad, mad or sad but, rather, that situational, cultural and circumstantial factors drive them down that road in a vengeful way. However, there is a small percentage of serious CWBs performed consistently by individuals who are pro-active not reactive. That is, their own personality and values lead them to commit a strong CWB. The clue is in their personal history: bad eggs have a past, often starting in adolescence, which foretells how they behave as adults. Many are duplicitously dishonest and disingenuous. Worse, they are very aggressive or criminal in their everyday behavior.

Second, these bad eggs are relatively rare and, hopefully, screened out of most organizations. They do not, in general, reach senior levels before being "found out"; but some do, and cause great mayhem. Paradoxically, some exploit their pathology and succeed very well in climbing the greasy pole in organizational life.

Third, it is important to think dimensionally not categorically. Although we talk in categorical terms: *he* is a psychopath, *she* is Machiavellian, *they* are criminals, it is apparent that there are degrees of normality and abnormality; goodness or wickedness. Many people inhabit they gray areas between normal and abnormal, healthy and unhealthy, adapted and maladapted. Further, some, through stress or change, can "cross the line" between the adapted and the sick.

There are – and always will be – bad, conscienceless, psychopaths who commit serious and petty organizational crimes. We can explain their behavior primarily in terms of their pathology – but they are the exception, not the rule. They may be high profile in media stories but, mercifully, very rare. They are, as statisticians say, *a low base-rate phenomenon*. As we have consistently noted, by far the most common motive for organization deviancy is the way people feel they have been treated by the organization.

Much has been written about the concept of the criminal personality: the idea that certain people are predisposed to commit crimes. How to explain lying, stealing and cheating at work? This section lists typical *internal* personal, "bad person" type explanations given by psychiatrists, psychologists, journalists and ordinary people who are victims or simply observers of "nasty" people in the workplace. While there are clearly occasions where the stealing, cheating and other CWBs are attributable primarily to the characteristics of individuals – namely, their personal pathology – it is nearly always the case that CWBs are not performed by "sick", "deranged" or "wicked" individuals but, rather, by those who, for one reason or another, are pushed over the brink!

The wrong focus

Psychologists have noted the *fundamental attribution error* – which is, essentially, the idea that people like to explain the behavior of others by using personality trait, internal or dispositional causes rather than external or situation causes. Their attributions are erroneous: their belief in cause is misplaced. Thus, asked to explain why someone is frequently absent or has many accidents, they prefer to explain the former behavior in terms, say, of hypochondria or laziness and the latter behavior in terms of clumsiness or simply accident proneness. Most people ignore or underplay the many other external and situational factors that might play a role. Thus, a person may be frequently absent because of a dying parent or accident-prone because of poor factory layout, machinery or safety rules in an organization. There are, quite simply, both internal and external causes of behavior.

We often err in explaining *others'* behaviors in terms of internal, stable dispositions like their personality, or moral integrity, or ability. We often explain *our* behavior in terms of the circumstances that shape, reward, constrain us, but *others* in terms of their personality. We, who are observers of other people, be they good or bad leaders and managers, tend to attribute (explain) their behavior as being primarily caused (motivated, shaped) by intrapersonal factors (that is, things about them). So, we talk of people's ability, motives and personality as the primary shapes of behavior. They argue that we completely neglect to understand the situational forces that shape behavior. We make the error which is fundamental to so many explanations of neglecting the forces and factors that shape behavior.

This difference is immediately apparent when people are asked to describe or explain their behavior. For instance, a person gives a bad speech: observers say the speaker was nervous, insecure or unprepared while the actors (speaker) notes the bright lights, the audience hostility, the unfamiliar gadgets.

Following from this, is it correct to say simply that it is bad people who do bad things? There are corrupt, egocentric, selfish people happy to break the law and cause misery to many others to further their own ends. Is this, quite simply an attribution error?

Thus, various researchers have talked about the *banality of evil*; others, the *banality of courage*. What they mean by this is that both the behavior of villains *and* heroes cannot, and should not, be (exclusively) explained in terms of their pathology or personal make-up. These intrapersonal explanations neglect situational and system factors.

For instance, those studying Nazi criminals often remarked at both the ordinariness and normality of those they cross-examined. They did not find sociopathic, callous monsters – though, no doubt, some did exist. Rather, they found people who "went along with the rules", obeyed orders and did "what was required of them".

Thus, a child growing up in an environment that is disorderly and unpredictable, and where they have to "fend for themselves" to survive, could easily behave like a psychopath. Equally, growing up in a criminal family or being part of a criminal gang may teach a child criminal ways. Similarly, there are lawless societies and those which approve of, even encourage, evil behaviors.

It is, therefore, argued that people who find themselves in bad societies, systems or organizations are often confronted by situations that encourage and, even, require bad behavior while discouraging good behavior. There are, therefore, not so much bad apples as bad orchards, bad packing crates.

Vengeful litigation

Over the last decade or so, many people could not help noticing print, radio and television companies funding advertisements from organizations offering to get compensation for "victims of accidents at work". Furthermore, there are now many cases of people suing hospitals and the military, religious institutions and social clubs, schools and universities, for some form of mistreatment. Priests and surgeons, generals and professors, as well as managers and whole companies, are forced to defend allegations of everything from incompetence to sexual accusations of many kinds.

This desire to take issues to law could be seen as spiteful, vengeful behavior of greedy, wicked people, or else a legitimate quest for justice. The idea that litigation is drastically on the increase can be seen as an indicator of the rise of bad bosses or bad processes at work, the increase of "ambulance-chasing" legal firms, the increased concern with restitutional justice or some combination of these.

There is no doubt that legal action and fear of litigation is a powerful motivator in many organizations. As employment legislation continues to become more complicated and law suits larger, companies find it "cost-effective" to employ full-time lawyers.

There have been distinct trends in workplace litigation. Overall, this seems to be increasing in most (western) countries, though various historical and legal factors seem to determine how steep the gradient. Next, whereas earlier most cases seemed to be about the design and enforcement of organized practices and procedures, now there are many cases about racial and sexual discrimination, harassment and other "inappropriate actions". Also, the costs and claims have risen astronomically.

The cost of law suits can be staggeringly high. They take a long time and require many resources. Companies have to gather evidence justifying their behavior as well as provide evidence requested by the "other side". The cost of winning can be high, but nothing like the cost of losing where compensation *and* legal costs have to be paid.

Fear of litigation, as a consequence, drives organizational practices. Paradoxically, this does not always ensure good practice and organizational justice. They may be cured simply by minimizing the likelihood and costs of lawsuits. Yet, the very attempts to avoid litigation may actually encourage it.

Thus, devious, dishonest, incompetent and lazy staff may be "kept on", if they threaten litigation. Promotion may be more based on legal threat than merit or hard work. Plants may be moved closer or redesigned to avoid legal issues in some countries.

What does it say about a manager or an organization that they have consistently been the target of lawsuits ranging from the ever-on-the-increase bullying and harassment to racial discrimination or using unsafe practices? Is this a good index of bad management? Clearly, one factor must be the history of the case: that is, where the managers or the organization are more often found innocent or guilty.

Perhaps the more interesting question is not so much the target of the litigation but, rather, the nature of the litigant. *What* sort of people regularly – and, indeed, happily – resort to litigation while others prefer not to do that. *Why* do they do it? *Which* targeted person or organization do they choose?

One approach would suggest greedy, vengeful, people purely in search of self-interest (more publicity, revenge) target people and companies most able to pay "compensation". Another would suggest often courageous people with a strong sense of justice for all workers sue large, arrogant companies that care little for the welfare of their workers and customers.

Economic models of litigation are straight forward. People sue to get money. Lawyers are happy to help them, of course; there are probabilities, costs and benefits associated with all law suits. However, the data suggests the homo-economical model is insufficient to explain who sues who, when and why.

The naming, blaming, claiming approach is different to simple complaining. It involves attributing cause, confrontation and then litigation. Some bad apples take advantage of these new trends.

The criminal personality

Every human characteristic is normally distributed; that is, there is a bell curve with a few people scoring very high (on height, creativity, the ability to sing), a few scoring very low, but many being in the middle. This applies to traits (extraversion), abilities (intelligence), values (equality) and beliefs. This is true, too, of integrity, honesty and law-abidingness. To this extent, there are people, relatively few, that score low on this dimension. This could be considered a stable consistent trait like behavior: that is, there are criminal types.

Early criminologists, like Lambrosso and Sheldon, argued for a criminal type, born with an innate disposition to criminality and anti-social behavior, but these ideas were (and are) angrily dismissed by criminologists, sociologists and others who claim they ignore all important social factors. For some fifty years, the trait position was disregarded (though enthusiastically supported by Eysenck) but has returned (with a vengeance), especially with the development in behavior genetics.

There is no shortage of theories about the cause of crime and criminality. Early *demonological* theory (criminals are evil, sinners, etc.) was replaced by Marxist *economic* theories (social class inequality, lack of opportunity), then early *biological* theories (mental/moral/physical deficiency), and then *psychological* theories (unconscious processes, peer learning). Most criminology has been dominated by sociological theories that emphasize social processes, labeling and conflict.

For a long time, both psychologists and sociologists argued that *crime was learnt*. Early ideas can be expressed thus:

1   Criminal behavior is learned.
2   The learning is through association with other people.
3   The main part of the learning occurs within close personal groups.
4   The learning includes techniques to execute particular crimes and also specific attitudes, drives and motives conducive toward crime.
5   The direction of the drives and motives is learned from perception of the law as either favorable or unfavorable.
6   A person becomes criminal when their definitions favorable to breaking the law outweigh their definitions favorable to non-violation.
7   The learning experiences – differential associations – will vary in frequency, intensity and importance for each individual.
8   The process of learning criminal behavior is no different from the learning of any other behavior, like altruism, selling or negotiating with others.
9   Although criminal behavior is an expression of needs and values, crime cannot be explained in terms of those needs and values (e.g., it is not the need for money which causes crime; rather, it is the method used to acquire the money, the method is learnt).

The learning approach, advocated by behaviorists, is that people develop *a sense of* – and, more importantly, *behaviors associated with* – right and

Table 4.1 Early risk factors for later delinquency

Individual factors	▷ Early antisocial behavior (physical aggression, biting, cruelty to animals) ▷ Poor cognitive development, low intelligence ▷ Hyperactivity, impulsivity, ADHD
Family factors	▷ Maltreatment, family violence, parental psychopathology and antisocial behaviors, teenage parenthood
School and community factors	▷ Poor academic performance ▷ Low academic aspirations ▷ Living in a poor, maladjusted family ▷ Disorganized neighborhoods ▷ Delinquent peer groups

wrong by the way they are socialized through processes of reward and punishment. Thus, children learn to be good but some learn better, faster and more efficiently than others.

Criminologists have studied the development of antisocial and criminal behavior and offending patterns as people *learn to become criminals*. They note certain risk factors for being delinquent and criminal, as well as the life events on a criminal career. Thus, individual, family, and school and community circumstances have been noted as early risk factors for later delinquency (Table 4.1).

There are many risk factors associated with youth crime. The Joseph Rowntree Foundation Social Policy Research Document 93 (1996) lists nine (Table 4.2).

Personality, intelligence and crime

Any theory of crime must explain the data, whether it is a psychological, psychiatric or sociological theory. Farrington (2003: 223–4) identifies 10 assumptions about offending that theories must explain:

1 Offending prevalence peaks between 15 and 19 years of age – that is, adolescence.
2 Onset offending peaks between 8 and 14 and begins to decline between 20 and 29. Crime, in short, is committed by young people.
3 Early onset nearly always shows a long criminal record and the committing of many different offenses.
4 There is continuity in offending over the life-span. High offenders in one period tend to be high offenders in the next, even though most eventually desist from crime. In this sense, we see trait criminality.
5 Chronic offenders nearly always have an early onset, high offense frequency of many types of crime, and long criminal careers.

Table 4.2   Risk factors associated with youth crime

Prenatal and perinatal	Early child-bearing (i.e. young mothers) increases the risks of such undesirable outcomes for children and is associated with low school attainment, antisocial behaviour, substance use and early sexual activity. An increased risk of offending among children of teenage mothers is associated with low income, poor housing, absent fathers and poor child rearing methods.
Personality	Impulsiveness, hyperactivity, restlessness and limited ability to concentrate are associated with low attainment in school and a poor ability to foresee the consequences of offending.
Intelligence and attainment	Low intelligence and poor performance in school, although important statistical predictors of offending, are difficult to disentangle from each other. One plausible explanation of the link between low intelligence and crime is its association with a poor ability to manipulate abstract concepts and to appreciate the feelings of victims.
Parental supervision and discipline	Harsh or erratic-parental discipline and cold or rejecting parental attitudes have been linked to delinquency and are associated with children's lack of internal inhibitions against offending. Physical abuse by parents has also been associated with an increased risk of the children themselves becoming violent offenders in later life.
Parental conflict and separation	Living in a home affected by separation or divorce is more strongly related to delinquency than when the disruption has been caused by the death of one parent. However, it may not be a "broken home" that creates an increased risk of offending so much as the parental conflict that lead to the separation.
Socioeconomic status	Social and economic deprivation are important predictors of antisocial behaviour and crime, but low family income and poor housing are better measurements than the prestige of parents' occupations.
Delinquent friends	Delinquents tend to have delinquent friends. But it is not certain whether membership of a delinquent peer group leads to offending or whether delinquents simply gravitate towards each other's company (or both). Breaking up with delinquent friends often coincides with desisting from crime.
School influences	The prevalence of offending by pupils varies widely between secondary schools. But it is not clear how far schools themselves have an effect on delinquency (for example, by paying insufficient attention to bullying or providing too much punishment and too little praise), or whether it is simply that troublesome children tend to go to high delinquency-rate schools.
Community influences	The risks of becoming criminally involved are higher for young people raised in disorganised inner city areas, characterised by physical deterioration, overcrowded households, publicly subsidised renting and high residential mobility, It is not clear, however, whether this is due to a direct influence on children, or whether environmental stress causes family adversities which in turn cause delinquency.

Source: Joseph Rowntree Foundation Social Policy Research Document 93 (1996).

6   Offenders are versatile rather than specialized in the crimes they commit, with violent offenders indistinguishable from other frequent offenders. Criminals can, and do, turn their hand to many types of crime.
7   Offenders are versatile at many forms of antisocial behavior such as bullying, drug-taking, stealing, truancy, and heavy drinking.
8   Crimes in the teenage years tend to take place in groups, while offenses after age 20 are committed alone – that is, early crime is much more a social activity, undertaken in groups.
9   Prior to age 20, revenge, excitement, or anger may motivate offenders, while after this age more pragmatic factors, such as earning money, become more common.
10 The onset of different types of offenses occur at different ages. Shoplifting takes place sooner than burglary, which occurs before robbery.

Farrington's "antisocial potential" theory posits that relatively few people have the potential to commit antisocial acts. Long-term Antisocial Potential (AP) involves impulsiveness, strain and life events, while short-term AP depends on situational and motivating factors. Desires for material goods, peer status, excitement and sexual experience, combined with anti-social means of satisfying these needs that are denied legitimately, result in high AP.

Individual difference researchers have been concerned with intelligence and personality correlates of criminality; certainly, there is plenty of evidence of the relationship between crime and intelligence. However, it may be that the less intelligent are simply likely to be caught or that intelligence is correlated with social class, which is the real determinant of crime.

The "cycle" goes something like this: less intelligent children, often of less intelligent parents, are more vulnerable and receive poor parenting. This leads to less control, more impulsivity and being more venturesome. At school, the double disadvantage of low intelligence and poor socialization (manners, respect, attentiveness) can lead to frustration and, hence, aggression and various behavioral problems, which alienate both teachers and parents, which increases the disordered behavior. Further, if the parents are themselves "deviant" or the low-IQ child finds no good but many bad peer models, the problems, already great, are compounded. So, potential criminals get into a negative spiral: less school success lead to fewer skills and less likelihood of obtaining a good job.

Personality theories of crime have identified a whole range of factors that appear to differentiate between those prone and those not prone to crime. Feldman (1993) has identified a number (Table 4.3).

Further, some researchers have come up with categories/types: the under-socialized, boisterous, destructive and disobedient type; the socialized, opportunist, trivializing type; the attention-seeking, impulsive, preoccupied type; and the anxious-withdrawn, shy and hypersensitive type.

Table 4.3   Factors indicating potential criminality

Time orientation	Criminals are "now" rather than future orientated.
Impulsivity	Criminals are particularly poor at delaying gratification.
Sensation-seeking	Offenders have an abnormally high need for stimulation.
Fatalism	Criminals tend to have an external focus of control believing that luck, fate or chance determines their life events.
Self-concept	Criminals have lower self-worth, self-esteem than non-offenders.
Aggression	Most criminals are under-controlled, being more prone to violence of many types

Source: Feldman (1993).

Eysenck's Theory of the Criminal Personality

Perhaps the most robust and fecund of the theories of the criminal personality is that of Hans Eysenck (1977). Feldman (1993: 166) has noted: "One of the theory's great merits is that it makes predictions which are clear-cut, testable and refutable".

The idea is beguilingly simple. Eysenck believed that sociological theory has little to offer society on the causes of crime, arguing that psychological theories have more explanatory power (Eysenck and Gudjonsson, 1989). Eysenck suggests that criminal behavior is not the product of either environment *or* biology alone but, rather, is an interaction of *both* (Eysenck and Eysenck, 1973). This extends his original belief that biology played the largest part in determining criminality when he first declared his theory on criminality in his book *Crime and Personality* (1964). Eysenck suggested that some people are born with cortical and autonomic nervous systems that affect their ability to learn from their environment, which leads some to be prone to illegal and criminal acts.

There are three biologically-based heritable and distinct personality factors, each of which relates to a conditionability – notably, the learning of rules of society:

Extraverts (E) are social and impulsive. They are excitement-seekers interested in novel experiences and being venturesome. This leads them to be poorer learners than introverts at many tasks, including the acquisition of general social rules. They are often, therefore, naughty children who turn into juvenile delinquents and, hence, criminals.

Neurotics (N) are anxious and moody, restless and rigid. They react strongly to threat, often with great fear to painful stimulation. This means they also don't learn social rules well and are "inefficient learners", particularly with respect to punishment.

Tough-minded psychoticism (P) is associated with aggressive, egocentric, insensitive, inhumane, uncaring and troublesome behavior.

Thus, the Eysenckian criminal personality theory is:

▷ Personality traits (P, E, N) are biologically based.
▷ Personality is consistent over time and stable across social situations.
▷ Personality traits are related to the personality disorders.
▷ Odd/eccentric/*Psychotism* (paranoid, schizoid, schizotypal); dramatic/*Extraverted* (histrionic, narcissistic, antisocial borderline); anxious/fearful/*Neurotic* (avoidant, dependent, compulsive, passive–aggressive).
▷ There is a significant negative relationship between intelligence and crime, but this is mediated by social class, educational attainment, race and gender.
▷ Prosocial (unselfish, altruistic, law-abiding) behavior has to be learned. Certain personalities do not learn as well as others.
▷ Psychoticism is the most important predictor of criminality.
▷ Different profiles lead to different types of criminals; high P, high E, low N turn into con-men; high P, low E, low N into thieves, and so on.

Thus, it is the people that score high on all three dimensions that are least conditioned, least socially restrained. They are aggressive, hedonistic, impulsive and reckless.

Eysenck and Gudjonsson (1989) have summarized their position thus:

1   There exists a general behavior pattern of antisocial behavior and criminality, marking the opposite end of the continuum to that constituted by prosocial, altruistic behavior.
2   Within the antisocial and criminal type of behavior, there is a certain amount of heterogeneity, marked particularly by the opposition between active and inadequate criminals, but probably also including differences according to type of crime committed.
3   Criminality is related to certain dimensions of personality, in particular that labeled "psychoticism", which is apparent in all age groups and under all conditions studied.
4   There is a strong tendency for extraversion to be linked to criminality, particularly in younger samples and among more active criminals; inadequate older criminals do not show high extraversion and may indeed be below average on this trait.
5   Most criminals are characterized by a high degree of neuroticism, but this may not be found as markedly in children and youngsters.
6   Scores on the L (lie scale – a measure of dissimulation or faking) are regarded in these studies as a measure of conformity (rather than of dissimulation) and tend to correlate negatively with antisocial and criminal conduct, both in children and in adolescents and adults.
7   The criminality scale, made up of the most diagnostic items of the Eysenck Personality Questionnaire, tends to discriminate significantly between criminals and non-criminals.

8   Primary personality traits – such as impulsiveness, being venturesome, risk-taking, empathy and others – correlate, in predictable directions, with antisocial and criminal conduct.

9   These relationships are observed also in conditions where self-report of antisocial behavior is the major criterion. Thus, personality–criminality correlations are not confined to legal definitions of crime or incarcerated criminals.

10   The observed personality – criminality correlations have cross-cultural validity, appearing in different countries and culture with equal prominence.

11   Personality traits characterizing antisocial and criminal behavior are also found correlated with behavior that is not criminal but that is regarded as antisocial (such as smoking, drug users), whether legal or illegal, tend to show high P, E and N scores. Studies show high P and N scores among drug users, but E scores are elevated only among drug users convicted of other crimes.

Eysenck and Gudjonsson (1989) in their later book are considered in their conclusions. Note the following:

> The main theme that runs through the book is that *psychological factors and individual differences related to the personality are of central importance in relation to both the causes of crime and its control.* This does not mean to say that other factors, such as sociological and economic ones, are not important. Indeed, in many instances they are. We believe that sociological theories are particularly relevant in relation to victimless crimes and less so in the case of victimful crimes.
>
> Psychological factors in criminality, we argue, relate to genetic and constitutional causes and to personality and other sources of individual differences. This does not mean that some people are *destined* to commit crimes. Criminal behavior as such is not innate. What is inherited are certain peculiarities of the brain and nervous system that interact with certain environmental factors and thereby increase the likelihood that a given person will act in a particular antisocial manner in a given situation. (Eysenck and Gudjonsson, 1989: 247)
>
> We agree that much criminal behavior may be construed as the end product of a chain of processes. The first stage consists of the desire for certain goods or outlets. Most commonly, this involves a desire for material goods, status among peers, excitement, sexual gratification, and the relief of anger and hostility. Second, illegal and socially disapproved methods are chosen as acceptable means for satisfying these needs and desires. The reasons for this may be many fold. They may involve faulty learning and inadequate moral development, the tendency to respond to stress in a particular way, and distorted attitudes and attributions. The third and final stage involves a number of situational and opportunity factors, where the criminal act is the outcome of a decision-making process involving perceptions of benefits and costs at any one point in time. (Eysenck and Gudjonsson, 1989: 248)

There are, of course, critiques of 20–30 questionnaire studies linking self-reported personality to self-reported crime and delinquency. The following points are often made:

▷ Self-report measures of both crime/delinquency *and* personality are open to dissimulation; lying, denial or exaggeration.
▷ Caught criminals are unrepresentative of the population. Most criminals are, alas, not caught.
▷ Criminals and delinquents are far from homogeneous (i.e. murderers are very different from con-men; violent offenders from property offenders).
▷ Incarceration may affect personality – increased Neuroticism, reduced Extraversion (i.e. prisoners may change as a function of that imprisonment).
▷ Few studies separate cause and effect. Correlation is not cause.
▷ Personality theories are far from complete, especially with regard to the development of the crucial delinquent personality.
▷ Social/environmental factors are ignored and down-played.

This final issue is the nub of objection, especially from sociologists and educationalists. Life circumstances – that is, poverty, growing up in a criminal family or an unruly (ungovernable) society, economic inequality, opportunities to commit crime – are all more powerful predictors of criminality than an individual's personality.

Eysenck's position did develop and change over time. He placed more emphasis on the role of psychoticism and admitted more the possibility of the social causes of crime. Over the years, various studies in different countries – Australia (Heaven *et al.*, 2004), Iceland (Gudjonsson *et al.*, 2006) – provided support for the theory.

However, it has been the longitudinal studies that have perhaps offered most support for the theory. Using a large sample followed from birth, Caspi *et al.* (1994) and Wright *et al.* (1999) replicated the Eysenkian hypothesized personality – crime relationships across country, gender race and method. Poor social control (impulsivity, hyperactivity etc.) predicted weak social bonds, adolescent delinquency and later criminality.

In a large meta-analytic review, Miller and Lynam (2001) note that developments in personality theory and in data analysis have permitted a second look at the criminal personality idea. They concluded:

> From the overall results, it is possible to generate a description of the personality traits that are characteristic of antisocial individuals. Individuals who commit crimes tend to be hostile, self-centered, spiteful, jealous, and indifferent to others (i.e., low in Agreeableness). They tend to lack ambition, motivation, and perseverance, have difficulty controlling their impulses, and hold non-traditional and unconventional values and beliefs (i.e., are low in Conscientiousness). It is informative that by beginning with the criminal, we arrived at a description very similar to the one offered by Gottfredson and Hirschi (1990) who began with the crime. Gottfredson and Hirschi (1990)

offer that individuals who are low in self control (1) have difficulty delaying gratification and instead respond to tangible stimuli in the immediate environment; (2) lack diligence, tenacity, or persistence in a task; (3) tend to be adventurous, physical, and active rather than cautious, cognitive, and verbal; (4) are little interested in, and unprepared for, long-term occupational pursuits; (5) are self-centered, indifferent, or insensitive to the suffering and needs of others; (6) are gregarious and social people; and (7) have minimal frustration tolerance. The first four characteristics map on very well to the dimension of Conscientiousness or Constraint. Similarly, the fifth and seventh characteristics are clear indicators of low Agreeableness. The only significant disagreement between our descriptions concerns the sixth characteristic – sociability; we found that dimensions related to Extraversion were not related to ASB. (Miller and Lynham, 2001: 780)

They believe personality relates to anti-social behavior in general, and crime in particular, in distal and proximal ways. Personality predicts how people react to situations, how other people react to them and, indeed, the situations they find themselves in. Personality also predicts decision-making.

They believe criminologists should be less hostile to personality and individual differences, because they help to explain the relative stability of anti-social behavior as well as prevention of crime.

Weighing the evidence leads to the following conclusions: there have been various reviews of the Eysenckian position, including attempts at analysis of the now many studies that have tested his theory. These are studies not only of adult criminals and adolescent delinquents, but also "normal" non-criminal individuals. Most studies look at the relationships between scores derived from Eysenck's famous personality test and some other measures, such as self-reported crime (Furnham and Thompson, 1991). Thus, it is possible to give an individual both a personality test and a self-reported measure of delinquent behavior including everything from traffic violation to acts of "minor vandalism", as well as petty theft.

Overall, the results provide mixed, but largely positive evidence for the criminal personality theory. Certainly, when the relationships are significant, they show the higher people score on (in this order) psychoticism, extroversion and neuroticism, the more likely they are to have been involved in criminal, anti-social and delinquent behavior.

The anti-social personality, the psychopath or moral imbecile

The personality disorder most obviously implicated in the "dark side of behavior at work" is the psychopath – now called the anti-social personality. Are those who lie, steal or cheat mentally deranged? We know that around one third of all people in prison can be diagnosed as anti-social people. Are they psychopaths who seem to have no moral control over self-destructive, anti-social behavior? The most conspicuous and dangerous signs of anti-social people or psychopaths include an absence of guilt, conscience or anxiety about the future; lack of feeling of affection for others; and impulsivity and inability to control behavior in the light of probable consequences, although those are known and fully understood.

In his famous book *The Mask of Insanity*, Cleckley (1941) first set out 10 criteria (Table 4.4). The book is, indeed, a classic in psychology and

Table 4.4   Cleckley's criteria and personality traits

Criteria	Personality traits
Superficial charm and intelligence	Superficial charm and good "intelligence"
Absence of anxiety in stressful situations	Absence of delusions and other signs of irrational thinking
Insincerity and lack of truthfulness	Absence of "nervousness" or psychoneurotic manifestations
Lack of remorse and shame	Unreliability
Inability to experience love or genuine emotion	Untruthfulness and insincerity
Unreliability and irresponsibility	Lack of remorse or shame
Impulsivity and disregard for socially acceptable behavior	Inadequately motivated antisocial behavior
Clear-headedness with an absence of delusions or irrational thinking	Poor judgment and failure to learn by experience
Inability to profit from experience	Pathologic egocentricity and incapacity for love
Lack of insight	General poverty in major affective reactions
	Specific loss of insight
	Unresponsiveness in general interpersonal relations
	Fantastic and uninviting behavior with drink and sometimes without
	Suicide rarely carried out
	Sex life impersonal, trivial and poorly integrated
	Failure to follow any life plan

Source: Cleckley (1941).

psychiatry because of its insight. Cleckley noted the slick but callous business person, the smooth-talking and manipulative lawyer, and the arrogant and deceptive politicians as psychopaths. Cleckley also identified 16 personality traits that, through his work with such individuals, he believed captured the essence of the psychopathic personality (Table 4.4).

Cleckley stressed the personality dimensions of this disorder, and clearly believed that most psychopaths are not violent. While he acknowledged that a substantial proportion of incarcerated individuals exhibit psychopathic traits, he asserted that the majority of psychopaths are not incarcerated. According to Cleckley (1941: 19), the psychopath:

> is not likely to commit major crimes that result in long prison terms. He is also distinguished by his ability to escape ordinary legal punishments and restraints. Though he regularly makes trouble for society, as well as for himself, and frequently is handled by the police, his characteristic behaviour does not usually include committing felonies which would bring about permanent or adequate restrictions of his activities. He is often arrested, perhaps one hundred times or more. But he nearly always regains his freedom and returns to his old patterns of maladjustment.

The psychopath is both overtly antisocial yet has superficial charm. They are superficial, grandiose, and manipulative. They lack empathy, long-term goals and remorse. They are both personally irresponsible and refuse to take responsibility for their behavior. If good-looking and intelligent, they can be lethal with their superficial charm.

Furnham (2003: 18) re-interpreted the latest American Psychiatric Manual (DSM IV) for the Psychopath – now called the Anti-Social Personality – into (hopefully) everyday language. Psychopaths:

> show a disregard for, and violation of, the rights of others. They often have a history of being difficult, delinquent or dangerous. They show a failure to conform to social norms with respect to lawful behaviours (repeatedly performing acts that are grounds for arrest, imprisonment and serious detention). This includes lying, stealing and cheating. They are always deceitful, as indicated by repeated lying, use of aliases, or conning others for personal profit or pleasure. They are nasty, aggressive, con artists – the sort who often get profiled on business crime programmes. They are massively impulsive and fail to plan ahead. They live only in, and for, the present. They show irritability and aggressiveness, as indicated by repeated physical fights or assaults. They can't seem to keep still – ever. They manifest a terrifying reckless disregard for the physical and psychological safety for others – or the business in general. They are famous for being consistently irresponsible. Repeated failure to sustain consistent work behaviour or to honour financial obligations are their hallmark. Most frustrating of all, they show a lack of remorse. They are indifferent to, or rationalise, having hurt, mistreated, or stolen from another. They never learn from their mistakes. It can seem like labelling them as anti-social is a serious understatement.

Usually, they are thought to have two major characteristics: anti-social or asocial behavior, and immaturity and lack of guilt or shame. The following are typical characteristics:

1   Thrill-seeking behavior and disregard of conventions
2   Inability to control impulses or delay gratification
3   Rejection of authority and discipline
4   Poor judgment about behavior but good judgment about abstract situations
5   Failure to alter behavior punished in the past
6   Pathological shamelessness and constant lying
7   Asocial and antisocial behavior.

There is no doubt whatsoever that psychopaths are bad apples – often, very bad apples.

Hogan and Hogan (2001) call the anti-social person *Mischievous*. They note that these types expect that others will like them and find them charming. They expect to be able to extract favors, promises, money and other resources from other people with relative ease. However, they see others as merely to be exploited, and therefore have problems maintaining commitments and are unconcerned about social, moral and economic expectations. They are self-confident to the point of feeling invulnerable, and have an air of daring and sangfroid that others can find attractive and, even, irresistible. In industries where bold risk-taking is expected, they can seem a very desirable person for a senior management position.

Miller (2008) calls psychopathic bosses *Predators*. He claims they think "It's a dog-eat-dog world. Look out for number one. Rules are for losers. I'm smarter than all these suckers...My needs come first. I can get over anyone." (p. 58). Miller (2008) notes that psychopathic bosses are prototype cut-throat, chainsaw type entrepreneurs. The interpersonal inquisitiveness is more about getting to know how to manipulate people than befriend them. They take joy in outsmarting "suckers", reinforcing their personal sense of cleverness and powerfulness. They can easily become experts, cheats, embezzlers or harassers. Curiously, they often risk a great deal for a little because of their love of thrill and excitement.

Miller (2008) notes two types of psychopathic bosses: the bright devious, cunning, conning, natural manipulator – this is the plotting smooth operator; and the less bright psychopathic boss – who is more likely to use bullying and intimidation.

Dotlick and Cairo (2003) notes that the mischievous psychopath knows that the rules are really "only suggestions". They are rebels without a cause, rule-breakers who believe rules, laws and other restrictions are tedious and unnecessary. They clearly have destructive impulses and a preference for making impulsive decisions without considering any consequences. They can, and do, speak their mind and use their charms and creativity – but for no clear business goal.

They document five signs and symptoms:

▷ Staff question the mischievous leader's commitments and projects they have initiated but subsequently neglected.
▷ they hardly ever take time or effort to win people over.
▷ everything rates as a challenge to them.
▷ they are easily bored.
▷ they have to spend a lot of effort covering up cock-ups and mistakes.

They have been called hollow – their relationships are superficial and they have no loyalty to anyone except themselves. They have little sense of who they are, and have no value system or long-range goals. Most of all, they cannot bide time. They like the here and now – and an exciting one, at that. They eschew stability and routine: They like lots of excitement. Further, they seem often devoid of anxiety.

Psychopaths have nearly always been in trouble with the law. What gets them into trouble is their impulsiveness. They are not planners, and think little about either the victim of their crime or the consequences for themselves. Crimes are often petty, deceitful and thefts but, most often, fraud, forgery and failure to pay debts. The first response to being caught is to escape, leaving colleagues, family or debtors to pick up the pieces. They do so without a qualm. The next response is to lie with apparent candor and sincerity even under oath and to parents and loved ones. They behave as if social rules and regulations do not apply to them. They have no respect for authorities and institutions.

They are at mercy of their impulses. Whereas neurotics tend to be over-controlled, the psychopath shows inadequate control. They are often child-like in their demands for immediate gratification. They seek also thrills often associated with alcohol, drugs, gambling and sex. They never learn from experience consistently repeating illegal and immoral acts. They maintain their lying, swindling, thieving and deserting despite being frequently caught and punished because they tend to be careless about being caught. They make poor efforts to conceal wrongdoing, believing they have special protection, privileges or immunity to punishment. They have to keep "on the move" because they come to be known in the community. Their geographic and vocational mobility is, indeed, a good index of their pathology.

Curiously, when asked about justice and morality in abstract, they tend to give "correct" conventional answers. They just don't apply this knowledge of right and wrong to themselves. This is particularly the case when their judgment conflicts with their personal demands for immediate gratification.

Psychopaths have problematic relationships. They seem incapable of love and deep friendship for several reasons. They manifest a near complete absence of empathy, gratefulness and altruism. They are selfish, not self-sacrificial. They appear not to understand others' emotions. They seem completely ungrateful for the help and affection of others. It is difficult to have a good relationship with a self-centered, selfish, egocentric individual. Others are seen as a source of gain and pleasure irrespective of their discomfort, disappointment or pain. Others' needs are too trivial.

Lack of empathy and vanity (a lethal combination) means the psychopath finds it difficult to predict how others will behave and which of their many behaviors will lead to punishment. The psychopath is, in essence, completely amoral. They accept no responsibility for their actions and, therefore, no blame, guilt, shame or remorse. They are able to mouth trite excuses and rationalizations for the benefit of others. Indeed, they often have a convincing façade of competence and maturity. They can appear attentive, charming, mature and reliable ... but have difficulty maintaining the façade. They can do so long enough to get a job or even get married, but not to sustain either. The restlessness, impetuous, selfishness soon emerges.

The first question is why they are attracted to certain jobs and employers to them. They seem attracted to entrepreneurial, start-up businesses or those in the business of radical change, such as when de-layering. It is when businesses are chaotic that they are often at their best.

Hare (1999) noted how many were "trust-mongers" who, through charm and guile, obtained, and then very callously betrayed, the trust of others. He notes how they make excellent imposters and how they frequently target the vulnerable. They target and exploit people's gullibility, naïvety and Rousseauian view of the goodness of man.

He calls them *subcriminal psychopaths* who can thrive as academics, cult-leaders, doctors, police officers and writers. They violate rules, conventions and ethical standards always just crossing legal boundaries. He also gives a rich case study description of what he calls a *corporate psychopath*. He notes that there is certainly no shortage of opportunities for psychopaths who think big. It is also lucrative. "They are fast talking, charming, self-assured, at ease in social situations, cool under pressure, unfazed by the possibility of being found out, and totally ruthless" (Hare, 1999: 121).

Babiak and Hare (2006) believe most of us will interact with a psychopath every day. However, their skills and abilities make them difficult to spot. Often, they tend to be charming, emotionally literate and socially skilled. Next, they are often highly articulate. Also, they are brilliant and chameleon-like in their impression management. Given his or her powerful manipulation skills, it is little wonder why seeing a "psychopathic" personality beneath someone's charming, engaging surface is so difficult.

Not all psychopaths are smooth operators, though. Some do not have enough social or communicative skill or education to interact successfully with others, relying instead on threats, coercion, intimidation and violence to dominate others and to get what they want. Typically such individuals are manifestly aggressive and rather nasty and unlikely to charm victims into submission, relying on the bullying approach instead. (Babiak and Hare, 2006: 19).

The successful psychopath has, essentially, a manipulative approach to life. Their sole aim is to get what they want by means of effort, emotion or fear, whether they deserve it or not. Hence the importance of various groups that may be called "the organizational police": auditors, human resources, quality controllers whose job it is to ensure compliance with standards.

There is a small but growing literature on the successful – that is, non-institutionalized – psychopath. They are described as carefree, aggressive, charming and impulsively irresponsible. They have the essential personality characteristics of the psychopath but seem to refrain from really serious anti-social behavior, though it is often illegal and almost always immoral. Researchers have identified many politicians and business leaders as non-criminal psychopaths. They are duplicitous, but not illegally so. They show many patterns of misconduct but seem not to get caught. They seem brilliant at tactical impression management and are drawn to unstable, chaotic, rapidly-changing situations where they can more easily operate. Successful, non-incarcerated psychopaths seem to have compensatory factors that buffer them against criminal behavior, like higher social class and intelligence. In this sense, the successful psychopath has a wider set of coping mechanisms than less-privileged and less-able psychopaths, who soon get caught. It is the articulate, good-looking, educated psychopath that is most dangerous at work.

In his book entitled *Bad Boys, Bad Men*, Black (1999) reviews the literature on Antisocial Personality Disorder (APD). He considers, amongst other things, "hidden antisocials", which he calls *successful bad boys* and what others have called either "successful" or "industrial" psychopaths, as well as murderers. Bad boys grow up into bad men. He notes the diagnostic criteria for adolescent conduct disorders, which include aggression to people and animals, destruction of property, deceitfulness and theft, as well as serious violation of rules.

To help readers diagnose anti-social personality disorder (ASP) he notes "I have provided a list of questions to offer a rough guideline of queries that psychiatrists and other mental health professionals may use to explore the possibility of ASP. The questions are not part of any formal questionnaire, do not follow any particular order, and have no special meaning aside from the fact that they represent the types of problems, behaviors, and attitudes that are common to antisocials." Black's list is presented in Table 4.5.

Black (1999) looks at the story of (the natural history of) APD, as well as theories as to its cause. These include genetics, hormones and diet, brain damage, "quirks" of the nervous system and childhood abuse. He also looks at prevention and treatment. He provides advice to both families with an ASP (APD) person as well as the person themselves. His advice to the ASP (APD) person is that they should:

▷ accept that they suffer from ASP.
▷ not use the diagnosis of ASP as an excuse to continue in antisocial activities.
▷ use the diagnosis of ASP as a reason to seek help and to learn.
▷ accept that ASP is a disorder that will be with them for life.
▷ acknowledge the affect that ASP has had on their family.

Table 4.5 Black's rough guideline of queries to explore the possibility of antisocial personality disorder

1	Do you have a short fuse and a hair-trigger temper?	26	Have you ever thought about harming or killing someone?
2	When in trouble, do you blame others?	27	Do you tend to disregard laws that you don't like, such as those against speeding?
3	Have you had trouble keeping a job?	28	Have you ever beaten or abused your children?
4	Have you ever quit a job out of anger without another one to go to?	29	Are you sexually promiscuous?
5	Do you get into frequent fights?	30	Did you ever use a weapon in a fight as a child?
6	Have you ever physically or verbally hurt your spouse?	31	Did you engage in sexual activity before most of your peers?
7	Have you ever not paid child support required by law?	32	Have you ever abused alcohol or other drugs?
8	Have you ever not followed through on financial obligations?	33	Have you ever mugged anyone?
9	Have you ever vandalized or destroyed property?	34	Have you been fired from jobs because of personality problems?
10	Have you ever pursued an illegal occupation like selling drugs or prostituting yourself?	35	As a child, did you ever lie to authority figures, like parents, teachers, or supervisors?
11	Have you ever harassed or stalked others?	36	Have you ever been arrested or convicted of a felony?
12	As a child, did you ever skip school?	37	Was your behavior incorrigible as a youngster?
13	Have you ever been cruel to small animals, like cats or dogs?	38	Did you ever have to go to a reform school or detention center as a juvenile?
14	Have you ever moved to a new location without having a job lined up?	39	Have you ever been jailed or imprisoned?
15	Have you ever been homeless or lacked a fixed address?	40	Have you ever squandered money on personal items rather than buying necessities for your family?
16	Have you ever wandered around the country without any clear goal in mind about where you were going?	41	Are you relatively unconcerned about having hurt or mistreated others?

cont'd

Table 4.5   continued

17	Have you ever stolen or burglarized?	42	Did you ever run away from home as a child?
18	If you were in the military, did you ever go AWOL?	43	Were you ever adopted or placed in foster care as a child?
19	Did you ever get a tattoo?	44	Have you ever snatched a purse or picked someone's pocket?
20	Have you ever used an alias or gone by another name?	45	Did you ever move in order to avoid the authorities?
21	Do you tend to be impulsive and make decisions without reflection?	46	Have you ever forged someone else's name on a document, like a check?
22	Have you ever run a "scam" or tried to con others?	47	Have you been married and divorced more than twice?
23	Have you ever lied in order to obtain sexual favors from another?	48	Do you feel that you are better than everyone else and therefore above the law?
24	Were you ever suspended or expelled from school because of your behavior?	49	Do you feel that the world owes you a living?
25	As a child, did you ever set fires?	50	Have you ever forced someone to have sexual relations with you?

Source: Black (1999): 73–5.

▷ realize that whilst a good lawyer can help them avoid the consequences of their bad behavior, this actually does more harm than good because it delays the seeking of appropriate support.
▷ make determined efforts to control their temper.
▷ learn to acknowledge guilt and to share and learn trust.
▷ resist the temptation to dwell on past events.
▷ seek help for any other problems they may experience.
▷ seek out and join groups that can offer support.
▷ not expect therapy to be an instant miracle cure but, rather, should be patient as the therapy runs its course.

Finally, he notes:

The problem of individuals who proceed through life outside all manner of social regulation has long been with us under many names: *manie sans delire, moral insanity, psychopathy, sociopathic personality, ASP*. Whatever we call it, the condition remains all around us, largely unrecognized. It is time for that to change. The men I have described throughout these pages could be neighbors, family members, or friends whose behavior swings from simply frustrating to deeply disturbing. Directly or indirectly, nearly all of us are affected by ASP at some point. We know antisocials, are victims of their misdeeds, fear them, or even grapple with the disorder ourselves. ASP explains a long-standing observation about the human condition: Some of us seem to be born bad. Now more than ever, psychiatry and society have the means to explore why bad boys become bad men, how we can stop them, and how to mend the damage they cause. Progress will continue if we begin to see this phenomenon more clearly and commit ourselves to doing something about it. If nothing else, confronting ASP will teach us something more about what it means to be part of a family, a community, and a culture, bound as we are by certain rules, expectations, and our own sense of conscience. In seeing what antisocials lack, we may be all the more grateful for what we have. (Black, 1999: 205–6)

Stout (2005) in a popular book entitled *The Sociopath Next Door* has on the cover the statement: "1 in 25 ordinary Americans secretly has no conscience and can do anything at all without feeling guilty". Her emphasis is on the role of conscience in everyday affairs and its role in good, moral behavior:

> About one in twenty-five individuals are sociopathic, meaning, essentially, that they do not have a conscience. It is not that this group fails to grasp the difference between good and bad; it is that the distinction fails to limit their behavior. The intellectual difference between right and wrong does not bring on the emotional sirens and flashing blue lights, or the fear of God, that it does for the rest of us. Without the slightest blip of guilt or remorse, *one in twenty-five people can do anything at all.*
>
> The high incidence of sociopathy in human society has a profound effect on the rest of us who must live on this planet, too, even those of us who have not been clinically traumatized. The individuals who constitute this 4 percent drain our relationships, our bank-accounts, our accomplishments, our self-esteem, our very peace on earth. Yet surprisingly, many people know nothing about this disorder, or if they do, they think only in terms of violent psychopathy – murderers, serial killers, mass murderers – people who have conspicuously broken the law many times over, and who, if caught, will be imprisoned, maybe even put to death by our legal system. We are not commonly aware of, nor do we usually identify, the larger number of nonviolent sociopaths among us, people who often are not blatant lawbreakers, and against whom our formal legal system provides little defense. (Stout, 2005: 9)

She further notes:

> If anything, people without conscience tend to believe their way of being in the world is superior to ours. They often speak of the naïveté of other people and their ridiculous scruples, or of their curiosity about why so many people are unwilling to manipulate others, even in the service of their most important ambitions. Or they theorize that all people are the same—unscrupulous, like them—but are dishonestly playacting something mythical called "conscience." By this latter proposition, the only straightforward and honest people in the world are they themselves. They are being "real" in a society of phonies. (Stout, 2005: 50)

Yet, later she concludes:

> Put differently, most identified criminals are not sociopaths. Rather, they are people with more normal underlying personalities whose behavior is the product of negative social forces such as the drug culture, child abuse, domestic violence, and cross-generational poverty. The statistics mean also that very few sociopathic crimes are ever brought to the attention of our legal system – that very few sociopaths are criminals in the formal sense. The most common sociopathic profile involves ongoing deception and camouflage, and only the most flagrant crimes (kidnapping, murder, and so forth) are difficult for a reasonably intelligent sociopath to conceal. Some – by no means all – of the sociopathic armed robbers and kidnappers get caught. Even when they do get caught, in the sense of being found out, they are rarely prosecuted. The result is that most sociopaths are not incarcerated. They are out here in the world with you and me. (Stout, 2005: 82)

Recent research into APD (i.e., psychopaths and sociopaths) has been fruitful. It certainly indicates the dangerousness of this disorder in society, particularly when psychopaths are intelligent, articulate and good-looking.

Criminal personality disorder

Can one talk legitimately of a criminal personality disorder? Raine (1993) has provided good evidence in favor of his theory that much criminal behavior can be seen as a type of individual clinical or personality disorder. He notes:

> It is argued that there are good reasons to believe that a variety of *social and biological factors exist that predispose the individual toward criminal behavior.* In combination with the fact that criminal behavior also meets a number of the definitions of disorder, it is concluded that there is a reasonable evidence either to directly support the view that crime is a disorder or alternatively to give serious consideration to this possibility. At the very least, there is sufficient evidence in favor of the notion that crime is a disorder to place the burden of proof on those wishing to disprove this position. That is, unless there are convincing arguments to the contrary, we should at least consider the possibility that if crime was identified by any other name which which was free of all societal connotations placed on it, ("ecrim" for example), then in the light of this substantive body of evidence, it is likely that ecrim would be more readily considered a disorder. (Raine, 1993: 292)

He provides 10 sources of data in support of his theories (Table 4.6).

The idea that crime can be largely explained in terms of a specific set of disorders or traits does run into problems, especially the concept of *criminal personality disorder.* The following challenges have been made to this position:

1   There are major age, gender and ethnic differences in rates of criminal behavior; such demographic effects are inconsistent with the view that crime is a disorder.

Table 4.6   Biological factors predisposing an individual to criminal behavior

Evolutionary evidence	There are evolutionary explanations both for the development and inhibition of cheating.
Genetics	Twin and adoption studies provide strong evidence of the heritability of criminality proneness.
Biochemistry	Antisocials have reduced serotonin and nonepinephrosom which supports behavioral disinhibition theory, which, in part explains antisocial behavior.
Neuropsychology	Frontal (front-temporal-lubic) structures characterize antisocial behavior and it could be assured there are neuropsychological correlates of the criminal personality.
Brain imaging	PET scanning supports the idea of frontal dysfunction.
Other biological factors	Body-build, raised testosterone, minor physical abnormalities, characterize the criminal personality.
Cognitive factors	IQ (verbal), learning disabilities, poor social information processing, lower moral reasoning, overt sensitivity to rewards.
Familial factors	1 Parental crime 2 Child abuse 3 Maternal deprivation 4 Divorce/separation 5 Poor parental supervision 6 Erratic and inconsistent punishment 7 Negative affect 8 Marital conflict 9 Neglect.
Extra familial factors	1 Negative peer influences 2 Academic failure 3 Bad schools 4 Large family sizes 5 Parental and self social class 6 Unemployment 7 Urban living 8 Poor housing 9 Overcrowding.

Source: Raine (1993): 292–4.

2   There have been major changes in crime rates, over time, that are inconsistent with viewing crime as a disorder.

3   There are important cross-cultural variations in the rates of crime that invalidate crime as a disorder.

4   Crime is a heterogeneous concept, so it cannot represent a unitary disorder identified by a discrete cluster of trails.

5   Crime is a socio-political-legal construction that can be changed by changing the law, whereas psychiatric disorders are determined by biological and social forces and, as such, represent more fundamental, fixed concepts.

6   Crime cannot be a disorder because it is so pervasive in society; we all commit crime, and the whole population cannot be viewed as "disordered".

7   The group of criminals that the disorder argument is being applied to cannot be definitely delineated; the inability for precise identification of the target population rules crime out as a disorder.

8   Some research shows that the same factors found to underlay severe criminal behavior also characterize less severe forms of antisocial behavior; this suggests that there is no discrete category of offenders to whom the notion of a disorder can be applied.

9   Crime is committed by groups and organizations, not by individuals; therefore, crime cannot be a disorder because organizations cannot be psychiatrically disordered.

10   Crime cannot be cured, so it probably is not a disorder.

11   Criminal behavior differs from other psychiatric disorders in that criminals pose harm to others; this delimits it from other disorders.

12   Crime is an aberration of behavior, whereas disorders represent aberration of mental functioning; crime, therefore, is not a disorder in the same sense as other disorders.

13   Criminal behavior is voluntary, whereas other disorders are involuntary.

The debate continues between psychologists and psychiatrists who favor inter-personal explanations of crime and delinquency, and criminologists and sociologists who favor sociological explanations.

Case study

There are some fascinating case studies of what maybe termed "industrial psychopaths". Babiak (1995) presented the case of Dave, who worked for a highly profitable American electronics company (Case study 4.1).

Babiak (1995) found five characteristics in the many studies of industrial psychopathy:

Comparison of the behaviour of the three subjects observed to date revealed some similarities: each (a) began by building a **network of one-to-one relationships** with powerful and useful individuals, (b) **avoided virtually all group meetings** where maintaining multiple facades may have been too difficult, and (c) **created conflicts** which kept co-workers from sharing information about him. Once their power bases were established, (d) **coworkers who were no longer useful were abandoned** and (e) **detractors were neutralised** by systematically raising doubts about their competence and loyalty. In addition, unstable cultural factors, inadequate measurement systems, and general lack of trust typical of organizations undergoing rapid, chaotic change may have provided an acceptable cover for psychopathic behaviour. (Babiak, 1995: 184–5) (authors' emphasis)

Case study 4.1   Dave

Dave was in his mid-thirties, a good looking, well spoken professional, married for the third time with four children. He had a degree from a large university and had been hired into a newly created position during a hiring surge. Dave interviewed well, impressing his prospective boss as well as the department director with his creative mind, high energy level, and technical expertise. Routine reference checks seemed positive as did a security check. Dave had come across as such a perfect fit with the organization that Frank was surprised when things started to go wrong.

During his second week of employment Dave stormed into Frank's office and demanded that the department secretary be fired because she had not demonstrated sufficient respect for him. According to her, Dave had been rude and condescending, and was upset that she would not drop everything to cater to his requests.

Although Dave often arrived early and stayed late, making a positive impression on everyone in the office, the quality and quantity of his work was actually less than it first appeared. Frank discovered that Dave's first major report included plagiarised material. When questioned, Dave brushed aside the concern, commenting that he did not think it a good use of his time and talents to "reinvent the wheel". Subsequently, Dave would "forget" to work on uninteresting projects, claimed that he was being overworked, and frequently complained that some projects were beneath him.

Disruptive behaviours included verbal tirades during staff meetings which he often showed up both unprepared and late. He frequently left during the middle of meetings in order to make "important" phone calls, and denounced meetings as a waste of time, preferring to conduct all of his business in one-on-one conversations. When assigned to a task force he dominated the discussions and verbally bullied other team members into supporting his ideas. However, he would alternate berating others with compliments, begging for forgiveness, and promising to return favours.

After three months Frank spoke with Dave about his inability to get along with others in the department, his inappropriate emotionality, and unwillingness to assume a greater number of assignments. Dave acted surprised that anyone thought there was a problem and denied causing any disruption, adding that fighting and aggression were necessary in order to achieve greater things in life. By the fourth month of Dave's employment, Frank was warned by a colleague who was leaving the organization to "watch out for Dave" (pp.177–8).

Dave was frequently described as taking advantage of the organization and many of its members. Dave once convinced a manager to lend him an expensive piece of equipment, swearing that he would lock it up before going home. The equipment was found by security that evening in an open hallway. On three occasions Dave attempted to take specialized tools and equipment home at the weekend without authorization. In each instance he argued with the security guard insisting that he was too well known in the company to need a property pass and his work was too important to be questioned.

There were several individuals in the company whom he was said to have "wrapped around his finger". These included a middle-aged staff assistant through whom Dave interacted with the company grapevine, a young female security guard who worked at the entrance of the building in the early evening, and a professional in another department who was described by some as Dave's "soul mate" and by others as the person who was really completing Dave's assignments. Dave frequently showed up at this person's office in an agitated state and she would allegedly "counsel" him. All made positive, glowing comments about Dave, and one described him as a nice guy, "an artist who was misunderstood".

Some of the stories told about Dave were humorous. One secretary reported a time when he knelt down at her desk to beg for something he wanted. Another reported that her boss asked her to change his own travel itinerary so that he did not have to fly on the same plane as Dave. Several people said that Dave saw himself as a "ladies man", Dave offered a co-worker a drink, and then tried to leave without paying for it. The woman reminded him of his offer and Dave caused a scene by arguing with the waitress over the price of the drink (p. 179).

In reviewing Dave's credentials several discrepancies were discovered. Dave had listed four major fields of study on his resumé, application blank, and other documents. When confronted, he dismissed the discrepancies with a comment that there was nothing wrong in using different major designations for different purposes because he had taken courses in these subjects. (He did not possess a degree in the field for which he was hired.) Further investigation revealed expense reports containing numerous undocumented charges. When confronted, Dave became irate and stated that the request for receipts was a symptom of a sick organization. This writer was also shown a memo from the purchasing manager warning Dave to stop ordering merchandise and supplies directly from vendors, without authorization (p. 180).

Dave consistently made favorable first impressions. Over time, however, the perceptions of some organization members grew increasingly negative. The discrepant views in organization members' perceptions seemed to vary as a function of the frequency of interaction with Dave and the finesse he used to influence them based on their current utility to him (p. 182).

One of the most important ways to differentiate personal style from personality disorder is flexibility. There are many difficult people at work but relatively few whose rigid, maladaptive behaviors mean they continually have disruptive, troubled lives. It is their *inflexible, repetitive, poor stress-coping responses* that are marks of a disorder.

Personality disorders influence the *sense of self* – the way people think and feel about themselves and how other people see them. The disorders often powerfully influence *interpersonal relations* and *work*. They reveal themselves in how people "complete tasks, take and/or give orders, make decisions, plan, handle external and internal demands, take or give criticism, obey rules, take and delegate responsibility, and co-operate with people" (Oldham and Morris, 1991: 24). The antisocial, obsessive, compulsive, passive–aggressive and dependent types are particularly problematic in the workplace.

People with personality disorders have difficulty expressing and understanding emotions. It is the intensity with which they express them and their variability that make them odd. More importantly, they often have serious problems with self-control.

Narcissistic bosses

Just as there are problem or sick employees there are sick bosses; bad apples who poison those around them. They, too, can suffer the kind of personality disorder described in the previous sections but, in addition, they can be subject to their own particular kind of syndrome. The effect can be far more wide-reaching in the workplace. A single employee might make life hell for those in his or her immediate vicinity. The influence of a boss can affect many more than their immediate friends and family. If anyone is going to turn a worker from a passive condition of alienation (see Chapter 8) to more active aggression and revenge, the cultures created by these people will ensure it.

Students of personality disorders have long implicated narcissism in management derailment. Thus, some have argued that Narcissistic Personality Disorder explains many CWBs at work. Penney and Spector (2002) have shown that narcissism is directly and indirectly related to CWBs.

Essentially, the difference between a narcissistic person and those with high self-esteem (sometimes described as "vain") is that, for the latter, positive self-evaluation is grounded in reality. The narcissist, on the other hand, has an inflated or grandiose self-image that is unstable, paradoxically uncertain, and in need of constant support. Narcissists unrealistically expect to be dominant, successful and admired in all situations. If this is not forthcoming, the way they traditionally maintain their (bizarre) self-image is to express aggression, anger, violence and disdain towards those who threaten their self-view. Expressing anger to the ego-threat from others potentially serves different functions. It punishes, discourages further negative feedback or evaluations, and signifies dominance over another.

Thus, the narcissist, not grounded in reality, is likely to experience many work-situated challenges to their (inappropriately inflated) self-appraisals. These ego-threatening challenges lead to frequent outbursts of anger, frustration or hostility that are manifest as constant aggression.

In the workplace, often, various constraints (time, money, equipment) obstruct or reduce successful job performance, which affects ability to do the job and is therefore ego-threatening. The narcissist is particularly sensitive to any indication that they are not better than everyone else and, therefore, are hypersensitive to constraints which lead to anything from manifestations of minor annoyance to great rage.

In their study, Penney and Spector (2002) found exactly what they hypothesized. Narcissists experienced more anger more frequently and engaged more in CWBs. It fits well with the theory of threatened egoism. Job constraints were important: when a non-narcissist experienced job constraints it did not lead to CWBs; for a narcissist, the more perceived job constraints, the more CWBs. In this sense, people respond to the same levels of constraint differently. Thus, personality factors (traits and disorders) seem to be effective predictors of CWBs under difficult, trying or stressful work circumstances.

The bullying boss

The idea of the manager as a bully is a much more common lay explanation for why workers may react badly at work. Very occasionally sabotage or stealing, or some other dark-side behavior, is the direct result of the bullying behavior of one or more supervisors or boss. CWBs are usually the attempt of a deeply frustrated individual or group to have their revenge for the humiliation, hurt and powerlessness that they have felt at the hands of a bullying boss.

Often, the vengeful act may be directed particularly to the individual. Their car tires maybe let down, their computer "infected", their office set on fire. Malicious, possibly exaggerated or untrue rumors may be spread. However, frequently the vengeful act can be less specifically targeted at the bully but, rather, at the wider organization – either because of the inability to revenge only the individual or else because the bullied see the bully as acting with the approval of the organization as a whole.

Indeed, some organizations or parts of them may approve, even require a bullying culture. That is, it is normative to bully. So what is workplace bullying? There are no agreed definitions but they all share certain themes: it is inappropriate, repeated and unreasonable behavior that is experienced as demeaning, humiliating, insulting, intimidating, offensive, even physically painful.

It is possible to distinguish between *personal* bullying, which can range from teasing, practical jokes, rumor-mongering to persistent targeted criticism. There is also *procedural, corporate culture* bullying, which may involve excessive workloads, unreasonable and demands that cannot be fulfilled, and paranoid monitoring of work.

The list of bullying behaviors specified by the literature in the area is, indeed, long. It includes:

▷ Verbal abuse – name-calling, rudeness, screaming, profanities.
▷ Ridicule via insults, slander, belittling or patronizing comments.
▷ Malicious teasing, pranks and practical jokes.
▷ Unwanted and inappropriate physical contact.
▷ Consistent criticism, accusations and blame.
▷ Isolation, ignoring or giving the person the "silent treatment".
▷ Unreasonable/impossible targets, deadlines, tasks, pressure.
▷ Assigned meaningless, pointless, dirty-work tasks.
▷ Devaluing work efforts, giving no credit for effort/outcome.
▷ Withholding and distorting work-related information.
▷ Refusing reasonable requests for training, equipment.
▷ Unexplained, unnecessary, erratic changes introduced.

▷ Constant threats of job loss.
▷ Tampering with a worker's individual property or work equipment.

Bullying is a difficult problem because it can be so subjective: one man's firm and directive supervision is another's bullying. To this extent, it is in the eye of the beholder. Jokes can be seen as insults; promotion refusal attributed to bullying rather than poor progress.

The law tends to side with the person who is complaining and, if the employer fails to deal adequately with the complaint, a worker may be able to resign and claim constructive unfair dismissal. If the bullying is serious, the worker may also be able to bring a civil or criminal claim (Kibling and Lewis, 2000: 241).

It has been argued that some people have a "victim-mentality" with widespread anxieties, fears and uncertainties, and experience practically everything as bullying. Equally, in a struggling organization that has had to change radically and restructure, some resentful or inadequate individuals may table reasonable and necessary requests as bullying. It could, therefore, be argued that it is better and more cost-effective to invest in teaching coping skills and stress resilience in the workforce than trying to catch, punish and rehabilitate bullies.

This renders "statistics" particularly problematic. Thus, self-report surveys show anything from 3% to 93% of people report some form of workplace bullying taking place over the past month/year. However, it does seem that some groups are more vulnerable than others: older and younger people, casual/temporary staff; low-status/few skills/poorly educated staff; those with impairments/disabilities; and those with minority beliefs/lifestyles.

What is clear is that perceived or real (if distinguishable) bullying has powerful consequences on the bully, the bullied and the work group. Usually, the most manifold consequences of bullying are on the health and well-being of the bullied. But there are usually noticeable increases in absenteeism and staff turnover, and a decrease in productivity.

Some researchers have attempted to count the costs and benefits of taking no action, such as the introduction of prevention and redress measures. Much of this is about creating awareness and providing employees with support systems, as well as managing incidents well.

A central question is why some managers bully. Is it a result of the personality, leadership style or lack of skill? Is it because of different expectations, or even an awareness of their behavior on others? Are bullies simply people with low social/emotional intelligence with an inability to influence and persuade? And, as a result, should they be punished or helped or both?

This book is not about the cause of bullying but, rather, possible reactions to it. Some people who feel bullied simply resign, others retreat, some complain, others take revenge. It seems logical that dark-side behavioral revenge against individuals and organizations can be significantly reduced by developing both a healthy workplace culture, and a sensitive and sensible set of procedures to deal with bullies.

In a sense, corporate cultures that condone bullying, explicitly or inexplicitly, invite revenge. Certainly, all organizations can experience problems, particularly at times of change and restructuring. Handled well, the incidences of reported bullying should decrease, as well as some of the negative consequences of those who felt bullied.

The toxic boss

Another person-explanation in lay terms rather than "psychobabble" is the idea of the toxic boss. Results from studies on the origin of delinquency and criminality make for depressing reading. As does coming across young children in a clearly toxic family; one feels they really have so little chance of growing up as healthy, responsible, adaptable individuals. The anti-social personality has often had a miserable upbringing which, alas, he or she often perpetuates, producing a cycle of misfortune, neglect, unhappiness and crime.

Reading the list of typical characteristics of the dysfunctional parent in the toxic family, it is not difficult to see why children from these families end up as they do. Moody, egocentric, uneducated, immoral "care-givers" give little care. Instead of providing the loving, stable environment, they do the opposite – which can have a disastrous long-term effect on the child.

> *Power tends to corrupt and absolute power corrupts absolutely: great men are almost always bad.*
>
> (Lord Acton (1834–1902), English historian)

And the same can happen at work. Dysfunctional managers create toxic offices. They manage, often in a brief period of time, to create mayhem, distrust and disaffection. And, even in stable adults, this can have long-term consequences. That perfidious issue of "stress at work" and its more serious cousin, the nervous breakdown, are often caused by the dysfunctional manager.

To many, especially young people, a manager is *in loco parentis*. They can have considerable influence over one's health, happiness and future. They can create an environment that allows employees to give of their best. They can stretch their staff by setting reachable but challenging goals, and they can give them support in doing so. They can be helpful and encouraging and consistent – or not.

But there are some seriously poor managers who create a working environment at the precise opposite end of the spectrum. What are the symptoms of the dysfunctional manager? Check the list in Table 4.7.

The dysfunctional boss, like the delinquent child, may have come from a dysfunctional home or been socialized in a dysfunctional organization. Management consultants often talk about management practices they have come across that are little short of startling. They cause unhappiness and reduce productivity and morale, which, over time, can lead to the breakdown of the staff.

Table 4.7 Symptoms of the dysfunctional manager

Inconsistency and unpredictability	This is often the hallmark of the type. They are unpredictable to staff, to clients and customers – even their family. You can never be sure about what they will say or do. They are fickle and capricious. The job of a parent and manager is often to create stability in a world of chaos, a sense of security in an insecure world, not the opposite. A dysfunctional manager is often more than inconsistent in that they give contradictory and mixed messages that are very difficult to interpret.
Low tolerance of provocation and emotional sensitivity	Dysfunctional managers fly off the handle. They are known for their moodiness. One has quite literally to tread around them very gently. Jokes backfire – unless, of course, they make them. They take offence, harbor grudges and can show great mood swings, especially when stressed.
Hedonism and self-indulgence	The dysfunctional manager is no puritan: they like pleasure. The golf round on a Friday afternoon, those expensive meals, that overpriced office furniture are all ways of a dysfunctional manager pleasing himself or herself. Further, they are often deeply selfish about them. There can be real problems if their pleasures are addictive, which so often they can be. The hedonistic, addictive personality is a real nightmare, not only from a financial point of view.
Nowness and no long-term planning	The dysfunctional parent and dysfunctional manager live everyday as it comes – not for religious reasons, but because they cannot or will not plan for the future. They never understood postponement of gratification. Hence, they experience serious setbacks when unexpected things happen. Saving for a rainy day is not part of their reputation. They can't or won't plan for future eventualities.
Restlessness and excitement-seeking	The dysfunctional manager is always on the go. They get bored easily, can't pay attention. They look as if they have an adult form of ADHD. They look as it they need thrills and variety to keep them going. And, inevitably, they find themselves in situations that are commercially, even physically, dangerous. They chop and change all the time. They cannot sit still and rarely pay attention to others.
Learning problems	Dysfunctional managers do not learn from their mistakes. In fact, they do not like learning at all. The skill-based seminar is not for them. Outward bound perhaps, but not the conference centre. Many have few educational qualifications. They don't value them in their staff or themselves. Hence, they do not encourage learning of any sort, often pooh-poohing the educated staff member.
Poor emotional control	They let feelings hang out. Dysfunctional managers are the opposite of the stereotypic reserved and controlled Englishman. They shout and weep, sulk and gush with little embarrassment or control. This is not the result of some California-based therapy: in fact, they have poor self-control. They become well-known for their outbursts.
Placing little value on skill attainment	The dysfunctional manager does not have an MBA. They despise attempts of their staff to upgrade their skills. They talk about gut feelings, experience or, worse still, luck. They are loath to invest in training on the job.
Perpetual low-grade physical illness	Dysfunctional bosses always seem to be ill. They get coughs, colds, chills – whatever is going around. They certainly are not health conscious, and are very liable to absenteeism.

It has been observed by the business guru Manfred Kets de Vries that whole organizations can become toxic because of the character of senior managers. Toxic senior managers see the world in a particular way, which influences their selection, self-perception and style.

The workplace can become psychologically, as well as physically, toxic. The dysfunctional manager is a sort of *Typhus Mary of stress and incompetence*, taking the disease around with them wherever they go. Worse, they model dysfunctionality to young staff, who may consider their behavior normal. The cure, alas, is often not worth the candle. Dysfunctional managers need more than counseling: they really need canceling.

Conclusion

This section has concentrated on various "within-person" explanations for CWBs. They tend to describe the thief, liar, saboteur or whistle-blower as sad, bad or mad. Further, some assert the "pathology" or personality of the individual is necessary and sufficient to explain their often outrageous, immoral or illegal behavior. We have the criminal personality concept, the anti-social personality disorder and other psychiatry terms to explain much bad behavior.

While it is no doubt true that, for select individuals, this type of explanation is important, the evidence suggests that a great deal of CWBs at work are not committed by angry, sick or evil individuals. The vast majority of people who take part in counter-productive acts are neither immoral nor insane. They react in a series of circumstances that confront them. It is often bad bosses rather than bad individuals that are the problem. They cause temporary, vengeful and criminal behavior. They might feel aggrieved or wronged by clear injustice, they might be part of a group that not only condones but enforces thieving, or they may be driven by personal circumstances to act in the way that they do.

Indeed, for instance, whistle-blowers are often portrayed as highly moral people acting with courage and integrity. Equally, some possibly less hardworking staff have accused their boss of being a bully, toxic and incompetent when all that he or she is doing is ensuring that productivity reaches an acceptable and necessary standard.

Bad person theories are, too often, the easy option for employers or employees to "explain away" bad behavior. They do not take into consideration sufficiently the complexity of forces acting on individuals when they commit CWBs at work. The theories may be "psychologically satisfying", but they are often misleading. As we have pointed out elsewhere, many different forces have to be implicated to explain the sort of behaviors we are dealing with in this book.

5 Measuring Dark- and Bright-Side Attitudes, Beliefs and Behaviors

Introduction

Both the researcher and the manager want to measure CWBs: the former for research, the latter for decision-making; and also to check the efficacy of preventative intervention. It is important to audit CWBs so as to manage them. As a result, various people have tried to develop questionnaires that supposedly measure CWBs. Some of these are described as "integrity tests" (see Chapter7). They give an insight into the attitudes, beliefs, behaviors and values of those who commit CWBs.

The central question for all parties is their validity. Do they measure what they say they are measuring? Most crucially, do they have predictive validity; that is, do scores on the test actually relate to CWBs in organizations? To develop a strong psychometric test is a long and expensive business. Researchers need to show a test is reliable and valid. This is particularly difficult in some areas like CWBs because the topic is taboo. Few people are happy to admit to doing CWBs and there is, this, the possibility of faking and distortion. Nevertheless, there has been a recent concerted effort to develop such questionnaires.

Researchers have, however, been more active in measuring "bright-side" attitudes like job commitment and engagement. By looking at the opposite phenomena, one can often get an insight into the issue of job satisfaction itself. The question is whether alienation and detachment is the opposite of commitment and engagement, or qualitatively different. Frequently, the absence of one thing does not imply the presence of another. It may, then, not be possible to measure the dark side by testing the bright side … or vice versa.

The organization of work

Without doubt, the most interesting work in this field has been that of Gerald Mars. In his thoughtful and well-researched book looking at the anthropology of work crime, Mars (1984) looks at a typology of research at work.

Anthropologists have taken a very different approach to occupational deviance and bad apples at work. In a series of books and papers, Mars (1984, 2006) showed much cheating at work was a consequence of how jobs were organized. He concentrated not on individuals but, rather, on groups and job families. He agreed that, though people were recruited and socialized at work and through the particular nature of controls, some deviance took place. Further, the peculiar and particular relationship between staff and management is important.

His initial focus is on the sorts of "rewards" people receive at work. These he divided into three categories:

▷ *Formal* – usually linked to official "compensation" systems usually involving money.
▷ *Informal* – which include perks, tips, over-time, time off.
▷ *Hidden* – taking goods/stock, overcharging customers and so on.

When people cannot easily increase their formal rewards at work, they can increase the other two, which may makeup a large part of their income. Further, it is the nature of the job that dictates the number and type of informal and hidden rewards.

Mars (1984) described *four* types of cheats at work also defined by a two-by-two grid. Mars (1984) developed a grid by group typology. Grids essentially measure the extent to which people are controlled by impersonal forces. Thus, jobs with a strong grid limit autonomy and restrict competition. Strong grids tend to insulate people from others and prescribe the expectations that others have of the job-holder. The grid dimension refers to the extent to which a person is dependent on, controlled by and protected by his or her work group. Strong group jobs are characterized by frequent, involved interaction. Strong groups often bind together at and after work.

This classification yields four types of jobs: Hawks, Donkeys, Wolves and Vultures.

Hawks (*weak-grid and weak-group*) refer to occupations that emphasize individuality, autonomy, competition. Hawks emphasize entrepreneurship. Individual flair, charm and cunning work best. Success can be indicated by the number of others a person controls. Thus, those who find new and better ways of doing things, and are innovative, do best. Mars (1982) notes that Hawks are individualists, inventors, small businessmen.

Hawks are typically entrepreneurial managers, owner-businessmen, successful academics, pundits, the prima donnas among salesmen, and the more independent professionals and journalists. Alliances among Hawks tend to shift with expediency, and a climate of suspicion is more common than one of trust. Successful Hawks have to be skilled at manipulating people and procedures. They are experts in beating the system's inherent rigidities, and dealing principally in information. Hawks work out alone where systems are inefficient and try to do something about it.

Donkeys (strong grid and weak group) are characterized by both isolation and subordination. An example today may be a "live in" nanny to a wealthy household with many children.

Donkeys are in the paradoxical position of being either or both powerless or powerful. They are powerless, if they passively accept the constraints they face. They can also be extremely disruptive, at least for a time. Resentment at the impositions caused by such jobs is common, and the most typical response is to change jobs. Other forms of "withdrawal from work", such as sickness and absenteeism, are also higher than normal. Where constraints are at their strongest, sabotage is not infrequent as a response, particularly where constraints are mechanized.

People dislike being treated like a programmed robot, and fiddling makes a job much more interesting; it gives new targets and a sense of challenge, as well as hitting at a boss where it hurts.

Wolves (strong grid and strong group) – this group is the home of those "traditional" rapidly disappearing working-class occupations such as miners. These are occupations based on groups with interdependent and stratified roles: garbage collection crews, airplane crews, and stratified groups who both live and work in "total institutions" such as prisons, hospitals, oil rigs and some hotels. Where workers do live in, or close, to the premises in which they work, group activities in one area are reinforced by cohesion in others. Such groups then come to possess considerable control over the resources of their individual members. Once they join such groups, individuals tend to stay as members. The independent individualist does not thrive: teamwork is vital and valued highly, both for success and for security.

Vultures (weak grid but with a strong group) Vulture jobs include sales representatives and travelers of various kinds, like driver-deliverers. They are linked by their common employer, common work base and common task, but have considerable freedom and discretion during their working day. These are jobs that offer autonomy and freedom to transact but, also, this freedom is subject to bureaucratic control that treats workers collectively and, employs them in units. Workers in these occupations are members of a group of co-workers for some purposes only, and they can, and do, act individually and competitively for others. They are not as free from constraint as are Hawks, but neither are they as constrained as Donkeys; the group is not as intrusive or controlling as are Wolf packs.

Thus, Wolves work often in packs and have a strong sense of their group and their place in it. Hawks are competitive, fixers who do their own thing. Vultures are less concerned with rank but do, sometimes, help each other, while Donkeys are isolated and constrained.

Mars (2006) noted that these groups form their own ideology, world-view and values. They make sense of their situation, and their values follow from this. Thus, wolf packs value control, discipline and order. Hawks value autonomy, freedom and independence. Vultures tend to be suspicious outsiders.

Mars (2006) attempted to update his analysis for issues in the twenty-first century. He notes three major changes that have occurred at work and their possible impact on "scams, fiddles and sabotage".

1 *Technical changes*: While the widespread introduction of computers has had dramatic effects, for most it has reduced their control; for others, it has increased it. Computers can be used to regulate and monitor behavior, but they do offer many new opportunities for sabotage. Angry, disenchanted people can introduce a computer virus; they can destroy, distort and delete databases; they can disseminate confidential information or deny access. Most of these examples are not about increasing opportunities to make money but, rather, to take revenge on others.

2 *Psycho-social changes*: Mars (2006) focuses on the growth of individualism and the fact that fewer people seem bound by social groups or group allegiances. This means a reduced respect for hierarchies and the relaxation of group controls, occupational specialization, the flattening of hierarchies and the increase in delegation offer people more autonomy.

3 *Globalization*: Young multinational people, because of their aspiration, education and ideology, seem more divorced from the communities in which they work. This can marginalize migrant labor, who move in search of work. It also means that local companies get bought by large, foreign companies, which is associated with thefts.

The crucial point that Mars is making is that the job itself largely dictates what sort of CWBs are possible and preferable. Further, that some CWBs are done effectively in groups with coordinated team work.

Measuring CWBs by questionnaire

To develop a good, sensitive and psychometric measure of CWBs is difficult. It must be compressive but parsimonious: all relevant CWBs must be included, but not those which are marginally or only very occasionally CWBs. It must also be sensitive to distinctions made earlier: severity target, anonymity. Ideally, it could be used across a wide variety of job categories, sectors and organizations.

Marcus *et al.* (2002) developed and tested a German language questionnaire with eight factors. They found intelligence (cognitive ability) was not related to CWBs, but self-control and integrity was. Self-control, defined as the general tendency "to avoid acts whose long-term costs exceed the momentary benefits". was the best predictor of not getting involved in CWBs. This may be seen as deferment of gratification or simply being "grown-up". The second-best predictor was integrity, as measured by an integrity test.

Their 74-item scale details typical CWBs. The first 20 items are presented in Table 5.1.

Table 5.1   Top 20 typical CWBs

	Item content
1	I argued with people from outside the organization (e.g. customers or visitors).
2	I left my workplace during working hours without permission.
3	I stayed away from work without excuse.
4	I was intoxicated during working hours.
5	I intentionally worked slowly or carelessly.
6	I sought revenge from colleagues.
7	I came to work late or went home early.
8	I've got physically rough with other employees (co-workers, colleagues or superiors).
9	I exceeded a break for more than five minutes.
10	I spread rumors about the firm.
11	There were occasions when I skipped work.
12	I worked less in the absence of my supervisor.
13	I had drunk too much during working hours.
14	I arrived at work at least 10 minutes late.
15	I talk within the firm to shirk working.
16	I presented ideas of colleagues as my own.
17	I shirked unpleasant tasks.
18	I stayed away from work, although I was actually healthy.
19	I overheard discussions of co-workers to take personal advantage of it.
20	I pretended to work to avoid a new work order.

Source: Adapted from Marcus *et al.* (2002).

One recent study asked people to rate CWBs on a 9-point scale from 1 = Petty to 9 = Very Serious (Stieger *et al.*, 2010). This gives a good indication of what ordinary people (in this case, Austrians) think is more or less serious (Table 5.2).

Most of the work in this area relies on people reporting on their *own* CWBs. This may be via standard questionnaire or through interview. There are well-known problems with this methodology. The most obvious is called "impression management and social desirability" – which means, in short, people not telling the truth. Equally, when reporting on others there is often evidence of either (or both) "horns" or "halo" effects. This refers to seeing somebody as wholly good or wholly bad and not differentiating their behaviors. There is also the problem of cognitive dissonance reduction, where

Table 5.2   Means and standard deviations, Austria

		X	SD
1	Purposely wasted the company's materials or supplies	4.89	1.90
2	Spent too much time daydreaming	5.35	1.80
3	Told people outside the job what a lousy organization s/he worked in	5.66	2.18
4	Being late to work without permission	5.88	1.87
5	Stayed at home from work and said s/he was sick when s/he wasn't	6.93	1.81
6	Purposely dirtied or littered his/her surroundings at work	5.65	1.97
7	Stole something belonging to the company	8.08	1.46
8	Started, or continuing, a damaging or harmful rumor at work	6.29	2.04
9	Was nasty or rude to a client/customer	7.27	1.54
10	Refused to take an assignment when asked by a supervisor	6.57	1.86
11	Arrived late at an appointment or meeting without permission	5.80	1.89
12	Failed to report a problem with the intention of making it worse.	7.25	1.56
13	Took a longer break than is allowed.	3.41	1.96
14	Purposely failed to follow instructions.	6.46	1.56
15	Left work earlier than is allowed	4.84	2.09
16	Insulted a fellow employee about his/her performance	5.53	1.82
17	Made fun of someone's personal life	5.56	2.10
18	Took supplies or tools home without permission	5.38	2.16
19	Tried to look busy while doing nothing	5.68	1.78
20	Put in to be paid for more hours than s/he worked	6.89	1.65
21	Took money from the company without permission	8.55	0.91
22	Made fun of someone's physical deformity (e.g. facial disfigurement)	6.87	2.01
23	Deliberately ignored someone at work	5.24	2.11
24	Refused to help someone at work when asked for assistance	6.27	1.74
25	Withheld needed information from someone at work	6.92	1.52
26	Purposely interfered with someone at work doing his/her job	5.05	1.82
27	Blamed someone else for an error s/he made.	7.30	1.49
28	Started an argument with someone at work	6.14	1.84

cont'd

Table 5.2   continued

		X	SD
29	Verbally abused someone at work	6.80	1.58
30	Made an obscene gesture to someone at work	6.02	2.04
31	Threatened a subordinate at work with violence	8.15	1.13
32	Hid something so someone at work could not find it	5.78	2.16
33	Physically attacked someone at work	8.34	1.10
34	Did something to make someone at work look bad	6.74	1.57
35	Took credit for the work of a colleague	7.36	1.52
36	Played a prank to embarrass at work	5.06	2.21
37	Looked through someone at work's private mail or property without permission	6.04	2.29
38	Insulted or made fun of someone at work	6.41	1.78
39	Worked on a personal matter instead of work for the company	5.70	1.82
40	Falsified a receipt to get reimbursed for more money than s/he did on business expenses	7.86	1.51
41	Made an inappropriate ethnic, religious or racial remark or joke at work	6.44	2.24
42	Intentionally worked slower than s/he could have	5.37	1.77
43	Discussed confidential company information with an unauthorized person	7.52	1.54
44	Used an illegal drug or consumed alcohol on the job	7.96	1.57
45	Made an inappropriate sexist remark or joke at work	6.51	2.10
46	Wore inappropriate (seductive/over-casual) clothing to work	4.08	2.09
47	Sabotaged the organization's tools or equipment	7.39	1.63
48	Threatened to expose a scandal at the firm	7.43	1.64

Note: 1 = Petty; 9 = Very Serious.
Source: Adapted from Stieger *et al.* (2010).

people resolve their cognitive discomfort to some degree by explaining away antisocial behavior.

A very important problem lies in the self-evidence fact of *low-base rate behaviors*. This really means that, for many CWBs, they represent the exception not the rule. Very few people get involved in sabotage or serious acts of violence. This presents problems for researchers, particularly when CWBs are influenced by many complex factors.

One possibility is to group these CWBs into, say, *property deviance* (theft, sabotage) and *production deviance* (tardiness, alcohol abuse). Another approach is to talk about *CWBs towards the organization* and CWBs towards other *organizational members*. It also should be noted that some acts are *public* (i.e. absence), others are private (theft).

The *opposite* of a CWB may be called "citizenship" or "pro-social behavior": supporting the organization, persistence, diligence, dutifulness. It is quite possible that a set of organizational variables (good management, fair appraisal system) lead to citizenship behavior. Citizenship behavior can be measured at the individual level in terms of the support people at work give to others (peers, subordinates, boss) and to the organization as a whole, and their level of persistence with extra effort despite difficult conditions. Give people a reasonable and equitable workload in a relatively conflict-free environment, and you are likely to achieve organizational citizenship behaviors (OCBs). On the other hand, frustrate them with few or poor resources, interruptions, restrictions and unreasonable rules and procedures, and poor training and you get CWBs (Miles *et al.*, 2002).

One question for both the researcher and the manager is the relationship between CWBs and OCBs. Thus, are they opposites? Is the absence of one an indicator of the presence of another? Could people be low on both? Or could

Table 5.3 Items comprising the OCB and CWB measures

OCB	
1	Helping other employees with their work when they have been absent.
2	Volunteering to do things not formally required by the job.
3	Taking the initiative to orient new employees to the department even though it is not part of my job description.
4	Helping others when their workload increases (assisting others until they get over the hurdles).
5	Assisting supervisor with his/her duties.
6	Making innovative suggestions to improve the overall quality of the department.
7	Punctuality in arriving at work on time in the morning, and after lunch and breaks.
8	Exhibiting attendance at work beyond the norm, for example, taking fewer days off than most individuals or fewer than allowed.

CWB	
1	Exaggerated your hours worked.
2	Started negative rumors about your company.
3	Gossiped about your co-workers.
4	Covered up your mistakes.
5	Competed with your co-workers in an unproductive way.
6	Gossiped about your supervisor.
7	Stayed out of sight to avoid work.
8	Taken company equipment or merchandise.
9	Blamed your co-workers for your mistakes.
10	Intentionally worked slow.

Source: Adapted from Kelloway *et al.* (2002): 150.

they swing wildly being high on both? One study (Kelloway *et al.*, 2002) measured both on two short scales (Table 5.3) and found they were unique, unrelated constructs. In this sense, they are not opposites. Presumably, the factors that may control the one (particular personality traits, special organizational circumstances) may be quite different from those that control the other. However, much depends on the nature of the job. Where jobs are very well-structured and rule-bound (such as working on a manufacturing conveyor belt), OCBs might be distracting and, paradoxically, lead to lower performance.

Another way to devise a self-report measure of CWBs is to take an established questionnaire and see which particular questions are related to CWBs. This is what Hakstian *et al.* (2002) did. Using a student sample, they first created a CWB that measured nine factors (Table 5.4). Then, they derived an 80-item scale based on a very well-established measure called the Californian Personality Inventory. The respondent simply puts true or false against each statement. To give an example of this measure, 10 true and 10 false items are displayed in Table 5.4. This means that, if you put "true" to all true items and "false" to all false items, you would get the maximum score.

The authors, in an excellent example of how to validate a psychometric measure, showed how their measure was significantly and logically related to such things as personality traits (i.e. high neuroticism, low conscientiousness, low responsibility, low self-control), all of the above measures on

Table 5.4   10 of the 80 CPI items selected for the CPI-Cp scale as an example

Item No.	Item statement
True	
26	It's a good thing to know people in the right places so you can get traffic tickets, and such things, taken care of.
77	When I get bored I like to stir up some excitement.
101	I must admit that I often do as little work as I can get by with.
191	I can remember "playing sick" to get out of something.
203	When things go wrong, I sometimes blame the other person.
False	
14	I always follow the rule: business before pleasure.
69	I would disapprove of anyone's drinking to the point of intoxication at a party.
96	I take a rather serious attitude toward ethical and moral issues.
286	I have never done anything dangerous for the thrill of it.
380	I am known as a hard and steady worker.

Source: Adapted from Hakstian *et al.* (2002).

specific CWBs, as well as supervisor ratings of trustworthiness, the work ethic, use of time, desire to improve and overall performance.

Nine scales were devised statistically (Table 5.5) that show how various behaviors are grouped systematically into specific areas.

Some of these questionnaires have been developed to be "user friendly". Thus, Jones *et al.* (2002) developed and reported the validity of a measure (Applicant Potential Inventory) which can be administered by fax, internet, personal computer and telephone. It measures:

1   Honesty: attitudes to theft and previous theft related behavior
2   Drug avoidance: likelihood to sell or use drugs

Table 5.5   Questionnaire to measure commitment

1	I am willing to put in a great deal of effort beyond that normally expected in order to help this organization be successful.
2	I talk up this organization to my friends as a great organization to work for.
3	I feel very little loyalty to this organization. ®
4	I would accept almost any type of job assignment in order to keep working for this organization.
5	I find that my values and the organizations' values are very similar.
6	I am proud to tell others that I am part of this organization.
7	I could just as well be working for a different organization as long as the type of work is similar. ®
8	This organization really inspires the very best in me in the way of job performance.
9	It would take very little change in my present circumstances to cause me to leave this organization. ®
10	I am extremely glad that I chose this organization to work for, over others I was considering at the time I joined.
11	There's not too much to be gained by sticking with this organization indefinitely. ®
12	Often, I find it difficult to agree with this organization's policies on important matters relating to its employees. ®
13	I really care about the fate of this organization.
14	For me this is the best of all possible organizations for which to work.
15	Deciding to work for this organization was a definite mistake on my part. ®

Notes:
1   Responses: Strongly disagree; Moderately disagree; Slightly disagree; Neither disagree nor agree; Slightly agree; Moderately agree; Strongly agree; scored 1 to 7, respectively.
2   ® is a reverse item.

Source: Porter and Smith (1970).

3   Employee relations: tendency to cooperation and courteousness
4   Safety: safety consciousness
5   Work values: attitude to work and work habits
6   Supervision attitudes: likelihood of appropriate responses to supervision
7   Tenure: likelihood not to quit after a short time
8   Customer service: attitudes to and understanding of customers.

Clearly, this is a general commercial instrument that only, in part, attempts to measure CWBs.

Others have attempted to see whether these instruments "travel well" not only across work sectors, but also countries. Fortmann *et al.* (2002) provided reasonable evidence of this contrasting South African and Latin American data collected on people at work.

Can you assess a potentially counter-productive person at interview? Interestingly, Blackman and Funder (2002) have shown structured interviews to be better at detecting CWBs because they appear to both parties as more informal and relaxed, which reduces the candidate pressure to fake "good". They believe the interviewer is more a "social partner" and are likely to let down their guard. It seems that good interviewers get more out of structured interviews because they can "get at" and probe better. Detection at interview depends on:

1   *The good judge*: Socially-skilled extraverts seem best, particularly those motivated to detect dissent.
2   *The ideal target*: It is more difficult to detect dissent in inconsistent, erratic, unstable responses. Indeed, inconsistencies of any sort (i.e. between verbal and non-verbal behavior: between emotional states; between action, beliefs and deeds) are all good indicators of bad news.
3   *The particular trait*: Some personality traits are easier to see than others. Extraversion, neuroticism and agreeableness are easier to see in interview than conscientiousness, which previous employees see very evidently. You cannot see the trait of counter-productivity in an interview, but you can see its correlates.
4   *Good information*: The more information collected from different sources over time is clearly best.

The interview may not be the best way of catching potential liars, cheats, thieves and saboteurs but, under specific circumstances, they can do rather well.

Alienation, engagement, commitment, citizenship and attachment

How do people feel toward their boss, their organization and their work? It has been said that people join organizations, but leave bosses: that they are attracted to the values and images of organizations, but leave because of the way they are treated by individuals.

People can feel alienated in, and by, organizations. Equally, they can be deeply committed to them, sacrificing a great deal so that the organization survives or prospers. There are three different research areas that deal with these related issues. There is a literature on the concept of *alienation*, much discussed by sociologists, political scientists and others. There is a smaller, but growing literature on *attachment*, which looks at how attachment to others may be, in part, a function of early attachments to care-givers. There is also a fairly extensive literature on organizational *commitment*.

Researchers have distinguished and tried to measure work alienation at one end of the continuum and work commitment, and involvement and attachment at the other. Commitment is seen as a broad attitude towards one's employing organization – especially loyalty, acceptance of goals and values, and desire to be a member. Job attachment is a more focused concept, being an attitude to one's job rather than towards the organization as a whole. Other related concepts are organizational identification and loyalty.

People can experience both *social* and *self*-alienation. Social alienation occurs when the person finds the department organization or society in which they live to be oppressive or incompatible with their values: they are socially estranged. The self-alienated person loses contact with inclinations or desires that are not in agreement with prevailing social patterns and feels incapable of controlling their own actions.

The loyal, proud worker is one who derives satisfaction from the job activity and/or the output of work: hence the job satisfaction among craftsmen. One can derive satisfaction or be alienated from the work itself or the job function … or both.

There are many questionnaires (e.g. Seemann, 1959) that attempt to measure work alienation and they appear to tap into the following issues:

▷ whether people feel they have enough authority to do their job well.
▷ whether people at work value and respect one's expertise, experience and training.
▷ whether one's work gives a sense of pride and accomplishment.
▷ whether work offers an opportunity to make independent decisions when carrying out tasks.

Shepherd (1972) offers a more extensive list of questions and statements devised to ascertain the extent to which people feel alienated at work. These give a good insight into what is meant by alienation:

Powerlessness: To what extent can you vary the steps involved in doing your job? To what extent can you move from your immediate work area during working hours? To what extent can you control how much work you produce? To what extent can you help decide on the methods and procedures used in your job? To what extent do you have influence over what happens to you at work?

Meaninglessness: To what extent do you know how your job fits into the total work organization? To what extent do you know how your work contributes to company products? To what extent does management give workers enough information about what is going on in the company? To what extent do you know how your job fits into the work of other departments? To what extent do you know how your work affects the jobs of others you work with? To what extent do you know how your job fits in with other jobs in the company?

Normlessness: To what extent do you feel that people who get ahead in the company deserve it? To what extent do you feel that pull and connection get a person ahead in the company? To what extent do you feel that, to get ahead in the company, you would have to become a good "politician"? To what extent do you feel that getting ahead in the company is based on ability?

Instrumental work orientation: Your job is something you do to earn a living – most of your real interests are centered outside your job. Money is the most rewarding reason for working. Working is a necessary evil to provide things your family and you want.

Self-evaluative involvement: You would like people to judge you, for the most part, by what you spend your money on, rather than by how you make your money. Success in the things you do away from the job is more important to your opinion of yourself than success in your work career. To you, your work is only a small part of who you are.

Other questionnaires look at related issues, like the propensity to leave, as well as organizational frustration. The latter looks at things like people believing there are too many petty and arbitrary rules at work; that work is boring, monotonous and unfulfilling; and that people feel trapped in the job.

Alienated workers may be passive or aggressive but, most likely, are passive–aggressive. While they may not become actively involved in betrayal by theft or whistle-blowing, it may be that they do not report others they know are doing so, or may even encourage them.

Most researchers agree that people at the bottom of hierarchies are most likely to feel alienation from their work. However, the work role, the group or department, and the organizational context all have an effect on alienation. It is often a clear function of the social controls that people experience at work.

One way to try to understand the concept of work alienation is to see how researchers have tried to measure it. One group (Aiken and Hage, 1966) differentiated alienation from work (disappointed with career, professional development and inability to fulfill professional norms) and alienation from expressive relations (dissatisfaction with social relations, supervisors and fellow workers). Eight questions were posed to arrive at this concept. They covered concepts such as how satisfied the respondent is with their present job, supervisor, or their fellow workers.

Is the alienated worker one who is likely to steal, cheat or partake in sabotage? Often proactive acts like stealing, sabotage or whistle-blowing are the result of anger. At the heart of alienation is passivity, withdrawal and inaction. The alienated are certainly more likely to go absent and follow commands to strike. They are likely to "work-to-rule" and be unproductive, but not likely to be active participants in CWBs.

It could be argued that alienation, if not "the mother of deviance", is certainly a cousin. That is, most organization deviants feel alienated from their organization. How they come to feel that way can take many forms. However, it may be true that alienated employees are more likely to become disengaged than destructive. There seems at the heart of the concept of alienation notions of apathy, of withdrawal and of passivity, rather than pro-activity. The alienated may be differentiated from the angry, though it is possible that there is stage-wise process with the two strong emotions preceding one another.

Organizational commitment and attachment

This concept refers to positive feelings toward the organization. Commitment is not the same as satisfaction: it refers to the extent to which employees identify with, are involved with, and are unwilling to leave their organization. Commitment is generally viewed as a broad but very relevant attitude to one's employing organization and is about loyalty, endorsing of values and acceptance of goals. People at work have multiple commitments: to their work group, their supervisor, top management and the organization as a whole. The committed worker is "embedded in the organization". Attachment is more focused on the particular job rather than the organization as a whole. Job commitment is related to low levels of absenteeism and voluntary turnover. More important, perhaps, it is related to a high level of willingness to share and make personal sacrifices to benefit the organization as a whole.

There are many similar constructs in this area: occupational commitment (strength of motivation to work in a chosen career role), organizational commitment (strength of identification with and involvement in a particular organization), job involvement (state of psychological identification with the job), and work involvement (work attitudes about the job in general). Hackett *et al.* (2001) believe they are related thus: *work involvement determines job involvement which predicts both occupational and organizational commitment which in turn predicts people's intention to withdraw from the job.*

Researchers have distinguished between the focus of commitment and the bases of commitment. Consider, first, the focus of commitment that is about who you are committed to within the organization (Becker and Bellings, 1993). One can have quite different feelings of commitment to top management, boss or supervisor, colleagues and clients, the union, support staff:

▷ those with low commitment to both boss/work group and top management/organization are *uncommitted.*

▷ those with high commitment to both are clearly *committed*.
▷ those committed only to their work group but not to top management are thought of as *weakly committed*.
▷ those committed to top management but not their boss are described as *globally committed*.

It is not unusual for people to be "locally committed". They feel loyalty and affection to their boss and colleagues and their local department, but care little for the organization as a whole. Propinquity or frequent contact are the real determinants of affection – and, thence, commitment.

Organizational commitment may be differentiated into different types. *First*, there is *investment* commitment. Over time people invest in organizations not only through buying shares and through compulsory pension plans, but also through their hard work and knowledge. People talk of "having given their best years" to an organization, knowing that beyond a certain age their chances of employment become reduced. They make a cost–benefit type judgment and conclude that leaving the organization is more costly than staying in it.

Second, there is *value or goal congruence* and commitment. This essentially means that people perceive that their personal goals are nicely aligned to that of the organization. These values may be about a wide range of issues but lead some people to being committed to organizations not widely popular.

Third, there is *social* commitment. For many colleagues, friends at work are very important. One's entire social network may be built around the workplace. Social identity, social support and social contact are latent benefits of the work experiences. It is not unusual for the major source of a person's commitment to be other people in the organization.

Essentially, organizational commitment has three separate but related components:

▷ acceptance of the explicit and implicit goals and values of the organization.
▷ a willingness to work on behalf of, and exert effort for the organization.
▷ having a strong desire to remain loyal to, and affiliated with the organization.

There seem to be both personal and organizational factors that are related to commitment. Naturally, these are related to *job characteristics*, (jobs with responsibility, opportunity to demonstrate skills), *nature of reward* (salary, profit-sharing schemes), *alternative employment opportunities* (one's worth in the job market) treatment of newcomers and so on. There are a number of personal factors that appear to relate to commitment (Schultz and Schultz, 1998):

▷ older employees with a loyalty ethos are more likely to feel commitment to the organization.

▷ length of service is important, but the relationship is not simple and linear – that is, more service = more commitment.
▷ those with fewer personal financial difficulties and problems tend to be more committed.
▷ people who are sent abroad for overseas sojourn are more committed to their parent company at home provided they have a good overseas experience.
▷ engineers and scientists seem less committed than other occupational groups, though this is a generalization with many exceptions and the cause is not clear.
▷ universally, in all countries, government and public sector employees seem less committed than employees in private, entrepreneurial organizations.

The organizational factors are relatively easy to predict:

▷ The most important is the employees perception of how committed they felt their organization was to them.
▷ The more people felt their managers and colleagues supported them, the more committed they feel.
▷ The more diverse or heterogeneous the workforce, the lower the commitment.
▷ Curiously, the more women in the work group, the lower the commitment among the men; the more men in the work group, the higher the commitment of women.

There are a whole range of questionnaires on organizations' commitment. Many have questions divided into sections that attempt to measure identification with the organization (adopting as one's own the goals and values of the organization), job involvement, loyalty (feeling of affection for and attachment to the organization), willingness to uphold the norms and rules of the organization, dedication to continuing commitment. The questions refer to pride in the organization, to a desire to stay working there, to feeling part of the organization.

How does one measure commitment? There is no shortage of questionnaires that have been well-tested. Porter and Smith (1970) saw commitment as a stable affective reaction that means that people are willing to give something of themselves in order to contribute to their organization. They see commitment as having three factors: a strong belief in, and acceptance of, the organization's goals and values; a readiness to exert considerable effort on behalf of the organization; and a strong desire to remain a member of that organization. Their questionnaire has 15 attitude statements that cover issues such as the pride they feel in the organization, concern with the success of the organization, and having an alignment of values between their own and those of the organization.

Buchanan (1974: 533) devised a 23-item, three-factor scale to measure commitment defined as "a partisan, affective attachment to the goals and values of an organization, to one's role in relation to goals and values, and to the organization for its own sake, apart from its purely instrumental worth".

A few researchers have attempted to measure *job attachment*. Koch and Steers (1978) defined attachment as congruence between one's actual and ideal jobs, an identification with one's chosen occupation, and a reluctance to seek different employment. Their measure had just four questions, which related to an ideal job, thoughts of job changes, and job features thought to be important to the individual.

Organizational citizenship

There is yet another concept in this area known as "organizational citizenship behavior" (OCB), and this is commonly defined as exceeding job requirements. It is, however, not clear where the boundary is between in-role or extra-role behavior or, in other words, the formal job requirements and extra activities. It is also not clear what sort of behaviors might makeup this list. For instance, Morrison (1994) in a study of day-time clerical employees in a large American medical centre specified 20 possible OCBs including helping others, volunteering, updating skills, and being punctual, reliable and hard-working.

Interestingly, many of these employees saw these behaviors as in-role rather than out-of-role, in the sense that they were expected.

In another study, Organ and Lingl (1995) measured 18 OCBs, which included respecting company rules and regulations, being concerned with organizational image and reputation, and sharing personal property with others in order to help them. They found that these 18 behaviors broke down into three factors they labeled "generalized compliance", "altruism" and "time/attendance". They found, as predicted, that the more satisfied employee tended to take part in most citizenship behaviors. They also found that the personality variable of "conscientiousness" was directly related to OCBs.

Ethical climates and cultures

It has been suggested that one can take the *ethical pulse* of an organization; that one can sense and see the ethical codes of conduct of an organization. In short, there is an ethical work climate – and, of course, its opposite This concerns what employees see to be the ethical practices *within* the organization, observed misconduct by others (as well as self-reported misconduct), perceived pressures to compromise ethical standards, as well as reasons for reporting and not reporting misconduct.

As a consequence, attempts have been made to devise questionnaires to measure ethical climate and culture. Items in Victor and Cullen's (1988) measure of ethical climate concern showing respect for others and the institution, as well as following rules. Victor and Cullen (1988) argued that an ethical climate inside an organization provides employees with guidance for what to do in ethical situations and, hence, solve "ethical dilemmas".

Others have preferred the idea or concept of "ethical culture", which is usually defined as a shared set of beliefs, norms and practices within an organization. Consider the measure that Key (1999) used, which asked people whether they thought the organization rewarded integrity, moral behavior, and ethical behavior or, in fact, punished it.

The idea is that management practices lead to the development and maintenance of a corporate culture that supports and encourages good behavior or, in fact, turns a blind eye to CWBs.

Disengagement at work

Popular polls suggest that around one quarter of people at work would, if they could, fire their boss. Around one half say they distrust their senior managers. An equal number describe themselves as cynical, burnt out, disengaged.

Disengagement is the opposite of engagement, which has different features. It has a *cognitive* component: "I identify with my work"; an *emotional* component: "work brings me joy"; a *physical* component: "I am prepared to work hard"; and an *existential* component: "work gives meaning to my life".

Engagement and disengagement is more than job satisfaction involvement or commitment. Certainly, some personality characteristics are related to engagement, which appears fairly stable. Yet, organization and team can both suppress and increase engagement. The engaged person is characterized by energy and vigor; by total concentration and absorption; by work enthusiasm and pride; by a sense of empowerment and control; and by work providing a sense of meaning and purpose. Thus, disengagement is associated with exhaustion and ennui. It would not be difficult to devise a disengagement scale. Consider the following:

▷ At work I feel bored and listless.
▷ I never look forward to going to work in the morning.
▷ I seem never to be able to concentrate at work.
▷ I am easily made despondent at work.
▷ Nothing inspires me at work.
▷ I am not at all proud of the work I do.
▷ I am totally lacking in enthusiasm about my job.
▷ Time drags at work.
▷ I never think about my job outside work.
▷ I am never absorbed by my work.

Many factors can lead to disengagement: a cold, selfish, bullying boss; a lack of control over one's work; office politics; poor decisions by senior managers.

People who feel safe to be themselves and say what they feel, who feel valued and valuable, who feel the work place is just, and who believe their work is important feel engaged. Lack of these things does not necessarily lead to disengagement; rather, non-engagement.

People express varying amounts of trust or distrust in their institutions: government, police, education, religious bodies. Their general trustworthiness is a function of their perceived competence, concern for the public interest, honesty and wastefulness. This can be measured by the extent to which people are happy to support various institutions, as well as the extent to which they are proud to be part of them.

Cynicism is different from skepticism: it is more negative. There are various different measures of political trust which could be easily adapted to organizational skepticism. Consider the extent to which you believe the following to be true:

1   If a senior manager sticks to his ideals and principles, he is unlikely to reach the board or director level.
2   No person can hope to stay honest once he/she enters top management.
3   Despite what some people say, most business leaders try to keep their promises.
4   Most directors are practically the agents of some pressure group or other.
5   Almost all directors will sell out their ideals or break their promises, if it will increase their power.
6   Most CEOs do a lot of talking, but they do little to solve the really important issues facing the organization.
7   Most CEOs are in business for what they can get out of it personally.
8   Most CEOs are really willing to be truthful with the share-holders.
9   CEOs are supposed to be servants of the organization, but too many of them try to be our masters.
10 All CEOs are bad – some are just worse than others.
11 Most CEOs are dedicated men and women, and we should be grateful to them for the work they do.
12 Most business leaders are willing to stand up for what they believe is right, even when nothing/the going gets rough.

The cynical disengaged employee is clearly potentially dangerous.

Conclusion

This chapter has been about measurement of work-related beliefs and values. Attitudes shape behavior, and vice versa. The amount of commitment, engagement and involvement people feel at work is related to their pro and antisocial behavior. The same is true if we look at opposite "negative attitudes", like alienation, cynicism, mistrust. Individuals may or may not share the beliefs of their group who may, as a collective, be happy or unhappy at work. What is true, however, is that these attitudes and beliefs can change very quickly. An unhappy and unsuccessful management buy-out or a failed merger can easily change attitudes from positive to negative and then start bad-apple behavior.

Attitudes and behaviors can be measured at the individual group or organizational level. The jobs people do and the way work is organized provide opportunities for certain CWBs and not others.

It has been asserted that you can only manage what you measure. Managers need to know the work climate and practices which may be, in reality, rather different than is superficially portrayed. Hence the importance of regular, general and specific surveys to obtain information about what employees think, feel and do at work.

6 Deception, Dissimulation, Impression Management, Lying and the Truth

Introduction

Cheating, sabotage, stealing and whistle-blowing at work, almost by definition, involves deception of one sort or another. This chapter will look at detection of deception. How easy and reliable is it to spot people lying? Can you be taught how to detect lie-telling accurately? Are some people simply better liars and liar-spotters than others? Can the conscience – free, psychopathic, liar – ever be detected?

Psychologists talk of dissimulation rather than lying. Further, they distinguish between *self-deception* and *impression management*, both of which are, technically, lies. Self-deception is the "unconscious" telling of lies, in the sense that people say things about themselves which are untrue, but they (naïvely, genuinely, bizarrely) believe to be true. It may be that they *are* more (sometimes less) attractive, intelligent and insightful than they say they are. The second type of lie – impression management – is a deliberate falsehood, perhaps only an exaggeration, designed to give an impression that is not true.

Lying is at the centre of ethical and moral codes. It is essentially a false communication that benefits the communicator. It is deliberate and may or may not be partly or fully successful. To be accused of being a liar, as opposed to occasionally telling lies, is serious business. There is a bewildering array of words and concepts that deal with those who don't quite tell the truth, the whole truth, and nothing but the truth. Fibs, fabrications, falsehoods and fudgings. Politicians "spin" the facts to the public. Organizations use public relations gurus to "sex up" products, messages and services. Individuals, as part of daily intercourse and to save embarrassment and hurt, say things directly or indirectly (possibly through euphemism) to each other. Notice the way negative as opposed to positive feedback is dealt with at work.

One reason why the public is as well- (or badly) informed about psychological issues is the number of popular articles on the topic. Some are based on reviews with authors, others on a sort of popularized precis of a book review.

The issue of truth and lying has certainly attracted a number of famous quotes:

Box 6.1   The issue of truth and lying

The issue of truth and lying has certainly attracted a number of famous quotes:

As a general rule, if you want to get at the truth – hear both sides and believe neither.

Josh Billings (1818–85) American humorist

FAMOUS AMERICAN LIES

The check is in the mail.

I'll start my diet tomorrow.

We service what we sell.

Give me your number and the doctor will call you right back.

Money cheerfully refunded.

One size fits all.

This offer is limited to the first one hundred people who call in.

Your luggage isn't lost, it's only misplaced.

Leave your resume and we'll keep it on file.

This hurts me more than it hurts you.

I only need five minutes of your time.

Your table will be ready in a few minutes.

Open wide, it won't hurt a bit.

Let's have lunch sometime.

It's not the money, it's the principle.

Anonymous

If you tell the truth, you don't have to remember anything.

Mark Twain (1835–1910), American author

The liar's punishment is not in the least that he is not believed, but that he cannot believe anyone else.

George Bernard Shaw (1856–1950), British playwright and social reformer

Trust in Allah, but tie to your camel.

Arab proverb

A verbal contract isn't worth the paper it's written on.

Samuel Goldwyn (1882–1974), American motion-picture producer

He who speaks the truth must have one foot in the stirrup.

Armenian proverb

The moment a man talks to his fellows he begins to lie.

Hilaire Belloc, "The Silence of the Sea"

Woe unto them that call evil good and good evil; that put darkness for light, and light for darkness; that put bitter for sweet, and sweet for bitter!

***Bible**: Isaiah 5:20*

Nobody speaks the truth when there's something they must have.

(*The House in Paris*, ch. 5)

Elizabeth Bowen (1899–1973), Irish novelist.

A liar is worse than a thief.

Proverb

Bad apples dissent, dissemble, dissimulate: this is *trait statement* and it implies consistent, deliberate and habitual lying. They tell "bare-faced" lies not to prevent hurt in others, but to prevent them personally being caught. It is about self-serving untruths aimed at cover-up behavior. It is about denying things that did happen (or are planned) and denying those that did. It is morally, legally and ethically, frequently indefensible. Liars can choose *not* to lie. It is a deliberate act which may be done by a good or bad person, with or without good justification. Most liars prefer concealment to falsification which is easier.

The term *deception* does not have to involve lying. Camouflage, be it on animals or on soldiers' tents, is an attempt to deceive. It could be argued that make-up and plastic surgery are also attempts at deception. False hair, false teeth, false padding are used not only by actors, criminals and spies, but also by all sorts of ordinary people to attempt to disguise their real appearance. Many of these attempts at deception are considered to be socially acceptable, even necessary. There are essentially only two ways of lying: to conceal or to falsify.

A lie is quite simply a falsehood; an untruth.

A broken promise, a failure to recall and a misinterpretation of an ambiguous statement are not really lies. Note what Ekman (2001: 23) writes:

I have come to believe that examining how and when people lie and tell the truth can help in understanding many human relationships. There are few that do not involve deceit or at least the possibility of it. Parents lie to their children about sex to spare them knowledge they think their children are not

Freud noted: *No mortal can keep a secret. If his lips are silent, he chatters with his finger tips: betrayal oozes out of him at every pore.*

ready for, just as their children, when they become adolescents, will conceal sexual adventures because the parents won't understand. Lies occur between friends (even your best won't tell you), teacher and student, doctor and patient, husband and wife, witness and jury, lawyer and client, salesperson and customer.

Lying is such a central characteristic of life that better understanding of it is relevant to almost all human affairs. Some might shudder at that statement, because they view lying as reprehensible. I do not share that view. It is too simple to hold that no one in any relationship must ever lie; nor would I prescribe that every lie be unmasked. Advice columnist Ann Landers has a point when she advises her readers that truth can be used as a bludgeon, cruelly inflicting pain. Lies can be cruel too, but all lies aren't. Some lies, many fewer than liars will claim, are altruistic. Some social relationships are enjoyed because of the myths they preserve. But no liar should presume too easily that a victim desires to be misled. And no lie catcher should too easily presume the right to expose every lie. Some lies are harmless, even humane. Unmasking certain lies may humiliate the victim or a third party.

There are a number of distinctions that can be made in this area:

Errors of omission vs. commission: The former (omission) refers to leaving out (usually) undesirable facts. Thus, a job applicant may choose not to mention his/her age, (lack of) education, jail sentences or bankruptcy. People believe that failing to declare something is quite different (and more acceptable) than telling a deliberate lie. That, of course, depends on the situation and the ethical code of the judge. Errors of commission are quite simply telling lies. These may involve exaggeration or fabrication, and are done consciously with a specific purpose in mind.

Self-deception vs. impression management: Self-deception involves conscious deception that a person does not believe is a lie. It is people believing in their own positive reports. Thus, a person may falsify an exam grade they felt they deserved or hoped for, rather than admit the one they received. And they feel this to be a quite acceptable act: certainly, not a lie. They may also – as they would say: "in all honesty" – report (of their feelings) intentions and behaviors that are patently at odds with those of others.

They are, in a sense, deluded – but they do not have to have a mental illness to be in this position. Impression management is about what is now called "spin". Reports may be "sexed up" to make them more appealing.

Popular books and simple advice

There is no shortage of popular books, often written by people who claim that they work for government and security services (FBI, MI5, Ministry of Defence) that offer a sort of self-help guide to lying.

Walters (2000), in a book called *The Truth about Lying* and subtitled *How to spot a lie and protect yourself from deception*, begins by giving a list of synonyms for the act of lying: adulterate, equivocate, obfuscate and so on, claiming that essentially three factors have to be present for deception:

▷ Choice – lying is a conscious decision; few people are "forced" to lie.
▷ Ability – intellect and communication skills to "carry off" the deceit.
▷ Opportunity – control over a situation where one can lie.

He cautions: "As a general rule it is better not to tell people about signs of deception" (Walters, 2000: 11), partly because they become self-aware and guarded, but also because of making them upset and angry.

Most people, it is argued, deceive by evasion: lies of omission rather than commission, with many statements "based" on the truth. You deal best with evasion – a favorite trick of politicians – by asking direct questions and demanding an answer.

Walters (2000) notes, like other experts in the field, that lay people are poor at spotting deception because they tend to look in the wrong place. Folk wisdom is misleading. Often, clues like eye-gaze avoidance, cross-ing arms, speech errors are unreliable signs. He notes four channels that give away lies: body language, voice quality, speech content and micro-expressions. There are, Walters (2000) notes, seven keys to spotting lies (Table 6.1).

Walters (2000) also notes *verbal* signs of lying. *First* is *voice quality*, looking at pitch, volume and speech rate. People who lie have more speech dysfunctions than when telling the truth. *Second* is *voice clarity*, looking at stuttering, stammering, muttering, pausing, sighing and nervous laugh-ter. Of course, there is also speech context and various signs of unclear thinking.

As for *non-verbal* communication, Walters (2000) notes we are all more aware of the signals we give around the head than any other part of the body. The implication is we "leak" most and, thus, we are best able to detect lying body signs in other parts of the body. Issues around the *head* include tilt and movement, hands to head movements, as well as facial expressions. The eyes

Table 6.1 Keys to spotting lies

	Observation
1	Establish base-rate behavior, namely a person's average, normal, consistent behavior. In this way you can see what changes due to evasion or stress.
2	Look for changes when different behaviors occur or regular patterns stop. Note what is being said at this point.
3	Look for clusters of verbal and non-verbal behavior which occur and re-occur. Don't put much trust in single behaviors (i.e. nose-touching, stuttering).
4	Look for consistency in reaction to particular events or topics in the conversation.
5	Try not to have preconceptions or misconceptions about a person lying before your contact. The more open-minded and observant you are the better.
6	Remember that other people react to you – this may affect the accuracy of their observations.
7	Cross-check and validate your observations, particularly if you really believe lying has occurred.

Source: Walters (2000).

are important for looking at eye contact patterns, blinking rates, as well as evidence of tears and crying.

The arms, shoulders (shrugging) and hands can give many clues, particularly the way people use their hands to illustrate or facilitate their speech. Legs and feet can be very good indicators of stress, partly because people forget about them. Body posture, too, gives signals. However, as Walters (2000: 109) and all others in this area are bound to point out: "All deception signals are a form of stress but not all stress responses indicate that a person is lying to you". He recommends when "interrogating" others to be neither naïve nor cynical, believing neither that everything is either truth nor a lie. He also notes: "in a third person remark, a person all but admits to having been deceptive, but he acts as if it were done by an imaginary person" (p. 119).

Other factors noted are:

▷ bargaining – where people admit partly, or underestimate the consequences of, their actions.
▷ soliciting sympathy by being friendly, even flirting.
▷ religious statements appealing to "higher moral authorities".
▷ personal moral stance or upbringing – suggesting they rigorously obey a code of conduct.
▷ excessive courtesy – a clever disguise.

Most people use *denial*. They claim to forget – which is unlikely, given that the event was significant. They use a lot of "flag expressions" like "trust me"; "believe me"; "honestly"; "truthfully". They use, typically, expressions used as "escape clauses" in legal contracts like "I hardly ever do it"; "most of the time"; "it was sort of". They also use *blocking* statements like "Why would I ever do something like that?"; "Why would anybody be involved in an activity like that?" They might overuse *bridging* statements that connect two parts of a story but hide crucial material "after a while", "later on that morning", "suddenly and without warning".

Displacement statements try to imply like-minded others and co-conspirators: "Everybody was up to it"; "the other guys were also involved". Some use *stalling* statements, which answer a question with a question; repeat the question or ask the interrogator to answer the question. Others use surgical, legislative, clever wordplay. The aim is to give an answer which is either technically true or makes the questioner define their terms. Thus, to reply to "Were you alone in the bedroom?" you respond "What do you mean by alone?" People who tell lies experience stress, which may manifest itself as anger: verbal and non-verbal. Others may signal depression.

Jaskolka (2004) suggests liars can't help giving themselves away. She writes:

> Scientific research shows that even the most accomplished of liars cannot control the automatic or reflex reactions that occur within the body when we tell a lie.

Lying creates stress, which can range from a slight tension to an intense fear. Our blood pressure and pulse rate rise, our breathing patterns change and our face may become pale as the blood is drained away. Stress affects the digestive juices, causing the stomach to churn. This may be accompanied by swift and violent bowel movements. Blushing and sweating can also occur in inexperienced liars. (p. 159)

She notes, as do others, various body language signs of dissent (Table 6.2).

She suggests some exercises like the following:

This is an eye observation exercise. It will enable you to determine in which direction a person tends to shift their eyes when telling the truth and, conversely, when being deceitful.

▷ In normal conversation ask an acquaintance a routine question that you know the answer to.
▷ Observe in which horizontal direction they shift their eyes as they look downwards to prepare a truthful answer. You now know which way their eyes shift when they are telling the truth.
▷ Now ask a question to which you feel they might be tempted to respond untruthfully.
▷ Observe whether their eyes shift in the same or a different direction. If they shift in a different direction, it is highly likely that this person is indeed being untruthful. (p. 165)

Table 6.2 Body language signs of dissent

	Sign	Activity
1	Posture	Leaning backwards, squirming in one's seat
2	Head positions	Rigid with little movement and minimal expressions
3	Facial expressions	Grimacing and blushing
4	Eye signals	Blinking or staring
5	Mouth expression	Covering the mouth, touching, rubbing or scratching the chin
6	Hand gestures	Open-palmed hands with shoulder shrugs
7	Body contact	Reduced from the normal pattern
8	Arms	Used as barriers
9	Legs	Foot tapping, twitching and jerking
10	Clothes	Loosening and touching clothes

Source: Adapted from Jaskolka (2004).

This could be seen as dangerous advice based on insufficient research, making the detection of lying seem too easy and reliable where it is not the case.

Pease and Pease (2006) talk of the three wise monkeys who "hear no evil, see no evil and speak no evil". They argue that, when people lie, they are more likely to cover their ears, eyes or mouths. They do note one needs to look for clusters of body language behaviors that tend to occur when people are uncomfortable because of the lies they are telling. They argue, somewhat controversially, that because women are better at reading emotions they are "therefore better at manipulating others with an appropriate lie" (p. 147).

They argue, no doubt correctly, that it is hard to lie: "most people believe that when someone is lying they smile more than usual, but research shows the opposite is true – they smile less". They suggest that the difficulty with lying is that the subconscious mind acts automatically and independently of our verbal lie, so our body language gives us away. This is why people who rarely tell lies are easily caught, regardless of how convincing they may sound. The moment they begin to lie, their body sends out contradictory signals, and these give us a feeling that they're not telling the truth. During the lie, the "subconscious mind" sends out nervous energy, which appears as a gesture that can contradict what was said.

Professional liars – such as politicians, lawyers, actors and television announcers – have refined their body gestures to the point where it is difficult to "see" the lie, and people fall for it, hook, line and sinker. They do it in one of two ways. First, they practice what "feel" like the right gestures when they tell the lie, but this only works when they have practiced telling many lies over long periods of time. Second, they can reduce their gesturing so that they don't use any positive or negative gestures while lying, but that's also hard to do.

Many researchers have documented "micro-gestures" or very small body languages changes that neither the person themselves or those observing them "pick up". These occur particularly when a person is trying hard, while lying, to suppress all these signs. They include things like faster blinking, knitting of the eye-brows, light sweating and blushing and perhaps biting the mouth. Researchers have investigated this by using slow-motion cameras where they study behavior frame-by-frame. One very famous clip looks at the eye-brow movements of the notorious British spy Kim Philby when he lied on British television. The problem for the "spy catcher" or "detector of lies" is that these micro-expressions are fleeting and subtle and therefore very hard to detect.

We all know it is much easier to detect liars when you can concentrate and not have to interact with them. So watching someone talk to another through a one-way screen helps, as does shining a bright light on them. Also, they are harder to catch when we cannot see the whole of their bodies because they are obscured by a desk or panel.

Table 6.3   The most common lying gestures

	Sign	Interpretation
1	The *mouth cover*	Alerts one to something being withheld
2	The *nose touch*	Because of the (genuine) swelling of the nose
3	The *eye rub*	Blocking out that which they do not want to see (see no evil)
4	The *ear grab*	A sign of anxiety (hear no evil)
5	The *neck scratch*	Showing doubt and uncertainty
6	The *collar pull*	May be a result of the discomfort which occurs with increased blood pressure
7	*Fingers-in-the-mouth*	A breast substitute to regain comfort

Source: Adapted from Pease and Pease (2006).

Pease and Pease (2006) list what they call the "most common lying gestures" (Table 6.3).

They note various other common gestures that could be indicative of lying. These include chin-stroking (indicating decision-making), head-rubbing and slapping gestures.

Equally, and surprisingly commonly, these books attempt to teach people simultaneously to catch liars but also learn how to lie. In a section called "Fake it till you make it", Pease and Pease write:

> If you avoid Hand-to-Face gestures and always talk using openness signals, does this mean you can tell some real whoppers and get away with it? Well...not necessarily, because if you use open positions when you *know* you're lying, your palms are likely to sweat, your cheeks may twitch and your pupils constrict. The most competent liars are those who can go into their acting role and act as if they actually believe the lie. A professional actor who can do this better than anyone else is presented with an Oscar. While we are not suggesting you tell lies, there is powerful evidence that if you practise the positive skills we've mentioned throughout this book, they will become second nature to you and serve you well for the rest of your life. (Pease and Pease, 2006: 355)

James (2008: 175–6) presents a list of things to spot if "your partner" is lying. It is a curious mix of empirically informed observations and wild speculations:

▷ First of all: ask yourself if you really do want to expose their lies. If you're happier being fooled then you might collude with the lie and only look for evidence of honesty.
▷ Value your gut reaction – it's based on very complex information processing.

▷ Remind yourself of your partner's normal, honest body-language behaviors. Invest some time in studying them more closely to spot patterns of behaviour.

▷ Beware the error Othello made if you do decide to confront your partner. Being placed under pressure by being accused can produce shifty-looking body language signals in the most innocent person.

▷ Look for changes in normal behaviour, like working longer or different hours, more time spent away at courses or conferences, etc.

▷ Check for different smells. People having affairs often wash more or change their perfume or aftershave.

▷ They also buy new underwear.

▷ Their vocabulary changes as they pick up new words from their new love.

▷ As does their body language – look for new gestures. And don't overlook changes in their musical taste – they'll start to extend their CD collection.

▷ Don't be fooled if they start looking at you more. You might take this for affection but it's more likely they're evaluating you against their new lover.

▷ Don't expect nicer behaviour. Guilt will often make your partner more picky and argumentative. They're finding flaws in you so they don't feel as guilty.

▷ Look for extended pauses or playing for time if and when you ask questions.

▷ Watch for eye movement – it's not set in stone but eyes going up to the right can mean imagination or fabrication, to the left can mean recalled memory.

▷ Watch for cut-offs at the moment of the lie, like dropping their eyes, looking away or face-covering.

▷ Watch for signs of increased pressure, which can cause an adrenalin buzz. This can mean a dry mouth with extra swallowing or lip-licking, shallow breathing, increased blink-rate and muscle tension of the jaw and shoulder area.

In a more recent and very popular book entitled *What Every BODY is Saying*, Navarro and Karlins (2008) offer *An Ex-FBI Agent's Guide to Speed-Reading People*. They are:

1 Be a competent observer of your environment (be aware, use your senses).

2 Observing *in context* is the key: to what situational cues are people responding.

3 Learn to recognize and decode universal signals.

4 Equally learn to recognize and decode idiosyncratic signals unique to a particular individual.

5 Establish an individual's "baseline", normal, relaxed behavior.

6   Watch for multiple tells – behaviors in the jigsaw that occur in clusters or in quick succession.
7   Look for changes that signal changes in emotions, intent, interest or thoughts.
8   Learn to detect false or misleading nonverbal signals; some behaviors that are honest; others dishonest.
9   Focus on behaviors that reflect comfort, contentment and relaxation and those that reflect discomfort (anxiety, tension, stress).
10 Be subtle when observing others – being observed changes behavior.

They mention the well known *freeze–flight–fight* response to stress. They also describe the many pacifying behaviors (touching the face/neck; body hugging) that people use to try to restore normality and comfort.

Like others before them, Navarro and Karlins point out that often our feet and legs are the most "honest part of our body", both because we are less aware of them but also these are hard-wired to respond to stress. People shift their feet forwards and away from others, signaling engagement or disengagement. The feet can wave goodbye long before an individual does. People cross their legs when contented and uncross them when alarmed. Legs can be used as a barrier or to increase space. However, it is perhaps leg and foot movements that are most telling. Whilst some people freeze with anxiety, others move their foot up and down (leg-kick response) rigorosly when stressed.

They note, for instance, the usefulness of looking at "pacifiers", which are gestures people use to comfort themselves in distress.

In order to gain knowledge about a person through nonverbal pacifiers, there are a few guidelines you need to follow:

1   Recognize pacifying behaviors when they occur.
2   Establish a pacifying baseline for an individual. That way you can note any increase and/or intensity in that person's pacifying behaviors and react accordingly.
3   When you see a person make a pacifying gesture, stop and ask yourself, "What caused him to do that?" You know the individual feels uneasy about something. Your job, as a collector of nonverbal intelligence, is to find out what that something is.
4   Understand that pacifying behaviors almost always are used to calm a person after a stressful event occurs. Thus, as a general principle, you can assume that if an individual is engaged in pacifying behavior, some stressful event or stimulus has preceded it and caused it to happen.
5   The ability to link a pacifying behavior with the specific stressor that caused it can help you better understand the person with whom you are interacting.
6   In certain circumstances you can actually say or do something to see if it stresses an individual (as reflected in an increase in pacifying behaviors) to better understand his thoughts and intentions.

7   Note what part of the body a person pacifies. This is significant, because the higher the stress, the greater the amount of facial or neck stroking is involved.

8   Remember, the greater the stress or discomfort, the greater the likelihood of pacifying behaviors to follow.

Pacifiers are a great way to assess for comfort and discomfort. In a sense, pacifying behaviors are "supporting players" in our limbic reactions. Yet they reveal much about our emotional state and how we are truly feeling (Navarro and Karlins, 2008: 49–50).

The best books in this area recommend caution. They often reflect the tension between the marketing demands of a book that "it lets the reader (with ease and high benefits) identify secret messages in body language" and the empirical literature and testimony of (real) experts who point out how difficult and problematic it is.

Navarro and Karlins (2008) end up with caution:

> There are no nonverbal behaviors that, in and of themselves, are clearly indicative of deception. Therefore, in order to sort fact from fiction, our only realistic recourse is to rely on those behaviors indicative of comfort/discomfort, synchrony, and emphasis to guide us. They are a guide or paradigm, and that is all.

> A person who is not comfortable, not emphasizing, and whose communication is out of synchrony is, at best, communicating poorly or, at worst, being deceptive. Discomfort may originate from many sources, including antipathy between those involved in the discussion, the setting in which the conversation is held, or nervousness during an interview process. It can also, obviously, be a result of culpability, guilty knowledge, having to hide information, or plain lying. The possibilities are many, but now that you know how better to question others, recognize their signs of discomfort, and the importance of putting their behaviors into context, at least you have a starting point. Only further inquiry, observation, and corroboration can assure us of veracity. There is no way we can prevent people from lying to us, but at least we can be on guard when they attempt to deceive us.

> Last, be careful not to label someone a liar with limited information or based on one observation. Many good relationships have been ruined this way. Remember, when it comes to detecting deception, even the best experts, including myself, are only a blink away from chance, and have a fifty-fifty probability of being right or wrong. Plainly put, that's just not good enough! (Navarro and Karlins, 2008: 230–1)

Why do people lie?

According to Vrij (2000), people lie to make a positive impression on others, protect themselves from embarrassment/disapproval, obtain advantage, avoid punishment, to benefit others, and to facilitate social relationships. Thus, one can tell a white lie not to offend somebody but also a blatant, bare-faced lie to cover someone's back.

Ekman (2003: 329–30) believes there are essentially, nine main reasons for lying (Table 6.4).

There is, of course, one other reason which one may call state sponsored deceit. This refers to government security services who train certain of their staff to present themselves as someone else. They do this to collect information from others (i.e. terrorists and other enemies of the state). They have to present themselves as someone other than a government official and thereby lie their way into the others' confidence.

Table 6.4 Main reasons for lying

	Purpose	Reason
1	To avoid being punished	This is the most frequently mentioned motive by either children or adults. The punishment may be for a misdeed or for an accidental mistake
2	To obtain reward not otherwise readily obtainable	This is the second most commonly mentioned motive, by both children and adults
3	To protect another person from being punished	
4	To protect oneself from the threat of physical harm	This is different from being punished, for the threat of harm is not for a misdeed. An example would be a child is home alone telling a stranger at the door that his father is asleep now, and to come back later
5	To win the admiration of others	
6	To get out of an awkward social situation	Examples are claiming to have a babysitter problem to get out of a dull party, or ending a telephone conversation by saying there is someone at the door
7	To avoid embarrassment	The child who claims the wet seat resulted from water spilling, not from wetting her pants, is an example if the child did not fear punishment, only embarrassment
8	To maintain privacy	Without giving notification of the intention to maintain some information as private
9	To exercise power over others	By controlling the information the target has

Source: Adapted from Ekman (2003): 329–30.

Catching liars: Why they fail

According to Ekman (2001) there are essentially five reasons why liars get caught in the act of lying. They leak cues to their deceit in their body, voice, or words. One reason is about thinking, the other is about feeling.

Lack of preparation (bad lines): A good lie requires preparation, rehearsal and memorization. A good liar should be able to anticipate when it is appropriate or necessary to lie, when to be inventive, that they must remain internally consistent, when the story must fit the known/revealed facts. The right words must be used, but the liar must not take time thinking about it. Lies take rehearsal and being word-perfect. Curiously, where people are over-rehearsed, over-consistent and over-whelmingly convincing, they also may be caught through their over-preparation. Con-men, used to telling the same series of well-prepared lies over and over again, succeed because of their preparation.

Lying about feelings: Lies that involve emotions are more difficult than lies about actions, facts, intentions, plans or thoughts. When a person is made angry, frightened or saddened, physiological changes (in the central nervous system) occur without choice or selection. Strong emotions triggered by particular memories are hard to conceal and control. Trying to look angry when one is not or calm when frightened is not easy. Feeling upset or angry takes considerable acting skill. Perhaps even harder is concealing strong emotions.

Feelings about lying: If a person feels guilty, silly, vulnerable about their deception (tax evasion, embezzlement, plagiarism), appropriate emotions are triggered that may be difficult to conceal.

Fear of being caught: This is also called *detection apprehension* and concerns being fearful about being caught and punished for their deception in the first place. Their fear is a function of a number of things: belief in the aptitude and skill of lie detector. Some people are believed to be particularly good at detection: police officers, psychologists and psychiatrists, customs officers. They are likely to increase fear in the liar, which may show up in a variety of emotional expressions. Some people seem natural liars and others easily detected when telling any lies. Natural liars (excluding psychopaths) tend to be individualistic and competitive. Another factor of importance is how high the stakes are (what is involved for the liar). The more at stake the more the detection apprehension. There are two punishments for every lie: that for the lie failing and that for telling the lie. The latter is about losing trust and being labeled a liar.

According to Ekman (2001: 641) apprehensiveness about being detected telling a lie is greatest under eight very specific circumstances:

▷ The target has a reputation for being tough to fool.
▷ The target starts out being suspicious.
▷ The liar has had little practice and no record of success.
▷ The liar is specially vulnerable to the fear of being caught.

▷ The stakes are high.
▷ Both rewards and punishments are at stake; or, if it is only one or the other, punishment is at stake.
▷ The punishment for being caught lying is great, or the punishment for what the lie is about is so great that there is no incentive to confess.
▷ The target in no way benefits from the lie.

Deception guilt: This refers to feelings about lying, not feelings about guilt. At extremes, this guilt can induce shame and affect feelings of self-worth, which can be very quickly physically manifested. People with a strict, moral upbringing naturally tend to be the most guilt-prone. The psychopath, of course, does not suffer from this problem.

There are a number of highly specific conditions which seem either to exacerbate or to reduce deception guilt. Again, Ekman (2001: 75–6) has specified eight of these.

▷ The target is unwilling.
▷ The deceit is totally selfish, and the target derives no benefit from being misled and loses as much as or more than the liar gains.
▷ The deceit is unauthorized, and the situation is one in which honesty is authorized.
▷ The liar has not been practicing the deceit for a long time.
▷ The liar and the target share social values.
▷ The liar is personally acquainted with the target.
▷ The target can't easily be faulted as mean or gullible.
▷ There is reason for the target to expect to be misled; just the opposite, the liar has acted to win confidence in his trustworthiness.

Duping delight: Some liars get caught, paradoxically, because of the post-lie relief, pride, even smugness. Again, if these feelings are not concealed – and that can be difficult – it can lead to the liar getting caught. People can tempt fate, enjoy "misleading others" and play games, only to be caught by duping delight. This problem occurs particularly, according to Ekman (2001: 79), under three circumstances:

▷ The target poses a challenge, having a reputation for being difficult to fool.
▷ The lie is a challenge, either because of what must be concealed or the nature of what must be fabricated.
▷ Others are watching or know about the lie and appreciate the liar's skilful performance.

Yet, people remain bad at detecting lies for many reasons. Vrij (2000) lists seven:

▷ First, people do not actually want to know the truth.
▷ Next, there are no typical deceptive behaviors for all people.

▷ Third, the differences between liars and truth-tellers are very small.

▷ Fourth, conversation rules prevent lie detectors from carefully analyzing an accused liar properly.

▷ Fifth, observers judgments are often affected by their personal bias, misbeliefs and systematic errors.

▷ Next, nervous behavior does not mean lying behavior, though many believe that to be true.

▷ Finally, most observers fail to take individual differences into account.

Vrij (2000: 98) provides the following:

Guidelines for the detection of deception via behavioural cues

1   Lies may only be detectable via non-verbal cues if the liar experiences fear, guilt or excitement (or any other emotion), or if the lie is difficult to fabricate.

2   It is important to pay attention to mismatches between speech content and non-verbal behaviour, and to try to explain these mismatches. Keep in mind the possibility that the person is lying, but consider this as only one of the possible reasons for this mismatch.

    Attention should be directed towards deviations from a person's "normal" or usual patterns of behaviour, if these are known. The explanation for such deviations should be established. Each deviation may indicate that the person is lying, but do not disregard other explanations for these deviations.

3   The judgement of untruthfulness should only be made when all other possible explanations have been negated.

4   A person suspected of deception should be encouraged to talk. This is necessary to negate the alternative options regarding a person's behaviour. Moreover, the more a liar talks, the more likely it is that they will finally give their lies away via verbal and/or non-verbal cues (as they continuously have to pay attention to both speech content and non-verbal behaviour). Bear in mind that probing in itself might elicit behavioral changes.

5   There are stereotyped ideas about cues to deception (such as gaze aversion, fidgeting, and so on), which research has shown to be unreliable indicators of deception. These can be a guide, but bear in mind that not everyone will exhibit these cues during deception and the presence of such cues may indicate deception, but does not do so in every case.

The clues to deceit

People communicate using verbal, vocal and visual cues. The words they choose, their voice quality and numerous body cues all provide information about their emotional and cognitive state, and whether they may be lying. The lie-catcher needs to notice and interpret these manifold and subtle cues. The expert, professional, lie-catcher differs from the (often misguided) amateur by the cues he/she looks for, the trust they have in them, and the way they are interpreted.

Table 6.5 Overview and descriptions of the non-verbal behaviors

Vocal characteristics

1	*Speech hesitations*	Use of the words "ah", "um", "er", and so on
2	*Speech errors*	Word and/or sentence repetition, sentence change, incomplete sentences, slips of the tongue, and so on
3	*Pitch of voice*	Changes in pitch of voice, such as a rise or fall in pitch
4	*Speech rate*	Number of spoken words in a certain period of time
5	*Latency period*	Period of silence between question and answer
6	*Frequency of pauses*	Frequency of silent periods during speech
7	*Pause durations*	Length of silent periods during speech

Facial characteristics

1	*Gaze*	Looking at the face of the conversation partner
2	*Smile*	Smiling and laughing
3	*Blinking*	Blinking of the eyes

Movements

1	*Self-manipulations*	Scratching the head, wrists, and so on
2	*Illustrators*	Functional hand and arm movements designed to modify and/or supplement what is being said verbally
3	*Hand and finger movements*	Non-functional movements of hands or fingers without moving the arms
4	*Leg and foot movements*	Movements of the feet and legs
5	*Head movements*	Head nods and head shakes
6	*Trunk movements*	Movements of the trunk (usually accompanied by head movements)
7	*Shifting position*	Movements made to change the sitting position (usually accompanied by trunk and foot/leg movements)

Source: Adapted from Vrij (2000): 33.

Liars try hard to cover-up their deceit but it is difficult trying to control your words, voice, face, feet and hands all at the same time. The voice and the face carry important cues. Vrij (2000: 33) has identified 17 non-verbal behaviors that may be directly related to lying (Table 6.5)

Vrij (2000: 104) has also given seven specifically verbal indicators that often relate to lying (Table 6.6).

There are some findings that are clearly true about lying: First, you can observe stress signals produced by the liar's autonomic nervous system: dry mouth but sweaty palms, shallow uneven breathing, "tickly" nose and throat, blushing or blanching. These are observable when someone is under stress, whether they are lying or not. It is very easy to confuse the two. Most people in interviews are – initially, at any rate – anxious. Also, people are less conscious of their feet or legs: the further you are from the face, the nearer you get to the truth. Sudden changes in foot-tapping, pointing feet to the exit ("I want to get out of here"), simultaneous tight arm- and foot-crossing have been taken to indicate lying. Foot movements may be as reliable as an index of boredom as they are of lying. The frequent crossing of legs may simply indicate an uncomfortable chair.

Posture is probably more sincere than gesture: it can be seen as more unnatural and forced when people lie. Because people seem less aware of their total posture, they may secretly signal various desires (to leave) or

Table 6.6 Specific verbal indicators

	Verbal characteristic	Description
1	Negative statements	Statements indicating aversion towards an object, person or opinion, such as denials and disparaging statements; and statements indicating a negative mood
2	Plausible answers	Statements which make sense and which sound credible and reasonable
3	Irrelevant information	Information which is irrelevant to the context, and which has not been asked for
4	Over-generalised statement	The use of words such as "always", "never", "nobody", "everybody", and so on
5	Self-references	The use of words referring to the speaker himself or herself, such as "I", "me" or "mine"
6	Direct answers	To-the-point and straightforward statements (for example, "I like John" is more direct than "I like John's company")
7	Response length	Length of the answer or number of spoken words.

Source: Vrij (2000): 104.

that they are holding back the truth. However, the shape and comfort of furniture naturally have something to do with it. Interestingly, giveaway, expansive *gestures* decline: because they feel they may be caught by excessive gestures people tend to sit on their hands, fold their arms, clap their hands together. The lack of spontaneity may be an index of lying or fear – the fear of being caught. And, of course, some people are not simply as gesturally expressive as others.

Most people know about the shifty *gaze* of liars: when children are lying, they look down or away. They look guilty but do not look you in the eye. Many an innocent person has been accused of lying through the avoidance of eye contact, but people avoid eye contact for many different reasons – uncertainty about opinion, trying to remember facts, social embarrassment. Indeed, it is impolite in some cultures to look one in the eye. And, as we shall see, some liars we caught because, knowing this "rule", they state too much. In this sense, they "protesteth" too much and hence got caught.

Liars tend to be most careful, thoughtful and involved in their choice and use of words. They can rehearse, practice and become word-perfect. They are also very conscious of their *facial expressions* during the lying episodes. But it is the voice and body that perhaps give most away ... and therefore the cues to watch to catch the naïve and sophisticated. People are betrayed by their words if they are careless, if they make a (Freudian) slip of the tongue or the emotional tirade when words pour, rather than slip out. We also know that there are various vocal indexes of deceit relating to lying pauses, hesitations, and tone and pitch of voice.

There are a number of important, subtle body indexes of deceit including gestures, emblems, illustrations and manipulations. Emblems are well-known gestures with precise meanings; illustrations are movements that accentuate speech; manipulations are movements like grooming, massaging, rubbing, holding, pinching, picking, scratching. The autonomic nervous system changes with emotional arousal. Certain body changes occur – sweating, blushing, pupil dilation, breathing pattern, frequency of swallowing – which are difficult to inhibit. They are the basis of the lie detectors/polygraph, as we have seen.

Experts in the area, like Ekman (2001), have stressed facial clues to deceit and how facial expressions can serve a lie, but also provide manifold and very subtle cues to the truth. He argues that the face can show which emotion is felt – anger, fear, sadness, disgust, distress, happiness, contentment, excitement, surprise and contempt can all be conveyed by distinctive expressions. The face can also show whether two emotions are blended together – often, two emotions are felt and the face registers elements of each. The face also shows the strength of the felt emotion – each emotion can vary in intensity, from annoyance to rage, apprehension to terror, and so on (p. 125).

People, through growing up, learn facial display rules. But to the skilled observer there are a range of micro-expressions which yield the emotions behind them. There are all sorts of technical terms that help describe expressions. For instance, a squelched expression is one where one (possibly natural) expression is masked or covered by another). Experts look for asymmetrical facial expressions which show up on only one side of the face, the exact location of these expressions, the timing of the expression (with both words and other expressions).

To the expert like Ekman, the face really is the mirror of the soul. He believes one can distinguish between 18 different types of smile – from the contemptuous, dampened and miserable to the flirtatious, embarrassed and compliant smile. He also documents some of the characteristics which often accompany particular lies. False smiles are often inappropriate (when they occur, how long they last); they are often asymmetrical, they are not accompanied by the involvement of the many muscles around the eye, and they only cover the actions of the lower face and lower eyelid.

Ekman (2001: 161) concluded thus:

> The face may contain many different clues to deceit: micros, squelched expressions, leakage in the reliable facial muscles, blinking, pupil dilation, tearing, blushing and blanching, asymmetry, mistakes in timing, mistakes in location, and false smiles. Some of these clues provide leakage, betraying concealed information; others provide deception clues indicating that something is being concealed but not what; and others mark an expression to be false.

> These facial signs of deceit, like the clues to deceit in words, voice, and body described in the last chapter, vary in the precision of the information they convey. Some clues to deceit reveal exactly which emotion is actually felt, even though the liar tries to conceal that feeling. Other clues to deceit reveal only whether the emotion concealed is positive or negative and don't reveal exactly which negative emotion or which positive emotion the liar feels. Still other clues are even more undifferentiated, betraying only that the liar feels some emotion but not revealing whether the concealed feeling is positive or negative. That may be enough. Knowing that some emotion is felt sometimes can suggest that a person is lying, if the situation is one in which except for lying the person would not be likely to feel any emotion at all. Other times a lie won't be betrayed without more precise information about which concealed emotion is felt. It depends upon the lie, the line taken by the person suspected of lying, the situation, and the alternative explanations available, apart from lying, to account for why an emotion might be felt but concealed.

Furnham (2000) provided another, similar list of the following list of factors that help "give away" liars:

Verbal cues: (spoken language):

▷ *Response latency* or the time elapsing between the end of a question and the beginning of their response. Liars take longer. They hesitate more, than when not lying.

▷ *Linguistic distance* – not saying I, he, she, but talking in the abstract even when recalling incidents in which they were involved.

▷ *Slow but uneven speech* – as they try to think while speaking but get caught out. They might suddenly speak fast implying something is less significant.

It is the change in pace as a function of a particular question that gives a clue that something is not right.

▷ *Too eager to fill silences* – to keep talking when it is unnecessary. Liars overcompensate and seem uncomfortable with what are often quite short pauses.

▷ *Too many "pitch raises"* – that is, instead of the pitch dropping at the end of a reply it raises like a question. It may sound like "Do you believe me now?"

Non-verbal:

▷ *Squirming*/shifting around too much in the chair.

▷ *Having too much* – rather than too little – eye contact as liars tend to over compensate. They know that liars avoid mutual gaze so they "prove they are not lying" by a lot of looking … but "a tad too much".

▷ *Micro-expression* or flickers of expressions (of surprise, hurt, anger) difficult to see unless frames are "freezed".

▷ *An increase in comfort gestures* – self-touching the face and upper body.

▷ *An increase in stuttering*, slurring and, of course, Freudian slips – generally an increase in speech errors.

▷ *A loss of resonance in the voice* – it becomes flatter, less deep, more monotonous.

For many observers, the problem is distinguishing between lying and anxiety. The well-trained and arrogant liar may, thus, look innocent; the truthful but nervous witness the liar. The fast nervous ticks of the latter may be seen as classic signs of subordination – as if caught. There are not hard and fast practices about catching liars. At interview, it is good to relax them (to get them off their guard) and then to talk as much as possible. The more said, the more opportunities to be caught.

Collett (2003) used the concept of "tell" to specify signals or actions that "tell you" what somebody is thinking, even if that person does not know it themselves:

Detection tells: Whereas most people believe they are good at detecting lies, the opposite appears to be the case. They seem to fail at this all important skill for five reasons. *First*, people prefer *blissful ignorance*, not wanting to admit that the other person is lying. *Second*, people set their *detection threshold very high*, but highly suspicious people might set it very low. *Third*, people who rely on *intuition* and "gut feelings" do not do as well as those who look for clues to deception. *Fourth*, people forget that all behaviors have *multiple causes* and that there are few single, simple indicators of lying. *Fifth*, people *look in the wrong places* and for the wrong cues – fidgeting as opposed to smiling. He then considered classic lying tells.

Eye tells: People know about gaze patterns and control them, but continuous rapid blinking and unusually intent staring may be signs of lying.

Body tells: Despite popular beliefs, hand movements and fidgeting are under conscious control and therefore unreliable indexes of lying. However, other neglected things like leg and feet movements and self-touching are better indicators. Further, just as many liars appear to freeze more rather than become increasingly animated when lying.

Nose tells: Touching the nose really represents covering the mouth. The "Pinocchio syndrome" may be simply due to anxiety and it remains unclear whether vasoconstriction (blood draining from the face/nose) or vasodilation (blood increasing in the face/nose) occurs when people lie.

Masking tells: These are masks (often smiles) that people use to cover or mask their negative feelings about lying. The straight or crypto-relaxed face masks seem to work best.

Smiling tells: Smiles are used extensively by experienced liars because they both make others feel positive and also tend to be less suspicious about them lying. But there are many types of smile – blended, miserable, counterfeit. Clues to the counterfeit smile lie in the duration (they last longer), assembly (they are put together and dismantled more quickly), location (confined to the lower part of the face), symmetry (less symmetrical).

Micro tells: These are very fast, short-lived, micro-moment expressions that are difficult to see live but can be seen on second-by-second videotape playback. They may relate to tension release or anger, or a whole range of emotions associated with lying.

Talking tells: Despite the fact that most people believe non-verbal cues are better than verbal cues to lying, it actually appears the opposite way around. Collett (2003) lists 11 of these:

1 Circumlocution: beating around the bush with long-winded digression
2 Outlining: broad-brush account lacking detail: liars rarely expand when asked; truth-tellers do
3 Smoke screens: confusing, non-sensible statements
4 Negatives: liars are more likely to use negative statements
5 Word-choice: fewer self-references (I, me) and more generalizations (everybody, always)
6 Disclaimers: excessive use of "I know this sound strange", "Let me assure you", and "You won't believe this but ..."
7 Formality: becoming more tense and formal, they say things like "do not" instead of "don't"
8 Tense: liars use the past tense more to distance themselves from the event they are describing
9 Speed: liars slow down because of the strain on their various capacities
10 Pause: liars pause more with more traditional dysfluences like "um" and "er"
11 Pitch: this rises with emotion.

Collett (2003: 239–40) provides the would-be lie-catcher with some good advice:

Although there is no guaranteed method of detecting lies, there are certain things that you can do to increase your chances of spotting a liar:

▷ To detect a lie successfully you need to set your criteria so that they're neither too high nor too low. That way you'll avoid coming to the conclusion that nobody ever tells a lie, or that everybody lies all the time.

▷ Where possible, the actions that someone performs while they are supposedly lying should be compared with how they behave when they are telling the truth.

▷ To be a good lie detector you should also concentrate on behaviour that falls outside conscious control or that people are likely to ignore.

▷ Given the opportunity, focus your attention on what people say and how they say it, rather than on what they do.

▷ It's important to work out whether the lie is likely to be spontaneous or rehearsed, and whether it's a high-stakes or a low-stakes lie. When the stakes are low or the lie has been rehearsed, the task of detecting the lie is much more difficult.

▷ To spot a lie you should always focus on a broad range of behavioural and speech clues. If you think you can spot a liar on the basis of a single clue, you're deceiving yourself.

Despite the fact there are numerous popular books and articles that seem to imply that you can "read people like a book" and relatively easily catch liars, experts in the field say the precise opposite. One's ability to detect lies is multi-faceted and problematic. In short, it depends: it depends on the nature of the lie, the personality and experience of both the liar and the person trying to detect the lie, and the context/situation in which the lie is told.

In short, Ekman (2001: 8) notes:

Success in distinguishing when a person is lying and when a person is telling the truth is highest when:

▷ The lie is being told for the first time;

▷ The person has not told this type of lie before;

▷ The stakes are high – most importantly the threat of severe punishment;

▷ The interviewer is truly open-minded, and does not jump to conclusions quickly;

▷ The interviewer knows how to encourage the interviewee to tell his or her story (the more words spoken the better the chance of distinguishing lies from truthfulness);

▷ The interviewer and interviewee come from the same cultural background and speak the same language;

▷ The interviewer regards the clues as hot spots, marking where it is important to get more information, rather than as proof of lying;

▷ The interviewer is aware of the difficulties of identifying the truthful, innocent person who is under suspicion of having committed an offence.

From other research, Furnham (2000) pointed out that there are both verbal and non-verbal cues to deceit and that, contrary to popular belief, verbal/vocal cues may be as accurate and sensitive an index as body language. Indeed, it is precisely because liars believe there is more potential to catch them through their body than their voice that they concentrate too much on their body language and not on what they are saying or how they are saying it.

How do professional lie-catchers (i.e. police, customs officers) go about catching liars? Indeed, are they better at it than non-professionals? Vrij (2000) reported on one study that showed large differences in the beliefs of different groups.

There are some simple but important strategies for everyone to bear in mind when trying to catch liars:

First, establish base rate behavior. This means, in essence, what people are like when they are normal, relaxed and telling the truth. Give people time to relax and see what they are like when it is unlikely they are lying. Some people fidget more than others.

Second, look for *sudden changes* in various behaviors (verbal, vocal, visual at the same time): movements and such. It is when behavior noticeably alters that it is most meaningful. It is particularly important when changes take place that are not restricted to a single modality (i.e. face or voice). It is always better to interpret the changes in behavior rather than one particular idiosyncratic feature.

Third, formulate a hypothesis as to the cause. What are they lying about, what is the sensitive issue? Not everything is a lie. Why should they be lying about some issues and not others? It is important to consider the possibility of an alternative explanation that shows the person is *not* lying. Test the theory by bringing up a particular topic (the area of the lies) and see if the non-verbal pattern reoccurs. If there are persistent indicators of discomfort when particular topics are reintroduced into the conversation, one may assume a stronger possibility of lying.

But the experts caution against feeling confident, particularly in the hard job of distinguishing, "disbelieving-the-truth" and just as easily "believing a lie". Clearly, absence of a sign of deceit is not evidence of truth. One problem, as noted above, is the ever-present idiosyncratic individual differences.

As Ekman (2001: 166) notes:

> The poker player in this example set up and exploited a disbelieving-the-truth mistake, profiting from being judged to be lying. More often when a lie-catcher makes a disbelieving-the-truth mistake, the person who is mistakenly identified as lying suffers. It is not deviousness that causes some people to be judged lying when they are truthful but a quirk in their behaviour, an idiosyncrasy in their expressive style. What for most people might be a clue to deceit is not for such a person. Some people:

▷ Are indirect and circumlocutious in their speech;
▷ Speak with many or short or long pauses between words;
▷ Make many speech errors;
▷ Use few illustrators;
▷ Make many body manipulators;

▷ Often show signs of fear, distress, or anger in their facial expressions, regardless of how they actually feel;

▷ Show asymmetrical facial expressions.

There are enormous differences among individuals in all of these behaviours; and these differences produce not only disbelieving-the-truth but also believing-a-lie mistakes. Calling the truthful person who characteristically speaks indirectly a liar is a disbelieving-the-truth mistake; calling the lying smooth-talker truthful is a believing-a-lie mistake. Even though such a talker's speech when lying may become more indirect and have more errors, it may escape notice because it still is so much smoother than speech usually is for most people.

A check list for the detecting of lies

How easy is it to determine whether somebody is lying? What factors make it easier for the liar to avoid detection, and which factors make it easier for the detective to catch the liar? Essentially, the hardest lies to tell are those when the liar has to try to conceal many strong emotions while telling the lie (Table 6.7).

Some researchers and practitioners have begun to look carefully at the structured interview and a careful analysis of the content and qualities of statements. These are called "criteria based content analyses" and look systematically at things like the structure of the logic, the quantity of details, reproduction of conversations, details about the mental state of different parties involved, admitting lack of memory and the like. Often, look for the inappropriateness of language and knowledge, inconsistency in the statements and so on.

Faking on questionnaires

Some people dismiss and pooh-pooh personality (and other self-report) tests at work because they argue that nearly all people lie on them: They dissimulate with social desirability responding. That is, they do not tell the truth but give answers that they believe are acceptable, desirable and will, in effect, lead to some advantage like selection or promotion.

What is perhaps oddest about these cynical observations is that people who claim questionnaires are a waste of time because they are full of lies, deceits and half-truths never seem to think that the same criticism may be leveled at the interview, which is often little more than a charade: a smoke screen of mirrors.

The idea that people may not be telling the whole truth on questionnaires has occurred to test publishers. It is worth distinguishing between a number of generic and synonymous terms used in this area. The first is *response bias*, which is a generic term for a whole range of responses to interviews,

Table 6.7 Lying check list

		HARD for the lie catcher to detect	EASY for the lie catcher to detect
Questions about the lie			
1	Can the liar anticipate exactly when he or she has to lie?	YES Lie prepared and rehearsed	NO Lie not prepared
2	Does the lie involve concealment only, without any need to falsify?	YES	NO
3	Does the lie involve emotions felt at the moment?	NO	YES Especially difficult if: ▷ negative emotions such as anger, fear or distress must be concealed or falsified ▷ liar must appear emotionless and cannot use another emotion to mask felt emotions that have to be concealed
4	Would there be amnesty if liar confesses to lying?	NO Enhances liar's motive to succeed	YES Chance to induce confession
5	Are the stakes, in terms of either rewards or punishments, very high?	DIFFICULT TO PREDICT While high stakes may increase detection apprehension, it should also motivate the liar to try hard	
6	Are there severe punishments for being caught lying?	NO Low detection apprehension, but may produce carelessness	YES Enhances detection apprehension, but may also fear being disbelieved – producing false positive errors
7	Are there severe punishments for the very act of having lied, apart from the losses incurred from the deceit failing?	NO	YES Enhances detection apprehension: person may be dissuaded from embarking on lie if she or he knows that punishment for attempting to lie will be worse than the loss incurred by not lying
8	Does the target suffer no loss, or even benefit from the lie? Is the lie altruistic, not benefiting the liar?	YES Less deception guilt, if liar believes this to be so	NO Increases deception guilt

cont'd

Table 6.7 continued

		HARD for the lie catcher to detect	EASY for the lie catcher to detect
9	Is it a situation in which the target is likely to trust the liar, not suspecting that he or she may be misled?	YES	NO
10	Has liar successfully deceived the target before?	YES Decreases detection apprehension; and if target would be ashamed or otherwise suffer by having to acknowledge having been fooled, she or she may become a willing victim	NO
11	Do liar and target share values?	NO Decreases deception guilt	YES Increases deception guilt.
12	Is the lie authorized?	YES Decreases deception guilt	NO Increases the deception guilt
13	Is the target anonymous?	YES Decreases deception guilt	NO
14	Are target and liar personally acquainted?	NO	YES Lie-catcher will be more able to avoid errors due to individual differences
15	Must lie-catcher conceal his suspicions from the liar?	YES Lie-catcher may become enmeshed in his own need to conceal, and fail to be as alert to the liar's behavior	NO
16	Does lie-catcher have information that only a guilty, not an innocent, person would also have?	NO	YES Can try to use the guilty knowledge test if the suspect can be interrogated
17	Is there an audience who knows or suspects that the target is being deceived?	NO	YES May enhance duping delight, detection apprehension, or deception guilt

cont'd

Table 6.7 continued

		HARD for the lie catcher to detect	EASY for the lie catcher to detect
18	Do liar and lie-catcher come from similar language, national and cultural backgrounds?	NO More errors in judging clues to deceit	YES Better able to interpret clues to deceit

Questions about the liar

19	Is the liar practiced in lying?	YES Especially if practiced in this type of lie	NO
20	Is the liar inventive and clever in fabricating?	YES	NO
21	Does the liar have a good memory?	YES	NO
22	Is the liar a smooth-talker with a convincing manner?	YES	NO
23	Does the liar use the reliable facial muscles as conversational emphasizers?	YES Better able to conceal or falsify facial expressions	NO
24	Is the liar skilled as an actor, able to use the Stanislavski method?	YES	NO
25	Is the liar likely to convince himself of his lie, believing that what he says is true?	YES	NO
26	Is she or he a "natural liar" or psychopath?	YES	NO
27	Does the liar's personality make liar vulnerable either to fear, guilt or duping delight?	NO	YES
28	Is liar ashamed of what liar is concealing?	DIFFICULT TO PREDICT While shame works to prevent confession, leakage of that shame may betray the lie	
29	Might suspected liar, feel fear, guilt, shame or duping delight even if suspect is innocent and not lying, or lying about something else?	YES Can't interpret emotion clues	NO Signs of these emotions are clues to deceit

cont'd

Table 6.7 continued

		HARD for the lie catcher to detect	EASY for the lie catcher to detect
Questions about the lie-catcher			
30	Does the lie-catcher have a reputation of being tough to mislead?	NO If liar has in the past been successful in fooling the lie-catcher	YES lincreases detection apprehension; may also increase duping delight
31	Does the lie catcher have a reputation of being distrustful?	DIFFICULT TO PREDICT Such a reputation might decrease deception guilt; it may also increase detection apprehension	
32	Does the lie-catcher have a reputation of being fair-minded?	NO Liar less likely to feel guilt about deceiving the lie-catcher.	YES Increases deception guilt
33	Is the lie-catcher a denier who avoids problems, and tends always to think the best of people.	YES Probably will overlook clues to deceit; vulnerable to false negative errors	NO
34	Is lie-catcher unusually able to interpret expressive behaviors accurately?	NO	YES
35	Does the lie-catcher have preconceptions which bias the lie-catcher against the liar?	NO	YES Although lie-catcher will be alert to clues to deceit; he will be liable to false positive errors
36	Does the lie-catcher obtain any benefits from not detecting the lie?	YES Lie-catcher will ignore clues to deceit, deliberately or unwittingly	NO
37	Is lie-catcher unable to tolerate uncertainty about whether he is being deceived?	DIFFICULT TO PREDICT May cause either false positive or false negative errors	
38	Is lie-catcher seized by an emotional wildfire?	NO	YES Liars will be caught, but innocents will be judged to be lying (false positive error)

Source: Ekman (2001).

surveys or questionnaires which bias the response (from the correct, honest, accurate response). They include, for example, the social desirable or faking-good response as well as its, opposite faking-bad (or mad); acquiescence or yea-saying (the tendency to agree irrespective of the question) or its opposite, nay-saying; extremity response set (always choosing extreme opposites) or its opposite, mid-point response set. These response sets may be due to the nature of the question as much as the motives of the respondents.

A second set of synonymous terms *are faking, lying* and *dissimulating,* each of which refers to the fact that the respondent is concealing the truth under a feigned semblance of something different. Faking and dissimulating refers specifically to those occasions when a respondent is deliberately giving false responses in order to create a specific impression (that he or she is ill, merits a job, is mad). A much more specific term is *social desirability,* which has come to be used as a general phrase to represent tendencies to distort self-reports in a favorable direction. It has been defined as a person's tendency to "deny socially undesirable traits and to claim socially desirable ones, and the tendency to say things which place the speaker in a favorable light". Whereas faking and dissimulation refer to any sort of dishonest response, social desirability refers specifically to one sort of faking – the presentation of self in a positive light. That is, it should not be seen as self-deception but deliberate other-deception.

There are essentially five ways of catching liars:

▷ Instructions: Ask/tell/implore people not to lie.
▷ Devise a lie scale.
▷ Establish a "faking profile" by asking people to lie and observe their responses.
▷ Use forced-choice or ipsative measures.
▷ Time the response.

The first method is simple, yet can work well. If everybody faked, they would all give the same (desirable) response; there would be no randomness in the answers and the tests would have no validity. This is patently and obviously not the case. People do tend to "move in a positive direction", so simply reducing the variability. In the same way as people lie about their age, they tend to "knock off" five to eight years, not 20. Telling people not to lie and that they may be caught does have some effect. However, much more effort has gone into trying to devise and validate social desirability or lie scales.

For over 50 years, psychologists have tried to devise measures of social desirability. They have developed various tests and measures, various codes (e.g. lie scales) that measure this response set. The idea is that, if people can be shown to lie on these measures, one could happily and reasonably assume they are lying on all other measures that they are given to complete.

One of the earliest is still one of the best known: the Marlowe–Crowne Scale (Crowne and Marlowe, 1960). It contains 33 Yes/No questions. The items cover such issues as taking part in gossip, playing sick, and taking advantage of others. Some are keyed in the positive direction (i.e. agreeing means social desirability) and some in the negative direction (i.e. agreeing means low social desirability).

Another approach is to develop a "lie scale". The idea is that, if people score highly on the lie scale, they are probably lying on the other items as well. They ask respondents whether they have ever been cheeky, greedy, or nasty to others or taken advantage of them. They also ask whether the respondents are good, honest, and helpful.

More recently, Paulhus (1988) distinguished between two items of desirable responding called *self-deception* and *impression management*. Those who self-deceive tend to be repressors who tend to be very defensive. They try to avoid anxiety by denying or distancing themselves from unacceptable behaviors. To what extent they do this consciously is not clear. On the other hand, there are impression managers who attempt to create a positive image by distorting the truth.

As an example, consider six self-deception and six impression management items (Table 6.8).

This distinction is now well-recognized, though from a practical perspective both forms seem undesirable.

Table 6.8   Self-deception and impression management

Self-deception

5	I always know why I like things.
*6	When my emotions are aroused, it biases my thinking.
7	Once I've made up my mind, other people can seldom change my opinion.
*8	I am not a safe driver when I exceed the speed limit.
9	I am fully in control of my own fate.
*10	It's hard for me to shut off a disturbing thought.

Impression management

30	I always declare everything at customs.
*31	When I was young I sometimes stole things.
32	I have never dropped litter on the street.
*33	I sometimes drive faster than the speed limit.
34	I never read sexy books or magazines.
*35	I have done things that I don't tell other people about.

Note: These are scored on a "not true" to "very true" scale. The items with an asterisk (*) are reversed.
Source: Paulhus (1988).

A third approach is to develop a *faking profile*. This is done by giving a large group of individuals a particular test and telling them *not* to respond honestly but to "fake good". They might be asked to respond as they think an ideal candidate for a particular job may do. They are told to make a good impression; come out as healthy, adjusted, talented. They may be contrasted with a group not given these instructions. This means, in effect, that one can derive a template or profile of liars. That is, this method yields a response of typical liars because people have been asked to lie. In that sense, it is clear what liars say. Therefore, if a candidate has the same response as the lying group, it may be assumed they, too, are lying.

A fourth approach is to use forced choice or ipsative measures (Table 6.9). This can be used for negative or positive items where people are tempted either to reject both or to attract both.

There are all sorts of psychometric issues and debates about using these sorts of tests because they are essentially asking people to make comparisons with themselves. What is, however, most important is that the two statements must be, or equal, positivity or negativity, otherwise potential dissimulators will simply choose the best alternative.

Finally, there are other techniques which have been used to try to catch potential dissimulators. One is to measure "response latency", or how long it takes people to respond. If the questionnaire is administered by computer, this is relatively easy to do. The idea is that people "dither" over the ones they lie on and respond fastest when telling the truth.

Table 6.9 Forced choice or upsate measures

Negative

Which are you more likely to do?

A   Arrive late at work when your boss is on holiday;
B   Take a "sickie" when not at all ill.

Another choice:

C   Steal office stationery;
D   Send personal faxes on the office fax machine.

Positive

Which are you more likely to do?

A   Stay after work for 6–8 hours unpaid to help out in an emergency situation;
B   Accept a reduction in your salary when your organization is experiencing financial difficulty.

Another choice:

C   Report where you have mistakenly paid twice for the same work;
D   Volunteer to help coach two struggling colleagues in your own time after work.

Getting at the truth

There is, of course, a danger that we become obsessed with lying, or believe we are only getting the partial truth. Most people do tell the truth most of the time; the main problem is that either they can't always remember everything or they

> *A man's most valuable trait is a judicious sense of what not to believe.*
>
> (Euripides (ca 485–406 BC))

remember it incorrectly. Frustratingly, when people are trying to tell the truth and they repeat the story, very often there are differences in the two stories.

A woman claimed she always knew when her boyfriend was lying because the details of an evening changed when he was challenged to repeat the events a second time. She was surprised to hear that she should be more worried if the story was exactly the same the second time round. We do not remember these events perfectly unless we need to or we have practiced the lie. A word perfect repetition of an event is more suspicious than some small inconsistencies.

In the workplace, people spend a great deal of time acquiring information from others. At appraisal time, managers need to find out what the staff member really thinks about their performance; staff need to find out what their line manager really thinks about them. After a meeting with a client or customer, employees have to give an account of what happened to their colleagues or line managers. We all know the dangers and propensity of people exaggerating their own contribution or omitting significant facts. Sometimes these deceptions are more than simple self-aggrandisement – it can be to hide fraud, corruption or some other CWB.

The employer's job is to get the truth and, at the same time, to be sensitive to the possibility of deception. The question then, becomes: Is it possible to combine the two: elicit maximum information while maximizing the chances of detecting deceit? Are the techniques used incompatible?

In the earlier part of this chapter, we looked at detection techniques and the vulnerabilities of the liar. Here, we consider how best to elicit accurate information while staying aware of the possibility of deception.

At an early stage in an employee's career, management courses usually have courses on interviewing techniques, and anyone going on personnel management courses spends a great deal of time crafting and refining these skills. These are for the more formal type of interview. Some, such as the recruitment interview, suffer the swings of fashion and are variously held up to be the only way to find out about people and whether they will "fit in"; many human resources specialists have told us over recent years they are unreliable as a selection tool. In appraisal, they are important and for any fact-finding process they are almost irreplaceable. Cook (1998: 66), reviewing the interview process concludes:

> Psychologists are right to be wary of interviews, because the traditional one-to-one unstructured interview does have very low validity. At its worst it may

contribute virtually no useful information at all. Unstructured group interviews achieve slightly higher validity, but are still very inaccurate. Psychologists are however wrong in dismissing interviews all together, because structured interviews can achieve very high validity, arguably as good as any other method.

But the debate about their usefulness identifies an important issue – they can be unreliable. Given that, we may not have a choice. What, then, can an interviewer do to maximize the information elicited and increase the accuracy?

This problem was identified by a number of police forces in the 1980s. Until then – and, indeed, still today – much police interviewing training focused on types of questions (open, closed, leading) and "what, when, where, why and how". It began to dawn on the police and others involved in the judiciary process that mistakes were being made and potentially valuable information was being lost from friendly witnesses. Fisher and Geiselman (1992) developed what has become known as the *cognitive interview* (CI) and it is now widely used by police forces in the US, UK, Australia and Germany.

The purpose of the CI is to help the witness remember as much as possible about an incident, often where he has been an eye witness. The results of laboratory and field tests are impressive and show that, in both criminal investigations and other non-police fact-finding interviews, the CI increases recall. Test results vary but suggest that people recall between 30% and 50% more information without any increase in the number of incorrect facts (Fisher and Geiselman, 1992: 195–202). Their conclusions suggested that the CI can be applied in a wide variety of criminal and non-criminal investigations, especially when demands are made on the respondent's memory and communication skills.

At roughly the same time as Fisher and Geiselman were working on the CI, police in the UK were improving their own investigatory and interviewing techniques. Much of this was stimulated by the passing of the Police and Criminal Evidence Act (PACE) in 1984. Their work produced the interview system known as PEACE, which incorporates the concept of *conversation management*. This term was coined by Shepherd (2007) when he was training police in 1983 (Milne and Bull, 1999).

Conversation management puts the emphasis on how to handle a meeting with two or more people, whether or not they are in a formal interview situation. Shepherd (2007) provides a structure which is very similar to PEACE. Shepherd (1986) identified six skills important for the interviewer:

1 Observation and memory
2 Listening and assertion
3 Initiating and regulating through the process of control and social reinforcement
4 Appropriate questioning which allows elicitation and probing
5 Active listening and information processing
6 Confronting feelings, reflecting back and summarizing.

Having acquired these skills the interviewer can then move on to reach four higher skills:

1   The ability to detect changes in interviewee non-verbal behavior which might indicate evasion or deception
2   The ability to detect changes in emotional state motivation, attitude and disposition
3   The ability to build a global picture of the interview as a whole
4   The ability to identify indicators and patterns of vagueness, ambiguity and contradiction by evaluating the interviewee's account.

From the perspective of the lie detector, these procedures have already identified some useful techniques. Primary is that the interviewer establishes the base rate of the interviewee – how does this person react normally, what are their normal mannerisms, speech and voice patterns.

Cognitive interviewing takes the process of getting at the truth a stage further and introduces some further requirements of the interviewer. They also introduce a question which is particularly difficult for the liar.

The CI asks the interviewee to go over the event but from a different perspective: this could be through the eyes of someone else who was there, or a tradesman (say, a builder or lawyer) who might have been there. Or ask the interviewee to recall events in reverse chronological order – this is particularly difficult for the liar because he may have practiced the lie often, but not backwards.

The danger in this procedure is to ask the interviewee questions which they cannot reasonably answer. They might be tempted to answer anyway. However, properly trained interviewers will be aware of this weakness and not take their interviewees outside their knowledge zone.

Combining all three techniques, we provide a nine-phase procedure for maximizing the amount and accuracy of information, as well as maximizing the chances of detecting deception (Table 6.10).

The procedure presented in Table 6.11 provides the lie detector with a number of important advantages:

The base line: The whole interview and discussion is conducted in a relaxed friendly manner designed to give the interviewer the opportunity to establish the other person's baseline verbal and non-verbal behavior.

An opportunity to ask peculiar questions: With practice, it is possible to ask people some challenging questions, often under the guise of helping them (genuinely) to remember as much as possible.

The best chance to elicit accurate information: This is a well-researched method of extracting accurate information. The deceiver will not be able to provide the kind of detail which a truthful person can.

Choosing which areas to explore in greater depth: Being sensitive to a person's stress levels will help the interviewer identify which areas he or she needs to explore in greater depth.

Table 6.10   The five stages of a PEACE interview

Preparation/ planning	This involves the important and necessary time spent preparing for an interview. It comprises deciding on the objectives of the interview and getting "up to speed" on the case.
Explanation	Telling the interviewee honestly and clearly what is happening and how the interview will proceed.
Acquire	Asking relevant questions (open and closed) to obtain the necessary information and facts.
Conclusion	Summarizing the main points of the interview, and ensuring that the interviewee knows how to get back in touch should they remember anything else. It is also important to show full appreciation of their efforts.
Evaluation	Writing up the interview and analyzing the information to establish its value and any gaps or questions about its veracity.

Cognitive interviewing in the workplace

This process has been developed by police forces and applied typically to police-type interviews of willing witnesses. It may be possible in the workplace to replicate the interview but, mostly, people in the workplace acquire information in a much more informal manner. The challenge is to use the techniques without making it sound like a formal interview. It should be possible to do the following:

▷ Establish rapport, make it personal – this an important stage, as it establishes the base rate behavior; take your time.
▷ Ask the open question "You saw client A yesterday – how did it go?"
▷ Perhaps hardest of all, do not interrupt the account.
▷ Use active listening techniques.
▷ Ask the person questions from different perspectives – "How would client A be reporting this meeting back to his boss?", "You said that the meeting was interrupted by his secretary coming in – what was he saying immediately before that?"
▷ Do summarize regularly.

If the individual needs help remembering everything, then you could offer to help by telling him you will use CI techniques and then you can deploy the full process described earlier.

For the most part, there is little or no conflict between these two objectives. However, the requirements to establish a rapport and create a relaxed atmosphere might lead an interviewer to steer clear of conflict or applying pressure.

Table 6.11   Combined 9-phase procedure for interview

Preparation	Read any files, prepare room, drinks, turn off mobile and other telephones, plan – be clear about the objective of the session.
Welcome	Greet, personalize and establish rapport. Most people cut this part of the process short. It has to be judged correctly, but it is important.
Explanation	Explain what will happen in interview and include need to concentrate and report everything – in effect, transfer control to the interviewee, emphasize importance of not guessing.
Initiate free report	Remind person of the context of incident or meeting, ask open questions, encourage them to report everything, allow pauses, do not interrupt their flow, use active listening techniques – effectively, give them control of this time, let them determine how this part of the discussion should run; study not just the words, but their style of speech and their body language (establishing their base rate).
Fill the gaps	Once they have finished their narrative, go over your notes and fill in the gaps (the temptation is to do this during the narrative – resist it). Remind them that it is OK to say "I don't know".
Further retrieval	Ask them to go over the same ground but looking at it from a different perspective: how will the other person be reporting this meeting? If I had been there, what assessment would I have made of the situation? Please tell me what happened immediately before you mentioned the price of the project? Monitor the person's verbal and non-verbal reactions. Where stress or strong emotion is detected, find an opportunity to go over that ground again.
Summarize	Summarize throughout the session but also, at the end, take care over an overview summary.
Closure	Thank them, confirm or consider continued contact, give details of how to make contact with you.
Evaluate	Write up the session and consider what gaps remain and where there might be deception. Consider what follow-up action might be necessary or desirable.

We know from Ekman that people are more likely to show they are lying when they fear being caught or the consequences of being caught, or they are embarrassed because they are lying. The interviewer may need to remind them of these factors, perhaps subtly, during the conversation.

Conclusion

Training and experience does help in the business of lie detection. But it is by no means simple or foolproof. Because we are all used to lying, it is an everyday occurrence and to a large extent socially acceptable. People have quite different beliefs about when one can, should and should not lie. And they have considerable personal experience to catch liars. However, many are not well-informed and, as we have seen, either look for or misinterpret the lies (or truth) they observe. Hence the ability of many liars to get away with it!

There is considerable consistency and overlap between reviewers' and researchers' conclusions in this area. They show that many "lay theses" – that is, the theories of ordinary people – are wrong: almost dramatically opposed to popular belief. They also admit that it is not an easy business. Those who have made a life-time research project of studying the nature of lying admit that they can often get it wrong. But they also offer good advice.

Ekman (2001: 187–9), in fact, offered 10 specific suggestions that help people trying to detect lies doing a better, more reliable job. They are:

1   Try to make explicit the basis of any hunches and intuitions about whether or not someone is lying. By becoming more aware of how you interpret behavioural clues to deceit, you will learn to spot your mistakes and recognise when you don't have much chance to make a correct judgement.

2   Remember that there are two dangers in detecting deceit: disbelieving-the-truth (judging a truthful person to be lying) and believing-a-lie (judging a liar to be truthful). There is no way to completely avoid both mistakes. Consider the consequences of risking either mistake.

3   The absence of a sign of deceit is not evidence of truth; some people don't leak. The presence of a sign of deceit is not always evidence of lying; some people appear ill-at-ease or guilty even when they are truthful. You can decrease the Brokaw hazard, which is due to individual differences in expressive behaviour, by basing your judgements on a change in the suspect's behaviour.

4   Search your mind for any preconceptions you may have about the suspect. Consider whether your preconceptions will bias your chance of making a correct judgement. Don't try to judge whether or not someone is lying if you feel overcome by jealousy or in an emotional wildfire. Avoid the temptation to suspect lying because it explains otherwise inexplicable events.

5   Always consider the possibility that a sign of emotion is not a clue to deceit but a clue to how a truthful person feels about being suspected of lying. Discount the sign of an emotion as a clue to deceit if a truthful suspect might feel that emotion because of: the suspect's personality; the nature of your past relationship with the suspect; or the suspect's expectations.

6   Bear in mind that many clues to deceit are signs of more than one emotion, and that those that are must be discounted if one of those emotions could be felt if the suspect is truthful while another could be felt if the suspect is lying.

7   Consider whether or not the suspect knows he is under suspicion, and what the gains or losses in detecting deceit would be either way.

8   If you have knowledge that the suspect would also have only if he is lying, and you can afford to interrogate the suspect, construct a Guilty Knowledge Test.

9 Never reach a final conclusion about whether a suspect is lying or not based solely on your interpretation of behavioral clues to deceit. Behavioral clues to deceit should only serve to alert you to the need for further information and investigation. Behavioral clues, like the polygraph, can never provide absolute evidence.

10 Use the checklist provided in the previous section to evaluate the lie, the liar, and you, the lie catcher, to estimate the likelihood of making errors or correctly judging truthfulness.

7   Integrity Testing

Introduction

Of all the qualities people most want in their boss – inspiration, intelligence, kindness – the one they always rate top is *integrity*. The same is true for managers who want, above all else, honest staff. They want their staff to be straight forward, trustworthy and sincere. From childhood, most of us are taught that truthfulness is imperative: lying, whether simple distortion or worse, is sinful, antisocial, hurtful and wrong.

Despite this, it is surprising how comparatively little effort selectors put into trying to detect integrity in candidates. While recognizing its importance, it seems to most people too difficult or embarrassing to test effectively. Some people have favorite "ethical questions" like:

▷ "Under what circumstances, in your view, is it appropriate to lie?"
▷ "You're a young consultant who could lose your job if you don't bill enough hours. All your colleagues are padding their hours. Do you pad yours?"
▷ "Your next-door neighbor offers to hook you up with free cable television. Do you take the offer?"
▷ "You discover that your company is inflating its earnings. Your boss says to go along or you'll be fired. Do you comply?"
▷ "You don't have enough money to pay your taxes at the end of the year. Your accountant recommends some made-up deductions, saying the tax office doesn't audit anyone these days. Do you go along?"
▷ "You're a car salesman paid on commission. All the other salesmen are saying that the next shipment of the hot new model everyone wants is due in three weeks – when it's really six weeks. Do you also say three weeks?"

However, there is a paradox at the heart of this issue. People, of course, lie on integrity tests. The more face-valued, transparent and obvious the test is, the easier it is to fake. Thus, those who appear to have most integrity on some reports may have the least.

Also, it appears that honesty and integrity, and how that trait or values are shown, may be different for different cultures. But is there such a thing as trait-integrity?

For over 50 years, psychologists dreamt of devising robust and reliable tests to measure the integrity of people. The idea has been very attractive to many employers. The idea of having a good (cheap and efficient) way of testing honesty and integrity has been a holy grail. Fifty years of test development and evaluation has lead to the following conclusions:

> There is now a reasonable body of evidence showing that integrity tests have some validity for predicting a variety of criteria that are relevant to organizations. This research does not say that tests of this sort will eliminate theft or dishonesty at work, but it does suggest that individuals who receive poor scores on these tests tend to be less desirable employees. (Murphy, 1993: 215)

> Thus, a large body of validity evidence consistently shows scores on integrity tests to be positively related to both a range of counter-productive behaviours and supervisory ratings of overall performance. However, virtually all the research has been done by test publishers, leading sceptics to question whether only successes are publicised. (Sackett, 1994: 74)

> In general, however, the evidence indicates that integrity test scores can be trusted. (Hough, 1996: 103)

Yet, there remains doubt about exactly *what* these tests are measuring, *how* easy they are to fake, and how stable integrity is over time and across situation.

Estimates of the use and growth of integrity tests come almost exclusively from America. The following are typical estimates from the 1980s and 1990s. As early as 1990, it was estimated that 2.5 million integrity tests were administered annually in America (Bergman *et al.*, 1990).

1   Around 5000 companies use pre-employment integrity tests to screen around 5,000,000 applicants.
2   Somewhere between 5 and 20 per cent of all American companies use some form of testing for variable forms of job (high sensitive jobs in particular).
3   There are 40–50 commercially available tests in the market as well as various in-house measures developed for very specific purposes.

Every organization would prefer to have honest, dependable and trustworthy employees. In some organizations – like the police and security forces, banks, and the military – it is essential. Hence, they often invest a great deal in techniques for assessing honesty and integrity in selection. Equally, these techniques can be used to "vet" people in the organization or attempt to establish guilt after the event. However, it is in the area of pre-employment screening that they are most used.

Skeptics point to various issues with tests: legality, privacy, discrimination, union busting (Bergman *et al.*, 1990).

Leadership integrity

Despite the numerous academic and popular articles on the relevance and importance of integrity in leaders, it remains a confused and a theoretical area.

Palanski and Yammarino (2007b) attempted to categorize, critique and summarize this disparate literature. They found five themes in this literature.

1   *Integrity as wholeness*: integrity from integer or completeness. It is something which defines all of life, a pre-condition of all behavior.
2   *Integrity as consistency in words and actions*: It is stable across time and situation and means espoused values are displayed values.
3   *Integrity as consistency in adversity*: Able to withstand challenge and temptation – a positive choice to stand up for that which is right.
4   *Integrity as being true to oneself*: This is authenticity, being true to one's conscience.
5   *Integrity as manifesting or being driven by moral, ethical, honest ideals and codes.*

For Palanski and Yammarino, integrity is about the *consistency* of words and actions. They distinguish between *substantive* virtues – like compassion honesty, which are morally good in *themselves*), and *adjunctive* virtues – like authenticity and courage, which are, not necessarily good in themselves.

Kaptein (2003) argued that management integrity is represented by two facts: the extent to which a manager/leader is a person of integrity, and the extent to which he/she is able to develop, nurture or stimulate it in others. Thus, the manager of integrity is authentic, constructive and reliable while also having a gentle, protective and strong hand with respect to his/her employees.

Integrity has various meanings. It implies incorruptible, unimpeachable, but also whole and complete and integrated. Kaptein (2003) notes the manager with integrity has:

▷   Clear limits knowing about moral boundaries (i.e. the difference between the spirit and the letter of the law).
▷   Clear ethical and moral guidelines that are rigorously followed and obeyed.
▷   Consistent behavior to others and over time that is predictable and straightforward.
▷   Coherent behavior in terms of values and ethics so that personal beliefs, behaviors, and values are aligned and similar to those of the organization.
▷   Constant behavior, in that it is steadfast in the face of temptation.
▷   Creates financial-economic value, which is a moral duty to benefit all those in the organization.
▷   Creates ecological value to protect the environment and ensure the long-term survival of the organization.
▷   Creates social value that encourages unity of purpose between all sakeholders in the organization.

This list of traits and behaviors is very desirable; perhaps unachievable. The issue is how integrity develops in an individual and how prone to change it is.

Trickle-down integrity

Few dispute the fact that business leaders have a large role to play in CWBs at work. Leaders model – and therefore shape – ethical behavior.

Mayer *et al.* (2009) note two schools of thought on the relationship between leadership and CWBs of staff. The *first* is that "the tone at the top" pervades the organization inspiring (or not) staff to act ethically. The *second* approach is that supervisors are the greatest influence on staff because they are the most direct carriers of rewards and punishments. Both assert that followers/employees mimic or role-model the behaviors of their leaders/bosses. However, because employees deal mainly with their bosses, and often very little with senior managers it seems, it is likely that the influence of top management is mediated by the ethical behavior of supervisors.

Mayer *et al.* (2009) found evidence for their ideas; namely, that top management by the way they create, enforce, model and interpret staff policies influence their immediate reports (middle-managers and supervisors) who, in turn, influence workers. They argue their "research may serve as a wake-up call to executives about the importance of their modelling behaviour to the managers that look up to them" (p. 10). They conclude thus:

> Given the number of corporate scandals in recent years, employers are increasingly interested in the ethical behavior of their employees. The present study suggests that ethical leadership is associated with less counterproductive behavior and more positive behavior. An important caveat of this study is that while ethical leadership at all organizational levels is important, immediate supervisors are the lens through which employees see what the organization values and therefore they likely have the most direct influence on employee ethical behavior. (Mayer *et al.*, 2009: 11)

"Honesty" screening

One of the main reasons for the use of integrity tests at work is because of concern with employees faking on employment personality tests, despite the fact that there is little evidence of this (Hogan *et al.*, 2007). Similarly, it is believed interviewers cannot pick up lying in interviews, while there is sufficient evidence that they can (Townsend *et al.*, 2007).

An employer interested in "honesty" screening has a number of different options:

1 *Polygraph/lie detector*: These come in different forms. The old ones measured blood pressure, pulse, sweat gland activity and breathing. Newer models measure the electrical activity in the brain or voice stress analysis. Once popular in American, its use has never taken off so much in other countries and there is now serious doubt about its validity. It seems popularly accepted that eliciting an accurate confession depends more on the

skills of the examiner than the characteristics of the person being tested. Legislation in America and elsewhere has significantly reduced its usage.

2 *Vetting*: This is also called reference checking or background/biographical investigations. Essentially, this involves checking up on what applicants have said or written about themselves and their past work, education and reward. Typically referees are contacted by phone but so are educational establishments, banks, even medical staff. The latter is expensive and may require detective agencies. However, the former is common. Indeed, people are often happy to say things "off the record" which they would be much less happy to put on paper. Issues around slanderous (spoken) or libelous (written) communication has made people very conscious about defamation and hence "informers" are far less forthcoming, making this method problematic.

3 *Drug testing*: Taking urine and blood samples is useful and legal, but some companies prefer not to do it not only because of the sort of impression that it conveys, but also because of charges of invasion of privacy. Also, these tests cannot always pick up those likely in the future to have addictive problems.

4 *Application form/biolographical data research*: This method seeks retrospectively to look at the differences between honest and dishonest employees for signs of future possible problems. A weight is given to certain answers and, if that score exceeds a specific number, they are screened out. Consider the following characteristics found to predict in American supermarket employees:

▷ Does *not* want relative contacted in case of emergency.
▷ Substandard appearance on application.
▷ Does not own their own car.
▷ Applicant recently consulted a doctor.

These are well-known problems with method. It openly discriminates against certain groups and the weights/scores often seem very unreliable – that is, highly specific to the organization.

5 *Integrity interviewing*: This is often little more than a structured interview that asks obvious and predictable questions, and seeks to observe verbal, vocal and non-verbal signs of lying like higher voice pitch, speech errors, increased blinking, frequent swallowing, fast and shallow breathing, and false smiles. It does require some considerable expertise. The jury remains out on the validity of these methods.

6 *Personality tests and assessment*: These come in very many forms – for instance: *graphological* analysis (which has little or no evidence of validity), *projective tests* (where people tell stories about pictures they see and project their personality motives, but are still thought of as highly unreliable) and *personality* tests around issues of morality, conscientiousness. We will discuss these in detail.

Personality and integrity

Is integrity a personality variable like introversion-extroversion? That is, is it biologically based, stable over time and partly heritable? Is it separate from the well-established "big five" personality model? If not, can we derive a good measure from standard personality tests?

One study attempted to answer this question. Marcus *et al.* (2006) found that the evidence seemed to suggest that, if you examine the scores on certain personality dimensions and combine them, it is possible to get a good sense of a person's integrity. Three personality variables stood out as most important: neuroticism, agreeableness and conscientiousness – the more stable, agreeable and dependable the person, the greater their integrity. However, if one examines their results on a factual level, one can be more precise. The more a person scores *low* in angry hostility, impulsivity and vulnerable, and *high* on trust, straightforwardness and distrustfulness, the more integrity they show.

This is pretty self-evident. However, what it suggests is that standard personality tests can be very useful in measuring integrity.

Another review on the relationship between personality and absenteeism came to a similar conclusion. Ones *et al.* (2003) found good evidence of the predictive validity of personality based in accounting for absenteeism at work. They also noted the importance of three traits: Conscientiousness (dutifulness, dependability, reliability, impulse control, rule-following), Agreeableness (trust, rule following) and Emotional stability (stress tolerance).

Again and again, the results of the studies looking at the personality predictors of work success point to the importance of two traits: High Conscientiousness, Low Neuroticism. For integrity, it seems it is important to add Agreeableness.

More recently, in a meta-analysis, Berry *et al.* (2007) report the following data estimates of the correlations between overall workplace deviance and the big five personality variable: Agreeableness =.44; Conscientiousness =.35; Emotional stability =.26; Openness =.08; Extraversion =.03.

Other studies of teams have shown that those teams whose overall team score for conscientiousness, agreeableness and stability are low show poor social cohesion, poor communication, more social conflict and a lesser sense that the workload is equitably shared.

Byle and Holtgraves (2008) found the same result. They noted also that conscientious people are less prone to fake on integrity tests. Hence, they recommend using conscientiousness tests which are, in their words, "short, reliable and inexpensive" (p. 294).

Kumar *et al.* (2009) tested Indians and also found that not only agreeableness, conscientiousness and stability, but also extroversion related to organizational citizenship behavior – the very opposite of CWBs.

The question both for the researcher and the manager is this: Is it necessary to use integrity tests when a careful use of well-constructed psychometrical ordinary personality tests can do as well to predict dark-side behaviors at work. However, there is also evidence that the use of more clinical instruments – for instance, to measure psychopathic personality traits – may do even better in predicting bad behavior at work (Connelly *et al.*, 2006).

Integrity testing at work

Integrity tests, also called honesty tests, are pencil-and-paper questionnaires designed to assess a very wide variety of work-related behaviors. These include:

▷ dishonesty and general untrustworthiness: unauthorized use of company information, forgery.
▷ alcohol/drug abuse: selling, using on the job, coming to work with a hangover/intoxicated.
▷ deception and deliberate misrepresentation: tax fraud and cheating, bribery.
▷ violent behavior: physical assault on others at work.
▷ "maladjustment": blackmail.
▷ job instability/excessive absenteeism: turnover/time theft, coming late to work, using sick-leave when not sick.
▷ theft of cash, merchandise and property: misuse of discount privileges, embezzlement.
▷ poor conscientiousness/prudence: no work ethic, intentionally going slow or sloppy work.
▷ failure to implement company policy.
▷ alienation attitudes: the opposite of commitment and engagement.
▷ Inattention to safety rules: causing preventable accidents.
▷ Ludditism and damage to property: willful damage and waste, vandalism.
▷ poor time-keeping: – having unauthorized work breaks.
▷ sabotage.
▷ sexual harassment.

Integrity tests were first developed in the 1940s and there are now over 40 off-the-shelf integrity tests commercially available to organizations (Ones *et al.*, 2003). They fall into two rather different types: those that are essentially *personality tests* (measuring things like conformity, conscientiousness, dependability), and those that are more *overt* (that question about active lying, theft, wrongdoing and attitudes towards it). Here are typical overt questions from overt integrity tests:

▷ "How often do you tell the truth?"
▷ "Do you think it is stealing to take small items home from work?"
▷ "How easy is it to get away with stealing?"

On the other hand, covert or veiled purpose questions include:

▷ "How often do you make your bed?"
▷ "Are you an optimist?"
▷ "How often do you blush?"

Some integrity tests measure attitudes and beliefs; and others, behaviors.

The issue for all tests is essentially threefold: how many people are misclassified or incorrectly "diagnosed", how easy those tests are to fake, and the extent to which they invade privacy.

Anyone examining this list will be struck by two things: *first*, these behaviors go far beyond the simple concept of integrity and, *second*, the list contains diverse and unrelated issues. Depending on your view, alienation attitudes are somewhat different from sabotage! The idea, however, is that integrity/honesty is relevant to all of these behaviors because, in some sense, they all reflect a level of dishonesty.

Some tests try to veil or disguise their purpose. Others assume low integrity is associated with thrill-seeking, non-conformity and low conscientiousness. Many tests have traditionally been used either: to screen out undesirable applicants, to investigate crimes for current employees, to vet those being considered for promotion or transfer, or to assess the current moral beliefs of people within the organization. Integrity tests were typically used with supervisory level personnel, especially in retail and financial companies.

There has been a great growth of interest in, and use of, questionnaire integrity tests. However, personality and other similar tests have been used since the 1930s to identify "agitators, malcontents and thugs" (Zichar, 2001). There seems both demand and supply: the test publishers respond to the market need.

Another reason for the growth in integrity testing is quite simply the fact that the use of the lie detector/polygraph has become more problematic. So, with a favored method less available and respectable, and evidence of increasing CWBs, it seems natural to resort to any integrity tests on the market.

Reactions to integrity tests

How do people react when asked to do an integrity test? Are they offended, insulted or accepting (Ryan and Sackett, 1987)? One realistic study with *job applicants* Jones (1991) found the following:

▷ 90% felt it was appropriate for an employer to administer such a test.
▷ 4% would refuse to take such a test.
▷ 63% would enjoy being asked to take such a test.
▷ 11% felt this type of test was an invasion of privacy.

▷ 2% said that, if they had two comparable job offers, they would reject the company using such a test.

▷ 3% would resent being asked to take such a test.

▷ 82% felt that a test such as this is sometimes an appropriate selection procedure.

▷ 5% believe that administering a test such as this reflects negatively on the organization.

▷ 80% indicated that being asked to take such a test would not affect their view of the organization.

▷ 80% indicated that tests such as this are routinely used in industry.

One study looking at seasonal student employees found, as predicted, that those who were given clear advance notification of work-monitoring and thought it fair were much more likely to return to the organization the following year compared with employees that were given no warning or thought it unfair (Hovorka-Mead *et al.*, 2002). The central question is whether these tests measure loyalty or the opposite.

The issue is that there is a thin line between what may be seen as benign and what are perceived as intrusive/invasive monitoring technologies. Zweig and Webster (2002) found that employees' acceptance of monitoring systems was a function of their perceived usefulness, fairness and privacy invasion which, in turn, were dependent on the precise characteristics of the monitoring system involved and the justification for its use. They argue:

> There is a delicate balance in the line between benign and invasive. People form expectations about the degree of personal information they will communicate with others in their daily lives. Often, there are shared expectations that are respected by all and serve to guide social interactions among them. When these expectations are violated, people can experience feelings of discomfort, embarrassment and even anger. From these studies, it was suggested that when awareness systems are put in place, employees might be unsure about the expectations guiding their own and others' behaviours. That is, awareness systems appear to cross this line and are considered invasive. Thus, we believe that the notion of boundary violations represents a key construct in explaining employees' reactions to technologies such as awareness systems. Awareness systems violate boundaries for sharing personal information with others, constrain employees' ability to control how they present themselves to other, and are construed as unfair. Even if attempts are made to respect individuals through manipulations of the system's characteristics, overall violations of psychological boundaries can lead to rejection. (Zweig and Webster, 2002: 627–8)

What would be particularly interesting would be to compare these results with those from other tests. Would people be happier to complete ability or personality tests than honesty tests? Are people simply wary of tests in general? It seems many people tend to accept tests that are job-relevant, and many even find them enjoyable.

Much, no doubt, depends on the type of test used, the way it is presented and the candidate's previous experience of testing, as well as their personality and values. Certainly, results appear to indicate that neither extreme view is correct: people neither happily embrace the idea of being tested, nor find the whole idea irrelevant, immoral and offensive.

Self-report tests of integrity

There have been pencil-and-paper tests for over 50 years that have attempted to measure integrity. Those have tended to grow over the past decade or so, as issues with integrity appear to have increased. These tests are fairly varied but appear to concentrate on the following four areas: *first*, direct, explicit admissions of dishonest behavior (lying, cheating, stealing, whistle-blowing); *second*, opinions/attitudes about the acceptability of dishonest behavior (prevalence in society, justification of causes); *third*, traits, value systems and biographical factors thought to be associated with dishonesty; *fourth*, reactions to hypothetical situations that do or do not feature dishonest behavior.

Miner and Capps (1996) have provided some excellent examples from integrity tests. Simple items from a test used in World War II asked how frequently respondents lied, whether they had ever been expelled from school, and whether they thought people trusted them. Still others enquired about illegal or disapproved activities, such as drug-taking or forgery.

Another approach is to ask questions about honesty: how much respondents believe others are honest or dishonest, and how they themselves have behaved. Other questions are about personality attributes associated with dishonesty.

Miner and Capps (1996: 152–3) also offer various scenarios.

Hogan and Hogan (1989), for instance, describe the design and validation of a personality questionnaire that predicted individuals who engaged in various CWBs. It also predicted the opposite – that is, persons who were liked by co-workers and supervisors. Murphy and Lee (1994) showed that the trait of conscientiousness was powerfully correlated with integrity, as one may expect. Conscientiousness is associated with dependability, perseverance and achievement orientation, while integrity is about honesty; so, these are not interchangeable measures, but they are logically related. Marcus *et al.* (2000) noted integrity related to three personality variables: agreeableness, conscientiousness and emotional stability.

Often, these self-report measures can be distinguished in terms of whether they are overt, explicit, "clear purpose" tests, or personality-based, "veiled purpose" tests. The sort of issues that an overt test examines include: honesty attitudes/admission of previous dishonesty; substance abuse, drug avoidance; personal past achievements; service orientation, customer relations; work values; clerical, mathematical, verbal skills, abilities and aptitudes.

On the other hand, the "veiled purpose" tests are more likely to try to measure: conscientiousness, dependability, prudence; hostility to rules and regulations; impulsivity, thrill-seeking, disinhibition; alienation and lack of commitment.

Example 7.1   Examples of integrity test scenarios

Scenarios

In the test with which we were involved, there were a number of scenario items which use the following format:

> Jane works as a sales clerk in a store beside the Interstate Highway/Main Motorway. The store's customers are mostly tourists who stop to buy gasoline, snacks, and souvenirs. One day Jane accidentally gives a man change for a $10 bill when he actually had given her a $20 bill. After the man left, Jane saw the $20 bill in the cash drawer with the tens and realized what she had done. At this point Jane might react in several ways. Indicate whether you agree with each of these possibilities.

> 1 Jane decides to deny that she shortchanged the customer if he returns for his $10. That will save her a lot of embarrassment. Do you agree?
> Yet Yes_____   No_____

> 2 Jane regrets the incident, but decides to make the best of a bad situation. She takes $10 from the cash drawer and tells her supervisor she is sick and wants the rest of the day off. Do you agree?
>
> Yes_____   No_____

> 3 Jane will gladly return the $10 to the customer if she sees him again. Meanwhile, she turns the extra money over to the store manager and decides to make up for the mistake by contributing $10 of her own money to a local charity. Do you agree?
>
> Yes_____   No_____

> 4 Jane turns the extra money over to the store at the end of her shift because the customer has not returned. She also writes down everything she can remember about how the man looks. If he ever stops at the store again, she will repay him with her own money. Do you agree?
>
> Yes_____   No_____

Confession and honesty attitude questions such as the following make up the remainder of the test:

> If I saw a person accidentally throw away a winning ticket at a race track, I would hand it back to that person.
>
> Yes_____   No_____

> If I got caught stealing, I think I should be given another chance if it was the first time it ever happened.
>
> Yes_____   No_____

> Have you ever cheated on the number of hours you have worked for any employer?
>
> Yes_____   No_____

Source: Miner and Capps, 1996: 152–3.

Recently, Bennett and Robinson (2000) devised such a measure. This inevitably involves defining specific items that make-up deviance. Table 7.1 presents 28 items from an earlier measure.

In the end, Bennett and Robinson developed a two-part questionnaire: one part measuring *organizational* deviance (behaviors directly harmful to the organization), the other measuring *interpersonal* deviance (behaviors directly harmful to individuals). They also provided validity data for their questionnaire. Again, what is striking is the variability in behaviors from nearly trivial to very serious, from everyday to rare, from generally condoned to completely unacceptable. This is an important issue. The assumption is that honesty/integrity is a stable "trait" that informs *all* behavior at work. Some looking at these items may say those who are "grumpy" or "emotionally volatile" or who have significant responsibilities outside the work place are unfairly labeled as lacking in honesty.

Clearly, one obvious advantage of the so-called "veiled purpose test" is that they are less open to faking or not admitting wrongdoing. Faking threatens test reliability. However, it has been shown to be significantly reduced when people are aware that the investigators (potential employers) have (many) other sources of information about their honesty.

There are different themes tapped into by self-report integrity tests. Further, there is an assumption that the honest, reliable person with integrity acts somewhat differently from the dishonest person on this dimension. Thus, the following behaviors can be expected:

1   *Report incidences of explicit dishonesty*: Honest people will honestly report that they have been less dishonest in the past
2   *Leniency towards dishonesty*: Honest people are less likely to excuse, forgive or explain away dishonesty in others and themselves
3   *Rationalization for thieving*: Honest people are less likely to try to excuse or provide rationalization for theft in organizations
4   *Brooding and rumination about theft*: Honest people are less likely to even think (plan, plot, fantasize) about thieving from their organization
5   *Rejecting dishonest norms*: Honest people are likely to question or reject dishonest behavior of all sorts perceived within the organization as acceptable
6   *Impulse control*: Honest people are less likely to act on their impulses, preferring to think through an issue before acting
7   *Punitive attitude*: Honest people have less punitive attitudes to themselves and others.

Karren and Zacharias (2007) list four concerns with all paper-and-pencil self-report integrity tests:

1   The nature of what is being measured – integrity or some related construct (like conscientiousness), because tests do show a relationship with a wide range of work performance measures

Table 7.1 A veiled purpose test

	Item	Participation rate %
1	Worked on a personal matter instead of work for your employer	84.3
2	Taken property from work without permission	51.8
3	Spent too much time fantasising or daydreaming instead of working	77.4
4	Made fun of someone at work	77.8
5	Falsified a receipt to get reimbursed for more money than you spent on business expenses	24.6
6	Said something hurtful to someone at work	55.2
7	Taken an additional or a longer break than is acceptable at your workplace	78.5
8	Repeated a rumour or gossip about your company	72.5
9	Made an ethnic, religious, or racial remark or joke at work	52.5
10	Come in late to work without permission	70.0
11	Littered your work environment	28.5
12	Cursed someone at work	50.5
13	Called in sick when you were not	57.8
14	Told someone about the lousy place where you work	58.9
15	Lost temper while at work	78.8
16	Neglected to follow your boss's instructions	60.6
17	Intentionally worked slower than you could have worked	54.1
18	Discussed confidential company information with an unauthorised person	33.3
19	Left work early without permission	51.9
20	Played a mean prank on someone at work	35.7
21	Left your work for someone else to finish	48.6
22	Acted rudely toward someone at work	53.0
23	Repeated a rumour or gossip about your boss or co-workers	69.1
24	Made an obscene comment at work	48.4
25	Used an illegal drug or consumed alcohol on the job	25.9
26	Put little effort into your work	64.0
27	Publicly embarrassed someone at work	33.9
28	Dragged out work in order to get overtime	26.0

Note: Responses ranged from 1 (*never*) to 7 (*daily*). N = 226.
[a] Percentage of respondents who indicated that they had participated in the behavior at least once in the last year.

Source: Bennett and Robinson (2000).

2   Tests can and do lead to decision errors: *false positives* (where those with integrity are accused of not having it) and the opposite, *false negatives* (where dishonest respondents appear honest)

3   Recent studies show that faking, coaching or retaking integrity tests can affect scores

4   Tests may be considered an invasion of privacy because they seek intrusive information about past undesirable behavior.

Do integrity tests work?

The most obvious and fundamental questions about honesty testing must be about *validity*. What is the evidence that they measure (only) honesty and can differentiate between the honest and dishonest? Over the past decade, there have been various studious and excellent reviews. Those who are positive conclude that integrity tests are often good at detecting CWBs, as well as supervisors' ratings of good/poor performance. Others believe that the "jury is out" and that we need more high-quality disinterested and skeptical research before making a judgment. Whatever the evidence and however it is reviewed, it is apparent that debate for and against tests is driven by strong emotions.

While validity is always the single and simply most important criterion of any test, there are others, some of which have a direct effect on validity. These include reliability, dimensionality, and so on, but perhaps the most important is *fakability*. Can clever (and dishonest) people "beat the test" and come out looking virtuous when they are not. This problem applies to all tests, but particular honesty tests. Results suggest that one can catch dissimulators but that there is a general – and quite understandable – trend to over-emphasize honesty.

The issue with testing is the problem of false positives and negatives – that is, classifying the honest as dishonest and vice versa. Both are equally undesirable but have quite different consequences.

While it is not difficult to make a case for the use of integrity tests, it seems ironic that test publishers seem to make possibly fraudulent claims for the efficacy of their tests in detecting dishonest people, thence reducing theft and shrinkage problems. Honesty testing is a competitive business.

It is possible honesty testing in the future will attempt to measure very specific, rather than general, types of honesty. Further, it is likely that the tests will be computer-administered.

Is there evidence that these relatively simple questionnaires mean that people are more or less likely to engage in dishonest CWBs? Can they predict who will be honest or dishonest? There are various ways of checking the variability of test. They include:

1   *The "known" or contrast groups method*: People who are known to be both honest and dishonest are given the test, and the quantity and quality of the difference in response is recorded

2 *Background, biographical check*: A thorough background check (number of convictions) using police, school, organizations' records are related to test scores

3 *Admissions and confessions*: Separate (perhaps confidential) admissions to a wide range of tests covering dishonest behaviors from the trivial to the very serious are correlated with test scores

4 *Predictive or future method*: People are tested at organizational entry and scores are related to documented (proven) dishonest behaviors over their career

5 *Time series or historic method*: Before honesty tests are used in selection, all sorts of indices are collected (loss, shrinkage); the same data are collected after tests are used in selection to see whether there is a noticeable difference

6 *Correlations with polygraph or anonymous admissions*: of theft or absenteeism.

Each method has its limitations and failings. For instance, background checks will not show working on company time. Predictive methods can take a decade to get results. A reduction in shrinkage (stealing) may have as much to do with the installation of a new security system as it does the use of tests. Studies have shown individual differences on integrity test faking. For instance, it seems brighter people fake better than less intelligent people (Brown and Colthern, 2002).

Certainly, tests have been validated against very different criteria – theft, faking credentials, CWBs – and they do tend to produce rather different results. Working on company time, taking lunch breaks are called "time theft". Stealing office stationary (pens, paper) is strictly theft. But both of these could be considered trivial, certainly quite different from the theft of company secrets, or of valuable products used for production or the products themselves. But what is the latest thinking around these tests?

First, it is agreed that these tests are certainly useful. They are valid enough to help prevent various problems. *Second*, testing alone will not stop theft, dishonesty, sabotage, as many factors other than dishonest individuals cause them. *Third*, integrity tests may be measuring aspects of human personality which are stable over time, though it is not certain which. *Fourth*, there are problems in testing because some testing codes and standards insist that people being tested give informed consent on details about the test, such as what it measures. Hardly the best thing to give the dishonest person. *Fifth*, there may be legal issues in how "cut-off" scores are used and labeled. One could classify people as "pass/fail" or "very, highly, moderately dangerous". How this information is used or recorded can cause expensive legal action. *Sixth*, integrity tests are used to "select-out", not "select-in". They are designed to help people screen out high-risk applicants, not identify "angels".

The issue of the validity of integrity tests and interpreting the evidence is technical. Four issues are relevant:

1   What are the criteria against which test scores are measured? How specific or serious are these criteria? Global (like job performance) or specific (like absenteeism or stealing)?
2   What type of measure is made: subjective or objective? Is the measure recorded electronically (on camera), by others' disinterested observations or is this done by a person's own self-report?
3   What is the validation strategy? That is, is it concurrent – are things compared at the same time (test scores and cheating data), or is it predictive – when scores are seen to predict future behavior?
4   Who comprise the validation sample of people on whom to do the study? Job applicants or job incumbents?

Researchers argue that the best studies are those using predictive objective data and those sampling job incumbents. Objective data is better than subjective data because it avoids distortion. Predictive studies are best because that is how integrity tests are used: to attempt to predict behavior ahead of time. Job applicants are the best sample precisely because they are motivated to present themselves in the best possible light.

Miner and Capps (1996) provide a masterful review of reviews more positive than negative. They conclude, as others have, that it is quite possible to construct honesty/integrity tests and this has been done, but that it is essential to examine the validity evidence for each test. Yet, the controversy has not gone away – and probably will never – because the issue of using tests "goes beyond science into values: the very use of these tests infringes certain values and beliefs". Yet, they conclude: "we foresee a prosperous future for honesty testing. These tests serve a significant need. It is important that they be permitted to continue to serve that need, and we believe that society will have the good sense to let that happen" (p. 241).

Researchers have made extensive, critical and exhaustive reviews of integrity testing in organizations. Through a range of state-of-the-art statistical measures, they have concluded the following (Ones and Viswesvaran, 1998). They found them internally reliable and that they have very similar results (test-retest r =.80) on different occasions. They also looked at their validity for predicting job performance, CWBs, training success, accidents on the job and property damage. They noted that, although integrity tests were developed to predict theft, they can be used to predict much more widely.

Whereas personality psychologists want to emphasize personality trait prediction and correlates of CWBs, social psychologists want to stress how group, organizational and situational factors influence situations. Inevitably, the two interact. Related to this is whether the trait of integrity – if it exists – is immutable. Can it change over time as a consequence of experience?

As Fine *et al.* (2010: 73–4) pose in a new study, "Is good character good enough?":

> while many selection solutions assess personal variables among job applicants for predicting CWB very few of these solutions consider the effects of subsequent situational variables on these individuals, after they are hired. As a result, researchers and practitioners have been left with somewhat of an incomplete understanding for accurately predicting counterproductive behaviors in the workforce.

Their study aimed to describe how situational factors could model/rate the direct effects of integrity on CBWs. This study looked at three things: employee integrity, as measured by questionnaire; engagement (satisfaction, commitment, discretionary effort), as measured by questionnaire; and perception of security control norms (i.e. employees' understandings of what happens if they deviate from company policy and instruction).

The results were clear: for those with high integrity, neither their job engagement nor their perception of security norms had any effect on their CWBs. However, the case was quite different for those of low integrity. The more they were disengaged and the more they viewed security norms as weak, the more they committed CWBs. Fine *et al.* (2010: 81) conclude:

> The findings imply that these situational antecedents should be assessed and managed to help identify and minimize the risk of CWB, especially when integrity is low. In line with our expectations, high integrity seems to be a strong enough personal control to deter individuals from committing serious CWB, but that when this personal control is low, situational variables will influence behaviour.

Objections to integrity testing

Integrity testing techniques vary greatly in technology, if not in purpose. These can probably be broken down into three types:

1 *Physiologically-based assessments* like the polygraph/lie detector or those methods that seek to analyze voice stress patterns
2 *Behaviorally-based assessments* that look at visual and vocal concomitants of stress and deception like stuttering, nose touching and the like
3 *Self-report methods* based on an analysis of interviews (tape-recorded and transcribed), as well as by questionnaire.

They are, however, all based on the premise that response to questions about *past* attitudes, behaviors, values can be validly used to infer *future* levels of honesty. That is, that the score on a test (of whatever type) is able to predict a wide range of dishonest, illegal or unacceptable behaviors.

These tests naturally cause a great deal of interest and discussion. Some reject the idea of using them at all. Others object that they are of limited worth (validity) and frequently mislabel people. If tests were totally valid, people would be neatly and accurately categorized as honest or dishonest (given some cut-off score). But it is inevitable (as with our entire legal system) that guilty people are judged honest and, more importantly, vice versa. Some organizations argue that, even if the validity is not perfect, it may be better to reject a candidate who is honest, than let a dishonest person (or, indeed, many) join the organization. Most of the debate concerns the innocent labeled guilty, rather than the equally (or more) worrying situation of the dishonest being admitted to the workforce.

A *second* objection lies in the assumption that dishonesty is a stable characteristic of individuals. One side argues that dishonesty is primary a function of the individual – their personality, values, conscience – and therefore integrity tests are, in principle, useful. Others argue that honesty is much less stable and is a function of situational factors, like poor security, seeing others steal, being offered bribes. In this sense, people may be very honest in one situation and quite dishonest in another. Thus, some situations provoke dishonesty, others not. Equally, it could be argued that people are honest over some issues (their childhood, their leisure activities) but not others (tax and money issues, relationships and sex).

Over 80 years ago, psychologists found children seemed particularly variable in honesty behavior and a situational view presided. But later research and analysis of the data have shown stable individual differences in honesty. However, there remains sufficient substantial evidence to suggest that certain external and situational factors can aid in influencing honesty. This means that there are, inevitably, limits to what one can achieve with any integrity test, no matter of what kind.

A *third* objection is that, paradoxically, it is the more honest people that admit to dishonesty in the past. In this sense, tests are better at detecting "goodies" rather than "baddies". Tests assume that those who more freely admit dishonesty in the past are more likely to do so in the future, or that individuals who have relatively lenient attitudes toward wrongdoing may be more likely to violate laws and policies. Indeed, the opposite may apply.

A *fourth* objection is that cultural factors determine the meaning of honesty and dishonesty. A gift in one culture is a bribe in another. Traditional employment patterns in one society represent nepotism in another. The argument is that honesty and integrity are socially defined with no absolutes. Hence, it is wrong and unjust to judge a person by the dictates of a different national or, indeed, corporate culture. In short, integrity tests are culture-dependent.

A *fifth* objection is that some people do not know the difference between right and wrong. The law makes allowance for children and certain types of mental illness. The psychopath or sociopath is, in Victorian terminology, a moral imbecile, in the sense that they do (and cannot) distinguish between right and wrong. Tests – even the polygraph – will not detect them because they feel no guilt. The implication is that there are personality factors that are associated with wrongdoing.

Thus, integrity testing is controversial. However, there is comparatively little evidence that either job applicants or incumbents find them objectionable – in practice or in principle. Certainly, some people do indicate "principled dissent" to integrity testing, which is seen as non-job-related and an invasion of privacy. However, one study showed that, compared with non-drug users, drug users had stronger negative reactions to personality testing, overt integrity tests and urine analysis (Rosse *et al.*, 1996). One may be tempted to conclude that those who "protest too much" may be doing so for a good reason.

All forms of integrity testing are controversial. This is partly because of problems of misclassification. Thus, even if a test is 95% accurate (which is extremely unlikely), then, 5000 in every 100,000 would be misclassified. Further, the stigma of being classified "dishonest" (correctly or incorrectly) may have very enduring and negative consequences quite out of proportion with the initial "crime". The punishment (rejection) therefore does not fit the crime.

However, at the heart of the issue is another more important and more pervasive factor. It is this: research has shown that *honesty* is the single-most important quality that we rate in others. It is also (almost uniquely) one characteristic nobody rates themselves on as below average. It is therefore a very hot topic that has to be dealt with very sensitively. To accuse some of trait (that is, stable) dishonesty is, therefore, a very serious accusation that needs to be correct.

Reviewers (Sackett, 1994) have noted that several millions of integrity tests are administered to low-pay job entrants where employees have access to money or merchandise (financial services, retailing). The clear purpose: overt tests are most discussed which look at attitudes to dishonesty, as well as reports of dishonesty.

Public policy

In America in the 1980s, there were both inquiries and legislation concerning the lie detector. In the 1990s, the public, the media and politicians started to become interested in self-report integrity tests. By the early 1990s, 46 publishers and developers were identified that measured constructs like counter-productivity, honesty, job performance, integrity and reliability. Paradoxically, the integrity of integrity testers was questioned.

After the American Psychological Society published its report, many psychologists commented on it. Their reactions can be considered under various headings:

The jury is not out: tests are valid: Three researchers from different universities published a report that examined studies that were done on over half a million participants (Ones *et al.*, 1993, 1995). They note:

> Firstly, integrity tests predict supervisory ratings of overall job performance with a mean operational validity of .41. This is the predictive validity that is relevant when applicants are being selected. The operational validity of .41 for integrity tests for predicting overall job performance implies that integrity tests have higher validity than some of the more accepted forms of personnel selection, including

assessment centre ratings, biodata, and even mainstream personality inventories. In fact, integrity test validities for overall job performance are second only to the validities of ability tests, work sample tests, and job knowledge tests used in personnel selection.

Secondly, integrity tests predict non-self-report broad composites of counterproductive behaviours with operational validities of .39 and .29 (depending on the type of test).

Thirdly, integrity test validities generalise across tests, jobs, organizations, and settings. (p. 456)

They also believe that it is desirable for integrity tests to be broad-based. Further, they believe it is disingenuous to believe that test publishers' data are questionable.

Classification errors are not random: Some researchers claim that integrity tests do not mention morality but, more probably, conventionality, conformity and traditionalism (Lilienfeld *et al.*, 1995). In this sense, rather old-fashioned honest people can get systematically misclassified. Equally true, these tests have been shown to be highly susceptible to faking or work "coaching instructions".

Integrity, unlikability, is changeable/mutable: Just as criminals and delinquents can "go straight", and even make up for past sins, so those who score low on integrity can reform. But to penalize people for admissions of past misbehaviors condemns them to be "locked in" to their past (Lilienfeld *et al.*, 1995). Dim people cannot go smart but dishonest people can go straight and, of course, the honest can easily wander off "the straight and narrow".

Ability and personality tests do not confer value judgments or labels, whereas integrity tests do. Rieke and Guastello (1995) believe that, because the evidence for honesty tests is not compelling, they need to be particularly carefully regulated.

Measuring integrity

Situational judgment tests

Situational judgment tests (SJTs) have been used since the 1920s to measure "social intelligence"; "good judgment" and "wise decision-making". Though the tests differ in length, style and purpose, they are similar in that participants are given a number of *typical*, often problematic situations that they may encounter in their everyday work and a number of *plausible* responses or courses of action from which they are to choose. They are asked to select a response on either the likelihood that they personally would choose it (i.e. a particular response) or one that, in their judgment, would be the best/most efficacious response. There are many examples but the four presented in Example 7.2 will suffice.

Example 7.2   Examples of situational judgement tests

Scenario 1: You are facing a project deadline and are concerned that you may not complete the project by the time it is due. It is very important to your supervisor that you complete the project by the deadline. It is not possible to get anyone to help you with the work.

  i   Ask for an extension of the deadline.
  ii Let your supervisor know that you may not meet the deadline.
  iii Work as many hours as it takes to get the job done by the deadline.
  iv Explore different ways to do the work so it can be completed by the deadline. On the day it is due, hand in what you have done so far.
  v   Do the most critical parts of the project by the deadline and complete the remaining parts after the deadline
  vi Tell your supervisor that the deadline is unreasonable.
  vii Give your supervisor an update and express your concern about your ability to complete the project by the deadline
  viii Quit your job.

(Whetzel and McDaniel, 2009)

Scenario 2: You assigned a very high profile project to one of your project managers. The project is very complex and involves the coordination of several other project managers. During each of the project update meetings, your project manager indicates that everything is going as scheduled. Now, one week before the project is due, your project manager informs you that the project is less than 50% complete.

	Responses
A	Personally take over the project and meet with the customer to determine critical requirements.
B	Meet with the customer to extend the deadline. Talk with the project manager about how the lack of communication had jeopardized the company's relationship with the customer.
C	Fire the project manager and take over the project yourself.
D	Coach the project manager on how to handle the project more efficiently.
E	Do not assign any high profile jobs to this project manager in the future.

Scenario 3: You lead a project that requires specific, accurate data to make business decisions. The data-capturing methods currently being used do not provide you with the information you need. Another department promised to provide you with the information, but failed to do so at the last minute. This delayed your project and you are certain that you still require the information to complete your project accurately.

A	Do the time-consuming work yourself, even though it is technically not your responsibility.
B	Temporarily allocate some members of your team to capture the data.
C	Ask the customer for a deadline extension and explain that the other department failed to provide necessary information.
D	Ask your manager to pressure the other department to deliver the information

(McDaniel and Whetzel, 2003)

Scenario 4: You are under enormous pressure to accomplish your tasks on time. Yesterday, new trainees started in your department. They are unfamiliar with the workflow in your department. You have to interrupt your work to answer trainees' questions and to correct their mistakes. You are expected to do both, finish your work on time and to take care of the trainees. What would you do?

Least likely		Most likely
	I tell the trainees that I am available after work to answer their questions.	
	I openly say that I cannot take care of the trainees and work for better initial training of the trainees.	
	I sent the trainees to my colleagues when they have questions.	
	I try to get by without becoming stressed and worn out.	

(Bledow and Frese, 2009)

The central question for most researchers and practitioners is whether this sort of test has any advantage over other tests in this area. Many reviews and studies are very positive. Consider the following: "We conclude that situational judgement tests are a promising method for measuring personal initiative and may be a general means of improving the validity of measurement in organisations (Bledow and Frese, 2009: 229). Yet other researchers have pointed out that SJTs, like most self-measures, are susceptible to faking.

Video-based SJTs have been devised. Overall, these tests have proved to be reliable but there are questions around how they scored – based on some theory or expert judgments, or some other method. There are questions of what they really measure and some evidence to suggest they are, in fact, a reasonable measure of intelligence. There is some evidence that people can be sufficiently coached to take these tests.

The greatest concern has been with faking (Nguyen *et al.*, 2005). In a review of faking, Whetzel and McDaniel (2009) concluded thus:

In sum, these studies show mixed results regarding the fakability of SJTs. However, two general themes can be identified. First, people can fake. Consistently, people

Example 7.3   Examples from a situational judgment test to measure integrity

1   Your work team is in a meeting discussing how to sell a new product. Everyone seems to agree that the product should be offered to customers within the month. Your boss is all for this, and you know he does not like public disagreements. However, you have concerns because a recent report from the research department points to several potential safety problems with the product. Which of the following do you think you would most likely do?

   A   Try to understand why everyone else wants to offer the product to customers this month. Maybe your concerns are misplaced.   [-1]

   B   Voice your concerns with the product and explain why you believe the safety issues need to be addressed.   [1]

   C   Go along with what others want to do so that everyone feels good about the team.   [-1]

   D   Afterwards, talk with several other members of the team to see if they share your concerns.   [0]

8   You're a manager doing a performance evaluation for Jerry. Jerry has not performed well this year. He is mad because you gave him a rating of 3 ("met expectations") on quality of work, and he believes that he deserves a 5 ("exceeds expectations"). You believe the rating of 3 is fair and accurate, but Jerry threatens to go to your boss to complain. What would you most likely do?

   A   Tell Jerry to go to hell.   [-1]|

   B   Explain to Jerry why you gave him the rating that you did, but refuse to change your rating.   [1]

   C   Seek a compromise, such as giving Jerry a 4.   [-1]

   D   Schedule a meeting with your boss so that you and your boss can decide which rating is best.   [1]

10   You're a new clerk in a clothing store and are being trained by Angie, a veteran employee. She quietly tells you that because employees are paid minimum wage, most people sometimes take home clothes for themselves. Employees who don't are considered dumb and arrogant. At closing time, Angie hands you a scarf to take home. Which of the following would you most likely do?

   A   Take home the scarf and keep your mouth shut.   [-1]

   B   Take home the scarf, but return it to the shelf later without letting other employees see you.   [-1]

   C   Politely tell Angie that you don't need any more scarves.   [0]

   D   Tell Angie that you don't want to take home any clothes, now or ever.   [1]

> **19** A few days ago, one of your customers asked you when a certain shipment of your products would be delivered. You knew it would take at least two weeks until delivery, but to keep the customer from getting mad you told them it would be no more than one week. Had this actually happened, what would you be likely to do now?
>
> A   Let it go this time, but resolve not to do this again. Confide in several people you trust about what you did, and listen to their advice.   [0]
>
> B   Talk to shipping and see if they can get the shipment there in under two weeks. Make clear to them that it must arrive in under 10 days.   [-1]
>
> C   Call the customer back and tell them that you were mistaken and that the shipment will not arrive for at least two weeks.   [1]
>
> D   Understand that this sort of thing is necessary in business and that almost everyone knows that promises such as this might not be kept.   [-1]

instructed to fake can do so and to the extent that this changes the rank order of candidates in a high-stakes selection situation, this ability has serious implications for operational use of tests. Second, one may be able to reduce faking by using knowledge-based instructions. (e.g., what is the correct thing to do?, how effective is the behavior?)

What of the usefulness of SJTs to measure integrity? Becker (2005) devised a 20-item test. Example 7.3 presents four items from the test, together with the score you receive for each answer.

Becker tested engineers, production workers and service workers, and found evidence for the validity of his measures. Obviously, some of these items look highly naïve and fakable. However, in principle, this seems like a very useful avenue of research.

Upward reporting

Kaiser and Hogan (2010) found that people are usually "on their behaviour" when dealing with superiors but less so with subordinates. That is, they are "more themselves" when dealing with their staff. Hence, they conclude that subordinates upwards ratings are the best source of information about a manager's lack of integrity.

However, they do note that serious violations of integrity are rare (low base rate) and hard to see because they are usually covert rather than overt. They advise, therefore, that it may be helpful to ask employees not to rate what they see but, rather, in their opinion, the *likelihood* that a manager would engage in specific unethical behaviors. In this sense, they are measuring reputation. They argue that there is plenty of research that suggests people form reliable impressions of another person's trustworthiness and cooperativeness.

They note that management competence and incompetence is not the same as integrity or lack thereof; further, that the way we most often measure integrity often grossly underestimates the number of business people with "integrity issues". This is partly due to the fact that integrity is measured by self-report or "top-down" – that is, bosses make the ratings.

Others, too, have argued that still the best (most subtle, reliable, valid) way to measure a person's integrity is to look at their subordinates "estimates of the likelihood of a particular person they know and work with behaving badly".

Indeed, there is a well-established and validated measure for this called the Perceived Leader Integrity Scale. This was developed and validated by Craig and Gustafson (1998) and has proved useful ever since. Items cover issues such as whether respondents see their leader to be vengeful, vindictive, and hypocritical. It also looks as issues such as leaders' integrity, morality, and selfishness.

However, there are important issues associated with staff rating their boss on an ethical, or any other, issue.

There are clearly benefits:

▷ Subordinates tend to know their superior more than superiors know their subordinates. They see their bosses and know their moods, foibles and preferences; they know their adequacies, skills, strengths, limitations and things that they do and do not like doing. Anyone who had been managed by a number of bosses knows their idiosyncrasies of day-to-day management of tasks, individuals and groups. Being at the sharp end of his/her policies preferences, they are in a particularly privileged position to judge them.
▷ Because all subordinates rate their manager from a statistical point of view, these ratings tend to be more reliable – and the more subordinates who supply ratings, the better. Instead of the quirks and the biases of individual managers' ratings (some being over-lenient, others strict, some showing favoritism), the various ratings of the employees can be checked for their agreement in the ratings, and then converted so that (hopefully) they can be averaged into a representative, fair view. If the employees have very different views of their bosses (dividing into, say, two quite distinct groups) this can present problems, but represents very significant data that merit further investigation. Indeed, the patterns in the upwards feedback data are very revealing of managers' styles.
▷ Subordinates' ratings have more impact because it is more unusual to receive ratings by subordinates than by superiors. It is also surprising to bosses because, despite frequent protestations to the contrary, information flows down organizations more often, smoothly and comfortably than it flows up. So, when it flows up, it is quantitatively and quantitatively different.

However, there can be problems with this method. This can be observed by a "halo effect" or the over-use of mid-point ratings, where neither specific praise nor blame is given but, rather, bland, safe-ratings half-way up the scale are given.

▷ On the other hand, an anonymous rating might lead some employees to be extremely vindictive to a boss who, in the best interests of the company, is pushing his/her staff to do better. Individuals who attempt to "knife" their superior could easily be detected, however, because their ratings would be significantly different from (and much more negative) than their peers. But, if the whole subordinate group decides (justly or unjustly) to give consent and ally to give bad feedback, they can! Usually, however, consensually negative upwards feedback is a sure sign of poor management.

▷ There are also greater *costs* involved. More forms have to be processed (probably by computer program) than in the top-down method. Also, subordinates need to be given some later training on how (indeed, why) to rate individuals without falling into some of the well-known traps. Training courses, paperwork and computing software cost money.

Response latency

We know that lying takes time. Studies on verbal lies show that, while it is true that the research does not always support the idea, when people lie they take longer to respond. Certainly, it seems that people take longer when lying than telling the truth (Vrij, 2000). However, one reason for the conflicting evidence is associated with difficulty of measurement.

Response latency is reasonably easy to measure accurately via computer-administered questionnaires. It is not difficult to design a program that measures, in time, how long it takes to answer a question once it appears on the screen. Thus, it may take someone between three and six seconds to read a question and then think of the answer they decide to choose, be it a rating or choosing a particular response. Considerable work has gone on in the field, the early work being dominated by Holden (Holden and Hibbs, 1995). To prove their point, he got people to fake (sometimes good, other times bad) and compared their response latency to those asked not to fake. He showed that he achieved "hit rates" way above chance: often 66% vs. 33% or 75% vs. 50%.

In another more applied study, he got groups of students to complete a questionnaire online. Half (randomly selected) were told to respond accurately and honestly. The other half were given the following instructions (Holden and Hibbs, 1995: 365)

> Imagine that you are applying for a job. The job is a sensitive government position involving exposure to confidential material. As part of the application procedure, please complete the following personnel security survey. You wish, however, to respond so as to MAXIMISE YOUR CHANCES OF BEING HIRED. Therefore, do not necessarily answer the following statements

truthfully, but answer so that you WILL BE HIRED. FAKE this test so you will get the job. Although you may feel you would never represent yourself dishonestly, please try to do so for this study. However, BEWARE that the survey has certain features (WHICH YOU WANT TO AVOID) designed to detect "faking." Do your best to FAKE out the survey and get the job. All your responses are strictly CONFIDENTIAL. Please respond to all items even if some seem not applicable.

The results showed that it was possible to differentiate with 81.94% correct classification between those who were asked to respond honestly from those faking good.

The authors argue that response latency can therefore be used to detect faking. However, they are aware of the problems of these measures, as well as other factors that may influence the accuracy of latency. This includes things like the costs to the faker of being caught out, as well as the cost to the accuser of saying someone is lying.

Clearly, this is far from a "foolproof" method. Many factors – a person's personality, their awareness, as well as their integrity – influence the speed at which they answer questions verbally or on a computer-generated questionnaire. However, what is true is that this method can provide data that, in *addition* to other information, *could* indicate whether a person is lying.

CV checking and verification

Most organizations use application forms as part of the selection process. Further, most people have a curriculum vitae (CV) – or vita, as Americans call them. This is a short document of one or two pages, written by the individual, which gives "facts" about their life. It usually includes details about education, work experience, skills and hobbies, as well as their address and contact number. Some include demographic factors like age, marital status and family.

A central question is the veridicality of these documents. In other words, do people tell the truth on application forms and CVs. There are questions about what information is *omitted*, as opposed to what is a downright lie: that is, sins of omission, as opposed to commission. Some CVs have rather vague and often grand generalizations.

One report from a market-research company showed that around one fifth of the workforce confessed to "misleading" potential employers when applying for a job.

Given that many organizations place high emphasis on education, experience and skills as being important criteria at work, they often have to rely on the CV or application form as a major source of information to influence their decision.

As a consequence, there are now organizations – many of whom advertise on the web – that offer a CV verification or checking service. At the lowest (i.e. cheapest) level, someone will check out a person's current or previous address (through the electoral role), their highest educational qualification, their last two years of employment history, and details about a nominated referee.

The more you pay, the more information you can get checked. The fact that these "services" are growing so fast attests to the problem of "impression management" in CV writing.

There are many organizations that advertise for CV checking, integrity testing and pre-employment screening. They often maintain that it is too risky not to use screening of some sort or another. These are some of the benefits of these measures offered by one agency (in 2010, by the Warwickshire Investigative Agency).

▷ As an employer you are responsible for and have a duty of care to your current employees.
▷ You have a duty to protect stakeholder interests.
▷ Safeguard against employing illegal workers.
▷ As a business owner, you must protect your assets, both intellectual and physical.
▷ You reduce the risks associated with the "wrong people" infiltrating your business.
▷ You win effectively reduce staff turnover and the costs associated with costly employment marketing.
▷ You will protect your brand and business image.

The lie detector (polygraph)

The idea of having a reliable, physiologically-based way of catching liars has always appealed to people – more so in the twentieth century, with its love of science fiction. The appeal of physiology is that it is supposed that you cannot lie your way out of these tests. The polygraph (or lie detector) has been passionately discussed and debated over this period and scientists remain divided on the issue (Iacono and Lykken, 1997).

The earliest records of quasi lie detectors can be found in the ancient Hindu culture and the medieval church methods of finding the truth. Suspects were asked to chew various substances and then spit them out. The ease of spitting and glutinousness of the spittle reflected guilt. What these people had observed was that fear leads to saliva diminishing in volume and becoming viscid in consistency. Today, we would say that anxiety influences the activity of the autonomic nervous system that controls salivation.

In the nineteenth century, various scientists tried measuring other supposed physical concomitants of fear. These include the plethypmograph (which records pulse and blood pressure in a limb), finger-trembling, reaction time, word association and so on, all done while investigating suspects.

Lykken (1988) has reviewed the uses and abuses of the lie detector. He noted that William Marston, student of a famous American organizational psychologist at Harvard University, first coined the term "lie detector". He wrote a book, *The Lie Detector Test* published in 1938, but this was nearly 20 years after he first used the term and tried to publicize the machine. Marston was a publicist, not a scientist. It was a Californian police officer, John A. Larson – later a forensic psychiatrist – who started scientific work observing continuous measures of blood pressure and respiratory changes during interrogation. Larson wrote a book in 1932 which was, in essence, the first scholarly book on lying and lie detection. He was a skeptic to the end.

Two of his associates – Lee and Keeler, from the Berkley police force – took up the mantle. Lee developed a portable "field" polygraph and even a book for polygraph users, while Keeler developed his own portable machine, named after himself. Keeler moved to Chicago where he met others who were to proselytize this cause, including John Reid who also developed his own pseudonymous machine. Reid was a lawyer, who developed a College of Detection of Deception and new ideas regarding polygraphic interrogation.

Up until this period (World War II), the favored technique was the *R/I* (relevant/irrelevant questions) approach. This involves alternating between a mix of irrelevant and relevant questions; for example, "What day of the week is it?";"Who is Prime Minister?"; and "Where were you on the night in question?";"Did you know the victim?". It was a poor technique because the relevant questions could, and did, generate stress in the innocent.

Reid developed the Control Question Test, when subjects were asked questions like "Have you even stolen anything?", "Have you ever been late for an appointment?", "Have you ever taken credit for something you did not do?" If the questions were answered "No", it was highly likely that the subject was lying. Hence, one had a "base rate" measure or standard against which the really interesting questions could be asked. Reid also used what were called "guilt complex questions" to see how the subject behaved when questioned about a similar, utterly fictitious but related crime. This was a good control question. Reid also, very controversially, listed the typical behavioral symptoms of truthful vs. lying subjects.

People are asked neutral questions, relevant questions and control questions: the latter related to the crime but not referring to it. The main problem with the technique is that it is very different to devise plausible questions that would ensure the eliciting of stronger reactions in an innocent person than would be relevant to a question relating to the crime of which they had been accused (Bull, 1988).

Another American, Cleve Backster, introduced two important ideas. The first was the *zone of comparison* format, where only the totally adjacent relevant and control questions were compared to look for the person's reactivity over the course of the test. He also developed a scoring technique to score a person's relevant response over all channels and all repetitions of the same question to get a total score. The overall verdict is based entirely on the polygraphic record: not using case facts, behavior symptoms, and so on, and inevitably the polygraph examines pre-conceived ideas.

It was not until the 1960s that the lie detector emerged from the police forensic laboratory into the market place. Operators approached all sorts of companies, especially banks and rental stores, saying their machines could screen *job applicants* to determine whether their application forms were truthful and whether they had stolen from previous employers, ever used illegal drugs, had any outstanding debts, or had any undisclosed criminal records.

They also said that job incumbents could be effectively and efficiently screened for embezzlement, misappropriation of funds and theft. Soon, more than two million Americans were being tested every year. It was a multimillion dollar business. Further, some serious university-based researchers seemed to endorse the technique.

But, from the mid-1970s, various psychologists started serious investigations into the lie detector and all condemned it. In 1988, the Polygraph Protection Act prohibited American employers from requiring or requesting that employees be polygraphed. "Hundreds of journeymen polygraphers had to seek other employment and millions of citizens no longer had to face the humiliation of having their character vetted in an hour's time by some graduate of a six-week course in polygraphy" (Lykken, 1988: 37). However, in half of American states lie detector evidence can still be admitted. Polygraphs are now used throughout the world: Canada to Thailand, Israel to Taiwan, though their use is limited. The test is not used (at least, by the government) in the Netherlands and the UK.

According to Ekman (2001), over a million polygraph tests are still given every year in the United States. Private employers, criminal investigators, the federal government, and the Department of Defense are the big users.

How polygraphs work

The polygraph tries to measure autonomic nervous system activity by sensors attached to different parts of the body: chest, stomach, fingers. These sensors measure changes in breathing (depth and rate), cardiac activity (blood pressure) and perspiration. It is also possible to measure brain electrical activity (event-related potentials). The indicators only show physiological changes usually induced by emotion. The machine amplifies signals picked up from sensors put on specific parts of the body. It does not detect lies but, rather, physical changes that are results of specific emotions (fear, anger, guilt) but which are not clear. People are asked "hot" or relevant questions as well as "cool" or control questions. The assumption is that, for the innocent person, there is no physical difference in the way he/she responds to relevant and control questions.

Problems of individual differences arise, of course. Some people are more reactive than others. Drugs can be used to suppress autonomic nervous system activity and make any physiological recording inconclusive. More worryingly, people can be trained to defeat the test with a range of techniques. Tests would therefore not only be highly unreliable, but also counter-productive: alienating and misclassifying the innocent and letting the guilty get away scot-free.

The lie detector is still in use in three separate contexts: criminal investigation, security vetting and personnel selection. Some have argued the polygraph is worthless in selection because it can only speak to the past, not the future. But others argue that the past, indeed, predicts the future. There is much less research on pre-employment screening. Some argue the base rate of liars is too low to ever be accurate. Others suggest that the test causes a poor impression. However, some argue that taking the test, or being threatened they will have to take it, leads people to admitting important things they otherwise would not admit. Thus, a test can have utility even without accuracy.

Ekman (2001) contends that there are many important issues associated with the polygraph like:

▷ how the polygraph may be useful even if it is not accurate – that is, utility vs. accuracy.
▷ the base rate of lying – if there are very few liars in a group, the test may easily overestimate that number.
▷ the idea that the polygraph is a deterrent – that it may successfully reduce/inhibit lying, even if the procedure is faulty.

The validity of the lie detector

To be acceptable as a test, a lie detector (like any other devise) must minimally fulfill a number of criteria: *first*, there must be a standardized method of administration that is fully described, clear and repeatable. *Second*, there must be objective scoring; not subjective, based on personal-experience scoring. *Third*, there must be external valid criteria – it must be shown to differentiate between truth and lies.

Critics have noted the lie detector is not a test but an interrogation device because methods are semi-standardized, it requires clinical observation and validity data is poor (Lykken, 1988). Data on the lie detector comes from two sources: clinical case studies and experimental evidence.

It must be pointed out that, in "real life" cases, it is often very difficult to establish validity because many crimes are never solved and confession (often false) is the only real feedback. It is possible to use laboratory studies using students. But, as Lykken (1988: 84–5) observed, these also have problems.

Laboratory studies, however, have serious disadvantages for predicting lie detector accuracy in real-life criminal investigations.

1 The volunteer subjects are unlikely to be representative of criminal suspects in real life.
2 The volunteers may not feel a lifelike concern about mock crimes that they have been instructed to commit and about telling lies they are instructed to tell.
3 Compared to criminal suspects, who know they may be in real trouble should they fail the lie test, volunteers are unlikely to be as apprehensive about being tested, with respect to mock crimes for which they will not be punished, irrespective of the test's outcome.

4   The administration of the polygraph tests tends not to resemble the pro-
    cedures followed in real life. For example, unlike real-life tests, which are
    most often conducted well after the crime took place, laboratory subjects are
    typically tested immediately after they commit the mock crime. Moreover,
    in laboratory research, to make the study scientifically acceptable, there is
    an attempt to standardize the procedure (e.g. all subjects are asked identical
    questions), a factor that distinguishes these from real-life tests.

Most of the researchers in the field have tried to evaluate the more
widely-known methods of lie detection. The Control Question Technique
must emotionally arouse the innocent person with the control as much
as the crime-related questions, otherwise it makes an error. There is,
rightly, a tremendous concern with the innocent person being mislabeled
or judged guilty. This may easily occur in the nervous, anxious, person –
particularly if he/she believes polygraphs are fallible (which, of course,
they are) and when they can (often, relatively easily) detect the difference
between relevant and control questions. Innocent people might believe
the police/polygraph operators are fallible as are their machines, or that
they are unfair. Fearful, guilty, hostile, impulsive, volatile people react
badly to authority figures wiring them up. Their reactions may unfairly
condemn them. Further, an innocent person may be so unhappy or disturbed by a crime they did not do – but found the body, or knew the
victim – that they react physiologically dramatically, seeming to show
their guilt.

Vrij (2000) notes many criticisms of the Control Question Test.
The first is the possibility that innocent victims give larger physiological responses to control, rather than relevant, questions. The next is that
guilty suspects are not less concerned with control, rather than relevant,
questions. Further, examiners have to be experienced and subtle in the
choice and phrasing of the questions. It is easy to frighten, embarrass
and intimidate others, as well as to "leak" their own beliefs and suspicions non-verbally. Next, there is the judgment problem: how to interpret
the difference in responses to repress to control vs. relevant questions.
It depends not only on the size of the difference in response, but also
the base-rate: every individual that is a low-reactive person might show
the same absolute physical differences as a highly- reactive person but, in
effect, the former is much more dramatic than the latter. A related issue
is that scoring polygraph charts is still a "subjective art", rather than a
"precise science". Finally, there are ethical and legal problems in deceiving
people in some of the control questions.

The Guilty Knowledge Test, on the other hand, works on the assumption that the lie detector operator has information about the crime exclusive
to the guilty person (i.e. precisely how much was stolen; the denomination
of the notes). The idea is that, when questioned in detail, the guilty person
recognizes descriptions of events, objects, people linked to the crime, and
this rouses him/her, showing up on the polygraph recordings.

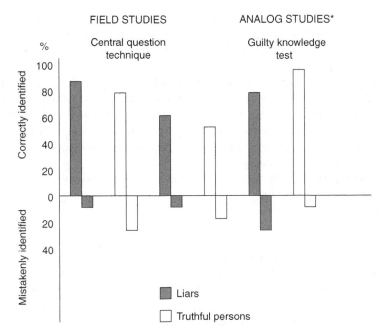

Note: The graph gives the averages, which are not always an accurate reflection of the range of research results. The ranges are as follows: for liars correctly identified in field studies, 71–99%; in analog studies using the control question technique, 35–100%; in analog studies using the guilty knowledge test, 61–95%. For truthful persons correctly identified: in field studies, 13–94%; in analog studies using the control question technique, 32–91%; in analog studies using the guilty knowledge test, 80–100%. For a truthful person incorrectly identified: in field studies, 0–75%; in analog studies using the control question technique, 2–51%; in analog studies using the guilty knowledge test, 0–12%. For liars correctly identified: in field studies, 0–29%: in analog studies using the control question technique, 0–29%; in analog studies using the guilty knowledge test, 5–39%.

Figure 7.1 **Polygraph accuracy**

Source: Miner and Capps (1996: 152–3).

Of course, it is not always easy to find appropriate questions and keep all details secret. Sometimes the criminal may not have noticed certain details that an innocent person at the scene of the crime might have. Problems arise in the questions, and a person may have guilty knowledge without being guilty. However, it is clear that experts in the area are much more likely to endorse the credibility of the Guilty Knowledge Test over the Controlled Question Test.

As noted, studies on the accuracy/validity of the polygraph can be categorized into two types: field studies of actual, real-life incidents; and analogue/experimental studies. Both have distinct advantages and disadvantages. There is actually a rarer type called "hybrid studies", where the researcher arranges for a crime to occur.

Ekman (2001) reviewed 30 studies: 10 field, 14 analogue, 6 hybrid. He concluded that accuracy was better in the field studies because there was more emotional arousal, less-educated people and less certainty about the ground truth. "Disbelieving-the-truth" mistakes and "believing-a-lie" mistakes are highest in the Guilty Knowledge Test. A figure originated by Ekman presenting his observations on the accuracy of polygraphs is given in Figure 7.1.

Ekman (2001) notes that some critics believe the figures underestimate accuracy, while some stress the precise opposite. He also believes more weight should be given to a test that shows innocence as an outcome, rather than lying. Further, even when a test suggests lying, this should only be used to pursue an investigation, rather than being enough evidence to proceed with a prosecution or a conviction.

Ekman (2001: 192) believes that one cannot properly evaluate the polygraph without understanding some fundamental concepts. Four are essential:

▷ the difference between *accuracy* and *utility* – how the polygraph might be useful even if it isn't accurate.
▷ the quest for *ground truth* – how hard it is to determine the accuracy of the polygraph without being absolutely certain who the liars are.
▷ *the base rate of lying* – how a very accurate test can produce many mistakes when the group of suspects includes very few liars.
▷ *deterring* lying – how the threat of being examined might inhibit some from lying, even if the examination procedure is faulty.

Vrij (2000) also reviewed various studies. Looking at laboratory studies of the Control Question Test, he found that 73% of guilty people and 66% of innocent people were correctly classified. Also, 9% of the guilty were judged innocent and 13% of the innocent falsely accused. Laboratory studies of the Guilty Knowledge Test were better: 96% of the innocent were correctly identified and only 4% falsely accused. Similarly, 82% of the guilty were correctly classified but 18% judged innocent.

A British evaluation

The British Psychological Society published a long edited book (Gale, 1988) called *The Polygraph Test: Lies, Truth and Science.*

The conclusion, stated at the beginning of the book, is a good example of British scientific diffidence and caution. On page 2 the editor writes "The truth is that we do not know the full truth about polygraphic lie-detection". Gale (1988) notes a little later: "Advances in science and technology are unlikely to leave our lives untouched, and the polygraph is no exception. The polygraph is a scientific instrument used for research into bodily responses and their relationships with psychological processes. As an instrument, it is reliable in producing a record of bodily events. However, this does not imply that the uses to which the polygraph might be put are also reliable. Some members of the British Psychological Society have expressed concern that the use of the polygraph for lie detection might reflect

Box 7.1   The Polygraph Test: Lies, Truth and Science

Field studies examining the accuracy of polygraph tests have shown that these tests (both CQTs and GKTs) make substantial numbers of mistakes. The proponents of the CQT test will probably argue that this conclusion is incorrect, and they will then refer to the accuracy scores obtained by original examiners in their field studies. The problem is that independent examiners were much less accurate. This suggests that extra, non-polygraph information, known to the original examiner but not to the independent evaluator, is essential for making an accurate decision. The accuracy of the test itself can only be reliably determined by using evaluators who have access solely to the test results, and their accuracy rates appeared to be less accurate.

Given the number of mistakes made in polygraph tests, I think that polygraph outcomes should not be allowed as a substantial piece of evidence in court... However, polygraph tests may make a valuable contribution to the detection of deceit. Polygraph outcomes might therefore be used as an additional piece of evidence in court (as long as more substantial evidence is presented as well), or as a tool in police investigations to eliminate potential suspects, to check the truthfulness of informants, or to examine contradictory statements of witnesses and suspects in the same case.

For this purpose, I prefer and advocate the use of the guilty knowledge polygraph tests. I do not do this for reasons of accuracy. Research has shown that Control Question Tests can be accurate, and their accuracy rates (at least in field studies) do exceed the accuracy rates of the guilty knowledge tests. I reject control question polygraph tests, because part of the procedure involves deceiving examinees. First, deception makes the test vulnerable, as people who read about a CQT will come to know, which will probably make the test less efficient. Secondly, in many countries the use of deception in criminal investigations is illegal. For example, in both the UK (the country where I work) and the Netherlands (my native country) it is illegal to lie to suspects in criminal investigations. This makes it illegal to conduct control question polygraph tests in these countries, and impossible to use the outcomes of such tests as evidence in criminal trials. This "deception is illegal" argument may be a typical European one.

Before guilty knowledge polygraph tests can be widely introduced in police investigations, several issues need to be clarified.

▶ More field studies with GKT are needed to test its accuracy. In these tests, the multiple perception of one item technique (asking about one detail several times) instead of the multiple item technique (asking about several details) might be worth testing, because this will probably improve the applicability of the test, as it is probably easier to design a test about one detail than a test about several details.

▶ It is important to ensure the quality of the polygraph examiners, as they have such an important role in polygraph testing. It might be a good idea to introduce university grades in polygraph testing, and only people with a "polygraph examination degree" would then be allowed to conduct tests.

▶ Polygraph tests should be carried out by institutions that are independent of the police force. There are several reasons to support this view. First, police officers often have pre-conceived ideas about the guilt of suspects, which

might influence the test. Secondly, police officers might make up polygraph outcomes in order to put suspects under pressure. This is not so likely to occur if
the tests are carried out by an independent organization. Thirdly, suspects may
distrust the police or may not have confidence in them. This may be particularly
so with regard to innocent suspects who are falsely accused by the police of
having committed a crime. It seems fair and reasonable that suspects should be
given an independent test.

It is necessary to check carefully confessions made by suspects after they have
failed a polygraph test. Polygraph tests may result in forced confessions, either
because suspects are going to believe that they have committed the crime...or
because they no longer see much opportunity to convince others of their innocence. (Gale, 1988: 205–7)

badly on its use in basic research. Criticism has also been made of the term "the
polygraph test", a misnomer which is said to give lie detection procedures some
respectability by their association with a scientific instrument". (p. 9)

The issue considered is the vexed question of various procedures, their
accuracy and validity; what we mean by truth and honesty, and whether,
indeed, the test measures it; what the test measures; whether the use of the
test will actually be useful and cost-effective in national security vetting and
the many legal and civil rights issues surrounding such tests.

Bull (1988) notes that the data are clear concerning the detection of lying
just by observation. It's difficult, highly unreliable and not easily trained.
One can, as Ekman (2001) has shown, never come to a final conclusion
from lie detector data on whether a person is lying or telling the truth. Bull
(1988), like all reviewers, was worried about misclassification – particularly
the innocent being judged guilty. All sorts of issues come into play: is the
person aware that they are lying; how valid do they believe the polygraph
to be; how good is the polygrapher? He concludes: "Until it is made absolutely clear on which forms of the testee's behaviours and responses, decisions about deceptions are based, there can be no proper scientific study of
the validity of the polygrapher's procedures" (Bull, 1988: 17–18).

Carroll (1988) did an early review on the accuracy of the polygraph based
on reliability (agreement between examiners; subject consistency across time)
and accuracy. He found both the reliability and validity data unconvincing,
and concluded thus:

If proponents wish to convince the scientific community of the merits of polygraph lie detection, I submit that they will have to develop a more convincing
case than the one currently on offer. Their case must be founded on studies which
include the necessary controls for non-polygraphic sources of information, that is,
studies which compare the accuracy of assessments derived from case-file material
and the subject's demeanour during questioning with that based on these sources
plus the polygraph record. I strongly suspect that such studies would confirm
what the available data suggest: that polygraph lie detection adds nothing positive
to conventional approaches to interrogation and assessment. (Carroll, 1988: 28)

In a very British, BBC and balanced way, the report allows the two famous American adversaries to describe and defend their position. In the pro-corner, Raskin (1988) – who addressed his essay thus, "Does science support polygraph testing?" – set about marshalling the pro-evidence. He concludes:

Careful consideration of the available evidence seems to indicate that there is scientific support for certain applications of polygraph techniques. Appropriate use of those techniques by qualified professionals in criminal investigation and forensic applications can achieve rates of accuracy that compare favourably with other forms of evidence, such as criminalistics, and are higher than common forms of evidence, such as eyewitness identification.

Polygraph testing can have serious problems of inaccuracy in the most common application, commercial pre-employment screening. That application most likely produces such high rates of error that tremendous social and personal damage results from its widespread use. There seems to be little scientific support for such uses of polygraphs.

Polygraph examinations in the context of national security programmes raise the most complex issues. Assessments of lifestyle and prior history produce problems similar to those that arise in commercial employment screening. The problems associated with low base rates of espionage in counter-intelligence contexts must be balanced against the need to identify spies because of the great security and monetary costs of failing to do so. Often, national security needs are pitted against the social and ethical needs of protecting individuals. Only the most careful programmes and techniques, coupled with research and development to minimize the errors, can help to reduce those problems. Ultimately, the future of government uses of polygraph methods will be determined by political and social considerations, hopefully enlightened by objective and thorough scientific evaluations. (Raskin, 1988: 109–10)

In the anti-corner, Lykken (1988) – a long-time opponent of the polygraph – presented, in equal measure, his analysis of the issue. Note how different his conclusion:

Unlike the fictional Pinocchio, we are not equipped with a distinctive physiological response that we emit involuntarily when, and only when, we lie. There are many reasons other than deception why a truthful person might show physiological disturbance in response to an accusatory question. Polygraphers cannot delude each innocent suspect into the belief that he or she has nothing to fear from the relevant questions but something important to fear from the "controls". The fact that one of several accusatory questions causes my heart to beat harder, my palms to sweat more, than the other questions do does not necessarily mean that I am guilty of that accusation. The assumptions on which the various forms of lie-detector test are based have only to be articulated to be seen to be implausible.

Many poorly designed badly controlled studies are to be found in the polygraph literature. The few relatively competent studies agree with each other and with what one might expect from the theory: polygraphic lie detection is wrong about one third of the time overall; it is seriously biased against the truthful subject; deceptive subjects with minimal coaching can deliberately produce augmented responses, undetected by the examiner, which will allow them to defeat at least one common type of lie test.

It seems to me that we must now acknowledge that this application of psychophysiology has been a failure; that polygraph lie detection does not and, in the foreseeable future, probably cannot work well enough to justify its continued use in the field. Polygraphic detection of guilty knowledge, based on entirely different and more plausible assumptions, has proved itself in the laboratory and deserves controlled study in the field of criminal investigation. (Lykken, 1988: 124–5)

Can you beat the lie detector? Essentially, there are two ways of doing this: physical or mental. Physical measures may involve self-inflicted pain (biting the tongue, kicking a drawing pin hidden in shoes; tensing and releasing muscles). Mental methods may include counting backwards and fantasizing. Physical measures are meant to give real, dramatic but misleading physiological responses picked up on the polygraph. The latter is meant to screen-out the questions, so making them indistinct. Studies have shown them equally effective, and there seems to be some evidence that people in security jobs are taught to use them effectively. But there are limitations. *First*, the person has to conceal carefully, precisely what they are doing. *Second*, it is harder to fake in the Guilty Knowledge Test than the Control Question Test.

Gudjonnson (1988) addressed the problem of how (best) to defeat the polygraph. This was his conclusion:

The use of different classes of counter-measures has been reported in the literature. The available evidence shows that mental counter-measures and the use of pharmacological substances (such as tranquilisers) are only moderately effective at best, whereas physical counter-measures can be highly effective under certain conditions. Two conditions appear important to the effective use of physical counter-measures. First, employing multiple counter-measures simultaneously improves the person's chances of defeating a polygraph test, at least as far as the control question technique is concerned. Second, physical counter-measures appear relatively ineffective unless people are given special training in their use. It is generally not sufficient merely to provide people with instructions about polygraph techniques and counter-measures.

Although there are clear individual differences in the ability to apply counter-measures effectively, training by experts in the use of physical counter-measures poses a potentially serious threat to the validity of polygraph techniques. For this reason it becomes very important that the use of counter-measures is readily identified by polygraph examiners. Unfortunately subtle and effective physical counter-measures are not readily observable without special expertise and equipment which are not generally available to field examiners. (Gudjonnson, 1988: 135–6)

It would, indeed, be naïve to believe there is a simple foolproof physiological method to detect deceit. Clearly, under certain circumstances the lie detector can be an extremely useful and impressive diagnostic. The worry, however, is the cost of misclassification – the innocent judged guilty and the guilty innocent. A reasonable question is that which asks for an alternative. In serious situations, where other material can be brought to bear in the decision, it seems reasonable at least to consider using the polygraph.

Increase in, or at least concern about, certain types of crime like sexual offences has led researchers to go back to the polygraph. Gannon *et al.* (2008) have looked again at what they call "polygraph-assisted risk assessment". They note that for *post-conviction*, polygraph testing can be seen as an excellent truth *facilitator*. That is, convicted offenders may say much more if polygraphed after being convicted, which may really help their treatment regimen. This allows for better risk assessment, which is particularly important in certain cases.

Conclusion

All people interested in selecting those whose integrity is fundamental to the job would like a simple, cheap, valid test that helped them *select in* those with integrity but *select out* those more likely to be compromised. They have an impressive choice ranging from simple questionnaires to new voice stress analyzers that may be used to analyze telephone calls.

The central issue for the researchers and the selector is validity. Any test that "labels" the guilty innocent, the psychopath full of integrity, or the deceiving employee a model worker has clearly failed in its primary duty. Equally – and, perhaps, more serious from both a morality and a libel point of view – is a test that erroneously judges the innocent guilty or those who do have integrity as not having it.

There are good tests and bad tests: those which have been properly devised and tested and those which are "quick-and-dirty" attempts to make publishers a great deal of money. Certainly, there are those implacably against tests and those who think they are useful. Looking at pen-and-paper tests, it seems the reviewers conclude they can be useful. The test results can usefully *aid* decision-making. That is, with test results and *other corroborative evidence* of guilt or innocence, it is possible to achieve significant improvement in the probability of detecting those who have commited, or will commit, CWBs.

Tests improve the *probability* of detection. Tests alone should never be relied upon to do this. This situation is even more the case with the polygraph, which has been very extensively tested. For some people, the idea of psychological – as opposed to self-report – responses is very attractive. It seems much harder to "beat the lie-detector" then come up as convincing on a questionnaire.

Yet, reviews have showed that, whatever technique is used, there are errors of classification. The optimist points to the overwhelming number of correct classifications, the pessimist to the errors – particularly those where the innocent are mislabeled. Again, used judiciously, and with supportive evidence, it seems that there are incidences where the polygraph may be useful. But this is more likely to be in the law court, rather than the office.

Many people who commit CWBs have no history of lack of integrity. They are often "pushed over the edge" by their work situation: the bullying boss, team pressure, clear inequity. But there are also those with a long history of disregard for the law, others' rights, and company property. There are correlates of integrity and these we can measure, and do so well. Those in the business of selection, then, need to consider carefully the issue of integrity testing and attempt a sensible route between rejection and naïve acceptance, if they want to select out those individuals likely to commit CWBs.

8   Protecting Your Assets

Introduction

Staff disillusionment and defiance is, at some time, almost inevitable. A head of research may go to the press and expose an environmentally damaging aspect of the company's work; an exchange floor dealer may cream off millions of dollars of profits; a medical researcher may claim a piece of work as original when it was stolen from someone else; a poison pen letter-writer may disrupt and reduce morale in the work force; an employee may put glass chips in baby food on sale on your shelves.

This chapter considers how to handle such incidents and how to minimize the damage they can do. A positive attitude to security from all employees in a company helps to reduce the incidence and impact of disloyalty.

How a company protects its knowledge, assets and secrets plays a significant part in creating its culture. Paradoxically, too heavy a hand, and productivity and loyalty will be significantly reduced. Excessive use of monitoring devices such as CCTV or physical searches, and staff will begin to feel they are not trusted, resentment may set in and opportunities to get back at the employer will be taken.

Security staff and departments rarely enjoy a good reputation in any organization. Security is expensive and it generates no profit – only substantial installation, maintenance and monitoring costs. Most companies recognize it can reduce the costs, but they would rather assign the subject to experts or consultants employed to conduct this rather seamy side of business. It is, however, a fact of business and corporate life.

If managers care about the fitness of the company, they cannot ignore the hygiene factors (i.e. quality of working environment), which contribute to a healthy corporate culture. Too much security or poorly applied rules stifle creativity and can infect the atmosphere with suspiciousness, even paranoia.

This chapter answers the following questions: How much is "enough security"? How to develop the right approach to security? Do strict security rules create the very distrust a company is seeking to avoid? Do all employees have to be treated in the same way? What specifically can a company do to protect its customers, investors, secrets and property? Will a company security policy formal document help and, if so, of what should it consist?

Issues around the security of property, computers and information will all be discussed in the context of: creating a positive attitude to security amongst employees, removing opportunities for mischief, handling miscreants who are discovered.

The chapter does not, however, provide detailed advice on specific physical security measures that might need to be deployed. Neither is it a comprehensive analysis of security measures needed to protect a company from all threats. Its focus is the people in the organization.

"Enough security"

It is much easier to put in a new security rule than it is to remove one. Creeping paralysis may well choke the organization; it takes a brave person to remove security rules. But the rules should be regularly reviewed, and with creativity as well as boldness. Further, it nearly always helps all the employees to be involved in making the rules and setting standards about security.

The objective should be to have "enough security" to protect the assets, material and non-material of an organization, but no more. The process starts with a risk and threat *assessment*. Properly done, this will identify those areas which need protection and the degree of protection required. Security experts and their consultants can do this, but the basic questions are very much the business of managers and the board, as well as individual employees. They have to make the important judgments about what are the critical areas.

The critical assets that need protection may include physical assets, including the property and offices. For many, the retention of key staff will be important. Others will identify customers, company reputation and investors.

This assessment also identifies the most likely threats to the assets. Table 8.1 illustrates the most common.

Each risk and threat will need different and proportionate measures. What follows will hopefully inform those who need to design a security policy the risks that need attention and how they might be tackled. By the end of the chapter, it will be possible to identify from a check list how to introduce "enough security" for each of the various risks and threats.

Detection

Many CWBs will go undetected, though some such as sabotage and whistle-blowing need, by their nature, publicity of some form. In all cases, the organization needs to ensure there is sufficient awareness amongst staff at all levels about the threats and what indicators to look for.

A policy of zero tolerance is needed, and the CEO has to be at the forefront of promoting that policy. Only then will staff feel comfortable about reporting suspicions and, with proper briefings, will know what to report and to whom.

At the time of writing, the incidence of CWBs is increasing. In part, this may be because organizations are having to cut costs and put more pressure on remaining staff.

In July 2010, BDO, one of the UK's largest accountancy firms, reported that fraud broke the £1 billion barrier in the first six months of 2010, almost

Table 8.1   Issues at risk

At risk	Internal threat or cause	External threat or cause
Buildings and fixed fittings	Sabotage	Vandalism
Staff resignations	Disillusion, bullying, failed expectations, new challenges, better pay	Head-hunters, seductive advertisements
Cash	Disaffected staff	Criminal individual or gangs breaking into property or taking advantage of absence
Company financial assets not held in cash	Criminal fraud with the advantage of insider information	Criminal fraud using insider information
Office consumables: e.g. stationery, printer cartridges, telephone calls, photocopier, furniture	Virtually every member of staff has access to this, and virtually everyone does it at some time in their career	Members of the public visiting and finding unprotected or easily stolen equipment
The company product itself: e.g. chocolates in a sweet factory, diamonds in a diamond mine	Employee theft	Retail shops suffer highly; criminals focus on small high value products
Research data on the company's new products	Disaffected staff	Competitors/consultants
Information about customers or clients	Disaffected staff	Competitors
Company reputation	Disaffected staff	Competitors

the same as for the whole of 2008. Simon Bevan, head of the Fraud Services Unit at BDO, believes that "as the recession continues we are starting to see the other side of the fraud equation, namely revenue dilution fraud. We are seeing companies where management commit fraud ... ." (http://www.bdo.uk.com).

This is echoed by PricewaterhouseCoopers (PwC) who, in their *Global Economic Crime Survey*, reported that the profile of the internal fraudster is changing rapidly:

Economic crimes committed by middle managers have risen very strongly, now accounting for 42% of all internal frauds, up from 26% in 2007"

...

The rise in frauds ... could be viewed in the context of increased financial pressures in the current economic climate and PWC go on to report that respondents to their questionnaires believe that crimes are committed to maintain living standards, with one in five believing that these crimes are committed by those jealous of higher earners whose compensation or bonuses were believed to be unfair. (PricewaterhouseCoopers, 2010)

The significance of this is twofold. *First*, as described elsewhere in this book, CWBs – and fraud, in particular – are on the increase; and, *second*, staff are a valuable source of information. In the UK in 2009, 21% of reported frauds were detected either because of internal tip off or by a whistle-blower. The full picture is shown in Figure 8.1.

The largest proportion of detection, taken together, is from the counter-formal fraud effort (fraud risk management, internal audit, law enforcement and corporate security), but these resources are under fire in the economic climate of the 2010s. Respondents to the PwC questionnaire reported that:

▷ Staff reductions have meant fewer resources are being deployed on internal controls.
▷ Internal audit is being asked to do more work with less staff, and that this has contributed to greater fraud risk.

(PricewaterhouseCoopers 2010)

The message from this is that companies and organizations need to increase their awareness programs and create an atmosphere not just of zero tolerance, but also where people feel able to report suspicious activity.

Where the CWB is not isolated to an individual and management suspect it is that the rotten apples are spreading, more intrusive methods may need to be employed to root out the corruption. The police have their "*Special Units*" which investigate internal corruption, and increasingly large

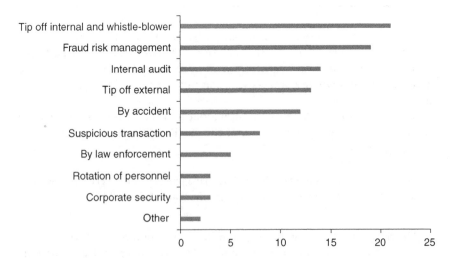

Figure 8.1   **Detection of reported frauds in percentages**

Source: Adapted from PricewaterhouseCoopers (2010).

companies are looking at ways of investigating internal crimes. Traditionally, they have three options:

1 to call in the police
2 to use their own security department
3 to ask an external company to investigate.

A fourth is beginning to emerge. Companies are setting up their own "Special Units" to conduct covert intelligence gathering, and analytical and investigation activities. These units, working within the law, recruit sources and deliver evidence to those who can then take action. Their activities are secret and only a few on the board may know of its existence. They need special accounting arrangements and many are run on the same basis as a small intelligence service.

Mostly, they are deployed where there is evidence of serious organized criminal activity. This usually means outside the company, but they need their insiders to pull off the bigger deals. These units are expensive, and there are potential risks if they are not run with strict ethical and professional codes.

Recruiting the right people

The recruitment criteria for staff often refer to the need for integrity, honesty, "impeccable character" and trustworthiness as essential qualities. Why do so many who fall short of these criteria get through the system? Is it possible to select out those who are dishonest? Can recruiters *select in* only the honest and reliable? Elsewhere in *Bad Apples* the issues of integrity testing and interviewing skills are discussed in some detail. From a security point of view, the recruitment of honest people who are not going to give secrets away, steal or commit sabotage is an *essential part* of maintaining the integrity of the company.

It is worth, however, pausing here to consider how best to probe at an interview, how to test someone's potential honesty. An interviewer might prepare an integrity question by identifying an incident when an employee had, in the past, not lived up to the standards of the organization – for example, the use of company credit cards. A question could be structured on the following basis:

> The rules state that employees may use a company credit card for personal use but must pay to the company outstanding personal balances in full at the end of every month. The company pays the credit card company independently. It is known that the accounts department does not check card repayments rigorously.

> It is December and you are short of cash for buying Christmas presents. You use the company card to pay for them. At the end of the month, when you get your

salary, you have insufficient funds to repay the debt and have no other credit cards available. What would you do in this situation?

(a) I would never use the company card for personal reasons – end of story (good)
(b) I would speak to my line manager and seek his or her advice on how I could repay the debt and interest later (good)
(c) I would go to the bank (or family or friends) and ask for a loan to pay the money I owed the company (average)
(d) I would save and pay the company at the end of January (poor)
(e) I would hope the debt would not be noticed, but if challenged would claim it was an oversight and pay as soon as possible (very poor).

Yet, the desirable answer to the question is blindingly obvious. A more subtle style of question would be to put the same situation to a candidate, but ask what he would do if he were the line manager who received the subordinate's admission that he could not pay the credit card debt. The responses of the line manager might be:

(a) The problem is a personal one for you to sort out. It's not my concern as your boss (average – the manager is effectively covering up a problem which might lead to dishonesty)
(b) How much is it – I will lend you the money to cover the debt (average)
(c) Don't worry – pay it next month, together with the interest – no one will ever notice (poor – condoning dishonesty)
(d) Speak to the accounts department and ask what can be done. Here is the number, let me know if you have any problems (average – the manager needs to ensure that the subordinate does report the incident)
(e) I would speak to accounts department and seek a solution (good).

The use of critical incidents in a structured interview needs training and diligence in preparing. Few staff are trained adequately in interviewing skills – a theme which is repeated often in this book.

Induction

The first few days in the office make a big impression on staff. They are usually apprehensive, excited and emotionally charged up. This is the moment that all trainers look for, when staff are at their most receptive. It is a great opportunity to put over messages about acceptable and desirable behavior. If, however, there is no clear message about security and related issues, and the new staff member is met by an indifferent attitude to security by their line manager, that impression will be carried forward and be difficult to change.

But how the message is delivered is also important. You can deliver the message well in one of three ways.

▷ *Give people new information*: what are the security regulations, what are the threats to the organization's security and what are the disciplinary procedures.
▷ *Give people new skills*: how to create and remember a new password, how to open a combination lock and how to set a security system.
▷ *Change people's attitude to issues*: they care about security, so they will not speak out loud the password or combination number, they will double-check their locks and clear their desks when they leave the office, they will set an example on security to newcomers to the office.

What should an induction program say about security and related insider threat issues? There is a difficult balance to achieve. On the one hand, there are some rules that need to be followed strictly, totally and always. But, to be effective, employees have to accept personal responsibility for security and be able to make judgment calls that rules cannot always predict. Employees need, therefore, to understand the security policy and what the organization is trying to protect.

Above all, induction is an opportunity to instill in the recruit feelings of loyalty and commitment, and to begin to establish the psychological contract. Skeats (1991: 91) contends that induction can engender "a feeling of belonging to a company [which] develops a commitment to organizational goals. The employer then maximises the contribution of the workforce and gets a faster return on investment". This is not to be confused with indoctrination, the blind or uncritical acceptance of company's policies and instructions. To be fully committed and loyal, staff need to feel they can contribute to the debate and question procedures. They should have an early opportunity to meet the top management who will become their role models.

> The head of training in a government department was having the usual sandwich lunch with new entrants on the second day of their induction. They were all a bit subdued and, when asked what presentations they had had that morning, they told him that it had all been about security. The lecturer had clearly been stern, and had certainly got her message over that security was important; but the new entrants were worried because she had implied the office listened in to all their mobile phone conversations, would certainly know when they transgressed, and the consequences would be grim.
>
> Some would argue that she had got her message over and changed their attitudes but, she had done so on the basis of fear and not understanding why security is important. Her problem was compounded because the implications she had made about the office listening in to telephone conversations was not true, and the new entrants would quickly find that out and so her whole message would be undermined.

Feedback

Does letting staff know the cost of theft/shrinkage have an effect? This, in part, depends on how accurate and reliable an organization's data on theft are. Obviously, it may not be possible to distinguish between external (customer) and internal (staff) theft, but figures suggest the latter is often much larger than the former.

One method is to give staff feedback on the "shrinkage" of particular items. One attempt proved more successful. Oliphant and Oliphant (2001) worked in an American chemist store and persuaded management to show, week by week, the total amount of money and items "missing" through shrinkage. After eight weeks, the store reported an 82% reduction in missing items and a 74% decrease in monetary good.

Owners of small (and large) businesses are often given advice about how to prevent (or, at least, reduce) CWBs in particular. None of the steps is surprising, but what is surprising is how infrequently they are done. The following are good recommendations:

▷ *Model good business ethics at the top.* Leaders and the top managers have to be role models in internal and external dealings. Having a widely trumpeted, official, corporate ethics policy and procedure is not enough. Expedient, blind-eye behavior has a trickle-down effect. Workers mirror managers' behavior. Start at the top.

▷ *Establish and communicate a clear policy.* On theft, fraud, sabotage etc. Many recommend zero tolerance and a default on sacking/termination. It may be helpful to have, in addition, a policy on alcohol and drug abuse, which can often lead to employee theft.

▷ Equally importantly, *make sure all policies are **uniformly** instituted and carried out.* This means no exceptions, which can be particularly problematic if there are many family members in the company or, indeed, it is a family firm. Favoritism breeds resentment, which soon leads to retaliation.

▷ *Put honesty and integrity firmly on the agenda when hiring.* Enquire about an applicant's history; check references, educational qualifications and criminal history.

▷ *Take all the financial control procedures seriously.* Restrict access to check books, cash and those who have authority to sign checks. Spread responsibility for financial issues among people. Have controlled and well-documented cash flow. Have regular spontaneous (i.e. unplanned) and independent auditors. Take large piles of cash to the bank regularly. Do the simple accounting stuff well – check invoices, payments and so on.

▷ *Consider financial support programs for staff.* If some people steal because they have financial problems, best get this out in the open and help them rather than wait until, out of desperation, they steal. Easier said than done – and with legal implications, but clearly worthwhile.

▷ *Act openly, immediately and decisively when faced with dishonesty.* This acts as a fine example to others. Do not prevaricate, dither or hide what is going on.

▷ *Make sure you act within the law.* Get and follow legal advice on procedures like dismissal. Where possible, obtain signed documents from employees admitting guilt and releasing the employer from all liability.

Need-to-know principle

This principle is one of the pillars of many civil service departments around the world and, increasingly, in companies. Where it applies, it should be introduced on day one of the induction course. It comes as no surprise, therefore, and employees' natural curiosity is, to some extent, controlled.

The beauty of the "need-to-know" principle is that it limits the information that has to be kept confidential, leaving most information to be freely exchanged. People can, therefore, have access to it if they need it in their work. The onus is on management to identify and justify why some information must be limited to only a few. If properly explained, particularly in the early days of their employment, staff will understand this readily enough and apply it. Many people do not want the burden of secrets and this principle releases them from the responsibility.

> A senior member of the UK civil service visited his daughter at her work. She was a secretary in a stock-broking firm. Having met the chairman and discussed business, and once the chairman had gone, the civil servant asked if (as a proud and interested father) he could see his daughter's office. She turned round and with great assurance and some aplomb, saying that would not be possible as he did not have clearance and it was the most sensitive area in the building. *But I have the highest clearance in the land,* he protested, being an ex-member of the Security Service. *Tough,* she said, *that doesn't count here!*
>
> Of course, she was right – there was no need for him to see or know anything about the business of the City.

However, a need to know principle applied insensitively can worsen the very problem it is trying to reduce (Davies, 2000: 56). If an employee needs to hide a problem, he could do so under the guise of need-to-know. Fewer people see the big picture and, therefore, fraud becomes easier to conceal. Need to know has a place in some organizations, but it should be applied in a balanced manner.

Password security

Passwords are everywhere: cash cards, email accounts, Internet banking, combination locks, computer logon procedures and many more. It is inevitable that people will take short cuts. It is impossible to remember them all and then to change them every six months.

The induction course is the ideal place to show people how to construct a strong password, and then how to remember it. Stories of people sharing computer passwords or writing them on pads near their PC are all too frequent. Just explaining the rules and telling people to follow them has little effect, if people are being asked to do something unreasonable. Any password system has to be simple as well as robust, and a little training will reduce the number of mistakes considerably.

Computers

The electronic age has brought many great advances and made many lives better. But it has also created a vast new set of problems for those with information to protect. For the paranoid, the PC represents unbounded opportunities to work out their condition. Even for the sensible but concerned managing director, the potential damage can seem overwhelming. Many find it too difficult to comprehend and give up or, ostrich-like, hope that it won't happen to them. Computer specialists are not always good at explaining the situation – some may deliberately do a bad job of it, to ensure their own indispensability or just to increase the size of their contract.

Examples of staff using company computers for nefarious purposes abound. It is not, however, too difficult to hold onto a few basic facts and to take appropriate action to protect the business.

The bad news:

> Everyone basically told us, *Software is a stupid thing to invest in because the assets walk out of the door at night.*
>
> (Ann Winblad, *Fortune*, October 1999)

▷ You can take vast quantities of information away on a CD or memory stick.
▷ They are easy to hide in a pocket or a bag.
▷ Information on laptops is particularly vulnerable, if the machine can be taken outside the office.
▷ Passwords provide comfort but little security unless properly administered and, even then, can often be broken by an internal hacker – your system administrator will be able to access all the company's information in the memory.
▷ If a PC is connected in any way to the Internet or other external information data machines, staff can send information outside without having to carry it away in their pocket or bag – any link to the Internet is inherently insecure.
▷ Staff can inadvertently send information to others not in the information loop.

The good news:

▷ Disc drives can easily be removed from a PC – this takes away one of the simplest methods of stealing information; an alternative method of backing up information may have to be provided.
▷ You can buy PCs that have removable hard discs (memory banks) – these can be locked away, so securing the information under lock and key.
▷ Laptops can easily be locked away to provide that extra protection, and their issue can be controlled.
▷ Passwords can be secure if staff change them regularly and know how to create them; better still, if they are given them and are trained to remember them or not to write them down in obvious places.

The bad outweighs the good, but it is not all doom and gloom. There will come a time when you will need to bring in a consultant or computer company to develop sophisticated IT and security systems. But, before calling in the consultant, consider the following:

▷ Identify who in your company has the sensitive information and who needs access to it.
▷ Ask whether their PCs really need to be linked to everyone else's in the company.
▷ Ask whether all the PCs need disc drives – if not, they can be removed from the PC or immobilized.
▷ Train staff in the use of passwords – they can provide some protection against the average computer user, but only if they are kept secret. Training should include how to memorize words, letters and numbers.

Where information can be held on a limited number of computers, consider using removable hard disc drives, so that they can be kept under lock and key. If the whole company has to have access to the same intranet and the information is really sensitive, consider buying a bespoke security package from a reputable software manufacturer. This limits access only to those who need the information, and it can also allow you to monitor who does access it. But training becomes even more important.

It is, however, all too easy to get carried away and to "worst case" the threat. A degree of proportionality is needed. Staff expect access to the Internet at work – indeed, managers expect them to use it. PCs are vulnerable, but the principles are not hard to understand. Managers should be able to influence what is needed and that is: enough, but no more.

Physical security

There are not many employers who can go to the lengths of searching staff as they leave their premises, though it may be done with those working with highly valuable objects such as jewels. The London and East India Dock Company at the beginning of the twentieth century, had no shortage of labor and could, and did, treat their workforce, most of which was casual anyway, without the consideration of today. The same is still true in diamond mining companies.

Less intrusive methods are becoming acceptable. Many government departments ask visitors to leave their mobile phones at the front desk, and some have random checks of staff bags. The purpose seems to be more about reminding honest staff that they should not take classified things home with them or to worry would be wrongdoers than it is to prevent them carrying anything out. More and more, what a person is bringing into an organization (rather than what a person is taking out of an organization) is perceived as an act requiring security cover.

We remain vigilant to the aircraft hijacker or bomber. Anyone traveling by air is used to having their luggage checked – quite often opened for inspection, and to being physically frisked. We accept that, but would we also accept similar treatment leaving the building in which we worked? It is unlikely. There may be some places where a physical check is acceptable but, to be effective in a normal office environment, it would have to be an intimate search. Floppy discs are easy to hide and papers, while less efficient, can be carried off easily enough.

Where, then, does an intrusive protection policy help an employer with staff who might physically remove company assets secrets? How far can an employer go, and is it effective? There are *three* things that an employer might want to prevent a member of staff from stealing: material items, cash, and information held on paper or in some electronic form. There is little that the employer can do to stop someone systematically taking information away in their head, however.

The larger the material item, the more difficult it is to hide and easier it is to detect. Diamond miners have an easier task of stealing than workers at a car manufacturer. Neither is impossible to perpetrate; neither is impossible to prevent. The problem for the employer becomes more difficult when the items leave the premises on company transport and are, therefore, under the control of the employee and not the employer.

Money can be easily removed from the petty cash or transferred to someone else's account, electronically or through the accounting and banking systems used by the company. Various methods have to be deployed to counter staff intent on such action. Some will be appropriate for you; others will not. Much depends on the threat assessment you made at the beginning.

Security officers at all exits

Security officers have the company's authority to stop people and ask them to open their bags, car boot or whatever. Their success relies largely on staff fearing a spot-check and being caught. Most people are not criminally minded and, while they might want to take out a half-used laser print cartridge or a few pens, they are likely to be discouraged by the fear of a search. The security officer must therefore do some unpredictable spot-searches. The number of exit points needs to be limited. This funnels staff through places where you can watch them more efficiently.

Security officers obviously need training. To search quickly and effectively is a skilled job; they also need to do it politely and with sensitivity. Too often, you see efficient security officers who create anger amongst staff because of the way they do their business: "I'm only doing my job" is not sufficient as a response. They may also get bored: they stop and search more to amuse themselves than catch others.

Companies are, at least partly, in the business of keeping staff happy. If spot-searches are necessary, then those being searched have to be treated with courtesy. The company needs to make it clear at recruitment this happens and remind staff regularly why it is necessary.

But we should be quite clear of the limitations of using searches at the exit points. At best, it is only going to find the casual and not very clever thief – and, even then, only a few of them. Their main purpose is to deter those who might be thinking about pinching stuff and who would do so if there were no checks. The truly determined pilferer will find a way around the security guard, who may be getting too expensive.

Electronic methods: closed circuit TV

Video cameras are now so sophisticated and so common that many of us have stopped noticing them. Others are carefully concealed so that we do not notice them. They peer at us in stores with their winking red lights, and some follow us around as we walk up and down the aisles. They can be used effectively inside the building, as well as at the exits. There is advantage to having them out. Staff feel they are being watched and therefore are reluctant to do anything wrong in front of them. The screens in the monitoring room do not, of course, have to be monitored all of the time. It is the fear of being caught and not knowing whether the CCTV cameras are on which is usually sufficient. Again, they are only likely to catch the amateur thief and to push the hard-core criminals into ever-more sophisticated methods, which will make your job that much more difficult.

CCTV *inside* the office is there principally for one reason and that is to monitor staff. This does not give an impression of trust; and that, in itself, generates feelings of resentment and can seriously undermine loyalty. Staff logic goes: if management does not trust its staff, then why should they show loyalty to the company. The argument can be taken too far and, with a proper communication policy to explain what you are doing, use of CCTV is possible. If not properly handled, the effect on staff of internal monitoring through CCTV can be negative.

It is possible to install more discreet cameras. These are more likely to catch people because they will assume they are not being watched but, come the day when you do catch someone, you will have to reveal your evidence. That means that staff will find out, which could cause even more problems for you.

Whether or not CCTV is discreet, companies have the problem of monitoring the screens. This means employing enough security officers to watch the TV screens and training them so they know what to look for and what to do, particularly if you are monitoring the screens in real time (i.e. as the action happens). Watching monitor recordings afterwards is a real bore, and catching the thief is unlikely.

X-ray machines can also be deployed at the exits to look for hardware items in bags leaving the building. If they are efficient and do not lead to the all too familiar queue at airports, they might just become part of the scenery and acceptable; but they are expensive and intrusive.

The gadget market is full of other electronic means to deploy. They include sophisticated software to track what employees are doing on their computers or telephones; using security cards not only to give people access to their office, but also to check their times in and out (a more sophisticated clocking-in system, but useful if staff are coming in and out at times when no one else will observe them in the office). It is possible to reduce the size of CCTV cameras so that they will not be spotted by employees. Locks can be fitted with devices to monitor how many times they have been opened.

Policing the police

Security officers have a hard job, and checking on staff is among the most thankless. Security staff are not high in a company's pecking order. Employers expect a great deal from them but give them limited status; they tend to be at the bottom of the pay scales and yet they are in charge of protecting valuable assets. The formula is not one that is likely to work out in the company's favor.

Security staff often feel they are undervalued – even despised. If so, they might not do their job well; or they might cause resentment in other staff, because they may anger other employees; or they will join the forces of evil and actually facilitate the misdemeanors. The answer is to ensure they are well-trained, properly managed and have adequate terms and conditions.

Employing physical methods to prevent the loss of material items can have a deterrent effect and may catch a few perpetrators. They are probably essential where the company has a high value product and employs relatively large numbers of staff who do not stay long with the company. The level of work the staff do is largely irrelevant; this can apply to rapidly changing staff in highly-paid sectors just as much as in the lower-paid areas.

Throughout, management has to communicate properly what they are doing and why it is necessary. The objective is to avoid innocent individuals feeling that they are not trusted. The measures are an unfortunate by-product of society, and most staff will understand that – so long as their own privacy is not invaded *unreasonably*. Proportionality and communication are the principles to guide managers.

Exit policy

Managing staff departures has a considerable impact on employees' perception of how the organization cares about people and is therefore of direct relevance to their loyalty. A well-administered but necessary and appropriate sacking need not lead to any resentment – sadness, probably, but not a feeling that the individual has been hard done by. When handled professionally, staff can leave expressing gratitude for the way they had been treated and expressing the view that this is the best option for both parties. This is discussed in greater detail in the next chapter, as it is more about developing loyalty than protecting assets.

The security department's concern is more short-term. Will the individual be taking with them secrets or goods of value to the company? Will they bad-mouth their previous employer, acting as a market terrorist? Some counsel asking departing staff (whether sacked or having resigned) to clear their desk immediately, under supervision, and then escorting them to the exit. This is hardly dignified and is likely only to make the individual more determined to pass on whatever information he has to competitors or others who may have an interest.

Clearly, however, there will be people intent on leaving with everything, and some may well attempt to sabotage their PCs if they really are feeling resentful or angry. Human resources and the security department have little choice then but to protect their assets in this very direct way. Wherever possible, staff should be treated with respect and allowed dignity – not just because it reduces the resentment they may feel, but also because other employees will be watching and the message that is sent out about how the company treats departing staff is easily transferred to how they treat people as a whole.

Anticipating trouble

A company can spend enormous sums of money putting in expensive electronic surveillance equipment and employing the best security guards, but it will be of little value if the managers are not sensitive to the causes and manifestations of problems in the first place. A manager's job is to maximize productivity by inspiring and supporting staff to greater efforts, and finding ever-more efficient methods of "delivering the goods". This effort, however, will be undermined if he is not able, at the same time, to spot the losses through pilfering, cheating or fraud. Neither will he or she be maximizing profits if staff are turning over at an unacceptable or sloppy rate.

What, then, should the company and its managers do to ensure they maximize the chances of discovering when trouble is brewing? There are five suggested "do"s for leaders and managers:

1   Set a good example – they need to be role models
2   Know their staff – take time to chat, be ready to talk football and opera
3   Know what to look for – be aware of the indicators of CWBs
4   Be skilled in interviewing – not just the formal one-to-one, but managed informal conversations as well
5   Establish clear and well-understood procedures for handling misdemeanors and those leaving.

If managers want their want staff to behave honestly, then their bosses must be seen to be honest and fair in their dealings. There are currently over a dozen American CEOs in prison convicted of high-level fraud. Not only do they have to show they themselves are not fiddling, but also they have to be seen to be earning their money. This can be demonstrated by increased profits, productivity and hard work. Many will see their managers working long hours. The very large earnings of some CEOs do raise questions in some staff minds, but it becomes a real problem when the company performs poorly under their stewardship. Staff will usually accede that the manager/CEO is new and has come in to sort out problems which everyone sees need to be addressed.

Managers need to know enough about their staff to be able to identify when their behavior changes, which might indicate a problem. We discuss below what to look for but they are only indicators and will vary for each individual (p. 243).

Neither should managers be unduly suspicious. If someone starts taking telephone calls and sounding embarrassed and putting the phone down quickly, this does not mean they are talking to a head-hunter or recruitment agency; they may be in the middle of a divorce, chatting to a new girlfriend or asking for medical results.

Managers need, at the very minimum, to be observant and to recognize the normal behavior patterns of their staff. Many can, and like to, go further – not for purely managerial reasons, but also because they are naturally interested in people and enjoy social contact at work. The problem can then become one of over-familiarity. It is much harder to take disciplinary action against those who are our friends. But that is a classic dilemma for the boss.

What, then, are the tell-tale signs which manifest themselves in staff whose loyalty and commitment is beginning to falter? Singer (1996) noted 12 danger signs that may indicate employees are embezzling from a company (Table 8.2).

Davies (2000) identifies 22 common indicators and risk factors when considering the potential for fraud in an organization (Table 8.3).

Table 8.2 Danger signs that may indicate embezzlement by employees

1	Rewriting records for the sake of "neatness"
2	Refusing to take vacations; never taking personal or sick days
3	Working overtime voluntarily and excessively, and refusing to release custody of records during the day
4	Unusually high standard of living, considering salary
5	Gambling in any form beyond ability to withstand losses
6	Refusal of promotion
7	Replying to questions with unreasonable explanations
8	Getting annoyed at reasonable questions
9	Inclination towards covering up inefficiencies and mistakes
10	Pronounced criticisms of others (to divert suspicion)
11	Frequent association with, and entertainment by, a member of supplier's staff
12	Excessive drinking or associating with questionable characters

According to Davies (2000) people commit fraud for a whole variety of reasons: pressure to perform (e.g. reach targets); personal pressures (gambling); the joy of beating the system (alienated hacker); greed, boredom and revenge. Fraudsters, he believes, come in four types: the boaster, the manipulator, the deceiver and the loner.

Davis (2000) clearly paints the picture of organizations that provide a fertile field for fraudsters. The downsized, de-layered organizations eager to outsource and in consistent flux and changes is typical where fraud occurs. A command and control organization with a blame culture and highly aggressive targets and a dysfunctional board is where fraud occurs most.

More generally, managers should look for these tendencies, which are often more difficult to spot in a busy office (Table 8.4).

In all the above, the emphasis is on *change* in behaviors. Dealing with the problem is the hardest. There are two essentials: the manager's ability, through discussion and interviewing, to find out what is happening or what has caused the change of behavior; and, that the manager follows the procedures for handling suspected misdemeanors.

Interviewing skills is a much-overlooked quality in managers. Most of us seem to reach positions of seniority in a company through impressing others. This puts a premium on talking and influencing. Of course, people listen to their bosses, and they are adept at picking up what the company wants from them. But they seem able to leap from an ability in those skills to an assumption that they are good at listening and elicitation (i.e.

Table 8.3 Common indicators and risk factors when considering the potential for fraud in an organization

1	Autocratic management style	12	Poor commitment to control
2	Mismatch of personality and status	13	No code of business ethics
3	Unusual behavior	14	Unquestioning obedience of staff
4	Illegal acts	15	Complex structures
5	Expensive lifestyles	16	Remote locations poorly supervised
6	Untaken holidays	17	Several firms of auditors
7	Poor quality staff	18	Poorly defined business strategy
8	Low morale	19	Profits well in excess of industry norms
9	High staff turnover	20	Mismatch between growth and systems development
10	Compensation tied to performance	21	Poor reputation
11	Results at any cost	22	Liquidity problems

Table 8.4 Signs of potential for fraud

Unusual absences	Frequent sick days, or unexpected half-days taken because of some minor crisis at home can indicate that the staff member has something else on their mind.
Longer lunch hours	Coming in late and leaving early can also indicate a distraction.
Refusal to share work	A refusal to let others share work or determination to keep an aspect of work exclusively to themselves might mean that they have something to hide, or that they want to keep this valuable access to information exclusively to themselves.
Change in personal habits	A change in personal habits or appearing permanently tired can show that the individual has a problem.
Increased use of phone	A change in their telephone habits or a long time spent with friends in the office can indicate a lessening of commitment.
Unusual wealth	Employees with new and unexplained material goods may well be funding this through the company.

interviewing) –assuming they believe it has any relevance at all in their work. But managers have to do it all the time, whether it is at the recruitment stage or during an appraisal interview, however formal the system employed by the company. The authors posit the view that most managers think they are good interviewers – but that most are not. They ask low-yield questions, seem lacking in insight and rarely correctly process the answers. Hence, the data show that interviews have very poor reliability.

An interview is held for one or more of three reasons: to pass on information, to extract information, or to influence an individual. In a good appraisal interview, all three motives are usually there.

When dealing with the early stages of handling a potential problem, the manager should mostly be in listening mode – and that is where so many managers fail. Without giving the person a chance to explain properly what is happening, there is no chance of progress. The manager has to do more, however; he or she has to probe further and find out what else might lie behind the manifestations of the problem. The real skill is about listening.

Such a practical skill is hard to teach through reading, and it is beyond the scope of this book. There are many good courses available to help develop good interviewing skills. The good news is that they are not hard to learn; neither do they take much time to acquire. A few days' learning how to interview properly is an investment well worth making.

Finally, managers should consider the following:

▷ *Ensure everybody in the organization takes at least two weeks leave in one break*: Many fraud cases are discovered when the perpetrators are away and someone else *has* to do their work.
▷ *Meet the family*: Include wives, husbands and children in some company social gatherings. It is, in any case, a good thing to do to further loyalty. If family feel they are included and can benefit from some of the company's largesse, they will encourage the breadwinner to stay. But it also gives the manager a chance to see if there are any seeds of discontent amongst close relatives.
▷ *Find ways to encourage staff to report to managers*: When they see wrong-doings amongst their colleagues. This may mean establishing a confidential or anonymous reporting procedure.
▷ *A good exit policy has a number of features*: Although there are some common elements, there are differences depending on whether you are asking the individual(s) to leave or whether they are resigning of their own accord.

Handling the press

When news of a security calamity (fraud, whistle-blowing, sabotage) breaks, the two most common responses are to blame the culprit or to say nothing. The former approach involves a company spokesperson saying that the company can hardly be held responsible for the problem, as it was either the culprit's malicious or illegal activity. Some may be tempted to assign a cause such as revenge or greed. This approach, however, is guaranteed to goad the individual into becoming more determined – and possibly more litigious. It will also paint a picture of the organization as being hard, unsympathetic and uncaring; the precise opposite of the "we care about our employees" image that most like to portray. Observers may also be tempted to ask whether there might be a problem inside the organization.

The second approach is to preserve a determined silence: the "no comments" option. The company lawyer, fearful of admitting any responsibility, may advise the public relations department to stay quiet. This strategy may seriously backfire. Imagine what the investigative media do when faced with silent public relations people and senior management. They hunt for a talkative secretary or a garrulous security guard – flattered by media attention, and more than happy to comment. The media may simply interview staff leaving the plant or office, and finding the angry, alienated employee who slates the company's management practices is an easy task. The media like to unroll a crisis, to keep a "human interest" story alive for as long as possible. These creeping crises are often more damaging than a "one-off" disaster. Seeing a company duck and dive, refuse to admit responsibility and appear callous about its victims leads to a true public relations disaster.

Organizations must learn they can only control that which they manage. They need to be prepared for what follows. What the public want to know is what happened and why, whose fault it was, when the company first thought it might happen, what they did immediately it did happen, and what they are doing now. In other words, they want to know the full story of the incident. They also want to know that it definitely will not happen again. Finally, they need to be convinced why they should trust the company again.

Conclusion

To be effective, the security department has to be embraced by all and respected by all. This is an area where there are no separate rules or procedures for top management. They have to follow the rules, as they have more sensitive information or access to assets than anyone else in the company, but they also have to walk the difficult tightrope of being human and recognizing that people do make mistakes and should not be punished. Above all else, a security department has to be approachable.

The following provides a basis for organizations to make a security health check:

Security policy: The starting point is a risk assessment: what really needs protection and who has access to it; limit sensitive information to those who need to know.

Induction:

▷ Reinforce messages of security standards during first few days of a new-comer's time in the office when they are at their most receptive.

Computers:

▷ Does everyone need access to disc drives?
▷ Does every computer have to be connected to the intranet/Internet?
▷ Train staff in use of memory for passwords.
▷ Consider locking up the most sensitive hard drives/PCs.
▷ Consider a reputable software company who could provide a system for you. But remember proportionality.

Physical security:

▷ Deploy guards at exits, but train them in how to do their job and to do it with charm.
▷ Funnel staff through a limited number of exits.
▷ Be aware of its limited value – largely deterrence.
▷ Police the police – treat the security officers well.
▷ Communicate to staff why it is necessary.

Exit policy:

▷ Treat staff with dignity and respect as they leave.

Management awareness:

▷ Set a good example and model desired behaviors.
▷ Know staff and use the appraisal process to understand their needs and concerns.
▷ Know what to look for when considering CWBs.
▷ Skill them in interviewing techniques.
▷ Clear procedures in handling misdemeanors.

9 Developing Loyalty and Commitment

Introduction

In Chapter 3, we broke down the factors which could stimulate CWBs into three groups: individual traits, the relationship between the individual and the employer, and external influences. In this chapter, we discuss what an employer can do to reduce the chances of CWBs by building a strategy which will develop in the workforce the CWB antidote: loyalty and commitment.

> *I walk into all these organizations, and I'm always puzzled when I realize that people still want to be there. Most people really want to love their organizations. We need that level of commitment ... Yet organizations have done very little to deserve that kind of staying-power.*
>
> (Margaret Wheatley, one of America's most sought-after and influential management philosophers, to Scott London, US national public radio series *Insight and Outlook*, January 1997)

Risk assessment

While there is plenty of literature on each CWB and how to manage it, there is little that describes *which* CWB is likely to hit an organization, *where* and *when* – if any at all. The logical place to start is to assess the risks. A risk assessment requires someone to look at the various threats, assess the likely motives of those who might want to conduct a CWB, judge the vulnerability of the organization and then to assess the likely impact of a CWB.

The whole point of a risk assessment is to make a judgment about *where* the negative impact of a CWB is likely to be high, and focus on that area to ensure the vulnerabilities are minimized. The alternatives are to spend too much money on protection, or to do nothing and wait for the worst to happen.

In a gold mine, it is clear that the metal was processed and that an ingot is highly desirable and a high target for thieves. The vault is likely, therefore, to be heavily strengthened and guarded. But where, after that, is the thief likely to hit? The mining operation itself will give the would-be thief plenty of opportunity to steal unprocessed chunks of gold, but might it be easier to steal and sell the vast quantities of diesel which the mine needs to dig and transport the gold?

In a pharmaceutical company, the high-value products might be the drugs produced. They are usually small in size and easily stolen, but the greater prize for competitors and insiders may well be the intellectual property which is held in the laboratories, particularly for the new products.

Towards a strategy

Davies (2000) urged those concerned with fraud to adopt a counter-fraud strategy by pulling together all the measures which a company should have in place to combat fraud. Many of these were discussed and identified in Chapter 8.

Table 9.1 Counter corruption practices in the police forces

Corruption is an *institutional failure*	Abandon the thought that corruption is an individual failure. Prevention and tackling corruption is about organizational cultural change.
Leadership	One of the most crucial factors is *leadership*. Not a disciplinarian or moralist person, but one who is a professional and a role model. The need is not just for the Chief Constable to be a role model but also top management – there needs to be a genuine culture of accountability.
Supervision	The first line of supervision is the first line of anti-corruption. The supervisor has to feel supported from above.
Risk assessment	Deviance and corruption in policing is a permanent occupational hazard, yet it tends to occur in highly predictable areas.
Red flags	Enquiries in any kind of disaster, from Pearl Harbor to 9/11, are littered with evidence about "indicators" – awareness by some that something was happening even if they did not know what. Organizations need to be in alert mode.
Somewhere to go	Employees need somewhere to go so they can report suspicions or concerns without fear of ostracization or worse from peers and perpetrators.
Special squads	In police forces, the history of the special squad is not illustrious – too many have fallen into corruption as well. But where they are effective, the public is unlikely to hear about them – their work has to be undercover. Such units can be set up in other industries.

Punch (2009: 239) recognizes that, while there are many sources to help write a counter-corruption strategy, the reality is that little will happen:

> Diverse agencies also offer seminars about combating corruption. These usually end up with the classroom walls enthusiastically covered with sheets of analysis and recommendations; but after this "revivalist" Sunday surge there is the return to reality on Monday and little happens.

He does, however, go on to offer advice on what should constitute a counter-corruption practice in the police forces. Table 9.1 presents practices that, amongst others, he identifies as important.

The list is applicable to most other professions and organizations. Indeed, they represent the kind of advice which is offered by many "Good Management and Leadership" books.

CWBs are conducted by people, and any strategy to combat them has to do with people – the emphasis in any policy to counter CWBs has to focus on management and leadership. In earlier chapters, we have discussed motivations stemming from perceived and real resentment. There is no doubt that poor management leads to CWBs in one form or another.

There are four critical areas for organizations to address as they build a strategy to reduce the incidence and cope with CWBs (Figure 9.1).

Values and standards

Codes and rules

Many organizations have a statement on values and standards, sometimes described as an ethical code. They also write vision, mission and ethical code statements which they may broadcast – as much for public relations as serious implementation. Some create simple but important *codes of behavior*, which are somewhere between rule books and etiquette books.

The emphasis is often on the positive, designed to encourage teamwork, professionalism, drive and other qualities to ensure customer satisfaction, productivity and, no doubt, profit – though that is rarely mentioned in such statements. The idea of some of these books and codes is to clarify standards and codes of behavior. They are about the behavioral "do"s and "don't"s.

There may be reluctance, however, to dwell on some of the negative issues, like the policy of theft, lateness for work and so on, though some organizations willingly and probably correctly do this. It is not inspiring to remind people not to take what is not theirs or to pass on unauthorized information.

Staff do need to know, however, *what is and what is not acceptable*. The rule book may exist somewhere, but it has to be accessible and readable. The main themes are clear and easily repeated. Organizations like to have

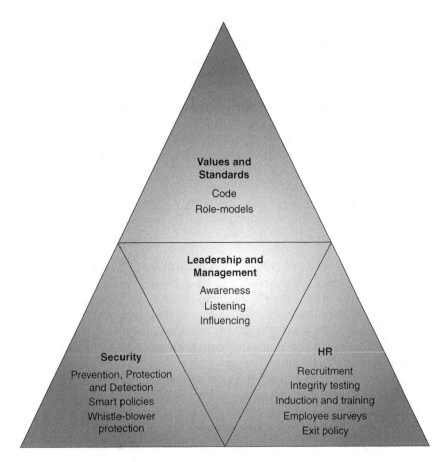

Figure 9.1 **A strategy for managers**

a catchy phrase, preferably alliterative. The danger is that it becomes too catchy and is therefore easily dismissed as part of the decoration.

At worst, the values and standards information is tediously dull, written in legalese, never properly disseminated, never read and generally reviled. The document is often given to a bewildered and overwhelmed newcomer who never reads it.

It is important that everyone knows and agrees to policies aimed at the "Insider threat" – that is, what the policy is with regard to fraud, malicious whistle-blowing and so on. It is best that these rules are regularly revised; also that representatives of various parts of the organization take part in their re-drafting, and take responsibility for their subsequent dissemination.

The British Army produced a pamphlet "Value and Standards of the British Army" (British Army, 2008). As to be expected in such a document, it is big on the positive qualities expected of soldiers and their commanders; but it is also uncompromising when describing what it expects of its staff as far as passing on unauthorized information and fraud, as well as abuse of drugs and alcohol. There is no doubt about what is and what is not acceptable. And, equally importantly, the message is not just for the soldiers but also for their commanders – in business language "their managers":

> Commanders create their command ethos and must ensure that Values and Standards are at the centre of it, through personal example and by educating and training their subordinates. The responsibility of commanders to be at the heart of this process cannot be delegated, and I hold you all accountable for it. (British Army, 2008)

Davies (2000: 257) puts values and ethics at the centre of his strategy against fraud: Organizations which successfully promote high standards of ethical conduct have a lower incidence of fraud and find out about fraud incidents earlier.

Davies further explained the need for clarity in areas which might be ambiguous. The distinction between a "facilitating payment" and a "bribe" is important. The first is usually acceptable; the latter, definitely not. The distinction becomes more important when dealing with different cultures where deals cannot be made without the use of agents who act as an intermediary between those in government (sometimes members of a Royal family) and British officials and business people.

In brief, an organization needs a clear and detailed description of its values and standards written in a style which is readable, inspiring and contains sufficient detail to be an effective guide. The values and rules need to be conspicuously followed openly and consistently.

Role models

Leaders and managers are ideally "beyond criticism", ethically. Otherwise, they are all too easily seen as hypocrites, not practicing what they preach and bringing the whole system into disrepute.

It does not take long in discussions about integrity with members of the Special Forces before the issue of writing books becomes a hot topic. Andy McNab (author of *Bravo Two-Zero*) may have made a fortune and no longer be held in great regard by those in the forces, yet, the real invective is for General Peter de la Billiere, who wrote extensively about his SAS career shortly after he left the army. If the General can write about such hitherto secret events so publicly, then why not the soldiers.

British ministers, opposition leaders and MPs were hounded in 2009 by the British press because they were guilty of corrupt or questionable financial practices. It is important, because they are in a position of trust and power; they set the example and, if it is acceptable for them to claim expenses which are personal rather than for professional services, then why should the rest of us not fiddle our expenses.

Perception is all important. Senior civil servants might want to combine an overseas visit with their partner. They may be scrupulous about paying for all the extra costs themselves, but they need to work the rumor mill as well.

Security processes

Prevention, protection, detection and deterrence

Security in most organizations is a fact of modern life, and people increasingly accept it as necessary. Entry passes, special access cards, random searches and password rules are commonplace. Security departments have to devise ever-smarter policies to defeat the determined worker (or outsider) who is trying to commit crime.

It is important, however, that employees see that security is the same for all, appropriate, taken seriously, and that the protective measures are good. This will ensure the opportunist will not take advantage just because it was easy.

How security departments explain their actions is, however, a feature which is not given much attention. A new device is installed or edict issued, often without much explanation. Some will accept them, but some will ignore them if they can, and some will be irritated. Few will be able to explain their importance to newcomers or visitors.

Security departments should work towards employees understanding the reasons *why* changes in security procedures have been introduced. It is the same for any significant change in a company should there be a change management procedure. The principles are simple and applicable to everything:

▷ Clear explanations (briefings) to all involved.
▷ Consultation with representatives of groups involved.
▷ Consistent implementation of the system.
▷ Modeling of the desirable behaviors, particularly by senior managers.

Whistle-blower protection

Whistle-blowing was discussed earlier as a potential threat to an organization – the whistle-blower using some wrong (possible correctly) in the organization to seek revenge for a management misdemeanor.

But whistle-blowers have their uses and, if their energies can be channeled within the organization, they can be enormously valuable. Every organization therefore needs an open, clear, whistle-blower policy. People with information about an internal wrong should be able to report on it without fear of reprisal or public exposure.

Human resources

Recruitment

Many companies rely on agencies, head-hunters or referrals from staff or others to identify potential candidates, particularly for very senior jobs. This may produce good results, but only if the recruiters know exactly what they are looking for to *select in* and *select out* candidates. Regular, detailed, explicit briefings are a pre-requisite; but good feedback on the referrals is also important. When they have put up someone who has fallen significantly below the standards required, the referees need to know. Where they get it right, they should also be told.

Where the company is large and there are many applicants, the initial recruitment procedures (sifting applications, preliminary interviews, initial security/identity checks conducted) can safely be outsourced to a properly briefed agency or consultancy. There should be sufficient evidence to produce a reliable short-list of suitable candidates, with most of those who might be disloyal sifted out. But from here on, employers need to involve people from the company; and not just those in human resources. Ideally, they should – for very senior, specialized or important security jobs – call in experts (i.e. psychologists who really know what they are looking for and, more importantly, indicators of "trouble").

Staff who are working in the areas where new recruits might be working or with whom new recruits can identify are an important asset at this stage of the recruitment process. These are the people who know what is required in the job and the sort of people who best fit in. They are also the people who the candidates need to meet, if they are to make an informed judgment about the company and whether it is the sort of place they want to work.

The administration of any interviews can still be outsourced or monitored by human resources to ensure appropriate recruitment standards are maintained, but the interviewing skills required are not hard to acquire. The advantages are considerable and worth the investment. Interviewing skills are an essential part of any manager's job, and training in them is rarely money wasted ... if done properly.

It is worth always bearing in mind that the selection interview is probably the first contact a person has with an organization. There is a lot of research on perceptions of fairness of the interview/process itself. In this sense, coping with insider threats starts very early on – even before people have actually joined the organization.

Selecting out potential bad apples

Chapter 6 addressed, in some detail, integrity testing – the basis of identifying those who may commit CWBs. Integrity testing is an important part of any strategy to reduce the incidence of CWBs.

Box 9.1   Essential loyalty checklist – How well does your company do?

1   Does the advert reflect the real values and actual work of the company?

2   Does the application form seek salient information which will inform the recruiters about all aspects of the candidate?

3   Are referees followed up by phone?

4   Are qualifications and other claims on the application form checked?

5   Where the recruitment process is outsourced, are they properly and regularly briefed in detail?

6   Are line managers introduced into the recruitment process early enough?

7   Are all recruiters properly trained/skilled for the purposes of the job?

8   Do candidates have enough opportunity to assess the company? Does the "interview" really present candidates with the full picture of the job?

9   Is the assessment centre designed to probe candidates' skills, motives and qualities in the areas important to your company, or is it off the shelf?

10   How rigorous are the checks on candidates' history and personality?

11   Is there someone on the panel who can interpret for the others the results of any personality tests?

Recruitment generally focuses on the positive; looking at the competencies and the extent to which candidates match those competencies. Much less frequently, there is a concerted effort to look for what the organization *does not want* in its employees.

Increasingly, candidates sit personality tests and these are used to help the recruiters assess what the person is like. They are used to assess a candidate's competencies as a team-player, his or her ability to get on with others, and curiosity. Recently, the psychometric test has become more sophisticated and of proven reliability.

There is now a body of academic literature which analyses the predictive validity of the "big five" traits with respect to CWBs. Bolton *et al.* (2010) built on the work of Spector *et al.* (2006), who had identified some factors such as "anger" which did correlate with abuse, though less closely to other CWBs such as sabotage. Bolton *et al.*'s work showed lower agreeableness and conscientiousness predicted more reports of all CWBs. More specifically, lower agreeableness was associated with more interpersonally-related behaviors, while lower conscientiousness was associated with more organizationally-directed behaviors.

Less obviously, the research indicated that "lower Extraversion predicted more theft, while higher Openness to experience predicted more production deviance" (Bolton *et al.*, 2010). However, Bolton *et al.* (2010) say more research is needed. At this stage, it would be wrong to exclude anyone from a job purely on the evidence of a psychometric test, but it could serve as a warning light and indicate the need to probe further.

Induction and training

Chapter 8 described in some detail how a security department should approach contributing to an induction course. It should be included in the strategy document because it has such potential importance in influencing new entrants. Trainers and security personnel should think carefully about their objectives and how to achieve them. In brief:

Some "don't"s:

▷ Don't frighten people or make claims about security department's abilities which are untrue.
▷ Don't present security as threatening to employees.
▷ Don't impose everything from above.

Some "do"s:

▷ Do encourage staff to see those in security as friendly, absolutely crucial and approachable.
▷ Do ensure trainers, managers and leaders demonstrate unconditional support for the security policy.
▷ Do explain the company's security policy openly – if there are areas that are more secret than others and where access is restricted then say so openly.
▷ Do train your security section on how to make presentations – all too often they come over as defensive or they overplay their hand by making their briefing sound threatening.
▷ Do establish good practices at the beginning.
▷ Do give a realistic picture of the threats to the company.
▷ Do tell people exactly what to do if they see, or are responsible for, a breach.
▷ Do encourage a non-blame culture.

Management – the big issue

So far, *Bad Apples* has produced significant evidence about the potential damage managers can cause to an organization. Some will seem obvious, and most readers will say "Well, I would never do that". Yet, repeated surveys tell us that sexual harassment in the workplace is all too common, that bullying is a regular occurrence, and that bosses are frequently uncivil. Bosses often have favorites, many do not follow their own rules and, often, their low emotional intelligence makes them clumsy, insensitive and cold.

But, even if bosses do not actively say or do bad things, they are often inadequate leaders of people because of what they do not do – come out of their office, provide clear direction, delegate and empower.

This is not, however, a treatise on how to be a good manager – it is a study about the impact managers may have on the insider threat. We believe the evidence is overpowering that bad managers not only miss the insider threat, but actively encourage staff to commit CWBs. In short, they are a main part of the cause that they seek so enthusiastically to cure.

> *I just hated all the swearing, particularly the four letter words and when they were directed at me and friends in the office – I just left.*
>
> (Civil servant, 2005)

Looking at the impact managers may have on the insider threat, organizations should promote three skills that managers should cultivate to reduce the threat of the insider, as well as creating an atmosphere which will actively promote loyalty and commitment. These three skills are summarized in Table 9.2.

Of course, an organization needs more from its managers – delivery on time and within budget. But, if one member of their staff turns bad, their efforts to produce efficiently will be seriously undermined – if not destroyed.

Awareness

Managers need a keen awareness and motivational insight (psychological mindedness) of what might motivate someone to commit a CWB, what indicators to look for, and how they can reduce the threat. Security, training and human resources departments need to encourage people in the organization to take more than just a passing interest.

Regular staff surveys are a good source of information about what happens in an organization. Staff need to feel such surveys are confidential, but

Table 9.2 Manager skills to reduce the threat of insiders

Awareness	Managers need to know more about themselves and other people, not just the staff who work for them but also the basics of personality and individual differences, what motivates staff, why staff might become disillusioned, and how managers and leaders contribute to the problem of the insider threat.
Listening	If something is beginning to go wrong, managers need to identify it early on, preferably before it becomes a problem. People need to feel they can talk to their boss, and tell him or her sensitive information and receive a sympathetic response. Real, active listening is at the core of interpersonal skills.
Influencing	But knowledge of what an insider might do, why they might do it and advance information of potential problems is not enough – managers have, then, to tackle the problem. It may be sufficient just to tell someone to change, but usually people need more persuasive tactics.

it does not take much to encourage a member of staff to discuss openly what they feel and what they perceive to be the problem.

A manager rarely has complete control over who comes to work in his or her department. Even when a manager does appoint someone and has a completely free hand, the individual will be a complex mix of personality, social and cultural background, as well as intellect and personal priorities. Few will be a perfect fit. The manager needs to know *how* to manage the imperfections. Maybe the person is not as conscientious as he would like; maybe they are just a little more neurotic than preferred; maybe they are bordering on the narcissistic. None would be enough to eliminate them from the recruitment process but, with this kind of profile, a manager would know that they are potentially more likely to be part of the insider threat.

The manager has to be able to spot the indicators and, unless they know what to look for, they will not be able to. Signs of distress, depression and anger are relatively easy to spot, once one has been given some training in the area.

Listening and other communication skills

A manager is responsible for production, managing other people, customer relations, analysis, alerting senior people or investors to potential problems, giving good news, negotiating – the list could go on. But, in every single function, one or other form of communication is needed.

There are at least four elements to communication: writing, speaking, reading and listening. The spoken and written words provide the hard evidence which people will use to feel comforted and happy, or to turn against the speaker or writer to claim an injustice. To be convincing, the body language has to be consistent with the words. Articulateness and vocabulary are related both to intelligence and education.

Harvey Thomas and Roy Lilley are both experts in the spoken word, and have advised Prime Ministers and CEOs on communicating skills. Their golden rule is: "If they haven't heard it, you haven't said it!" (Thomas and Lilley, 1995). People do not take on board everything that is said or written, and they have an alarming tendency to hear things that have not been said or to interpret the message in other ways.

There are four basic rules to any communication, written or spoken (Gower, 1987: 12, 24):

> *If language is not correct, then what is said is not what is meant; if what is said is not what is meant, then what ought to be done remains undone.*
>
> (Confucius (traditionally 551 BC–479 BC))

▷ *Simplicity*: Unusual words may show the writer or speaker to be clever and well educated, or more often a show-off, but simpler words have more impact and are therefore easily understood.

▷ *Brevity*: Any person can only absorb a finite amount of information. Only a small part of a long text or statement will therefore be remembered. Murphy's

Law will ensure that the important parts are the ones not committed to memory.

▷ *Humane*: Style is a contentious issue and people will hold on to their views. In office communications a degree of humanity helps the reader or listener relate to the messenger and the message. It should be friendly, sympathetic and natural.

▷ *Accurate*: An obvious statement perhaps but all too easily shaded or in the modern idiom, spun out of recognition.

Listening is the Cinderella of communication skills. It is also perhaps the most important when it comes to building and maintaining loyalty. There are two levels of listening:

▷ effective listening – sensitive, understanding and remembering what others really say.

▷ active listening – the listener demonstrates sympathetically that they are listening, and therefore encourages the other to reveal more. The active listener also interprets all the signals, verbal and non-verbal.

The key elements to active listening are:

▷ Time, that most elusive of commodities for a manager but, unless people are able to have sufficient time to collect and order their thoughts, important details will be missed. Many interviewers find that the nugget which reveals the real problem comes just as the person is leaving the room.

▷ Demonstrate you are listening through your responses, sometimes called the grunt factor – the occasional "umm" or "yes", nods of the head, paraphrasing of what has just been said all help to encourage a speaker because they believe they are being listened to.

> *Listening is a magnetic and strange thing, a creative force. The friends who listen to us are the ones we move toward. When we are listened to, it creates us, makes us unfold and expand.*
>
> (Karl A. Menninger (1893–1990), American psychiatrist)

▷ Avoidance of critical judgments – if someone feels their views are being challenged they will shut up, rather than argue or become defensive.

▷ The interviewer's body language – while it should be open and relaxed to encourage discussion, it should not be completely at odds with the other person. To some extent the body language should "mirror" that of the other, but avoid mimicry.

Skilled listeners collect complete and accurate information, as well as creating trusting relationships with others. It is the skill of the coach, counselor and psychiatrist. Facing a potential insider threat, these are essential tools for a manager. They will also help achieve other objectives. As with most skills, people need to practice in a learning or training environment before they reach the necessary level of competence. Most managers claim they are good listeners. Experience suggests otherwise. Developing good active listening skills is an essential part of effective management.

Influencing

So, what kind of action can a manager take? At its most basic, a manager can sack the insider but, as we have already discussed in the exit policy section, this may in itself cause more problems by increasing the resentment and feelings of revenge in the perpetrator. If the sacking is done with little respect for the dignity of the perpetrator, other members of staff will note that this is part of the "management style" of the company.

> *When dealing with people, remember we are not dealing with creatures of logic; we are dealing with creatures of emotion, creatures bristling with prejudices and motivated by pride and vanity.*
>
> (Dale Carnegie, *How to Win Friends and Influence People*, 1936)

It therefore falls to the manager to influence events and people in a way which, at the very least, limits the damage but also, wherever possible, persuades people to pursue a path which is more beneficial to the individual and the organization.

Most employees will obey the commands of their boss, but the best look not just for compliance, but also for a change in attitude. There are various methods available which a manager can deploy. Robert Cialdini (1993) identifies six specific strategies of persuasion which a manager can deploy (Table 9.3).

Honesty and transparency

If the culture of the organization is one where deception is the norm, where top managers are known to be taking money not properly earned, then the rest of the workforce will follow that example. Similarly, if employees cannot see or understand how decisions affecting their livelihood are being made, or they think these decisions are biased, unfair or even illegal, they will think the worst if things go against them.

Paternalistic management styles suggest that decision-makers know best what is in the interests of the worker. They may have been right but, in recent times, this view is constantly challenged by younger generations who believe they should be given insights into the process, if not the actual discussions. They want to see the evidence for decisions. References to personal gut feeling or instincts do not carry much weight to the modern graduate. They are more likely to see this, at best, as lazy thinking – there should be evidence, and a good mind will be able to identify the reasons for a decision rather than rely on the equivalent of reading tea leaves. At worst, they will believe decisions were taken based on the basis of bias, prejudice or old-fashioned thinking.

Table 9.3 Six specific strategies of persuasion a manager can deploy

Reciprocation	The idea that if you give someone something, they feel under an obligation to give something back. In management terms, the giving may not need to be much – a "thank you", or public recognition that the employee has done something good, will often suffice.
Commitment	Once someone is committed, they tend to stay with that person or organization. By getting people to state they are consulted, happy and loyal in part ensures they are consistent in their behavior. Most people have made the commitment when they are recruited and will keep to that commitment beyond the time when they may be better off leaving. The manager can do more by making sure the individual remains committed – pensions, strong development plans for the member of staff all help to reinforce the commitment.
Social proof	The fact that important, powerful, successful people think or act in a particular way is social proof of its value and importance. Being part of the club, the "in" group, the A-team – people like to feel they are, or can become, part of the social norm. Managers who create a good team atmosphere with the right values will automatically encourage others to follow suit.
Liking	We like people who like us and when we are more alike. We all tend to do things for people we like (that is not synonymous for weakness). People who dress well, who are courteous, who smile are all more likely to influence others.
Authority	Those who have power, status and rank command authority. People do respond to authority and will obey, even agreeing to do things which may cause harm to others or themselves, but the trick is to do it because they respect you, not just because you are the boss.
Scarcity	Things that are rare are more valuable. If the manager can make an individual feel special, that he or she is unique or involved in something exceptional, the more likely he is to influence that person to his way of thinking.

Johnson and Philips, in their book *Absolute Honesty* (2003: 49–51), note how to build a culture rooted in six laws of honesty:

▷ *Tell the truth*: When the news is good this is rarely a problem but when there is something unpalatable managers avoid the issue or try to sugar the pill to the extent that the real truth is obscured. In the long run telling the truth will earn managers respect and trust and encourage others to do likewise.

▷ *Tackle the problem*: Where there is disagreement people often take the apparently easy path and just go along with the idea and co-operate. This does not help and people should be encouraged to deal with the issues with constructive confrontation.

▷ *Disagree and commit*: The culture should allow people to disagree. Too often people attend meetings where consensus is reached but then go back to their colleagues or staff and lobby against the decision. People should feel free to

disagree with policies they believe to be wrong, particularly if they concern ethics, morals or the law.
▷ *Welcome the truth*: If a manager is justly criticized they should not become defensive, but accept they are in the wrong.
▷ *Reward the messenger*: Unpalatable information is never easy to pass on. When a subordinate does so to a senior manager the difficulties are much greater.
▷ *Build a platform of integrity*: Lead by example; even when things get tough stick to the principles and values that matter.

Exit policy

How a company treats staff who leave, for whatever reason, speaks volumes about that company's attitudes to its employees. An over-riding principle for employers is summed up in one word: "dignity".

If someone leaves and they feel badly treated, ignored, unappreciated, their already negative feelings will probably be compounded. There will be no restraints on what they say about the company; neither will they feel guilty about giving away what they can remember of the company's clients, research programs or other secrets. It is perhaps too much to expect staff who leave to remain loyal to their former employer but, with the right handling and aftercare, their propensity to be disloyal can be limited.

Geoffrey Wigand (the head of research at the tobacco company Brown & Williamsons who blew the whistle on their inclusion of narcotic substances

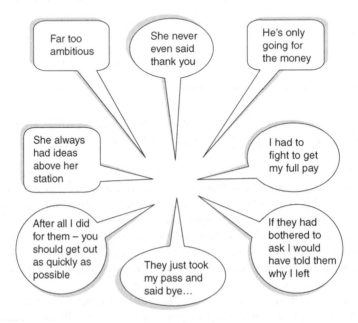

Figure 9.2 **A minefield of misunderstanding**

into cigarettes: see pp. 275–6) felt that he was reasonably well paid–off, and his first thoughts were not to "blow the whistle". It was only after he was called back, made to sign another confidentiality agreement and threatened that he became seriously disillusioned – with some encouragement from Lowell Bergman, the journalist from the US TV company CBS.

He felt badly treated by the tobacco company and resentment began to set in, leading to him break his confidentiality agreement and, therefore, his benefits. There was, of course, also a real desire to reveal what was happening in the tobacco company. If he had been treated more sympathetically, it is quite possible Wigand would not have gone through with the whistle-blowing.

Whenever someone leaves, whether through resignation or enforced departure, the rest of the organization is watching how that person is treated. If the organization is perceived to have treated them fairly, then staff feel comfortable and are that much more ready to remain loyal to the company. If, however, they see someone treated badly, the seeds for trouble will have been sown.

Handling resignations

However important the person is, or however critical he or she appears to be in the organization's work, the principles of handling their departure are the same:

▷ An expression of genuine (if appropriate) regret that they are leaving.
▷ Check conditions of employment and respond to any requests for exceptions with sympathy and, where possible, flexibility.
▷ Ask and listen to their reasons for leaving, particularly to any comment on how the organization might have been responsible for their decision.
▷ Make time to be with them for their last few hours in the office.
▷ Make best use of the exit questionnaire and interview information for future behaviors.
▷ Maintain contact after they leave. Ensure they feel welcome when they return.

The overall aim is to make the individual feel that their departure is a loss and that their work in the company has been valued. The purpose is twofold. Whatever the professed reason for leaving, there is a reasonable chance that their departure has something to do with failed expectations. They may be feeling disillusioned or unhappy with the company or their current boss.

Assuming the decision is final, the departure procedures should do nothing to reinforce any negative feelings. If possible, they should reverse them. Having left the company the individual will often speak about the company to prospective investors, customers, clients and, possibly, competitors. They may have useful information for others. It is possible for people to remain loyal to previous employers; if they depart with dignity, the chances of them not bad-mouthing the company and not passing on confidentialities are higher.

The second reason is even more compelling. Those staff who are left will be watching how the individual is treated on departure. They will have friends who are left and they will express their feelings forcefully. How those are treated on departure sends a strong message to those remaining about how the company really values its staff. Everyone leaves at some stage, even if it is retirement.

Circumstances may well cause employers to handle people differently. Staff may be working in a sensitive area. If they are leaving with feelings of resentment, access to their office should be immediately controlled. It is not easy to do this without compounding the feelings of resentment. Before taking this action, employers need to be sure that the individual is likely to take advantage of their continued access and remove goods or information.

If an employer does this, they are saying to the individual in unambiguous terms "We do not trust you". The individual is likely to respond "In that case, I have no reason to respect your goods or secrets, and I shall say and do what I like now."

The Public Interest Disclosure Act in the UK protects people in some cases, when they have information which is in the public interest to release. But staff have a duty of confidentiality, and this can be written into their terms and conditions of service. If confidentiality agreements are employed, staff leaving should be reminded of the terms of the agreement.

Enforced departures

Is there any hope for those forced to leave? The answer is yes, but there is a greater price put on the professionalism of managers and personnel department. Staff are forced to leave usually for one of four reasons: retirement, redundancy, inefficiency or disciplinary.

Retirement

This is the least threatening to organizations. Neither party need feel guilty. Both have (usually) honored their part of the deal, and the retiree may well be going off to do nothing more threatening than sail around the world, do voluntary work, garden or retire to the country and live off the company pension.

But there are some threats. Employees may still need to earn money to bolster their pension, and their biggest asset could be the knowledge they have accumulated over the years working for your company. Their value as a consultant to the industry could be considerable. Your competitors, be they business or institutional, will usually be only too happy to learn from their experiences in your company.

Staff that are retiring deserve the same minimum treatment defined above for staff resigning. They are more likely to appreciate some kind of contact after they have gone. Retirement is a shock to the system and many feel lonely, isolated, even abandoned. Company support systems are appreciated. Where they are absent, retirees may feel cross and abandoned.

Retirees usually need help to adjust. Many companies now run retirement courses and offer counseling to help retirees find new occupations – not necessarily in business, but something to fill the void of a hitherto active working life. If they are likely to go into alternative employment, then an outplacement agency will be able to monitor – and, indeed, influence – where they go.

Some organizations employ someone specifically to help staff thinking of leaving find new jobs. The value of this "person placing staff outside the organization" strategy outweighs the cost of employing him or her. The advantages are: staff leaving feel the company is still interested in them; the company can influence where ex-employees go when they leave – and therefore deter them from going to the opposition; the outplacement agency/individual can maintain contact with those leaving and organize any further contacts.

Redundancy

The early and unexpected sacking of people because the company no longer needs those staff is one of the cruelest turns of the employment hand of fate. Sometimes it is predictable and staff will have some warning but, either way, it is uncomfortable for all concerned. The numbers involved may affect the precise details of how you manage the news, but the principles are the same, whether for 20 or for a thousand (the law in the UK defines redundancy as 20 or more over a six-month period). The principles here apply equally for any number of staff being asked to leave a company for structural reasons.

Above all else, management needs to communicate well and fully to those who are leaving *and* to those staying. Sackings can be one of the most disruptive influences on productivity. People fear they may be next and will be looking even more carefully at the way the company treats those affected. The trade union, where it exists, will need consulting at some stage. Whoever gives the information, be sure they know how to deliver bad news. Managers, in particular, often need help and advice. They feel the need to sugar the pill with initial explanations about how the individual concerned has many qualities and is a good person. If people are treated properly and with respect, the company is more likely to receive respect and loyalty in return.

Sacking because of inefficiency, incompetence or indiscipline

It is a major part of a manager's job to maximize the output of those working for him or her. "Managing poor performance" is a management competence that is frequently found wanting. Failing to act should not be an option. Staff in the section can easily become disgruntled because they have to carry a person who is not pulling their weight. Alternatively, they will see that misdemeanors or poor performance are condoned and might follow their example. Sacking is the final option.

To avoid resentment, staff who are not up to the job need to be told in clear terms how they are under-performing and be given the opportunity, either through training or coaching, to improve. The processes have to be gone through, and each company should have clear standards about how to manage inefficiencies. This may not mean written regulations, but managers should explain what they are doing and be consistent. Written procedures can often help to ensure consistency, and that way staff know what to expect. ACAS in the UK produces useful guidelines on what to do and how.

If the rules are not clear and are imposed inconsistently, staff will have cause for complaint. Once the procedures have been exhausted and there is no alternative to sacking, managers need, again, to adhere to the minimum standards already outlined. Who does what may vary. The personnel manager might need to administer some, the line manager others. More senior people might have to be involved. But a plan of action needs to be drawn up and followed.

A well-administered sacking need not lead to any resentment – sadness, even guilt, but not a feeling that the individual has been hard done by. When handled professionally, staff can leave expressing gratitude for the way they have been treated and expressing the view that this is the best option for both parties.

Conclusion

Every organization has to deal with incompetence, or aggressive – or worse, vengeful – staff at times. Some organizations have particular problems and issues as a function of the sector they are in. Many have to protect important "secrets" or handle very sensitive information. Others can put many temptations in the path of managers and employers. In short, few organizations are immune from the insider threat, which takes many forms but has a limited number of causes and "cures".

Study of CWBs shows: *first*, almost anyone in the organization is a potential threat, in the sense that things can happen to people in and outside the organization to change a conscientious, moral and trust-worthy individual into a serious threat to the welfare of the organization. While it is true that some people are more vulnerable to being tempted to commit a range of CWBs, nearly every person has a "tipping point" where they are pushed over the edge.

Second, while there is a long list of CWBs from arson to whistle-blowing, the causes are surprisingly similar. They depend partly on the character of the individual and partly on the opportunity they have to committee particular CWBs. The solution to these issues lies partly in selection.

Third, the manager/supervisor–employee/worker relationship is crucial for the morale and engagement of individuals. It is said that people leave

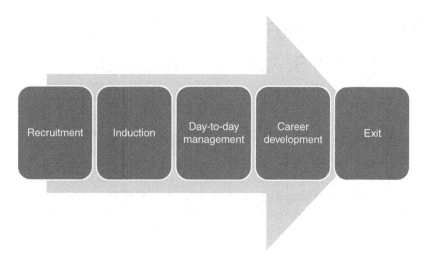

Figure 9.3 **The career path**

managers not organizations and that, equally, people are shaped by good teachers for the rest of their lives. While managers may not be responsible for many aspects of an employee's "pay and conditions", the way they manage can have a dramatic impact on a person's day-to-day well-being. Managers are often a significant cause of stress, demoralization, lack of trust, and perceptions of injustice. *Badly-managed people are the most common cause of turning a good worker into a threat to the organization.* In short, the insider threat is often from bad managers: bullies who show favoritism; those who give no support or control to their staff, only pressure; and those who are egotistically self-obsessed. The solution to this part of the problem lies, primarily, in management training.

Fourth, company policy and culture also play a part in all insider threats. Every organization has a culture – or, more often, cultures – which are patterns of behavior and shared beliefs. Some of these can condone certain CWBs, like unjustified absenteeism, "liberating stock" and "getting even" with bosses. These are difficult to change, and there needs to be "straight talk" about what is acceptable and what is not acceptable which all managers should seriously model.

Processes and procedures are necessary to contain the insider threat and to leave no ambiguity about organizational policy. It is also important to ensure these processes and procedures are justified, clear and relevant. A monocular, "We don't trust you" policy will probably have a low compliance; it could also increase staff resentment and, hence, the likelihood of further CWBs.

As organizations look to develop their strategy for avoiding CWBs, they could reflect on the final figure in this chapter and ask themselves if they are confident that they have the right procedures in each of the five stages pictured (Figure 9.3).

10 Counter-Productive Work Behaviors: Case Studies

The following case studies provide examples of CWBs, the personalities of the people involved and the consequences of their action. Prestigious companies collapsed, national security weakened and lives were lost. The finger pointed to one person, but what other factors might have played a part?

ALDRICH AMES: Betrayer of his employer – the CIA, and his country – the United States of America

Aldrich Ames, an employee of the CIA, became an agent of the Russian Intelligence Service, the KGB, in 1985. He betrayed not only his employer, but also his country – perhaps the ultimate form of treachery.

He received millions of dollars from the KGB for his work, and greed is certainly a major part of his motivation. For many commentators, including most of the press at the time, this was the only reason. But were there other factors influencing him?

On the face of it, Ames is an unlikely betrayer. He came from a middle-class family and his father was himself a member of the CIA. At no stage did Ames demonstrate that his political beliefs rejected democracy and capitalism, or favored communism and a command economy. Beliefs – or, as some would describe it, "ideology" – played no significant part in his decision to spy.

Neither was he persuaded by a Russian Intelligence officer to work for the KGB. He knew very well that they would be delighted to accept him as an agent, but there were no direct external influences pulling him towards espionage.

Personal relationships

Ames appeared to care about people and wanted good relationships. Both his mother and father, while demanding, were important to him. His sister's death was a major sadness. All died before he started working with the Russians.

He enjoyed a close relationship with his first wife and, while later it lacked passion, they were still able to conduct a civilized relationship without tension. When his wife took up politics in 1972 he joined in, probably against the rules of his employer. But their lives did drift apart, and Ames went on a posting to Mexico in 1981 alone. In Mexico, Ames had a number of affairs before meeting and falling in love with a Colombian diplomat. This relationship enjoyed much passion and survived until Ames' arrest in 1985.

Ames flirted with the theatre and magic. He enjoyed creating illusions and seemed comfortable with role-playing in the CIA training and operational activities.

> I recognise that I am often unable to open myself up fully or allow any true familiarity to show in many situations. I am not the sort of man who can talk easily about his feelings or gush with strangers. (Earley, 1997: 42–43)

Of his alcohol use he said:

> I guess I should mention that an enduring pattern to my drinking has been its social aspect. I have always felt inhibited, uncommunicative, unable to make small talk and to enjoy intimacy with others, even friends and colleague. Social drinking, together with the effects of alcohol itself, made me feel more able to relate to and deal with others. (Earley, 1997: 54)

There are friends from school and college who vouch for him as a good friend; there are others who found him less easy:

> He was an awkward boy. I remember he used to try and run after me and try to kiss me! He wore a sarong for a few days, but he didn't know how to sit properly. (Earley, 1997: 257)

Attitude to employers

Ames joined the CIA with the help of his father, having failed at university. His career in the CIA seems checkered. He did receive good reports, but he also received some poor ones. He had, by the time he started working for the KGB, become an expert in the KGB and been involved in running some major cases in New York.

There were some indications that Ames resented his treatment. He was passed over for promotion in 1985, and developed a reputation for "being argumentative, resentful" (Earley, 1997: 257).

He said, after his arrest:

> It's interesting to think how different not only my career but my own feelings and thoughts, too, might have been had I not encountered such a rogues' gallery

of incompetent and sometimes vicious [in the sense of behavior and habit] superiors in my field assignments. In Turkey, New York City, Mexico City, and to a
lesser extent Rome, I worked for a collection of men who were almost universally
despised, pitied, or condemned

...

I am not exaggerating about the nearly dozen men I say were incompetent and
generally contemptible, mostly professional but often personal as well. (Earley,
1997: 285)

Beliefs

Ames claims that, by the time he decided to turn to the KGB, his respect
and belief in the US and its political and intelligence institutions had
evaporated:

A lot of barriers which should have stopped me betraying my country were gone.
The first barrier was that political intelligence matters. It doesn't

...

I had also become to believe the CIA was morally corrupt... It was a dangerous
institution.

...

By 1985 I also felt that I knew more than anyone else about the real Soviet
threat, the real Soviet tiger, and I did not believe that what I was about to do
would harm this country.

...

And finally, I personally felt totally alienated from my own culture... I did not
feel part of our society

...

The truth is there was only one barrier left, and that was one of personal loyalty
to the people I knew and, unfortunately it was not a very strong one. (Earley,
1997: 145–6)

Money

Ames admits freely he needed money. He was in debt at the time, he thought
to the tune of $45,000. His first request to the KGB was for $50,000.
However, having received this payment he continued to work for the KGB
and eventually earned some millions of dollars.

Why did he need this money? Was it to buy security, power, freedom,
or to buy the love of his new wife, Rosario? Most commentators point to

the last, and there is no doubting her expensive tastes and love of the high life.

> It [continued work for and payment from the KGB] seemed to be the only way for me to guarantee that the us I desired so desperately would survive. It would make us possible and, therefore, make our love a lasting one. I wanted a future. I wanted what I saw we could have together. Taking the money was essential to the recreation of myself and the continuance of us as a couple. (Earley, 1997: 147)

Money was the prime motivator: he needed freedom from his debts and he needed to ensure his future through the love of Rosario.

External influences

There is no evidence that another party directly persuaded Ames to become a spy. The decisions were his own. But that is not to say others did not influence him, both in his decision to betray, and in the subsequent and sustained acts of betrayal.

Rosario resented having to renounce her Colombian citizenship, and lost few opportunities to remind Ames that she was a Colombian. She complained she could barely afford to buy groceries. She longed for the big city life with all its cultural trappings. Suburban life in Washington did not appeal. Rosario further undermined Ames' loyalty to the CIA and put considerable pressure on him to provide her with a comfortable and culturally rich life.

The KGB did not identify him and develop him as a potential agent, but they did look after him and sustained him as a source.

> I had walked away from the protection that the agency gave me and I was in the cold and I didn't like it so I moved to the other camp and said "Okay, guys, now you protect me"
>
> ...
>
> I do feel a sense of continuing obligation and gratitude to the KGB, and I think the men who became my handlers developed a genuine warmth and friendship for me. (Earley, 1997: 147)

Conclusion

Ames needed money to pay off debt and to give Rosario the life style he thought she needed to stay with him. That was the immediate and dominant motivation.

But money on its own would probably not have brought him to betrayal. The need for the love of others, his use of alcohol, the erosion of belief in the US political direction and resentment of CIA management all played their part.

NICK LEESON: Broke the rules and caused the collapse of The UK's oldest bank – Barings

Nick Leeson rose through the ranks of Barings Bank and, in 1994, was the floor manager of their trading operation on the Singapore International Monetary Exchange (SIMEX). He used a bogus account (known as the "88888" account), initially to cover a loss created by a junior work colleague. He subsequently used this account to cover other unsanctioned business. As the markets in 1994 fell the debts increased, and Leeson fled Singapore to escape the auditors.

The obvious conclusion is that he was trying to make money for himself – that he was, in short, greedy. But money was not his motive. At no stage did he stand to gain financially from his wrongdoing. The Serious Fraud Squad investigated the case and found insufficient evidence to make a case against him in the UK.

Leeson's mother pushed him to achieve from a young age. He had ambition, and planned his moves into the city and up the ladder to financial success. But there was nothing extraordinary in his behavior in these early years. He was unusually successful, but not a rebel.

By the time he joined Barings in 1989, he was seen as a hard-working competent employee. Later, he would comment on those early months:

> Although I wasn't that interested in who or what Barings was – it was just the next job for me – I did find out some of its history. It was hard not to when it was drummed into you every time you walked along any corridor to the gents. (Leeson, 1996: 32)

Whatever the induction process was, it clearly had little impact on Leeson. History and tradition permeated the company, but it did nothing in this case to swell Leeson's pride in Barings. Of his colleagues, Leeson commented at that time:

> I got my head down and stuck to it, and I wasn't afraid of asking the most stupid questions. People at the London end of Barings were all so know–all that nobody dared ask a stupid question in case they all looked silly in front of everyone else. (Leeson, 1996: 38)

Leeson moved to Singapore in 1992 to activate Barings' trading seat on the floor of SIMEX. Leeson was doing well at this stage, and the bank thought highly of him.

A few months after setting up the new operation, one of his staff made a mistake on the floor which cost £20,000, a great deal of money for Leeson at that stage. Leeson chose not to report it or to take action against the staff member, largely, he claims, because of the attitude of his immediate boss at that time. Instead, he hid the mistake, and took on responsibility for the loss himself by using the bogus 88888 account.

This was a critical time for Leeson. Whatever his subsequent motives, Leeson's explanation for his decision at this time were:

> It had been a madhouse. Nobody could have known what they were doing. It was all Simon Jones's fault, I swore, and Mike Killian's in Tokyo: the mean tight fisted bastards wouldn't let me employ anyone. They wanted to keep the costs down to the bone; Simon Jones hired this girl on a salary of £4000 a year. It was disgusting, and all so he could look good on the bottom line. Everyone else I'd wanted to employ had all been turned down, either because they cost too much or because the sales people didn't think the surge in volume would continue. (Leeson, 1996: 55)

His feelings for Baring were apparent. It is worth recalling that Leeson himself did nothing here for his own personal financial gain.

Throughout the saga, Leeson's feelings about management in Barings were never far away. He recalls a minute recording a meeting between Peter Baring and Brian Quinn, a director of the Bank of England, on 13 September 1993, in which Peter Baring is recorded as saying: "The recovery of profitability has been amazing following the reorganization, leaving Barings to conclude that it was not actually very difficult to make money in the securities business."

Leeson goes on to comment:

> As I stood in the box and grabbed phones, signaled to George or Fat Boy, bought and sold, watched the market lurch about, gobbled sweets and even chewed the trading cards themselves, I imagined Peter Baring's quiet voice in some splendid lofty office in the Bank of England as he sat back on a leather sofa and stirred his Earl Grey tea and admired his brightly polished toe caps.
>
> ...
>
> not actually terribly difficult
>
> ...
>
> They should have known better. Certainly Peter Baring should have known better. Making money is never easy. (Leeson, 1996: 98)

Insights into Leeson's personal motivation are also revealing. While he still felt that he had some control over the 88888 account, he wrote:

> I could see the whole picture. I was probably the only person in the world to be able to operate on both sides of the balance sheet. It became an addiction. (Leeson 1996: 87)

However, the markets continued to fall and Leeson became desperate. As he and his wife were fleeing Singapore in February 1995, he recalls:

> "It was for you", I almost said, "I did it to make you happy, because I could win that way." But then I knew it was also for me: I'd had to win that way so that I could run my own team, be my own boss, tower over the trading floor, earn my bonus. The pity of it was that now I realized Lisa would have loved me if I'd just joined my dad as a plasterer. (Leeson, 1996: 10)

Vanity, excitement and ambition all played a part. His wife Lisa is also an important player, but not directly. She remained unaware of his illegal activities and, when she was given glimpses, reacted strongly against and told him not to do it again. There could, therefore, be an element of fear of being caught by Lisa, as well as the authorities that played a part.

The dominant factor behind Leeson's actions was his feelings about the management of Baring. He was not alone. In July 1996, the *Daily Telegraph* commented in an editorial:

> The report reflects badly on the Bank of England, badly on Mr Leeson, but worst of all on the senor management of Barings ... it is the Board of Barings who emerge from this story as almost sublime incompetents, blithely counting their own booty on the promenade deck, oblivious of the torrent cascading into their ship from below the waterline.

Footnote

Leeson gave himself up, and the courts in Singapore sentenced him to six-and-a-half years' imprisonment for deceiving the auditors of Barings in a way "likely to cause harm to their reputation" and for cheating SIMEX.

In October 2003, Leeson gave an interview to the *Financial Times*. Nearly 10 years after the event, when asked if he was still driven by the same destructive influences that drove him to lose more and more money at Barings, he replied:

> "I certainly push boundaries and overstep them if they are not strong enough to stop me." he admits, remarkably frankly. "I'll go to the gym and come back completely exhausted. I just like to push hard."

> Would he say he was honest now? "Erm ... I'd like to think so", he replies, after a long pause. "I don't hide anything from Leona, maybe I'm too honest sometimes. But you know, I suppose I'm not really in a situation where I could do something dishonest." He takes another sip of tea and, for the first and last time during our chat, he cracks a mischievous smile. "But if I could fudge some expenses, I probably would." (*Financial Times*: 18 October 2003)

JEFFREY WIGAND: Revealed the illegal activities of his employers, Brown & Williamson, the US Tobacco giant, in the press and courts

Jeffrey Wigand was sacked by his employer Brown & Williamson (B&W), one of the seven largest tobacco companies in the world, in 1993. In 1994, Wigand embarked on a course which would lead to him appearing on nationwide TV in the US and in the US courts testifying against the tobacco industry, and B&W in particular.

Wigand has become a role model for whistle-blowers and has had a major film – *The Insider*, starring Al Pacino and Russell Crowe – made about his story. But the cost to him personally and financially has been significant. Was he motivated purely by ethical principles? Or were there other factors which influenced him?

Beliefs

There is no doubt that Wigand believed the tobacco industry was causing great harm to many people, including young teenagers. He also believed B&W management was cynically ignoring the health risks. A major part of his motivation was to expose these wrongs.

> He was disturbed by a report that on average children begin to smoke at 15 ... I used to come home tied in a knot. My kids would say "Hey, Daddy do you kill people?" I didn't like some of the things I saw. I felt uncomfortable. I felt dirty (*Vanity Fair*, May 1996).

And later, after he had left B&W:

> He was in his den with Lucretia [his wife] when he watched Andrew Tisch, the chairman of Lorillard, testify, "I believe nicotine is not addictive." Then he heard Thomas Sandefur [CEO B&W] say the same thing. Wigand was furious. "They lied with a straight face. Sandefur was arrogant! And that really irked me." (*Vanity Fair*, May 1996)

The management

Wigand was a good scientist. He had worked his way up the hierarchies of other firms, been successful and much appreciated. But his position changed soon after the appointment of Thomas Sandefur as CEO.

> Sandefur used to beat up on me for using big words. I never found anybody as stupid as Sandefur in terms of his ability to read or communicate ... In terms of

his understanding something and his intellectual capacity, Sandefur was like a farm boy.

Wigand felt that Sandefur, when presented with data which showed cigarettes contained cancer-causing ingredients, would do nothing to change the product, fearing that it would impact sales. On 24 March 1993, two months after Sandefur's appointment as CEO, B&W sacked Wigand.

B&W suspected he was talking about his previous employment and the company threatened to remove elements of his severance package, unless he signed a new and stricter confidentiality agreement. His reaction was:

> If Brown & Williamson had just left me alone, I probably would have gone away. I would have gotten a new job". (*Vanity Fair*, May 1996)

B&W's tough tactics and threats continued for a number of years. They served only to strengthen Wigand's resolve. He became deeply resentful of B&W.

Wigand's personality

Wigand is proud of his scientific achievements and skills. He had worked in the health care industry, including companies such as Boehringer Meinheim Corporation, Pfizer and Johnson & Johnson. He was brought up in a strict Catholic home in the Bronx, and became a talented biology and chemistry student.

His stubborn, rebellious nature comes out often. His brother James recalled in his interview with Marie Brenner:

> He suddenly announced to his parents that he was dropping out of college and joining the air force. "It was a rebellion to get away," James said. "My mother just about freaked out... but if you make someone so suppressed, the anger kind of builds up". (*Vanity Fair*, May 1996)

And Wigand, to Marie Brenner herself:

> I have a very bad problem – saying what's on my mind... I don't take too much crap from anybody (*Vanity Fair*, May 1996).

This determination combined with anger bordering on rage. During interviews with Marie Brenner, she frequently recalled such incidents:

> Wigand splutters with rage.
>
> ...

I am accustomed to his outbursts. A form of moral outrage ... he is often irascible and sometimes, on personal matters, relentlessly negative.

...

His need to control his emotions [at the office] caused him frequently to lose his temper at home, Lucretia remembered. (*Vanity Fair*, May 1996)

Alcohol also played its role.

Wigand himself had at one time been a drinker, but he stopped when he felt out of control. After he was fired he told me, it was not surprising he began to drink again. (*Vanity Fair*, May 1996)

Persuaders

More by accident than design, Lowell Bergman, producer on the CBS program *60 Minutes* met Wigand. Bergman needed help on an issue concerning another tobacco company: Philip Morris. Wigand could provide just the kind of technical advice Bergman wanted. Wigand was not, however, prepared to talk about his work at B&W – at least, initially.

It was the beginning of an extraordinary relationship. Bergman's presence in Wigand's life would eventually inspire him to come forward as a whistle-blower. (*Vanity Fair*, May 1996)

Bergman was perceptive, and recognized the problems:

The bottom line is that this was a man with significant information, but it wasn't just that he had to worry about the obvious, which is Brown & Williamson crushing him, he had to worry about what would happen in his personal life. (*Vanity Fair*, May 1996)

Wigand's relationship with the Food and Drug Administration, and with others from the government and the judiciary, were also important as they persuaded and coached him towards giving testimony, but none was as influential as Bergman.

Conclusion

Wigand's action can be partly explained by personal belief. B&W's management style contributed significantly to the situation. But Bergman's intervention was crucial and provides the third of the big three factors in this case.

JEROME KERVIEL: Made a series of unauthorized trades totaling as much as €50 billion

Jerome Kerviel was a junior financier in the risk management department of Société Générale. In 2005, he joined their futures trading team. Between 2006 and 2007, he made a series of unauthorized trades totaling as much as €50 billion. At the beginning of 2008, Société Générale announced that, as a result of closing these trades, it had lost about €4.9 billion.

Kerviel admitted to investigators that he had made huge bets on the downward movement of shares, and that he had become obsessed with winning. This had led him to take crazy risks, as if he were playing a computer game. The astronomical gains that he frequently made gave him "an orgasmic pleasure".

However, he insisted that his superiors knew about the scale of his trades and had turned a blind eye, so long as he was making profit. In a newspaper interview, Kerviel spoke about how his superiors described him as the human "cash machine". Kerviel also claimed that the €1.7 billion profit which he had made by the end of 2007 was used by the bank to cover the losses of his colleagues, and described their professed lack of knowledge of his activities as entirely hypocritical. Kerviel also insisted that his top concern was to "earn money for his bank and impress his superiors", rather than to make money himself. The desire to appear a success seemed more important than the personal financial reward.

> The desire to appear a success seemed more important than the personal financial reward.

Société Générale's own internal report on the losses indicated that Kerviel's activities had led to 75 internal alerts at the bank before the unauthorized trades were discovered in January 2008. Eric Cordelle, the deputy to Kerviel's supervisor, admitted that he had been approached by the bank's back-office staff in November 2007, following an inquiry from Eurex (the Frankfurt-based derivatives exchange) who were seeking explanations about Kerviel's trades. The fact that nothing was done seems to back-up Kerviel's own comment that "as long as you earn money and it isn't too obvious, and it's convenient, nobody says anything".

Société Générale identified five key points of failure in their internal report:

> Société Générale created an environment in which the traders were encouraged to take risks in return for profits. This became their primary motivation.

1 Kerviel had no direct supervisor for the majority of 2007. The old supervisor had resigned and no replacement had been appointed.
2 When a new supervisor was appointed, he was inexperienced. His superiors did not offset that lack of experience by increased levels of support.

3   Red flags were repeatedly ignored by senior Société Générale manage-
    ment. The report identifies 39 occasions when Kerviel's actions should
    have raised suspicion.
4   Back-office staff did not have the seniority to hold traders in check.
    Neither were they resourced to check the integrity of the trades.
5   Société Générale created an environment in which the traders were
    encouraged to take risks in return for profits. This became their primary
    motivation.

Conclusion

Kerviel's case demonstrates three failings:

1   The dangers of leaders failing to act as role-models and/or set a healthy
    corporate culture – lack of leadership.
2   The dangers of the construction of a risk-taking culture where no respect
    or seniority is granted to those who might otherwise act as checks and
    balances (the back-office staff).
3   Psychological contract-breaking became an issue after Kerviel's arrest.
    He had thought that his trades were "unofficially authorized" by his
    management. How else to explain how he could have got away with
    such flagrant behavior? So, when his unauthorized trades were wrapped
    up by Société Générale, Kerviel felt no compunction in speaking out
    against the bank. As it turns out, the investigating magistrate clearly
    had some sympathy for him and refused to charge him with attempted
    fraud.

DANIEL JAMES: Convicted of communicating information calculated to be useful to an enemy

Daniel James was a Lance Corporal in the Territorial Army who was convicted in November 2008 of "communicating information to another person that was calculated to be useful to an enemy". He was sentenced to 10
years' imprisonment.

James was an Iranian citizen who came to the United Kingdom as a teen-
ager, and became a UK citizen in 1986. James joined the Territorial Army in
1987 and, in March 2006, was sent to serve in Afghanistan as an interpreter
to General Richards, the Commanding Officer of the International Security
Assistance Force in Kabul. James met the Iranian Military Attaché in
Afghanistan in 2006 and, in September of that year, began an email contact
with him which lasted until James' arrest in December 2006. James' emails
to the Iranian Military Attaché suggested willingness to impart information
of use to the Iranian government. Investigators found that James had stored
NATO confidential documents about troop deployments in Afghanistan on

a memory stick. James was arrested before any material of this nature could be handed over.

Motivation

There appear to be three key motivations for James' actions: dual nationality, disenchantment with the Army and a narcissistic personality.

Dual Iranian/British nationality

James retained Iranian citizenship post his naturalization as a British citizen. This is assumed to have clouded his sense of loyalty to the UK, although James himself claimed that his loyalty remained wholly with the UK and the Army.

Disenchantment with the Army

Witnesses at James' trial said that he had become aggrieved and bitter at his lack of promotion. James began to complain to others about what he perceived as discrimination against him in the Army, linking racist attitudes to his lack of promotion. In a police interview, James complained of this lack of promotion and of being treated "like a f***ing foreigner", saying he had had enough of the Army.

Though only a Lance Corporal, James was doing a job classed at the rank of sergeant. But, as a Territorial, he was not eligible for consideration for promotion until he had returned from his tour. James said that he was promised promotion by General Richards but did not receive it. At James' trial, General Richards said that James understood that he was ineligible for promotion and that he had received that message "phlegmatically".

Narcissistic personality

A psychiatrist who examined James post his arrest testified that he had a narcissistic personality with an inflated view of his own importance. He was described by General Richards as a "Walter Mitty" character that enjoyed being the centre of attention. Others testified that James reveled in his position close to the General, and behaved in an arrogant fashion to those around him.

James' defense lawyer agreed that James' personality type made him a poor choice for such a sensitive role. James denied that he had spied for Iran, saying that he had a special purpose to act as a peacemaker, and that the information he had passed to the Iranian government was part of his attempts to set up a deal for Afghanistan to buy petrol from Iran. James intended that this deal would benefit all parties, as well as the USA, and help to bring peace – clearly, a grandiose plan for a Territorial Lance Corporal to be putting together independently.

Comment

This case illustrates:

▷ *Bullying/harassment*: James felt that racism played a part in his lack of promotion.
▷ *Perceived broken psychological contract*: In James' mind, he deserved (and had been promised) the promotion because he was doing a job of that rank.
▷ *Institutional failure on the part of the Army* in putting someone with dual UK/Iranian nationality and a narcissistic personality disorder in a sensitive position. James was not highly vetted and the Army did not note these points or his past criminal conviction for assault before posting him to the job. In the words of General Richards, "there was no alternative" to giving James the job – he was the only available soldier with the Farsi/Dari skills.

Bibliography

Aitken, M. and Hage, J. (1966) Organizational Alienation: A comparative analysis. *Journal of Applied Psychology, 65,* 497–501.

Alstete, J. (2006) Inside Advice on Educating Managers for Preventing Employee Theft. *International Journal of Retail and Distribution Management, 34,* 833–44.

Ambrose, M., Seabright, M. and Schminke, M. (2002) Sabotage in the Workplace: The role of organizational injustice. *Organizational Behaviour and Human Decision Processes, 89,* 947–65.

Babiak, P. (1995) When Psychopaths Go to Work: A case study of an industrial psychopath. *Applied Psychology, 44,* 171–88.

Babiak, P. and Hare, R. (2006) *Snakes in Suits.* New York: Regan Books.

Bakshi, A., Kumar, K. and Rani, E. (2009) Likening the "Big Five" personality demands to organisational citizenship behaviours. *International Journal of Psychological Studies, 1,* 73–821.

Bamfield, J. (2009) *Global Retail Theft Barometer.* Nottingham: Centre for Retail Research.

Barnes, P. and Webb, J. (2007) Organisational Susceptibility to Fraud and Theft, Organisational Size and the Effectiveness of Management Controls. *Managerial and Decision Economics, 28.*

Barnfield, I. (2006) Sed Quis Custsodiet? Employee theft in UK retailing. *International Journal of Retail and Distribution Management, 34,* 845–59.

Becker, T. (2005) Development and Validation of a Situational Judgement Test of Employee Integrity. *International Journal of Selection and Assessment, 13,* 225–332.

Becker, T. and Billings, R. (1993) Profiles of Commitment: An empirical test, *Journal of Organizational Behavior, 14,* 177–90.

Bennett, R. and Robinson, S. (2000) Development of a Measure of Workplace Deviance. *Journal of Applied Psychology, 85,* 349–60.

Bergmann, T., Mundt, D. and Illegen, E. (1990) The Evolution of Honesty Tests and Means for their Evolution. *Employee Responsibility and Rights Journal, 3,* 215–23.

Bernerth, J., Field, H., Giles, W. and Cole, M. (2006) Perceived Fairness in Employee Selection. *Journal of Business and Psychology, 20,* 545–63.

Berry, C., Ores, P. and Sackett, P. (2007) Interpersonal Deviance, Organizational Deviance and their Common Correlates. *Journal of Applied Psychology, 92,* 410–24.

Black, D. (1999) *Bad Boys, Bad Men.* Oxford: OUP.

Blackman, M. and Funder, D. (2002) Effective Interview Practices for Accurately Assessing Counter-Productive Traits. *International Journal of Selection and Assessment, 10,* 109–16.

Bledow, R. and Frese, M., (2009) A Situational Judgement Test of Personal Initiative and its Relationship to Performance. *Personnel Psychology, 62,* 229–58.

Bloomsbury Reference Book (2003) *Talking Shop.* London: Bloomsbury Publishing.

Bobocel, D., McCline, R. and Folger, R. (1997) Letting Them Down Gently: Conceptual advances in explaining controversial organizational policies. In C. Cooper and D. Rousseau (eds), *Trends in Organizational Behaviour,* Volume 4, 73–88.

Bolton, L.R., Becker, L.K. and Barber, L.K. (2010) Big Five Trait Predictors of Differential Counterproductive Work Behavior Dimensions. *Personality and Individual Differences, 49,* 537–41.

Broad, W. and Wade, N (1988) *Betrayers of the Truth: Fraud and deceit in science.* Oxford: OUP.

British Army (2008) Value and Standards of the British Army. Available at www.army.mod.uk/documents

Brockway, J., Carlson, K., Jones, S. and Bryant, F. (2002) Development and Validation of a Scale for Measuring Cynical Attitudes towards College. *Journal of Educational Psychology, 94,* 1–15.

Brown, R. and Colthern, C. (2002) Individual Differences in Faking Integrity Tests. *Psychological Reports, 91,* 691–702.

Buchanan, B. (1974) Building Organizational Commitment. *Administrative Science Quarterly, 19,* 533–46.

Bull, R. (1988) What is the Lie-Detector Test? In A. Gale (ed.) *The Polygraph Test.* London: Sage, 10–18.

Burnett, M., Williamson, I. and Bartel, K., (2009) The Moderating Effect of Personality on Employees Reaction to Procedural Fairness and Outcome Favourability. *Journal of Business Psychology, 24,* 469–84.

Butler, T. and Waldroop, J. (1999) Job Sculpting. *Harvard Business Review,* September/October.

Byle, K. and Holtgraves, I. (2008) Integrity Testing, Personality and Design. *Journal of Business Psychology, 22,* 257–95.

Calles, B. (2008) Corruption in the Police: The reality of the "dark side", *Police Journal, 81, 1,* 3–24.

Camara, W.E. and Schneider, D. (1995) Questions of Construct Breadth and Openness of Research in Integrity Testing. *American Psychologist, 50,* 459–60.

Carnegie, D. (1998) *How to Win Friends and Influence People.* London: Vermillion.

Carroll, D. (1988) How Accurate is Polygraph Lie Detection? In A. Gale (ed.) *The Polygraph Test.* London: Sage, 19–28.

Casal, J. and Zalkind, S. (1995) Consequences of Whistle-Blowing. *Psychological Reports, 77,* 795–802.

Caspi, A, Moffitt, T., Silva, P., Krueger, A. *et al.* (1994) Are Some People Crime Prone? *Criminology, 32,* 163–95.

Centre for Retail Research (2003) *European Retail Theft Barometer,* 3rd Report, Nottingham.

Cizek, G. (1999) *Cheating on Tests.* Mahway, NJ: LEA.

Cialdini, R. (1993) *Influence: The Psychology of Persuasion.* New York: William Morrow.

Cleckley, H. (1976) *The Mask of Sanity,* 5th edn. St Louis, MO: Mosby.

Cleckley, H. (1941) *The Mask of Sanity.* St Louis, MO: Mosby.

Colella, A., Paetzold, R., Zardkoohi, A. and Wesson, M. (2007) Exposing Pay Secrecy. *Academy of Management Review, 32,* 55–71.

Collett, P. (2003) *The Book of Tells.* London: Doubleday.

Connelly, B., Lilienfeld, S. and Schmeelk, K. (2006) Integrity Tests and Morality. *International Journal of Section and Assessment, 14,* 82–6.

Cook, M. (1998) *Personnel Selection.* Chichester: John Wiley & Sons.

Craig, S. and Gustafson, S. (1998) Perceived Leader Integrity Scale: An instrument for assessing employee perceptions of leader integrity. *Leadership Quarterly, 9,* 127–45.

Crino, M. (1994) Employee Sabotage: A random or preventable phenomenon. *Journal of Managerial Issues, 6,* 311–30.

Cropanzano, R. and Greenberg, J. (1997) Progress in Organizational Justice. In C. Cooper and I. Robertson (eds) *International Review of Industrial and Organizational Psychology,* Volume 12. New York: Wiley, 317–72.

Crowne, D. and Marlowe, D. (1964) *The Approval Motive.* New York: Wiley.

Crowne, D. and Marlowe, D. (1960) A New Scale of Social Desirability Independent of Psychology. *Journal of Consulting Psychology, 24,* 349–54.

Dailey, R. and Kirk, D. (1992) Distributive and Procedural Justice as Antecedents of Job Dissatisfaction and Intent to Turnover. *Human Relations, 45,* 305–17.

Davies, D. (2000) *Fraud Watch.* London: ABG.

Davis, J., Payne, G. and McMahan, G. (2007) A Few Bad Apples? Scandalous behaviour of mutual fund managers. *Journal of Business Ethics, 76,* 319–34.

Deck, G. (1985) Controlling Employee Fraud. *Public Budgeting and Finance, 6,* 52–62.

Di Battista, R. (1996) Forecasting Sabotage Events in the Workplace. *Public Personnel Management, 25,* 41–52.

Di Battista, R. (1991) Creating New Approaches to Recognise and Deter Sabotage. *Public Personnel Management, 20,* 347–53.

Dotlich, D. and Cairo, P. (2003) *Why CEOs Fail.* New York: Jossey Bass.

Douglas, M. (1986) *How Institutions Think.* New York: Syracuse University Press.

Earley, P. (1997) *Confessions of a Spy.* London: Hodder & Stoughton.

Ekman, P. (2003) *Emotions Revealed.* New York: Times Books

Ekman, P. (2001) *Telling Lies.* London: W.W. Norton.

Eoyang, C. (1994) Models of Espionage. In T. Sarbin (ed.) *Citizen Sabotage.* New York: Praeger, 69–92.

Eysenck, H. (1977) *Crime and Personality.* London: Routledge & Kegan Paul.

Eysenck, H. (1964) *Crime and Personality.* London: Routledge & Kegan Paul.

Eysenck, H. and Eysenck, S. (1973) The Personality of Female Prisoners. *British Journal of Psychiatry, 122,* 693–8.

Eysenck, H. and Gudjonsson, G. (1989) *The Causes and Cures of Criminality.* New York: Plenum.

Eysenck, S., Eysenck, H. and Barrett, P. (1985) A Revised Version of the Psychoticism Scale. *Personality and Individual Differences, 6,* 21–9.

Fallon, J., Avis, J., Kudish, J. Gornet, T. and Frost, A. (2000) Conscientiousness as a Predictor of Productive and Counterproductive Behaviours. *Journal of Business and Psychology, 15,* 339–50.

Farrington, D. (2003) Key results from the First Forty Years of the Cambridge Study in Delinquent Development. In T.P. Thornberry and M.D. Krohn (eds), *Taking Stock of Delinquency: An Overview of Findings from Contemporary Longitudinal Studies.* New York: Springer, 137–83.

Farrington, D. (1992) Criminal Career Research in the United Kingdom. *British Journal of Criminology, 32,* 521–36.

Feldman, P. (1993) *The Psychology of Crime.* Cambridge: Cambridge University Press.

Felps, W., Mitchell, T. and Byington, E. (2006) How, When and Why Bad Apples Spoil the Barrel. *Research in Organisational Behaviour, 27,* 175–222.

FBI (2000) Overview of the Law Enforcement Strategy to Control International Organized Crime.

Financial Times (2003) Article on Nick Leeson. 18 October.

Fine, S., Horowitz, I., Weigler, H. and Basis, L. (2010) Is Good Character Good Enough? *Human Resource Management Review, 20,* 73–84.

Fischer, L. (2000) *Treason 101: By the Numbers.* Columbus, OH: DSS/ Security Research Centre.

Fisher, R. and Geiselman, R. (1992) *Memory Enhancing Techniques for Investigative Interviewing. The Cognitive Interview.* Springfield, IL: Charles C. Thomas.

Fortmann, K., Leslie, C. and Cunningham, M. (2002) Cross-Cultural Comparison of the Reid Integrity Scale in Latin America and South Africa. *International Journal of Selection and Assessment, 10,* 98–108.

Franklin, J. (1975) Power and Commitment. *Human Relations, 28,* 737–53.

Furnham, A. (2005) *The Psychology of Behaviour at Work.* Hove: Psychology Press.

Furnham, A. (2003) *Mad, Sad and Bad Management.* Cirencester: Management Books.

Furnham, A. (2000) *The Hopeless, Hapless and Helpless Manager.* London: Whurr Publishers.

Furnham, A. (1999a) *The Psychology of Behaviour at Work.* Hove, UK: Psychology Press.

Furnham, A. (1999b) *Body Language at Work.* London: Chartered Institute of Personnel and Development.

Furnham, A. (1990a) The Fakability of the 16PF, Myers-Briggs and Firo-B Personality Measures. *Personality and Individual Differences, 11,* 711–16.

Furnham, A. (1990b) Faking Personality Questionnaires: Fabricating different profiles for different purposes. *Current Psychology, 9,* 46–55.

Furnham, A. and Petrova, E. (2010) *Body Language in Business.* Basingstoke: Palgrave McMillan

Furnham, A. and Taylor, J. (2004) *The Dark Side of Behaviour at Work.* London: Palgrave Macmillan.

Furnham, A. and Thompson, J. (1991) Personality and Self-Reported Delinquency. *Personality and Individual Differences, 12,* 585–93.

Gale, A. (1988) *The Polygraph Test: Lies, truth and science.* London: Sage.

Gannon, T., Beech, A. and Ward, T. (2008) Does the Polygraph Lead to Better Risk Prediction for Sexual Offenders. *Aggression and Violent Behaviour, 13,* 29–44.

Gillespie, I. (1996) From the Head of Department's Point of View. In S. Lock and F. Wells *Fraud and Misconduct in Medical Research.* London: BMJ Publishing Group.

Gino, F., Gu, J. and Zhong, C.-B. (2009) Contagion or Restitution? When bad apples can motivate ethical behaviour. *Journal of Experimental Social Psychology, 45, 6,* 1299–302.

Gobert, J. and Punch, M. (2003) *Rethinking Corporate Crime (Law in Context).* Oxford: Butterworths.

Goldberg, H. and Lewis, R. (1978) *Money Madness.* London: Springwood.

Gottfredson, M. and Hirschi, T. (1990) *A General Theory of Crime.* Stanford: Stanford University Press.

Gottschalk, P. (2008) *Criminal Entrepreneurship.* New York: Nova Publishers.

Gower, Sir E. (1987) *The Complete Plain Words.* London: Penguin Books.

Graham, H.T. and Bennett, R (1995) *Human Resources Management.* London: Pitman.

Greenberg, J. (2002) Who Stole The Money, and When? Individual and situational determinants of employee theft. *Organizational Behaviour and Human Decision Processes, 89,* 985–1003.

Greenberg, J. (1998) The Cognitive Geometry of Employee Theft: Negotiating "the line" between taking and theft. In R.W. Griffin, A. O'Leary-Kelly and J. Collins (eds) *Non-Violent Behaviors In Organizations, Vol. 2, Dysfunctional Behaviors in Organizations.* Greenwich, CT: JAI, 147–93.

Greenberg, L. and Barling, J. (1998) Predicting Employee Aggression against Co-Workers, Subordinates and Supervisors. *Journal of Organisational Behaviour, 20,* 897–913.

Greenberg, L. and Barling, J. (1996) Employee Theft. In C. Cooper and D. Rousseau (eds) *Trends in Organizational Behaviour.* Volume 3. Chichester: Wiley, 49–67.

Greenberg. J. and Scott, K. (1996) Why Do Workers Bite the Hands that Feed Them? *Research in Organizational Behaviour, 18,* 111–56.

Griffeth, R.W., Hom, P.W. and Gaertner, S. (2000) A Meta-Analysis of Antecedents and Correlates of Employee Turnover. *Journal of Management, 26,* 463–88.

Grover, S. (1993) Lying, Deceit and Subterfuge: A model of dishonesty in the workplace. *Organizational Science, 4,* 478–95.

Gudjonsson, G. (1988) How to Defeat the Polygraph Tests. In A. Gale *The Polygraph Test.* London: Sage, 126–36.

Gudjonsson, G., Einarsson, E., Bragason, O. and Sigurdsson, J. (2006) Personality Predictors of Self Reported Offending in Icelandic Students. *Psychology, Crime and Law, 12,* 383–93.

Hackett, R., Lapierre, L. and Hausdorf, P. (2001) Understanding the Links between Work Commitment Constructs. *Journal of Vocational Behaviour, 58,* 392–413.

Hakstian, A., Farrell, S. and Tweed, R. (2002) The Assessment of Counterproduction Tendencies by Means of the California Psychological Inventory. *International Journal of Selection and Assessment, 10,* 58–86.

Hare, R. (1999) *Without Conscience.* New York: Guilford Press.

Havorka-Mead, A., Ross, W., Whipple, T. and Renchin, M. (2002) Watching the Detectives. *Personnel Psychology, 55*, 329–62.

Hay Group (2001) *The Retention Dilemma*. Available at www.haygroup.com

Heaven, P., Newbury, K. and Wilson, V. (2004) The Eysenck Psychoticism Dimension and Delinquent Behaviours among Non-Criminals. *Personality and Individual Differences, 36*, 1817–25.

Heider, F. (1958) *The Psychology of Interpersonal Relations*. New York: Wiley.

Herriot, P., Manning, W. and Kidd, J. (1999) The Content of the Psychological Contract. *British Journal of Management, 8*, 151–62.

Heuer, R. (no date) Treason 101. Insider Threat, DSS/Security Research Centre.

Herzberg, F. (1992) *The Motivation to Work*. New York: Wiley.

Hogan, J., Barrett, P. and Hogan, R. (2007) Personality Measurement, Faking and Employment Selection. *Journal of Applied Psychology, 92*, 1270–85.

Hogan, J. and Hogan, R. (1989) How to Measure Employee Reliability. *Journal of Applied Psychology, 94*, 273–9.

Hogan, R. and Hogan, J. (1994) The Mask of Integrity. In T. Sarbin (ed.) *Citizen Espionage*. New York: Praeger, 93–105.

Hogan, R. and Hogan, J. (2001) Assessing Leadership: A view from the dark side. *International Journal of Selection and Assessment, 9*, 40–51.

Holden, R. and Hibbs, N. (1995) Incremental Validity of Response Latencies for Detecting Fakes on a Personality Test. *Journal of Research in Personality, 29*, 362–72.

Holder, R. (1998) Detecting Fakers on a Personnel Test. *Journal of Social Behaviour and Personality, 13*, 387–98.

Hollinger, R. (2001) *National Retail Security Survey Final Report*, University of Florida.

Hollyforde, S. and Whiddett S. (2002) *The Motivation Handbook*. London: Chartered Institute of Personnel and Development.

Hough, L. (1996) Can Integrity Tests Be Trusted? *Employment Testing, 5*, 97–111.

Howard, S. (2002) The Missing £7 Billion. *People Management*, 21 March 2001.

Huseman, R., Hatfield, J. and Miles, (1987) A New Perspective on Equity Theory. *Academy of Management Review, 12*, 222–34.

Iacono, W. and Lykker, D. (1997) The Validity of the Lie Detector: Two surveys of scientific opinion. *Journal of Applied Psychology, 82*, 426–33.

Jack L. Hayes International (2006) *18th Annual Retail Theft Survey*, 30 October.

Jackson, C., Levine, S., Furnham, A. and Burr, N. (2002) Predictors of Cheating Behaviour at University. *Journal of Applied Social Psychology, 32,* 1–18.

James, J. (2008) *The Body Language Bible.* London: Vermillion.

Jarrett, T. and Taylor, C. (2010) *Bribery Allegations and BAE Systems.* London: House of Commons Library.

Jaskolka, A. (2004) *How to Read and Use Body Language.* Slough: Foulsham.

Johnson, L and Phillips B. (2003) *Absolute Honesty.* New York: AMACOM.

Jones, J. (1991) *Pre-Employment Honesty Testing.* Westport, CT: Quorum Books.

Jones, J., Brasher, E. and Huff, J. (2002) Innovations in Integrity-Based Personnel Selection. *International Journal of Selection and Assessment, 10,* 87–97.

Joseph Rowntree Foundation (1996) Social Policy Research Document 93, Joseph Rowntree Foundation.

Kaiser, R. and Hogan, R. (2010) How to Assess the Integrity of Managers. Unpublished Manuscript. Tulsa, Oklahoma.

Kaptein, M. (2003) The Diamond of Managerial Integrity. *European Management Journal, 21,* 99–108.

Karren, R. and Zacharias, L. (2007) Integrity Tests: Critical issues. *Human Resource Management Review, 17,* 221–34.

Kayes, D., Stirling, D. and Nielsen, T. (2007) Building Organisational Integrity. *Business Horizons, 50,* 61–70.

Keenan, J. (1990) Upper-Level Managers and Whistle Blowing. *Journal of Business and Psychology, 5,* 223–35.

Keenan, T. (1997) Selection for Potential: The case for graduate recruitment. In N. Anderson and P. Herriot (eds) *International Handbook of Selection and Appraisal.* Chichester: Wiley.

Kelloway, E., Loughlin, C., Barling, J. and Nault, A. (2002) Self-Reported Counter-Productive Behaviours and Organizational Citizenship Behaviours. *International Journal of Selection and Assessment, 10,* 143–51.

Key, S. (1999) Organisational Ethical Culture: Real or imagined. *Journal of Business Ethics, 20,* 217 – 225.

Kibling, T. and Lewis, T. (2000), *Employment Law.* London: Legal Action Group.

Kish-Gephart, J., Harrison, D. and Trevino, L. (2010) Bad Apples, Bad Causes and Bad Barrels: Meta-analytic evidence about sources of unethical decisions at work. *Journal of Applied Psychology, 95,* 1–31.

Klein, R., Leong, G. and Silva, J. (1996) Employee Sabotage in the Workplace: A biopsychosocial model. *Journal of Forensic Sciences, 41,* 52–5.

Koch, J. and Steers, R. (1978) Job Attachment, Satisfaction and Turnover among Public Sector Employees. *Journal of Vocational Behaviour, 12,* 119–28.

Leeson, N. (1996) *Rogue Trader.* London: Warner Books.

Lilienfeld, S., Alliger, G. and Mitchell, K. (1995) Why Integrity Testing Remains Controversial. *American Psychologist, 50,* 457–58.

Lind, E., Greenberg, J., Scott, K., Welchans, T. (2000) The Winding Road from Employee to Complainant: Situational and psychological determinants of wrongful termination claims. *Administrative Science Quarterly, 45,* 557–90.

Lock, S. and Wells, F. (1996) *Fraud and Misconduct in Medical Research.* London: BMJ Publishing Group.

Logan, B. (1993) Product Tampering Crime: A review. *Journal of Forensic Sciences, 38,* 918–27.

Lykken, D. (1988) The Case against Polygraph Testing. In A. Gale (ed.) *The Polygraph Test.* London: Sage, 111–23.

McClelland, D. (1987) *Human Motivation.* Cambridge: CUP.

McDaniel, M. and Whetzel, D. (2005) Situational Judgement Test Research. *Intelligence, 33,* 515–25.

McLagan, G. (2004) *Bent Coppers: The Inside Story of Scotland Yard's Battle against Police Corruption.* London: Weidenfeld & Nicholson.

Maas, P. (2005) *Serpico: The Classic Story of the Cop who Couldn't Be Bought.* New York, HarperCollins.

Marchington, M. and Wilkinson A. (1997) *Core Personnel and Development.* London: Chartered Institute of Personnel and Development.

Marcus, B. (2000) *Towards a More Comprehensive Understanding of Counterproductive Behavior in Organizations.* Paper presented at the European Association of Personality Psychology, Germany.

Marcus, B., Hoft, S. and Riediger, M., (2006) Integrity Tests and the Five-Factor Model of Personality. *International Journal of Selection and Assessment, 14,* 113–30.

Marcus, N., Hoft, S., Riediger, M. and Schuler, H. (2000) *Integrity Tests and the Five-Factor Model of Personality.* Paper given at the American Psychological Association Conference, Washington.

Marcus, B., Schuler, H., Quell, P. and Hümpfner, G. (2002) Measuring Counter Productivity. *International Journal of Selection and Assessment, 10,* 18–35.

Mars, G. (2006) Changes in Occupational Deviance. *Crime, Law and Social Change, 4455* (4), 283–96.

Mars, G. (2000) Culture and Crime. In D. Canter and L. Alison (eds) *The Social Psychology of Crime*. Dartmouth, UK: Ashgate, 23–49.

Mars, G. (1984) *Cheats at Work*. London: Unwin.

Martinko, M., Gundlach, M. and Douglas, S. (2002) Towards an Integrative Theory of Counter Productive Workplace Behaviour. *International Journal of Selection and Assessment, 10*, 36–50.

Maslow, A. (1998) *Maslow on Management*. New York: John Wiley.

Maslow, A. (1970) *Motivation and Personality*. New York: Longman.

Mayer, D., Kuenzi, M., Greenbaum, R., Bardes, M. and Salvador, R. (2009) How Does Ethical Leadership Flow? Test of a Trickle-Down Mode. *Organizational Behavior and Human Decision Processes, 108*, 1–13.

Megargee, E. and Bohn, M. (1977) Empirically Determined Characteristics of Ten Types. *Criminal Justice and Behaviour 4*, 149–210.

Miceli, M., Dozier, J. and Near, J. (1991) Blowing the Whistle on Data Fudging. *Journal of Applied Social Psychology, 21*, 271–95.

Miceli, M., Near, J. and Dworkin, T. (2008) *Whistle-Blowing in Organisations*. Mahwah, NJ: LEA.

Miles, D., Borman, W., Spector, P. and Fox, S. (2002) Building an Integrative Model of Extra Role Work Behaviours. *International Journal of Selection and Assessment, 10*, 51–7.

Miller, D. (2001) Disrespect and the Experience of Injustice. *Annual Review of Psychology, 52*, 527–53.

Miller, J. and Lynam, D. (2001) Structural Models of Personality and their Relation to Antisocial Behaviour. *Criminology, 29*, 765–98.

Miller, L. (2008) *From Difficult to Disturbed*. New York: American Psychological Association.

Miller, L. (1999) Workplace Violence. *Psychotherapy, 36*, 160–9.

Milne, R. and Bull, R. (1999) *Investigative Interviewing. Psychology and Practice*. Chichester: John Wiley & Sons.

Miner, J. and Capps, M. (1996) *How Honesty Testing Works*. London: Quorum Books.

Ministry of Justice (2010) Bribery Act. London: HMSO.

Mishra, B. and Prasad, A. (2006) Minimising Retail Shrinkage due to Employee Theft. *International Journal of Retail and Distribution Management, 34*, 817–32.

Morris, J. and Moberg, D. (1994) Work Organization as Contexts for Trust and Betrayal. In T. Sarbin (ed.) *Citizen Espionage*. New York: Praeger, 189–202.

Morrison, E. (1994) Role Definitions and Organizational Citizenship Behaviour. *Academy of Management Journal, 37*, 1543–67.

Murphy, K. (1993) *Honesty in the Workplace.* Pacific Grove, LA: Brooks.

Murphy, K. and Lee, S. (1994) Personality Variables related to Integrity Test Scores. *Journal of Business and Psychology, 8,* 413–24.

Navarro, J. and Karlins, M. (2008) *What Every BODY Is Saying.* New York: HarperCollins.

Near, J. and Miceli, M. (1996) Whistle-Blowing: Myth and reality. *Journal of Management, 22,* 507–26.

Near, J. and Miceli, M. (1995) Effective Whistle-Blowing. *Academy of Management Review, 20,* 679–706.

Nguyen, N., Biderman, M. and McDaniel, M. (2005) Effects of Response Instructions on Faking a Situational Judgement Test. *International Journal of Selection and Assessment, 13,* 250–60.

Nichoff, B. and Paul, R. (2000) Causes of Employment Theft and Strategies that HR Managers can use for Prevention. *Human Resources Management, 39,* 51–69.

Office of Public Sector Information (OPSI) (2010) Bribery Act. London: HMSO.

Oldham, J. and Morris, L. (2000) *The New Personality Self-Portrait.* New York: Barton Books.

Oliphant, B.J. and Oliphant, G.C. (2001) Using a Behavior-Based Method to Identify and Reduce Employee Theft. *International Journal of Retail and Distribution Management, 29,* 442–51.

Ones, D.S. and Viswesvaran, C. (1998) Integrity Testing in Organizations. In R. Griffin, A. O'Leary-Kelly and J. Collins (eds) *Dysfunctional Behaviour in Organizations. Vol 23B. Non-Violent Dysfunctional Behaviour.* Greenwich, CT: JAI Press.

Ones, D.S., Viswesvaran, C. and Reiss, A. (1996) Roles of Social Desirability in Personality Testing for Personnel Selection: The red herring. *Journal of Applied Psychology, 81,* 660–79.

Ones, D.S., Viswesvaran, C. and Schmidt, F. (2003) Personality and Absenteeism: A meta-analysis of integrity tests. *European Journal of Personality, 17,* 519–38.

Ones, D.S., Viswesvaran, C. and Schmidt, F.L. (1995) Integrity Tests: Overlooked facts, resolved issues, and remaining questions. *American Psychologist, 50,* 456–7.

Organ, D. and Lingl, A. (1995) Personality, Satisfaction, and Organizational Citizenship Behaviour. *Journal of Social Psychology, 135,* 339–50.

Palanski, M. and Yammarino, F. (2007a) Integrity and Leadership: A multi-level conceptual framework. *European Management Journal, 25,* 171–84.

Palanski, M. and Yammarino, F., (2007b) Integrity and Leadership: A multi-level conceptual framework. *Leadership Quarterly, 20,* 405–20.

Patel, Hitesh (2010) KPMG Fraud Barometer. Available at www.KPMG.co.uk

Paulhus, D. (1988) *Assessing Self-Deception and Impression Management in Self-Reports: The Balanced Inventory of Desirable Responding*. Unpublished manual. Vancouver: University of British Columbia.

Paulhus, D. (1984) Two-Component Models of Socially Desirable Responding. *Journal of Personality and Social Psychology, 46,* 598–609.

Pearce, J. and Henderson, G. (2000) Understanding Acts of Betrayal. In C. Cooper and I. Robertson (eds) *International Review of Industrial and Organizational Psychology*, Volume 15. New York: Wiley, 163–87.

Pease, A. and Pease, B. (2006) *The Definitive Book of Body Language*. London: Orion.

Penney, L., Spector, P. (2002) Narcissism and Counterproductive Work Behaviour. Do bigger egos mean bigger problems? *International Journal of Selection and Assessment, 10,* 126–33.

Peters, H. and Lievens, F. (2005) Situational Judgement Tests and their Predictiveness of College Students' Success: The influence of faking. *Educational and Psychological Measurement, 65,* 70–89.

Piquero, A., Paternoster, R., Mazerolle, P., Brame, R. and Dean, C. (1999) Onset Age and Offence Specialisation. *Journal of Research in Crime and Delinquency, 36,* 3, 275–99.

Porter, L. and Smith, F. (1970) The Etiology of Organizational Commitment. Unpublished Paper. University of California, Irvine.

PricewaterhouseCoopers (2010) *Global Economic Crime Survey 2009*. UK: PricewaterhouseCoopers.

PricewaterhouseCoopers (2003) *Economic Crime Survey*. London: PricewaterhouseCoopers.

Punch, M. (2009) *Police Corruption: Deviance, accountability and reform in policing*. Cullompton, UK: Willan Publishing.

Raine, A. (1993) *The Psychopathology of Crime*. London: Academic Press.

Raskin, D. (1988) Does Science Support Polygraph Testing? In A. Gale (ed.) *The Polygraph Test*. London: Sage, 96–110.

Rieke, M. and Guastello, S. (1995) Unresolved Issues in Honesty and Integrity Testing. *American Psychologist, 50,* 458–59.

Robinson, S. and Bennett, R. (1997) Workplace Deviance: Its definition, its manifestations and its causes. *Research on Negotiations in Organizations, 6,* 3–27.

Robinson, S. and Bennett, R. (1995) A Typology of Deviant Work-Place Behaviours. *Academy of Management Journal, 38,* 2, 555–72.

Robinson, S. and O'Leary-Kelly, A. (1998) Monkey See, Monkey Do: The influence of work groups on the anti-social behaviour of employees. *Academy of Management Journal, 14,* 658–72.

Rosse, J., Miller, J. and Ringer, R. (1996) The Deterrent Value of Drug and Integrity Testing. *Journal of Business and Psychology, 10,* 477–85.

Rothschild, J. and Miethe, T. (1999) Whistle-Blower and Management Retaliation. *Work and Occupations, 26,* 107–25.

Ryan, A. and Sackett, P. (1987) Pre-Employment Honesty Testing. *Journal of Business and Psychology, 1,* 248–56.

Sackett, P. (2002) The Structure of Counterproductive Work Behaviours. *International Journal of Selection and Assessment, 10,* 5–11.

Sackett, P. (1994) Integrity Testing for Personnel Selection. *Current Directions in Psychological Science, 3,* 73–6.

Salgado, J. (2002) The Big Five Personality Dimensions and Counter-Productive Behaviours. *International Journal of Selection and Assessment, 10,* 117–25.

Schein, E. (1980) *Organizational Psychology.* Englewood Cliffs, NJ: Prentice Hall.

Schmitt, M., Baumert, A.,Gollwitzer, M. and Maes, J. (2009) *The Justice Sensitivity Inventory,* University of Koblenz.

Schmitt, M. and Dorfel, M. (1999) Procedural Injustice at work, Justice Sensitivity, Job Satisfaction and Psychosomatic Well-Being. *European Journal of Social Psychology, 29,* 443–53.

Schultz, D. and Schultz, S. (1998) *Psychology and Work Today.* New Jersey: Prentice Hall.

Seeman, M. (1959) On the Meaning of Alienation. *American Sociological Review, 24,* 783–91.

Shepherd, E. (2007) *Investigative Interviewing. The Conversation Management Approach.* Oxford: Oxford University Press.

Shepherd, E. (1986) Conversational Core of Policing. *Policing, 2,* 294–303.

Shepherd, J. (1972) Alienation as a Process. *Sociological Quarterly, 13,* 161–73.

Shore, L. and Tetrick, L. (1994) The Psychological Contract as an Explanatory Framework in the Employment Relationship. In C. Cooper and D. Rousseau (eds) *Trends in Organizational Behavior,* Volume 1. Chichester: Wiley, 91–109.

Sibbald, B., Bojke, C. and Gravelle, H. (2003) Primary Care: National survey of job satisfaction and retirement intentions amongst general practitioners in England. *British Medical Journal, 326,* 22.

Singer, T. (1996) Stop Thief! Are Your Employees Robbing You Blind? *Entrepreneur,* January, 148–53.

Skeats, J. (1991) *Successful Induction: How To Get The Best From Your Employees.* London: Kogan Page.

Somers, M. and Casal, J. (1994) Organizational Commitment and Whistle-Blowing. *Group and Organizational Management, 19,* 270–84.

Spector, P.E., Fox, S., Penney, L.M., Bruuresma, K., Goh, A. and Kessler, S. (2006) The Dimensionality of Counterproductivity. *Journal of Vocational Behavior, 68,* 446–60.

Stieger, S., Kastner, C., Voracek, M. and Furnham, A (2010) The Association between Fast World Beliefs and Perception of Counterproductive Behaviours at Work. Unpublished Paper.

Stout, M. (2005) *The Sociopath Next Door.* New York: Broadway Books.

Thomas, H. and Lilley, R. (1995) *If They Haven't Heard It, You Haven't Said It! A Guide to Better Communication.* Potters Bar, UK: Progress Press.

Townsend, R., Bacigalupi, S. and Blackman, M. (2007) The Accuracy of Lay Integrity Assessments in Simulated Employment Interviews. *Journal of Research in Personality, 41,* 540–57.

United Nations (2002) Results of a Pilot Survey of 40 Selected Organized Criminal Groups in Sixteen Countries. UN: Office of Drug and Crime.

Vanity Fare (1996) Article on Jeffrey Wigand, May.

Vardi, Y. and Weitz, E. (2004) *Misbehaviour in Organisations.* Mahwah, NJ: Len.

Victor, B. and Cullen, J. (1988) The Organisational Bases of Ethical Work Climates. *Administrative Science Quarterly, 33,* 101–26.

Vrij, A. (2000) *Detecting Lies and Deceit.* Chichester: Wiley.

Walters, S. (2000) *The Truth about Lying.* Naperville, IL: Sourcebook.

Warek, J. (1999) Integrity and Honesty Testing: What Do We Know? How Do We Use It? *International Journal of Selection and Assessment, 7,* 183–95.

Whetzel, D. and McDaniel, M. (2009) Situational Judgement Tests: An overview of current research. *Human Resource Management Review, 19,* 188–202.

Wimbush, J. and Dalton D. (1997) Base Rate for Employee Theft. *Journal of Applied Psychology 82,* 756–63.

Wright, B., Caspi, A., Moffitt, T. and Silva, P. (1999) Low Self-Control, Social Bonds and Crime. *Criminology, 37,* 479–513.

Zickar, M. (2001) Using Personality Inventories to Identify Things and Agitators. *Journal of Vocational Behaviour, 59,* 149–64.

Zweig, D. and Webster, J. (2002) Where is the Line between Benign and Invasive? An Examination of Psychological Barriers to the Acceptance of Awareness Monitoring Systems. *Journal of Organizational Behaviour, 23,* 605–33.

Index

Printed by MPG Printgroup, UK